MUIRHEAD LIBRARY OF PHILOSOPHY

AN admirable statement of the aims of the Library of Philosophy was provided by the first editor, the late Professor J. H. Muirhead, in his description of the original programme printed in Erdmann's *History of Philosophy* under the date 1890. This was slightly modified in subsequent volumes to take the form of the following statement:

'The Library of Philosophy was designed as a contribution to the History of Modern Philosophy under the heads: first of different Schools of Thought—Sensationalist, Realist, Idealist, Intuitivist; secondly of different Subjects—Psychology, Ethics, Aesthetics, Political Philosophy, Theology. While much had been done in England in tracing the course of evolution in nature, history, economics, morals and religion, little had been done in tracing the development of thought on these subjects. Yet "the evolution of opinion is part of the whole evolution".

'By the co-operation of different writers in carrying out this plan it was hoped that a thoroughness and completeness of treatment, otherwise unattainable, might be secured. It was believed also that from writers mainly British and American fuller consideration of English Philosophy than it had hitherto received might be looked for. In the earlier series of books containing, among others, Bosanquet's *History of Aesthetic*, Pfleiderer's *Rational Theology since Kant*, Albee's *History of English Utilitarianism*, Bonar's *Philosophy and Political Economy*, Brett's *History of Psychology*, Ritchie's *Natural Rights*, these objects were to a large extent effected.

'In the meantime original work of a high order was being produced both in England and America by such writers as Bradley, Stout, Bertrand Russell, Baldwin, Urban, Montague, and others, and a new interest in foreign works, German, French, and Italian, which had either become classical or were attracting public attention, had developed. The scope of the Library thus became extended into something more international, and it is entering on the fifth decade of its existence in the hope that it may contribute to that mutual understanding between countries which is so pressing a need of the present time.'

The need which Professor Muirhead stressed is no less pressing today, and few will deny that philosophy has much to do with enabling us to meet it, although no one, least of all Muirhead himself, would regard that as the sole, or even the main, object of philosophy. In view of Professor Muirhead's long and fruitful association with the Library of Philosophy to which he now also lends the distinction of his name, it seemed not inappropriate to allow him to recall us to these aims in his own words. The emphasis on the history of thought also seemed to me very timely; and the number of important works promised for the Library in the near future augur well for the continued fulfilment, in this and other ways, of the expectations of the original editor.

H. D. LEWIS

MUIRHEAD LIBRARY OF PHILOSOPHY

General Editor: Professor H. D. Lewis

Professor of History and Philosophy of Religion in the University of London

The Analysis of Mind. By BERTRAND RUSSELL. 6th impression.

Analytic Psychology. By PROFESSOR G. F. STOUT. 2 Vols. 5th Impression.

Coleridge as Philosopher. By PROFESSOR J. H. MUIRHEAD.

Contemporary British Philosophy. Edited by PROFESSOR J. H. MUIRHEAD.

Contemporary Indian Philosophy. Edited by RADHAKRISHNAN and PROFESSOR J. H. MUIRHEAD.

Development of Theology since Kant. By O. PFLEIDERER.

Dialogues on Metaphysics. By NICHOLAS MALEBRANCHE. Translated by Morris Ginsberg.

Ethics. By NICOLAI HARTMANN. Translated by Stanton Coit. 3 Vols.

The Good Will: A Study in the Coherence Theory of Goodness. By PROFESSOR H. J. PATON.

Hegel's Science of Logic. Translated by W. H. JOHNSTON and L. G. STRUTHERS. 2 Vols. 2nd Impression.

History of Aesthetic. By DR. B. BOSANQUET. 4th Edition. 5th Impression.

History of English Utilitarianism. By PROFESSOR E. ALBEE.

History of Psychology. By PROFESSOR G. S. BRETT. Edited by R. S. PETERS. Abridged one volume edition.

Human Knowledge. By BERTRAND RUSSELL.

A Hundred Years of British Philosophy. By DR. RUDOLF METZ. Translated by Professor J. W. Harvey, Professor T. E. Jessop, Henry Sturt. 2nd Impression.

Ideas: A General Introduction to Pure Phenomenology. By EDMUND HUSSERL. Translated by W. R. Boyce Gibson.

Indian Philosophy. By RADHAKRISHNAN. 2 Vols. Rev. 2nd Edition.

The Intelligible World: Metaphysics and Value. By PROFESSOR W. M. URBAN.

Introduction to Mathematical Philosophy. By BERTRAND RUSSELL. 2nd Edition. 8th Impression.

Kant's First Critique. By H. W. CASSIRER.

Kant's Metaphysic of Experience. By PROFESSOR H. J. PATON.

Know Thyself. By BERNARDINO VARISCO. Translated by Dr Guglielmo Salvadori.

Language and Reality. By WILBUR MARSHALL URBAN.

Matter and Memory. By HENRI BERGSON. Translated by N. M. Paul and W. S. Palmer. 6th Impression.

Modern Philosophy. By GUIDO de RUGGIERO. Translated by A. Howard Hannay and R. G. Collingwood.

The Modern Predicament. By H. J. PATON.

Moral Sense. By JAMES BONAR.

Natural Rights. By D. G. RITCHIE. 3rd Edition.

Nature, Mind, and Modern Science. By E. HARRIS.

The Nature of Thought. By BRAND BLANSHARD, B.SC., PH.D. 2nd Impression.

Personality and Reality. By J. E. TURNER.

The Phenomenology of Mind. By G. W. F. HEGEL. Translated by Sir James Baillie. Revised 2nd Edition. 3rd Impression.

Philosophy and Political Economy. By J. BONAR. 4th Impression.

The Platonic Tradition in Anglo-Saxon Philosophy. By PROFESSOR J. H. MUIRHEAD.

The Principal Upanisads. By RADHAKRISHNAN.

Some Main Problems of Philosophy. By G. E. MOORE.

Time and Free Will. By PROFESSOR HENRY BERGSON. Translated by F. G. Pogson. 6th Impression.

The Ways of Knowing: or, The Methods of Philosophy. By PROFESSOR W. P. MONTAGUE. 4th Impression.

The Muirhead Library of Philosophy

EDITED BY H. D. LEWIS

CONTEMPORARY
BRITISH PHILOSOPHY

CONTEMPORARY
BRITISH PHILOSOPHY

Personal Statements

THIRD SERIES

RICHARD I. AARON	W. C. KNEALE
H. B. ACTON	H. D. LEWIS
A. J. AYER	J. D. MABBOTT
WINSTON H. F. BARNES	D. M. MACKINNON
C. A. CAMPBELL	H. J. PATON
FREDERICK C. COPLESTON	K. R. POPPER
A. C. EWING	H. H. PRICE
J. N. FINDLAY	L. J. RUSSELL
STUART HAMPSHIRE	GILBERT RYLE
H. A. HODGES	F. WAISMANN

EDITED BY

H. D. LEWIS

LONDON: GEORGE ALLEN & UNWIN LTD
NEW YORK: THE MACMILLAN COMPANY

PRINTED IN GREAT BRITAIN
in 11 pt. Imprint type at
THE UNIVERSITY PRESS
ABERDEEN

EDITOR'S PREFACE

THERE have been very considerable changes in the philosophical scene since the publication of the first volumes of *Contemporary British Philosophy*. Those who wish to sharpen their impression of these changes at the start will be well advised to begin their study of this book with a perusal of the polished and witty contribution made to it by Professor Paton. I shall not attempt to add anything to what Professor Paton says, partly because there are already available admirable introductory studies of recent philosophy, and partly because it is the aim of the papers themselves to extend the original 'picture of present-day philosophy' by giving an impression of the state of philosophy in Britain today and of the reaction of leading thinkers to the issues most in debate amongst them. But there is one matter of a general nature to which I must venture to refer.

At the turn of this century, and in the early part of it, the view was widely held that there was a process of human development whose main lineaments could be fairly clearly discerned, and that philosophy should be viewed largely in relation to progress of this kind and as a means of bringing it to clearer awareness of itself. For good or ill, philosophers do not have the same unifying conception of their task today, and they tend also for other reasons, such as those indicated by Dr Waismann below, to view the problems of philosophy in sharper distinction from one another than used to be the case. This is one reason for the adoption by some contributors of one specific problem as a main topic of discussion. But it was also considered advisable, as a matter of general policy, to provide samples of the way philosophers today handle particular questions as well as general discussions of the method and scope of philosophy. It was thought thus to ensure for the volume a body and variety which it might otherwise lack, and I hope I do not exceed the bounds of editorial propriety in saying how gratified I was to observe the skill with which those contributors who concentrated most on a particular problem were able to set their discussion of it in its proper place against the background of their general view of philosophy and the features of it which seemed most important to them. In this I am sure they were carrying out effectively the aim which my predecessor, the late Professor J. H. Muirhead, had in mind in a sentence in his original preface which I ventured to quote as part of my general directions to those who kindly agreed to contribute. That sentence runs as follows:

"What has been aimed at in these volumes is in the first place to give the contributors an opportunity of stating authentically what they regard as the main problem of philosophy and what they have endeavoured to make central in their own speculation upon it."

In another regard, however, there is sharp deviation from the policy of my predecessor. It was my firm opinion, and also the opinion of those whom I consulted, that autobiographical sketches such as those which introduced papers in the first volumes, could not take their place well in a similar work today. For, in addition to changed conceptions of the way philosophy progresses, autobiography is apt to be rather bleak where it is not spontaneous, and it is hard to ensure evenness of quality and length in short autobiographies. If allowed to run to more than a very few brief paragraphs, they would give the work as a whole a not very satisfactory double aim and add much to its price. It did, however, seem likely to be of some advantage to readers abroad and in years to come to have a short factual description of the present position of the contributors and their achievements, somewhat in the manner of *Who's Who*. This will be found at the end of the volume, but the list of 'Main Publications' has been placed as before at the end of each paper. In most other respects I have followed fairly closely the lines laid down by Professor Muirhead. I have not, for example, invited contributions from those who have specialized mainly on the side of philosophical scholarship.

It is evident that there are one or two peculiarly regrettable omissions from the list of contributors, but I have the highest expectations that the outstanding writers who were unable to figure in this volume will have the time and inclination to form the nucleus of a similar volume to appear, I hope, very shortly after the present one. The latter prospect also eases the mind of the editor in yet another way, for it will afford means of including, in the enterprise as a whole, a number of notable younger philosophers whose names have come to the fore mainly since the war. If there is substance in the statement ascribed by Professor Paton to Mr. Richard Robinson, namely, that 'Never has there been such a blooming of philosophy in the whole history of the world', it will be clear how much harder my task has been than that of Professor Muirhead, and even he, long before the present expansion of philosophy in the universities and the renewed enthusiasm for the subject generally, had to overflow into a second volume. I hope that the omissions of the present work will be considerably repaired in the next.

My final and very pleasant task must be to acknowledge my indebtedness to those who have helped me. I wish first to thank the contributors themselves, not only for being willing to participate but also for their courtesy at every stage and their promptitude in providing a final draft of their work by the date suggested. My obligations are also considerable to members of my team who allowed me to consult them freely at the initial stages and later. It will be largely owing to their advice if this book should prove, as I hope may be the case, not unworthy of its predecessors in the series.

H. D. LEWIS.

CONTENTS

THE RATIONAL AND
THE EMPIRICAL

By RICHARD I. AARON

*Professor of Philosophy, University College
of Wales, Aberystwyth*

THE RATIONAL AND
THE EMPIRICAL

MY main interest in philosophy has been the growth and development of empiricism in its various forms. All these forms
presuppose a distinction between the rational and the empirical,
and it is this distinction which I should like to examine here.
I need hardly add that the distinction underlies many other systems of thought as well as the empiricist, for it is fundamentally
involved in realisms, idealisms, positivisms, and materialisms.
It is so much a part of our intellectual inheritance that we
tend to take it for granted. Even philosophers who are em-
phatic about the need for a fresh start, and who make the
strongest plea for liberation from past thinking, will frequently
be found to have assumed the truth of this distinction and to
have rested their philosophy upon it. Yet I venture to think that
it needs re-examination and re-appraisal. In what follows I shall
attempt to show that the absolute distinction made between the
purely rational and the purely empirical can be harmful, however useful less absolute forms may be. I do not deny that the
distinction between the rational and the empirical has its uses,
but I suspect it in certain of its forms. In treating it here I have
in mind considerations of theory of knowledge and metaphysics.
It is obvious that the problem affects other philosophical enquiries, particularly ethics. A re-examination of the distinction
might prove valuable in our attempts to answer ethical questions
but I do not propose to examine these questions here.

We may begin our examination of the distinction between
the rational and the empirical by attending to the first term and
asking what people have meant by 'rational' in this context. Most

interesting is the contemporary account according to which the rational is the purely logical (or even linguistic) as contrasted with the factual; but some mention must be made, too, of other views which have to some extent coloured the contemporary one.

There is the theory that genuine knowledge is that in which pure reason apprehends an eternal, non-empirical object. No empirical factors are involved, both the knowing and what is known being entirely non-sensory. This sort of view one associates traditionally with the name of Plato and certainly passages in his works, for instance in the *Republic*, seem to support it. Thus the Form of the Good is a non-empirical, eternal object apprehended not by *doxa*, not even by *dianoia*, but by *noesis*. An instance of such rationalism in modern philosophy would perhaps be Descartes' theory of the sheer intuition of the 'simple nature', but it is not easy to find indubitable examples in modern thought. Not every theory dubbed 'Platonist' is rationalist in this sense.[1] Nor would the physicist's knowledge of atoms and electrons provide us with an example. All such knowledge involves empirical factors, but truly rational knowledge in the present sense of the term involves none. Perhaps we should look to Whitehead's 'eternal objects' or Santayana's 'essences' or the 'ideal objects', mathematical entities, logical relations and universals of Meinong, Husserl, and the early Russell, for our example; but I doubt whether any of these theories would attain the standard of rationalist purity required. It looks as if no responsible philosopher now wishes to argue that human knowledge could ever consist in the apprehension by pure reason of wholly non-empirical objects in this 'Platonic' sense.

But though pure rationalism, in this sense of the term, seems to have few defenders, it yet makes its contribution to modern thought, for it sets forward a specific criterion of knowledge

[1]There is current a curious custom of describing every assertion of the reality of common characteristics as 'Platonist', as opposed to 'nominalist', so that Aristotle and even phenomenalists become 'Platonist'. Needless to say, this is not the sense of the term we now have in mind.

which is accepted by very different schools. Rational knowledge in the Platonic sense is, first, infallible knowledge and, secondly, eternally true knowledge. Infallibility and eternity become standards by which our fallible 'knowledge' of the ever-changing world is judged and found wanting. Thus we may pause to consider for a moment a very different kind of rationalism, that which appears in the traditional empiricism of the seventeenth and eighteenth centuries. The empiricists beginning with the view that all knowledge was empirically derived, were also influenced by these two ideals of rationalism. Now empirically derived knowledge did not possess the requisite certainty and eternity, but the empiricists found salvation in their predicament in a modified, conceptualist rationalism. Though knowledge begins with experience, we can fortunately abstract concepts or general ideas from experience. These concepts are the creations of our mind, but this does not prevent them from being fixed and so having a sort of eternity. Moreover, between these concepts we can apprehend relations which we know to be certainly true independently of experience. This new rationalism is different in certain respects from the Platonic; the eternal object known with certainty is now conceptual in character and not real; it is expressly the creation and invention of the mind, even when created on the 'suggestion' of experience. Yet the relation is apprehended by infallible reason and the conceptual, being fixed in meaning, has its own eternity. Moreover, the empirical derivation of these concepts need not be emphasized; it becomes increasingly irrelevant as the conception becomes more and more abstract. So something approaching a hard and fast distinction can be made between fallible knowledge in sense-perception and the certain, eternally true, rational knowledge of conceptual relations.

Thus rationalism was retained, but the realism was lost and a subjectivism was set in its place which invited criticism. Yet undoubtedly the main weakness of this type of rationalism was its resting on a very dubious account of conceiving. It thought of concepts as psychical entities, a species of internal accusatives, between which various relations could be grasped. Such an account of concepts and of conceiving has proved itself bankrupt. Concepts are not internal objects; they are more properly regarded as retentions of past experiences revealed, for instance, in the ways in which we are disposed to respond to natural signs, or to recall imagery or, most important of all, to use words. They are not occurrent entities that can themselves be rationally apprehended; nor are they *relata* between which relations can be grasped. And once these points are understood conceptualist rationalism of the traditional empiricist form must be rejected.

In any discussion of the contemporary distinction between the rational and the empirical it is natural to begin by contrasting two sorts of statement, those which are true by virtue of factual considerations and those which are true by virtue of logical rules, and we should look for the rational in the latter class of statements. 'John is playing on the lawn', we say, is a statement requiring empirical verification. Somebody must go out to see whether John is playing on the lawn. But 'John is or is not playing on the lawn' is quite another sort of statement, and we know that it is true without having to go out to see whether it is true or not. It is true by logic.

On this view a rational statement is one true by logic, and by this principle the rational can be distinguished from the empirical. Such a statement as 'John is or is not playing on the lawn' is necessary and so infallible, and since it holds timelessly, it is eternally true. But certain difficulties arise here which have to be faced. And, first, what is meant by saying that a statement is true 'by logic'? We might attempt to reply in this way. Consider the example given. Any statement which has this form 'x is or is not y', for instance, 'John is or is not playing on the lawn', is bound to be true. In this case 'or' and 'not' are logical constants though 'x' and 'y' are variables. I can speak of Tom rather than of John, of being in the wood rather than being on the lawn. But whatever statement I make, that statement is true if it exemplifies the form 'x is or is not y', and such a statement is precisely what we mean by a logically true statement. As Professor Quine puts it: 'If we suppose a prior inventory of *logical* particles, comprising "no", "un-", "not", "if", "then", "and", etc. then in general a logical truth is a statement which is true and remains true under all re-interpretations of its components other than the logical particles.'[1]

This is a useful description of logically true statements, and it enables us to demarcate precisely the class of such statements. But it is not, and does not pretend to be, an exact definition of '*logical* truth', for it uses the notion of logical particle in describing logical truth. Nor are we offered a definition of 'logical particles', but merely an inventory of them. I take this to mean that all that is being done here is to delimit the class of logical truths and show their differentiating characteristics. They will be true in the necessary and timeless way noted above, independently of changes in any components other than the logical particles. But there is no attempt to *explain* the special position of the logical constant. It might be said that these logical statements are true because they answer to our definition of 'true'. We might accept Tarski's definition and apply it not only to factual truths such as 'John is playing on the lawn' but also to logical. The sentence 'John is or is not playing on the lawn' is true, if, and only if, John is or is not playing on the lawn. This would then make clear what we mean by saying that the sentence is true. But since one and the same definition covers 'logically true' and 'empirically or factually true' it shows that what we are after, the difference between the logically and the empirically true, is not to be found here. Neither Tarski's paradigm nor Quine's description helps us to explain the fundamental distinction between logically true and empirically or factually true.

Would it help to say that the key to logical truth and to rational truth is to be found in the notion of analyticity? But we have been warned recently by more than one philosopher against the ambiguity of the term 'analytic'. Many statements which at first sight appear to be analytic reveal themselves to be synthetic, and the border line between analytic and synthetic is blurred.

[1]*From a Logical Point of View*, pp. 22–3.

Moreover, it is most difficult to give a precise account of what analyticity is. If we say that the analytic statement is one true in virtue of the meaning of the terms used, the term 'meaning' is likely to cause us trouble. Further, is not every statement true in virtue of the meaning of its terms, whatever more we have to say about the truth of some statements? If we say that the analytic statement is a statement true by virtue of definitions, the term 'definition' is itself most difficult to define unambiguously, especially if we begin to talk of 'synonymy' of words in trying to define the term. If we say that the analytic statement is one whose denial would involve us in inconsistency, the core of the statement is then revealed as a tautology, so that to say that the logically true is the analytic is to say that it is tautologous.

But we should persevere with this notion of consistency. Pure logical (and rational) statements are held to be denials or rejections of what is inconsistent. Thus any statement of the form 'a is non-a' is to be rejected. Every other statement, however synthetic, must, if true, be rational to this extent, that it possesses the inner consistency requisite for its acceptance as true by a rational being. A synthetic statement is not true just because it is self-consistent; many self-consistent statements are false. But no statement inconsistent with itself is true.

This demand for consistency or non-contradiction has a certain pervasiveness. A sign is itself and not another sign, and so with all symbols. If we are to argue rationally it is essential that we use our terms consistently. It would be disastrous if the term 'not' were used in one way at one point in an argument that claimed to be rational and in another at another point. It would be equally disastrous if the middle term in a syllogism meant one thing in the major premise and another thing in the minor. Again, we could not think rationally if, *per impossibile*, one and the same proposition p entailed the same proposition q on one occasion but did not entail it on another. Consistency is essential throughout for rational thinking. This does not mean that we never use words unambiguously or inconsistently— it is only too obvious that we do; but this is because we are not wholly rational creatures. A middle term may have a different meaning in the two premises and our syllogism have four terms and be invalid. But this is irrational. The rational must be consistent.

It would perhaps be an exaggeration to say that consistency is the sole mark of rationality for contemporary thought, but it seems to be one mark and also the most universal, the most widely accepted. The fundamental place still held in logic by the law of non-contradiction is witness to this fact; and even if we suppose in the modern fashion that we can arbitrarily decide what logical principles are to hold in a system, it is difficult to think of a system which lacks the principle of consistency. Incidentally, if the consistency principle is in fact necessary for every system of thought, an interesting consequence follows. There cannot be alternative logics, if we mean by alternative logics such as possess wholly different principles, for this principle of consistency would be common to all. In a loose sense we might admit alternative logics for disciplines somewhat remote from one another, say physics and sociology. We might argue that the fundamental principles of these enquiries are so different that we could talk in their case of alternative logics. But if both systems have an inner consistency, then there is that much in common between them logically. To establish alternative logics, in the full sense of the word, it would be necessary to prove that two systems differ from one another in every principle, and this would presumably not be the case so long as inner consistency were demanded of the two systems.

Let us now take this insistence upon consistency as our best clue in seeking to understand what philosophers today mean by logical or rational truths. Once we do this a crucial question arises, a question of greater importance than whether some statements which claim to be analytic are in fact analytic, or whether analyticity is or is not an ambiguous notion. Because this question is so fundamental it is difficult to put, but I may try in the following way. Why do I so emphatically say that the inconsistent is to be rejected? What precisely is the virtue of the consistent? Why do I as a rational being demand consistency in my own thinking (and indeed in my behaviour in general), and why do I demand it in others? More, why do I assume that whereas consistent thinking may apply to the world in which I live, any inconsistent statement about it can be dismissed at once as false just because of its inconsistency?

Some philosophers hold that all we need say here is that consistency is required if we are to use any language successfully and that this in itself explains the necessity of consistency, so that the logical principle and rationality can be explained in terms of the requirements of a language. I should answer that consistency is certainly required in one's use of a language, but that this answer is altogether too narrow. For we use language to speak of the world, and, if we do so successfully, does not this point to a certain relationship between the logical structure of language and the structure of the world? We have been warned recently on more than one occasion against the error of 'importing the mere procedure of thought into the fact of nature', and we should pay due heed to this warning. But it is quite as serious an error to ignore the applicability of our thought to the world, and to refuse to face the problems that arise once this be granted. And this, it seems to me, is the error of those who say that the linguistic is our sole concern here so that we need not go beyond it. Of course no objection can be made to the logician who says that he does not want to concern himself with these further problems, which belong anyway to philosophy rather than to logic. Such a person can do what he chooses; he is only at fault when he denies that these problems are there.

An alternative to the linguistic theory would be to return to the earlier form of rationalism and say that Reason teaches us that non-contradiction is a principle not only of thought but of the world. This appears to be metaphorical language; it does not seem to be true in the literal sense that a faculty, Reason, intervenes to teach me this principle. At any rate, I am never conscious of such intervention. Am I to suppose that this takes place below the threshold of my consciousness? Or is it rather that Reason is dragged in to disguise the dogmatic character of this assertion, namely, that the principles of thought and language are also principles of the world?

In addition to the linguistic and the rationalist there is another approach to this problem, namely, Mill's in his celebrated discussion of the principles of thought in the *System of Logic*—a discussion not altogether consistent with some things he says elsewhere on this topic. Here he holds that principles of thinking (he is speaking particularly of mathematical principles) are 'generalizations from observation' (II. v. 4). Now it is obvious that Mill is wrong. So many critics, from Meinong and Husserl onward, have thundered against this 'psychologism' that it is unnecessary to go into details in examining it. If we accepted this theory we could not explain the necessity of these principles. Seven apples and five apples have always made twelve apples, but perhaps on the very next observation they will make thirteen. If $7 + 5 = 12$ is a generalization from experience, we cannot be sure of its truth. On Mill's theory logical and mathematical laws would be empirical laws, i.e. (though Mill would not admit this) hypotheses never completely certain. But it is clear that these are not laws of this kind; they are not hypotheses to be tested by experiment. No conceivable experience could ever falsify them.

All this, I believe, has to be accepted, and it damages Mill's case, that the principles of mathematics (and logic) are conscious generalizations from experience, beyond repair. None the less when we ask how we acquired or learnt these principles and how it is that thinking in accordance with them has a certain applicability to the real world, an approach something like Mill's, though different too in essential features, is not only promising but is, it seems to me, the only approach possible. Consider such a principle as non-contradiction. On the theory I wish to suggest this principle is acquired through the impress of our world upon us. That world is a world in which things are separate, each thing is itself and not another. Each feature and quality of these things excludes other features. It need not be part of the theory that this world is itself controlled or ordered by the principle of non-contradiction, but it does assert that the world is such that we, in thinking of it, find it essential to think of it in terms of that principle. Thus it is our experience of the world that first disposes us to think in terms of non-contradiction and consistency, just as it disposes us to think, too, in terms of substances and attributes. In fact the same explanation accounts for our primitive notion of substance as accounts for this feeling for consistency. They both reveal the manner in which our experience of the world affects our minds, leaving permanent dispositions which explain our thinking. This is no 'generalization from observation', none the less it is learning from experience.

Now these explanations of how we first gain the principles which regulate our thought and speech are psychological in character and it is to psychologists that we should look for enlightenment about them. When we in general ask whether statements, including statements of principles, are valid or not, it is to the logician and not to the psychologist that we turn. He explains how such and such a statement is necessary, because to deny it would be to contradict oneself. But when we enquire about the validity of the principle of non-contradiction itself the logician, too, is at a loss. Theoretically he can choose or not choose to use this principle, and when he does use it in a thought system then, it may be said, he can show it to be necessary for that system. But this answer is unsatisfactory. We use the principle of non-contradiction or consistency long before we become aware of it and of the important part it plays in our thinking. Once we do become conscious of it we are then theoretically free to use it or not to use it. We reach a stage at which we can build up our logical systems as we choose and select the principles we choose. It may then be contended, and justifiably contended, that when we continue to demand at this stage that our logical system be consistent we do so because we see that our system requires it and this gives the principle validity. But it is also true, first, that no one does try to think without using consistency or non-contradiction as his guide, secondly, that to think consistently is to think in accordance with one's deepest tendencies. We are already disposed to assume without question that what contradicts itself is false. Hence the acceptability of this principle at any moment. On the other hand, we also find that thinking in accordance with this principle frequently helps us to improve our understanding of the real world. The principle of consistency is not alien to that world; on the contrary, if this theory is correct, it is something we have learnt from that world itself. Consequently, consistent thinking always has an applicability in principle to the real world; it may apply even when our thinking is of systems which appear very remote from the experienced world. To avoid misunderstanding it should, however, be added that consistency, though necessary, is never a sufficient condition of such applicability.

Now while logic, given the principle of non-contradiction or consistency, holds the key to validity, I cannot admit that the above argument has not some relevance to our fundamental problems in connection with non-contradiction. It explains why we find the principle so acceptable to ourselves and it explains, too, why consistent thinking helps us to understand our world. But if this is an element, one element only, in the full theory of reasoning in accordance with non-contradiction—and I claim no more for it—it is clearly an empirical element. Hence my doubts about the absolute distinction between reason and experience even from this rational side. When we say that the rational is 'argument in accordance with fixed logical principles' or even 'the proper use of fixed logical constants in statements' the empirical may at first appear to have little relevance to the rational in these senses. On the other hand, if we enquire about the consistency which seems logically fundamental whatever account we give of rational statement and argument, then, it seems to me, no answer which completely ignores the empirical is adequate. I should say, therefore, that even when, in abstract thinking, we find ourselves most removed from experience, there is still a link with the empirical in so far as non-contradiction is our guide. Not even thinking of this highly abstract order is purely rational with no taint of the empirical. For in so far as it is guided by non-contradiction it is guided by a principle which in the last resort is empirically derived (even though we may later voluntarily select it as our guide), a principle which might be different if the experienced universe were different. We cannot conceive thinking without the principle; more, *we cannot conceive any item of experience falsifying it.* But this shows the measure to which our experience of the world has moulded our thought. It shows the strength of the dispositions which our experience of the world has engendered within us. On the other hand, given the principle we then see the absolute necessity and universality of many statements, and these admittedly are necessary in a way in which empirical statements are never necessary. This difference still holds true, and is to be emphasized the more in view of the assertion of an empirical element within the rational, and the consequent denial of the purely rational.

If there is no purely rational the contrast between the purely rational and the purely empirical cannot be made, so that we have already established what we wished to establish. But we may now consider the matter from the angle of the alleged purely empirical and we shall find ourselves confirmed in our rejection of the contrast. First, we should note that in most of its uses today the term 'empirical' does not mean that which is wholly free from any rational element. If, for instance, a contrast is made between rational and empirical statements, on the ground that we expect the latter, but not the former, to be verified in experience, we do not then mean that there is no rational element within this experience. Usually our use of the word 'empirical' is not ruled by the contrast between a pure empirical and a pure rational. Yet when we begin to philosophize this contrast tends to become uppermost in our minds, and we think it necessary to search for a bare given or directly received which can be purely empirical. The more adequately any statement expresses this purely empirical the happier we are in calling it 'empirical' and the easier it becomes to contrast it absolutely with rational statement. Now it seems to me that these tendencies, in the main part, are the consequence of the traditional empiricist doctrine about sense-perception, and the easiest way to prove them erroneous is to show that this doctrine is unacceptable.

According to the traditional empiricist doctrine all human knowledge, however complex, is derived from basic experiences in sensation and—as it was found necessary to add—in introspection. This additional reference to introspection was not at first intended and was indeed something of a hindrance to the main theory, for the real interest was in our knowledge of the external world. Such knowledge was said to be derived from primitive experiences which consisted in 'having sensations' or 'having simple ideas' or, again 'receiving sense-data'. In these experiences the mind simply received certain material; it then set to work to combine, abstract, relate and so on. The purely empirical was what was thus received before the mind's work upon it began. As such it was something wholly and completely different from the rational.

The language in which this doctrine has been expressed has varied with different philosophers, but in some form or another it has been dominant, in British thought in particular, for some time. None the less it is undoubtedly very unsatisfactory. It would be foolish to deny that we have sensations, that is, that we feel a pain, feel giddy, and so on. But it is false to regard sense-perception as a construction out of 'sensations'. We may analyse sense-perception, and even wish to argue that elements of 'bare sensing' are involved, but this is different from saying that in sense-perception we begin by receiving into our minds so many simple ideas or sense-data or sensa, so many private objects, out of which we then proceed to construct more complex objects.

This is not the place to develop in detail any alternative theory, but it seems obviously more hopeful to think of sense-perception in terms of a prepared mind widening its horizons rather than of an empty mind receiving impressions. Over a lengthy period we have acquired a body of information about the external world; this information is retained, not necessarily in descriptive sentences but quite as much in our skills, techniques and in our expectations, and it is a mind informed in this way which now perceives. The perception is mostly recognition; but discovery of what is new and interpretation of what is new (that is, placing the newly discovered within the system of information already possessed) also occurs. But this is a discovery that comes to the trained mind only; moreover, it is a discovery of some further fact about the external world, not a discovery of private sensations.

Our sense-perceptions are not complexes of sensations and so sensations are not basic parts of these perceptions. If we set out theoretically to analyse the experience and isolate the 'sensing', this 'sensing' is no longer an actual experience which together with many other sensings could be thought to make up the percept. It was part of the false theory of sense-perception that all empirical statements could be reduced to basic statements describing the basic sensations. In so far as these sensations were unique and private it is difficult to see what language could describe them. We should need a special language of proper names applicable to sensations in their unique occurrence and used by one person only, being private to him. But could we ever invent such a language? In any case, if we are right in rejecting this view that perceptions are complexes of sensations, we are also justified in rejecting the doctrine that all empirical statements to be properly understood must be reduced to basic statements. Such reductionism becomes unnecessary on the alternative view of sense-perception.

Now if we think of the rational as the correct use of certain logical constants in language and as the correct application of logical principles in inference, we may find much of it present in sense-perception on this alternative account. For while our present perception is influenced by what has been retained in our skills, techniques and dispositions, it may equally well be influenced by our conscious inferences and deductions. Stress on the part which tendencies and dispositions of which we are not conscious play in the gaining of experience should not blind us to the part that is played in it by conscious inference. I am disposed by many factors to think that I am now seeing a house in the distance, but when I passed that way a month ago there was no house there and it is unlikely that a house could have been built in a month. Moreover, I know that that is National Trust property and no houses can be built on it. It must then be a rock I had not previously noticed. This is inference and it is part of my experience at the moment. But the traditional empiricism regarded it as subsequent to the bare experience of 'having the visual sensation of a grey sense-datum' and not itself part of the 'pure experience'. In this way the contrast between the purely empirical and the purely rational could be drawn, but it was false theory that made it possible. The rational is not here contrasted with the empirical but the empirical itself contains within it a rational element.

It is not possible then, to accept the absolute dualism between the purely rational and the purely empirical on these grounds. Empiricist insistence upon it, when it occurs, is mistaken and is the consequence of a false account of sense-perception. We should recall, too, an additional factor in the situation to which we have already referred. According to the traditional empiricism our sole knowledge of the external world was through the senses, but it was superficial and unreliable, and no certainty was possible. Hence certainty was sought in the apprehension of self-evident relations between 'ideas'. This was then held to be 'rational' apprehension and wholly different from deceptive sense-experience. Thus the curious position was reached, that even when empiricists rejected the rationalist's contention that true knowledge of the world was by way of reason, their very empiricism drove them forward to a new rationalism and to a further hardening of the distinction between experience and reason. Incidentally, this cannot be dismissed as so much past history, for the same forces are at work in the empiricism of the twentieth century, as witness the solace which positivists find today in the indubitabilities of the *a priori*.

But it is time now to sum up the argument and set down certain conclusions. In some senses the distinction between the rational and the empirical seems a justifiable and useful one; in others, I am convinced it is misleading. We know what we are talking about when we say that some people are more empirical in their methods than others whilst others are more rational; or that the French people are generally more rational than the English. We know what we mean when we distinguish between finding things out by experience and finding them out by reason. In the first case we pass no judgement until we have observed or carried out certain experiments. Is John on the lawn now? Let us go and see. In the second, we draw conclusions from premises and establish a truth by inference. Is this theorem correct? We work out the proof in accordance with strict mathematical laws and find out. Still more precisely, we can make, as we have seen, a very useful distinction between two sorts of statements, the empirical and the rational; the former being those which need verification by reference to experience, whereas the latter do not. All such distinctions between the empirical and the rational are both legitimate and helpful.

But the distinction which is misleading and dangerous is one between two wholly distinct powers or faculties, both of them cognitive powers, namely, Reason and Experience. We have long since rejected the Faculty Theory as such, but this much of it remains, and we seem to find it difficult to give it up. This may be because we think that such distinctions as those admitted in the previous paragraph necessitate it, but this would be a false view. Knowledge involving empirical verification on the one hand, and rational knowledge on the other, are certainly very different from one another. But is the difference absolute? Does it involve an absolute distinction between Reason and Experience? In my opinion only a superficial view of these matters leads us to think so; once we ask the deeper questions about the nature of experience on the one hand and of rational certainty on the other we cannot suppose that it does. For then rational elements are found present in what we call empirical knowledge, for instance, in sense-perception, whilst an empirical element is involved in the rational, in our feeling for consistency and in our rejection of the contradictory.

I conclude then, that we are not in fact driven inevitably

to assert the absolute distinction, and I should like to point out now why the assertion of it is dangerous, that is to say, dangerous within theory of knowledge (for I am still confining myself to this field). It leads us to take up extreme positions which we find impossible to maintain. We say that knowledge comes by way of Reason alone and we seek to wash it clean of any empirical stain, or we choose Experience and condemn speculation, putting our faith in 'bare and naked sensation'. But we soon find that these positions cannot be maintained. For as we come to realize the true nature of rational knowledge, we speak less of pure Reason unadulterated by experience; and as we move away from narrow traditional empiricism, Experience ceases to be the bare reception of material which the philosophers thought it to be.

As long as we maintain an absolute distinction between Reason and Experience, we find theory of knowledge subjected to very severe stresses and strains. For instance, it becomes acutely difficult to relate together different parts of human knowledge which seem to be related and yet, on this theory, are absolutely different. Thus an unbridgeable gulf is held to extend between the natural sciences on the one hand and logic and mathematics on the other, for the latter are supposed to be rational and utterly different from the former which are empirical. But can we at all admit that these sciences are so utterly different from one another? It is true that certain differences between them do exist and these are very important ones. In the natural sciences we seek to discover the nature of our world with the aid of observation and experiment; in logic our concern is with the character and possibility of various thought systems, some of which appear to have nothing to do with the external world, and with the notations used in the elaborations of these systems. These are very large differences, but they should not be exaggerated into absolute differences, as when we say that logic is purely rational knowledge as contrasted with the empirical knowledge which is natural science. For these natural sciences are clearly not empirical in this absolutist sense. Thus they have an obvious concern for notation and for the systems of thought useful to them, even if these matters are not their sole or primary concern. Moreover, the theorizing in the natural sciences is itself logical and part of its reasoning is mathematical. How, then, can an absolute distinction be set up between the natural sciences and logic and mathematics? Finally, the findings of logic and mathematics are applicable in principle to the natural sciences. This would be an utter mystery if logic and mathematics were purely rational and if the purely rational had no points of contact with the empirical.

To conclude, I cannot see how any theory of human knowledge could surmount the initial difficulty of an absolute distinction between Reason and Experience. The rational and the empirical are rather aspects of human knowledge, relatively but not absolutely different. In my opinion knowledge is best viewed as a process of continuing discovery, a discovery of ourselves, of other selves and of our universe. Now this discovery is only possible granted sense-perception, granted imagination and imaginative retention, granted intellectual powers including those of symbolization and speech and high level ratiocination, and so there is need for the empirical and the rational. Attempts to view knowledge in this more integrated way would be impossible if we were compelled to begin with a hard and fast distinction between the rational and the empirical; but it seems to me that the evidence when properly considered puts no such compulsion upon us.

MAIN PUBLICATIONS

The Nature of Knowing. Williams and Norgate. 1930.

Hanes Athroniaeth : O Descartes i Hegel. University of Wales Press Board. 1932.

An Early Draft of Locke's Essay (with Jocelyn Gibb). Oxford University Press. 1936.

John Locke. Oxford University Press. 1937, rev. ed., 1955.

Our Knowledge of Universals. Annual Philosophical Lecture to the British Academy. Oxford University Press. 1945.

The Theory of Universals. Oxford University Press. 1952.

The True and the Valid. Friends of Dr. Williams Library : Annual Lecture. 1955.

POLITICAL JUSTIFICATION

By H. B. ACTON

Professor of Philosophy in the University of London
(Bedford College)

POLITICAL JUSTIFICATION

I

THE question with which our discussion commences is this. We imagine a government and its officers on the one hand, and a citizen or group of citizens on the other. The government's officers are upholding some legal ordinance, and the citizen or group of citizens are considering whether they ought or ought not to obey. We suppose, furthermore, that, at any rate for a time, the question of obedience or disobedience is being discussed in as rational a manner as is possible. The question then is: how *could* such a matter be rationally discussed between two such parties? Clearly it could not be rationally discussed if there were no prospect whatever of the issue's being brought to an agreed conclusion. Disputation that cannot lead anywhere is not rational disputation at all, but rather a sort of unorganized amusement or disguised fight like competitive boasting that comes to an end merely because one of the parties can think of nothing more to say rather than because a conclusion has been reached. When there is an argument between a citizen and his government about whether the citizen should obey or not, by reference to what sort of consideration could one party hope rationally to convince the other that obedience or disobedience is the proper decision? We know, of course, that such arguments are seldom carried out on a purely rational plane, that, indeed, they are not intended to remain on the purely argumentative level at all. The questioning citizen will either obey or disobey, and the governmental party will terminate the discussion with an attempt at enforcement. But when these things have been done it will be possible to look back on them and consider

23

whether they were done rightly or wrongly and why they were right if they were right or why they were wrong if they were wrong. Both parties to the discussion, we are supposing, wish to act in a way that they can *justify*, and hence our question is about the nature of justification in politics. We want to know how it is possible, when the parties concerned are a government on the one side and a citizen on the other, for the one to justify its conduct to the other, whether it be the enforcement of obedience or an act or policy of disobedience.

In modern times the question has most often been put in terms of justifying obedience to government, but when the question is put in this way there is at any rate a suggestion that obedience is in greater need of justification than disobedience is. The situation we have in mind, however, is one in which one of the parties has open to him the alternatives of obeying or disobeying, and hence, if he is to justify his conduct he must be ready to justify obedience if that is the course he decides he should adopt, or disobedience if that is the course he decides he should adopt. The presumption against obedience has been encouraged, of course, by the theory of a State of Nature in which men are supposed to live without any political superior. For the masterless condition is, in the very act of being called 'natural', regarded as original and in some degree proper, so that it is the derivative civil state that is called upon to produce credentials. In fact, however, it is men who have been born in civil society and have lived their lives in it who may come, on occasion, to doubt whether they owe loyalty to the state, and therefore their position is more realistically described as one in which reasons are put forward in favour of disobedience than as one in which they ask why they should obey. The question 'Why should I obey the laws of the state?' might, therefore, be understood as a question about whether there ought to be any state or government at all rather than as a call for justification in a dispute between a citizen and his government. Justifying government is a very different thing from justifying the acts of this or that government or of this or that objector. It is the latter sort of justification that I wish to consider, since it seems more reasonable to set out from a situation that sometimes arises than to raise a question which is so abstract that we cannot even see how to begin answering it.

Obedience to government is a clear enough idea—there is a law or ordinance, and those people obey it who do what is prescribed to them in it. Disobedience, however, may take a variety of forms. It may take the form of refusing to obey and of then remaining passive to receive the penalties of disobedience. It may take the form of not obeying and of endeavouring to escape the legal consequences. Or it may take the form of not obeying and of endeavouring to overthrow the government by force and to replace it by some other government. The first form of disobedience is called, curiously enough, 'passive obedience', by virtue, I suppose, of the obedience given to the officers who apply the penalties. The second form of disobedience is of no interest to us in this paper, since either it is nothing but a sort of unprincipled subterfuge or else it leads to the third. The third form of disobedience is rebellion, and it is this that writers on the subject have mostly had in mind when they have considered the alternative to obeying the state authorities. I hope to show later that the first form of disobedience, that called 'passive obedience', has a very important role to play in the process of political justification.

It will be noticed that in the last two paragraphs I have very briefly commented on two important features of the Whig tradition in political philosophy. Whig political philosophers have generally assumed a 'natural', masterless condition from which men moved into civil society. Because of this assumption, Whigs have supposed that it is obedience rather than dis-obedience that needs to be justified. Whig political philosophers have also generally regarded forcible resistance rather than passive obedience as the proper counter to tyranny. I have now made the preliminary suggestion that, if we start our enquiry from the realistic situation of particular citizens in dispute with a particular government rather than from the abstract one of natural men and government in general, we shall get a more adequate idea of what political justification is.

II

'Justification', says Wittgenstein, 'consists in appealing to something independent.' The parties we are considering, the upholders of government on the one hand and the objector on the other, are both seeking to justify their position, are both seeking to justify, that is to say, the action they propose to take, and they both believe, therefore, that there is something they can both refer to that will somehow *show* that one course or the other is the right one. We must consider, therefore, what this independent thing can be, and wherein its independence consists.

It is natural to use the word 'appeal', and to think, in the first place, of the legal notions of laws, rules, courts, and judges. Of course, when the dispute is about obedience or disobedience the appeal cannot be made to the *actual* laws, since with regard to them the judge can only counsel obedience, except in so far as the disputed ordinance may be unconstitutional and obedience is deferred until this can be established by the appropriate court. Nevertheless, when the attempt is made to carry rational discussion of the sort of issue we are considering as far as it can be carried, as much as possible of the judicial atmosphere and procedure is retained. It is a matter of 'Let God be my judge' or 'I must lay my case before a Higher Court than that which now has me in its power'. This tendency to appeal beyond an actual court or positive law is present even when there is no dispute between government and subject, as can be seen from the frequency with which fundamental laws are regarded as of divine origin. It is only the most sophisticated governments which support their legislation by reference merely to their own fiat. In cases of dispute there is generally some attempt at putting both government and objector side by side before some common superior. If this were not done, neither governments nor objectors could take even the first step in justifying themselves, the former because they could do no more than threaten in their own name, the latter because disobedience undoubtedly is disobedience.

We are led in the first place, then, to laws which are held to bind governments no less than subjects. These laws are regarded both by the subject and the government as having authority over them. Neither party is in a position to change them. Neither party can claim to have made them. If they form part of any actual legislation, the legislator is not their creator or author but merely their transmitter. But what kind of law can this be, and how is it formulated? It does not help, except perhaps in a practical way, to say that it is divine, since either God *willed* it and it is arbitrary, or else he *transmits* it and we are back where we started. It is hard to get beyond the notion of laws which no one has made and which have authority over individuals and governments. When we say that they have authority over individuals and governments we mean that individuals and governments ought to submit to them. Submitting to them is using them to guide and justify conduct, and this could not be done unless there were some awareness of them. Moral laws are, of course, the main instance of this kind of law, and, for purposes of political justification it is they, along with customary law and Natural Law, that are appealed to. Natural Law is that part of the moral law that is relevant to political or other public concerns, so that for our present purposes we have to consider customary law and Natural Law. Customary laws are, of course, different in different parts of the world, whereas Natural Law is held to be universal. Furthermore, whereas Natural Law is held to be rational in a manner that is in some degree analogous to the intuitive rationality of some logical and mathematical axioms, customary law is obviously an historical growth which cannot claim anything in the slightest degree like logical or mathematical rationality. The obviousness, to members of a traditional society, of their customary laws, is the result of training and familiarity, while the obviousness of Natural Law has been thought to indicate a moral necessity analogous to logical necessity. Now when Wittgenstein said that justification consists in appealing to something independent, he had in mind, as the independent thing, something like a railway timetable. It is only when there is such a thing to refer to that an opinion about the official time of a train or a suggestion about when it will be necessary to leave home to catch it, can be justified, and the question arises whether customary law or Natural Law could be appealed to in any such way. Is customary law or Natural Law a public object that both parties to a dispute can have, so to say, before them as a means of settling their difference?

To refer to the customs of a society is, of course, much more complicated than referring to a railway timetable, but in principle there is a certain similarity. For example, there may be written records of some of these customs, and there may be recognized experts in them who, on being consulted, will give a definite and unanimous response. Unless this is so, it is in vain that appeal is made to customary law. If the authenticity of the documents or the bona fides of the experts are doubted, and if no revised documents or purified experts are forthcoming and acceptable, then justification of this sort has become impossible. It is logically impossible for A to justify a course of action to B if B rejects the authorities to which A appeals. To withdraw confidence from the texts and their interpreters just is to withdraw from this particular mode of justification. When faith in a traditional order is breaking down, those who have lost their faith say that the defenders of the old order are irrational. By this they mean that they are appealing to rules that have no authority. The revolutionaries in such a situation, therefore, are calling upon their opponents to submit the dispute to a new tribunal. This might conceivably be the customs of some other traditional society so that one individual point of reference would be substituted for another. But it is more usual, once the traditional order has been questioned, for the new appeal to be made to the universal system of Natural Law.

Now Natural Law is not individual and identifiable in the detailed way in which the customs of a particular society may be. It is said to be discoverable, of course, in the hearts and minds of all men, but policies of action cannot be justified by each party's proclaiming that something within him requires him to do what he is doing and the other man to do what he tells him. One's own inward conviction is not something independent that can be appealed to by *both* parties to the dispute. To refer inwards in this way may be to adopt the *arbitrary* attitude that is incompatible with justification of any kind. To this it may be replied that it is of the essence of Natural Law that each individual, looking within himself, finds the *same* principles, and that, this being so, it can *both* be found inwardly *and* serve as a common principle of justification. But how does any individual know that other men have discovered the same thing, by looking within themselves, that he has found by looking within himself? Only by comparing what they say with what he has found. Hence the existence of common principles of Natural Law written in each heart or mind can only be of practical relevance if they are also spoken or written in some common tongue. If, therefore, they are to serve as principles of justification in political disputes there must be some list of them, or some recognized custodian of them, to which common reference is made. At a time when philosopher-lawyers like Grotius or Pufendorf were held throughout Europe to be capable of formulating them in generally acceptable terms, there was still a possibility of appealing to them as to something independent of the particular whim or interest of some tyrant or fanatic. But when jurists and philosophers had each become specialists, the jurists concerning themselves almost exclusively with particular systems of positive law, and the philosophers, as Rousseau noted, striving at all costs to be original, the Natural Law, through being disregarded, ceased to serve as a source of justification, although if it came into regard once more, it might resume the office it has now relinquished.

Concrete principles of customary law, and the more abstract principles of Natural Law, have each their practical merits and defects as an independent point of reference in political justification. To appeal to the customs of a particular society is to appeal to something fairly definite. Furthermore, when such an appeal is made in a dispute between a government and a subject or group of subjects it is obvious that they both regard themselves as members of the same continuing society and

hence have a common concern of a pretty concrete kind. These
are the features of customary society that led Hegel to prefer it
as a less abstract and less arbitrary ('subjective') court of appeal
than Natural Law. When there is no single church or other
universal community to proclaim it, Natural Law suffers from
the two opposite defects of being, on the one hand platitudinous
and therefore settling nothing, or on the other hand of being
constantly added to and interpreted so that different parties
appeal to, or even manufacture, different parts of it. This second
defect may be illustrated by Berkeley's polemical device of
supporting his defence of passive obedience by claiming that it is
a precept of Natural Law. In general, Natural Law consists of
rules by which actions may be condemned or merely permitted
rather than rules that lead towards positive achievements. Since
it is largely negative, there can be no such attachment to it on the
part of individuals as exists when there is loyalty to a specific set
of institutions.

A third sort of independent thing to which appeal is made in
political justification is the common good or general happiness.
But before I pass on to discuss this it will be useful, I think, if I
linger somewhat on the notion, prominent, as I have already
said, in certain forms of Natural Law theory, of appealing to
practical maxims held to be revealed to the heart or mind or
reason of each individual. The appeal to conscience is often
regarded in this way, and Hegel, if what I have said above is
correct, was not without reason in suspecting a tendency towards
arbitrariness in this inward-looking procedure.   Let us, therefore, consider how the appeal to conscience is associated with
political justification.

III

We have imagined, it will be recalled, a dispute between a
government on the one hand and a subject on the other. The
latter is inclined to disobey some important legal command, and
the issue is to be discussed rationally and fairly between the
parties. We ask how either party could justify its decision to the

other, and the form of justification we now have to consider is that known as 'the appeal to conscience'. It is pointed out on the one hand that such an appeal may be quite whimsical and that crimes may be committed in the name of conscience no less than in the name of liberty. This was Hegel's opinion when he remarked that Robespierre's Reign of Virtue almost immediately became an unprincipled Reign of Terror. On the other hand, however, there is something respectable and impressive about the appeal to conscience which makes us reluctant to say that there is nothing in it but arbitrary whim.

According to the *Oxford English Dictionary*, one meaning of 'conscience' is 'consciousness of right and wrong', and when the word is understood in this way a man is not necessarily consulting some private voice when, as we say, he searches or consults his conscience. For a man who searches his conscience is trying to make up his mind about what he ought to do, and if he says that his conscience forbids him to obey, he means that he *ought* to disobey, and if asked why, he will refer, not to any private illumination, but to the considerations that have led him to make this decision. It would take me too far from the main object of this paper if I were to discuss in detail what sort of considerations these are. Some have already been mentioned when we discussed custom and Natural Law, but there will obviously be more specific ones relating to the particular situation of the agent and the people with whom he is connected. My point here is that they are normally open to formulation and discussion. Discussion between disagreeing parties can go on until action is necessary, and at that point both parties must act on the judgement they have by then reached.

It should be observed that each party may think that the other is right in opposing him. Let us suppose that A has decided that he ought to refuse obedience, and that B has decided that it is his duty to secure A's arrest in the event of A's doing this. It is quite possible that A thinks that B ought to arrest him and that B thinks that A ought to disobey. A, for example, may be a political leader who has told his followers that a certain measure should be disobeyed if it becomes law, and the measure may have become law and have been disobeyed already by some of A's followers. In such circumstances (which it would be tedious to elaborate) it might be A's duty to disobey even though he now recognizes that he ought not to have urged this in the first place, and B might agree that A ought to disobey though he believes it is his own duty to proceed against A for it. In such a situation, the conflict of the different people's duties is by no means a sign of arbitrariness. Indeed, the fact that each recognizes that the other ought to oppose him shows that both parties are guided by a similar view of the same system of social relationships within which they occupy different positions.

The next case to be considered is that in which one or both of the parties thinks that the other party is *not* doing what is right. Let us suppose, for example, that A thinks he ought to disobey and that B thinks that A ought to obey. B may nevertheless also think that A is quite sincere in holding his mistaken view and in endeavouring to pursue his wrong course of action. B might come to think, therefore, that A's false view of his duty being what it is, A ought to disobey. In such a case, B is able to consider A's duty from A's point of view, to contemplate the circumstances that A considers, and to see that if they were as A thought they were, then it *would* be A's duty to do what A now (mistakenly) thinks is right. This leads us to a most important step. For we now say: '*If* A had been aware of such and such, and had realized the relevance of this or that moral rule, then he would have seen that he ought to have done X; but the matter appeared differently to him at the time, and he therefore did right to follow his own conscience.' In these circumstances B may hold that A ought to follow his own conscience rather than to do what B has rightly told him to do. The case we considered in the last paragraph was of one individual recognizing that another ought to oppose him because of this other man's situation and the duties involved in it. The case we are now considering is of one individual recognizing that another man ought to oppose him because of this other man's sincerely held but false view of what his duty is. The essence of this second case is that a man ought to follow his own conscience rather than what someone else tells him to do when these two things come into conflict.

We must next consider, therefore, what it would be for someone to do what someone else told him to do instead of following his own conscience. The case we are considering is that in which A is doing what he has decided he ought to do notwithstanding B's arguments to the contrary. For this to happen, A must have *made up his mind* that he ought to disobey. If he is to do what B tells him to do rather than what his conscience tells him to do, he must have made up his mind he ought to disobey and must decide to obey notwithstanding this. That is to say, when the time for action comes he must fail to do what he is quite sure he ought to have done. He must therefore have been *tempted* in some way. In the case we are considering, in which B is an officer of the government, it is possible that A obeys him against his conscience out of fear. Or he may have been attracted by personal liking for him, or by general respect for his authority, or he might merely have been lazy, since conformity is generally the more immediately comfortable course. But once A has decided he ought to disobey he has also decided that submission to any of these or to any similar temptations would be wrong. For example, if he has decided that he ought to disobey notwithstanding his friendship for B, then if he allows this friendship to influence him into obedience, it must be, in his own eyes, a *reprehensible* act of friendship that he performs. It will be seen that we must distinguish here between a man's making up his mind what his duty is and then being tempted not to perform it, and his not being able to make up his mind or his making it up and then changing it. Thus, two of the temptations I have just mentioned, that of friendship and that of respect for authority, might not always be temptations in the way in which fear and laziness are. For A might first think he ought to disobey and then, when he considers his friendship for B or the many achievements of the government that B is serving, he may hesitate and finally conclude that, after all, these weigh the balance in favour of obedience.

There is, I think, a rather important conclusion to be drawn from this. If there is to be a clear case of anyone's acting against his conscience, he must have, so to say, a *definite* conscience, and must be, if not *absolutely* convinced, then at any rate pretty sure, of the direction in which his duty lies. When a man's moral situation is complicated (as is very often the case in political affairs) he may hesitate between different courses and finally take the course he does, not from any strong conviction of its rightness, but because events force *some* action upon him and this action seems at any rate not to be wrong. We might say that in such cases his conscience approves a *range* of actions or does not strongly disapprove of any single member of that range, so that to go against his conscience would be to go against this whole range. If so, then *following* his conscience would not be any very definite thing, but would involve a conviction of what ought *not* to be done along with doubts about the positive course. This indicates that in very complicated political situations it may be most misleading to suggest that there is any positive course that is a matter of conscience for any of the parties concerned, although it will always be possible to imagine actions which it would be wrong for any of them to perform. In such situations, honourable men may decide on a course because *some* decision *must* be taken and this one is not wrong.

Nevertheless, if someone *is* convinced that a particular course is his duty, then that is the course *he* ought to pursue. It is this proposition that has seemed to some philosophers to make conscience a variable and personal affair and to suggest that a man's duty is what he *thinks* is his duty. On the one hand it seems obvious that if a man thinks he ought to pursue a certain course, then that is the course he ought to pursue, and yet, on the other hand, it seems shocking to suggest that a man's duty just is what he *thinks* it is. Attempts have been made to resolve this conflict by distinguishing between subjective and objective duty, but it seems to me that the matter can be dealt with more convincingly in the following way. In the first place, as we have seen, a man does not have to look within himself for some purely private guide in order to find what it is that he thinks is his duty. He has to consider the situation in which he must act, relevant principles of behaviour, probable consequences of this or that course, other people's expectations, and so on. He may find it hard to decide what he ought to do, and if action is forced upon him there may not be any single action which his conscience prescribes. In such circumstances he may well take other people's advice, or even be persuaded or bullied by them, without acting contrary to his conscience, since on this matter his conscience is not formed or definite. In such a case, his duty to do what he thinks is his duty, is his duty to act cautiously and without fanaticism on a course that he is quite prepared to find is not the right one after all. But if, on the other hand, a man has come to a *definite* conclusion that he ought to act in a certain way, then this is the *only* way he can act in without going against his conscience.

There is a sense of 'think' in which it merely indicates that a view is actually held by someone, as in the sentence: 'He thinks that the Etruscans originally came from Asia Minor.' There is another sense of 'think' in which it indicates that the man who is said to think something is aware that his view is not certainly true, as in the sentence: 'He thinks that the Etruscans originally came from Asia Minor but is by no means dogmatic about it.' There is a third sense of 'think' in which someone who knows that someone else is in error may express this by saying, with emphasis on the main verb: 'That is what he *thinks*', or by saying some such thing as: 'He *thinks* that Napoleon was born in France.' In the sense of 'think' in which it refers to someone's actual moral belief, a man could not possibly do his duty without doing what he thinks is his duty, for there is nothing else that a man intent on doing his duty *could* do. In the sense of 'think' in which it indicates hesitation on the part of the person who is said to be thinking, no *definite* conscience can be said to exist, so that 'It is his duty to do what he thinks is his duty' means that it is his duty to do one of a certain range of actions, that he will not do wrong if he does any one of them, and that he will do wrong if he does none of them. In the sense of 'think' in which it indicates that the man who is said to think is wrong, 'It is his

4

duty to do what he thinks is his duty' means: 'He has a wrong view about what his duty is, but since he can only act on or against the view he actually has, then from the moral point of view he will do better to act on his wrong view than to be tempted away from it by laziness or self-interest or by some other non-moral consideration.' The dictum, therefore, that a man's duty is to do what he *thinks* is his duty, is not, when properly understood, either sceptical or nihilistic. It emphasizes that moral action is conscious action, and that conscious action is necessarily performed in the light of circumstances as they appear to the agent. It emphasizes, furthermore, that it is possible to make mistakes about what one ought to do without those mistakes being morally reprehensible, however unfortunate they may be in other respects.

It will be seen, therefore, that when we consider an action from the point of view of conscience we always consider it from the point of view of the person who performs it. No one can have a conscience about what someone else does—unless, indeed, he has induced this other person to do whatever it is that he has done. Talk about conscience, therefore, is necessarily about how an act or course of action accords or fails to accord with the agent's view of what he ought to have done. It follows from this that if one man knows what another man's conscience tells him to do, and if this, if done, would lead to actions which conflict with what the first man's conscience tells *him* to do, then the first man may both approve the actions of the other man and at the same time conscientiously oppose them. How does this affect the matter when the first man is an agent of the government and the second man is a conscientiously disobedient subject? Justification cannot be merely in terms of one's own inner tribunal. If it is to be distinguishable from an arbitrary fiat or egotistic coup there must be something independent to appeal to. But when consciences clash in the fundamental way I have just been describing, what is there to appeal to? There may be nothing but the rule that it is better for a man to follow his own conscience even though, in the view of other people, it is a wrong conscience (what Aquinas calls a *conscientia errans*), than for him

to follow any course that does not have the sanction of his conscience. This rule, by itself, can do very little to lead to practical
agreement between the parties who appeal to it. It can lead them
to respect one another, but if they are to co-operate practically
they must both of them be able to appeal to something more
definite and concrete than the personally centred principle of
merely following conscience whatever it may be.

There are some consequences of this that seem to me to
be rather important for political philosophy. If two parties are
to accept and act on the principle that a man ought to follow his
own conscience whether it be right or wrong, each must be able
to ascertain what the other party's conscience is. It is notorious
that in complex political circumstances this is very difficult and
that in consequence they give rise to a good deal of suspicion and
cynicism. If this is to be lessened—it can hardly be possible
to allay it altogether—a man who is appealing to an idiosyncratic
or minority conscience must have some means of showing that
it is indeed to his conscience that he is making his appeal. He
can only do this by the consistency of his behaviour in relation
to the peculiar principles he professes and, more particularly,
by his sticking to them when this results in his personal dis-
advantage. This is why I said above that 'passive obedience' has
an important part to play in the process of political justification.
Those who disobey the laws are often endeavouring to further
their own personal ends or to oust others from positions of
power and prestige, but when disobedience is accompanied by
submission to legal penalties the distinction between ambition
and personal integrity is marked as closely as it can be. It may
be marked, also, by the hardships which a revolutionary is
prepared to undergo in his unpopular cause, but who knows
what daydreams of an ultimate refined vengeance sustain him?
The distinction is marked too, though somewhat less drastically,
by the convention of some parliaments that a minister resigns if
some important policy or prediction of his comes to nought. The
failure may be due to no serious fault on his part, and he may be
the most suitable person to retrieve the situation, but he resigns
in order to demonstrate that his own career is of less real concern

to him than is the successful performance of the duties of his office. If a statesman thinks that the public good requires him to play the part of a trimmer, he runs the risk of obloquy and can at the best hope for no more than an ambiguous epitaph. Trimming, however high-minded it may be in a particular series of events, debases the political currency by increasing the difficulties of distinguishing between what is genuine and what is counterfeit.

I said above that when each party to a political dispute allows that the other is following his conscience, each will respect the other. Now this respect is something over and above the respect that consists in paying attention to the rights of others. The respect I am now calling attention to arises from a recognition that the individual who is respected is doing his duty as he sees it, and involves more, therefore, than a mere readiness to respect his rights. A question, here, for political philosophers concerns how, in what sort of action, one party can manifest his recognition that his opponent is following his conscience. There is no space to pursue this very far, but we may note that this sort of respect does not necessarily issue in leniency or indulgence, whether by government to subject or subject to government, since it is one thing to recognize that someone else is doing his duty and quite another to change one's own view of what one's own consists in. Indeed, an extreme readiness to give way before the moral challenge of others may, by making the profession of moral challenger an easy one, increase the occasions on which conscience is the cover for ambition. It is obvious that the sort of language the parties use in addressing one another is most important, and that abuse and contempt are quite incompatible with the recognition that the other party is following his conscience. The general point I should like to make here is that if this sort of respect is to be possible, fixed modes of manifesting it must exist; there must be etiquettes or rituals which all the parties understand and use. These may, of course, change, but if in some access of radicalism they are abolished, then justification in terms of conscience becomes quite impossible.

What has just been said, I think, throws some light on the nature of the liberal political ideal. Liberalism arose, in part, out of the struggle for religious toleration, in the course of which such men as Bayle and Locke appealed to the principle that it is wrong to require an individual to subscribe to religious principles that produce no conviction in him. Bayle argued that penalties against the profession of particular religious beliefs ignored that 'the first and most indispensable of our obligations is that of never acting against the inspiration of conscience', and Locke wrote that 'No way whatsoever that I shall walk in against the dictates of my conscience will ever bring me to the mansions of the blessed'. Now if what Bayle and Locke wrote and what I have just said is correct, it may follow that it is the duty of the persecutor to follow his persecuting conscience, though he should also respect the conscience of the religious dissenter by whatever means this sort of respect is exercised. It will certainly be the duty of the dissenter to undergo punishment or to go to some other country rather than to profess a religion that he believes is false. Thus the principle of respect for conscience cannot, on its own, provide a rule by which conflicting policies may be judged. Its inability in this respect is (or would be were it possible) still further increased when it is suggested that different people may act conscientiously in terms of opposed moral codes. Moral tolerance raises greater difficulties than religious tolerance does, and I am inclined to believe that the liberal principle of toleration is of little practical importance unless it is associated with more definite rules such as are comprised in Natural Law. We may ask, in this connection, whether there are rules of conduct which could not possibly function as principles of conscience. No one, for example, could be conscientiously wicked, in the sense of ascertaining what would be wrong for him to do and then deliberately doing it just because it was wrong. This is impossible because we mean by 'following conscience' the attempt to do what the agent believes is right. Could a man, then, make lying, or murder, a principle of conscience? He would have to believe that it was right for him to deceive other people, not only occasionally, but

regularly, and that it was right for him to take the lives of
innocent non-combatants. It is difficult to take at all seriously
the idea that someone who is at all capable of thinking in terms
of doing what is right should regard it as a matter of conscience
that he should follow a rule of deception or assassination. The
case of the Thugs (or Thags) of India is often cited in this
connection, but the fact that they gave only a part of their loot
to their goddess Kali and kept most of it for themselves suggests
that the *Encyclopaedia Britannica* is correct in describing them
as 'a confederacy of professional assassins'. Kant was substantially right when he said that 'in the case of natural laws
there can be no innocent errors'. Conscience is so incongruous
with systematic violation of Natural Law that we tend to believe
that someone who claims conscience for such violations is either
mad or a pretender. Moral tolerance, therefore, can only extend
to such moral differences as do not conflict with the basic moral
principles. Authenticity has no claim to respect (although it
may be admired as an animal or other natural object is admired)
unless it is consistent with these principles.

IV

I have said that a third independent thing that is appealed to
in political justification is the common good or general happiness.
The phrase 'common good', of course, is part of the vocabulary
of Natural Law theorists, but when this system fell into disrepute the idea arose that the general happiness was something
more definite which could be appealed to with greater prospect
of agreement. Indeed, Bentham and J. S. Mill believed that if
the utilitarian criterion was used, it would enable scientific
methods to be employed in matters of government and facilitate
social agreement thereby. Obedience or disobedience, or any
other disputed social decision, would be justified by appealing
to the knowledge that one course rather than the other would
in fact lead to the greatest happiness. Bentham, with his belief
that money could be used as an instrument for measuring happiness just as thermometers are used for measuring temperatures,

thought that this would be a simpler thing to do than it has in fact proved to be. In the last hundred years such things as statistics of death and disease, of output, incomes and consumption, along with the device of the retail price index, have been used in the hope that they would do what Bentham had hoped would be done with the money measure. Disputes about rights, it was thought, are as insoluble as the disputes of metaphysicians, and would be rendered obsolete, as metaphysics has been, by use of scientific methods.

This is a view that deserves a great deal more examination than it usually gets either from its supporters or opponents, and here I can only call attention to one or two fundamental points.

It will be noticed in the first place that stress is laid on the importance of ascertaining which course of conduct will in fact lead to the general happiness of the society in question. But the attempt to find out the most effective means of carrying out the policy it is desired to carry out is relevant not only to the utilitarian system of justification but also to the others I have mentioned, since *any* course that is undertaken is the better for being carried out in the light of the best available knowledge. It is not this aspect of scientific utilitarianism, therefore, that needs our attention here, but that part of it that concerns the end to be aimed at and its more or less accurate estimation.

In the second place, then, let us consider the end to be achieved. There are two features of it that need examination, its measurability on the one hand, and its singleness or individuality on the other.

As to the first, the utilitarian aim has been to secure as long life as possible along with as little disease and as little poverty as possible. The measurable content of happiness thus consists in longevity, health and the consumption of goods. Now it is obvious that there are many things besides these that are prized and form part of happiness. Some of these extra things, such as sport and artistic enjoyment, can be submitted to some sort of quantitative treatment, by such methods as enumerating the members of sports clubs or of books purchased or plays produced. Others, such as the happiness to be gained in love and friendship, do not seem to be amenable to this sort of treatment at all, and yet make up a large part of what is most satisfying in the lives of happy people. Why, then, should there be so much stress on the measurable aspects of happiness? Partly, no doubt, just because they *are* measurable in a fashion and so *can* provide *some* sort of basis for comparison. (We are all familiar with the method of justifying an educational policy in terms of money spent or buildings put up.) But it would be a mere irrational obsession with measurability to deny the existence or importance of those parts of happiness that cannot be measured. Another reason, no doubt, is that life, health and the consumption of (at least some) goods are conditions of there being any happiness at all. But why should we be asked to judge the whole happiness of a society in terms of what are so obviously only a part of it? I believe that there is only one answer to this that has any plausibility, namely, that it is believed that the standard enjoyments that all can have ought to be given priority over the more refined pleasures of which many people may be incapable. If this is so, then the measurable happiness criterion is not an independent one, but depends upon a view about just distribution and just timing which may or may not be correct but which must be judged in terms of rights and duties and other terms of traditional morality and Natural Law.

In conclusion something must be said about the singleness or individuality of the end referred to when appeal is made to the common good or general happiness. It cannot be doubted that when there are important disputes within a society, those who are sincerely aiming at a right solution regard the appeal to the common good as relevant and necessary. But what is this common good, and how can it be referred to in the process of political justification? The word 'common' in the phrase 'common good', and the word 'general' in the phrase 'general happiness', are clearly meant to contrast, in some way, with what is peculiar or particular. When individuals or groups are opposed to one another and wish to justify their case rationally, it will not constitute such a justification if each appeals to his *own* good. Hence 'common' cannot refer to some range of personal interests that every individual member of the society has—if it did our liability to service could never be more than limited. Perhaps, then, the appeal, in such circumstances, is to a rule that applies to all in the way that moral rules do. If so, it must be to a rule that concerns the society as a whole as well as each individual in it. Following out this line of thought, we can conceive of such rules as the following. 'All the members of this society are, together, more important than any single member of it.' 'No individual or group within this society has a right to ignore the rights and interests of the rest.' 'We all have a duty to try to maintain our society as a whole, even to the extent of risking personal extinction.' It seems to me that it is this sort of rule, with a reference to a *particular* society, that is appealed to in political justification. Furthermore, justification is by reference to a society rather than by reference to a number of individuals. I suppose it is true that the existence or survival of many individuals is more important than the existence or survival of one individual, though some might question this, and in any case it is difficult to be sure that the convincingness of the proposition is not due merely to the arithmetical truth that many are more than one. But the appeal to the common good seems to presuppose loyalty to a society that continues in being longer than does the membership of any set of contemporary individuals. Other principles of Natural Law, such as those about promises or gratitude, apply to any man anywhere. But the duty to have regard to the common good is different from these, and has some kinship with the older mode of justification by reference to the customs of a given society. The difference is that, whereas the appeal to custom was to fairly fixed rules of behaviour, the appeal to the common good in modern times involves reference to institutions that are known to be changing. This would be as uncertain as an appeal to a judge who could change the law whenever he wished, were it not that many of the changes are in accordance with aims that are shared and promoted by most members of the society. Even so, political justification in a modern society is a much less definite process than it was in earlier times, since the common good to which appeal is made is so much more volatile.

MAIN PUBLICATION

The Illusion of the Epoch: Marxism-Leninism as a Philosophical Creed. Cohen and West. 1955.

PHILOSOPHICAL SCEPTICISM

By A. J. AYER

*Grote Professor of Philosophy of Mind and Logic in the
University of London*

PHILOSOPHICAL SCEPTICISM

IT is now often said that philosophical scepticism is not serious, and there is a sense in which this is true. The philosopher who tells us that it is doubtful whether the sun will rise tomorrow is not issuing a warning, in the way that an astronomer might; he is not inviting us to take precautions against a natural catastrophe. The philosopher who protests that he has no good reason for believing that anyone besides himself can think or feel is not any the less ready to sympathize with his fellow men or to pay attention to their views. This is not to say that philosophic doubts of this kind have no influence at all upon the behaviour of those who entertain them. To be unable to see one's way out of the prison of solipsism may well produce a sense of isolation. Yielding to phenomenalism may make the world seem insubstantial: distrust of induction may make it seem perilous. And no doubt there are psychological reasons why philosophers adopt such positions; a psycho-analyst might be able to account for someone's finding these difficulties especially acute. But the point of philosophical scepticism does not lie in its effects; nor would the discovery of its causes, however interesting in itself, enable us to evaluate its content. It rests upon argument: if we wish to understand it, the argument has to be examined.

One way to bring out the peculiarity of the philosopher's doubts is to contrast them with the scientist's. The difference is not only that the scientist's doubt is commonly directed upon particular theories or propositions, whereas the philosopher's is more general, applying as it does indiscriminately to all forms of inductive reasoning, or to any statement about the past, or to any supposed perception of a physical object, irrespective of the circumstances. The scientist's doubt also may be general; what it puts in question may be not just some special theory, but a method of procedure, a standard of proof. But in such cases the suggestion is that the procedure works badly, that adherence to the standard of proof misleads us into accepting false propositions for true; there is the implication that other methods or other standards would serve us better. And this is a question which it is left to experience to decide: the merit of rival procedures is tested by their results. But it is characteristic of a philosophical doubt that it cannot in this way be settled by experience. A philosopher who calls the reality of the external world in question does not for that reason expect to observe anything different from one who thinks it undeniable. Experience cannot decide between them, for the subject of their dispute is just how any such experience is to be interpreted. A philosopher who finds fault with inductive reasoning is not suggesting that some other method would work better; he would still object to it however well it worked; for part of his case is that its working well is not a reason for accepting it. In general, the philosophical sceptic sets out to disqualify the various sources of knowledge. But this disqualification is carried out on *a priori* grounds. It is independent of the candidate's actual performances.

Because this type of scepticism makes no appeal to experience, some philosophers would say that it was senseless. They would argue that a claim to knowledge could legitimately be denied, or doubted, only on the ground that it failed to reach a standard which some other claim might satisfy. An examination is not genuine if it is impossible that any candidate should pass it. Thus it makes sense to condemn some perceptions as illusory by contrast with others which are veridical; it makes sense to treat some forms of historical record as unreliable by contrast with others which are not; some problematic arguments can be irrational as opposed to others which are rational. But to suggest that all perceptions were illusory, all records unreliable, all problematic reasonings irrational, whatever their particular character, would be nonsensical: the fact that they were no longer contrasted with anything would deprive the words 'illusory', 'unreliable', 'irrational' of their use. It is only if something is genuine that anything can be fraudulent.

I think that this objection holds. Its defect is that it is too summary. It disposes of the sceptic's conclusions without considering the reasons which lead him to them; and what is philosophically interesting about scepticism is not the result, which no one seriously accepts, but the steps by which it is reached. In some cases, too, the sceptic could meet the argument by slightly moderating his position. He might maintain, for example, not that all our perceptions are illusory, but only that we can never be sure that any given one is not: this is indeed the form which scepticism about our knowledge of the external world most commonly takes. The objection would still remain that one could not know that any perceptions were illusory unless one knew that some were not; or, since the sceptic would not mind saying that one never does know either of these things, that the only ground that there can be for distrusting any one perception is that one trusts some other. Similarly, in all other fields, there would be no reason for judging that some particular piece of evidence was unreliable unless there were reliable evidence with which it conflicted. But, while this argument too is sound, it does no more than make the point that the sceptic's position finds no support in experience, that his reasons for doubt are not empirical. The implication is that this condemns it, and perhaps it does. But merely to say that the sceptic's reasons for doubt are *a priori*, and therefore illegitimate, is not enough. What is established is that these philosophical doubts do not, and cannot, have the warrant that scientific doubts may have: they function in quite a different way. But it would be rash to conclude from this that they have no force at all.

Allowing that the sceptic's contentions are not always senseless, some philosophers would be disposed to say that in that case they are simply false. It is alleged that one can never know what another person is thinking or feeling, that it is not certain that any physical object exists, that one can not know what will happen in the future or even what happened in the past, in short that nothing can be known for certain except possibly that one's momentary private experience has the content that it has. But the fact is that we do very often know what other people are thinking and feeling; it is quite certain that a great many physical objects, this piece of paper, for example, or the table at which I am seated, exist; there are countless facts that every one of us knows about the past and many that we know about the future, as for instance that the sun will rise tomorrow. Once again the objection is well-founded. We do often know such things: it is in many cases certain that they are so. And it is important that this should be remembered. It is a commonsense corrective to the philosopher's undermining of our confidence. All the same, I am inclined to say that such rough rejoinders are beside the point. Our sceptic, if he is at all sophisticated, will be ready to admit that common usage entitles us to say that we know a number of facts about other minds and about the past and possibly about the future: he will allow that as the word 'certain' is conventionally used, it is certain that this piece of paper exists. But still he wants to say that it is not really certain. He wants to say that we do not really know what goes on in the minds of others, or at least that it is very doubtful if we ever really do.

But how if one knows something can one really not know it? How, if something is certain, can it really not be? If anything satisfies the criteria for being certain, as the word 'certain' is ordinarily used, then it is certain. There is no real meaning of the word 'certain', or of any other word for that matter, beyond the meaning, or meanings, that it is conventionally given. If the sceptic denies that it is a correct use of the word 'know' to say that I know that this is a piece of paper, or if he denies that the criteria for knowing are satisfied in this instance, he is in each case wrong. And if he is not denying either of these things, what can his position be?

It may be suggested that he is making not so much a statement as a proposal. When he says that we really do not know what we claim to know, his use of the word 'really' is not factual, as one would normally expect it to be, but prescriptive. What he is saying, in effect, is that we ought not to use words like 'know' and 'certain' in the ways that we ordinarily do use them. We ought to give them a different, stricter, sense, a sense in which the criteria for their application are not so easily satisfied; and it is in this stricter sense, which he is recommending to us, that we really do not know what, in the ordinary sense, we do. He may not realize that he is making a linguistic recommendation: if he did, he would hardly make it so deviously; but that is what it comes to.

There is much in this suggestion; but it cannot be accepted quite as it stands. For what would be the point of such a proposal? What difference would it make if we agreed to it? If we could be persuaded that it was somehow improper to use such words as 'know' or 'certain' in the ways that we commonly do, we might find some other use for them, or drop them altogether; and then we should probably feel the need to adapt, or invent, some other words to do the work that they do now. But what philosophical question would this help to answer? No doubt philosophers are, or should be, seriously concerned with the meaning of words; but it surely cannot be of any special interest to them that such and such a function is, in a given language, performed by this word rather than that. There is, therefore, no reason why they should be specially interested in a proposal that some particular word should be robbed of its employment or made to change it. Neither is it clear from what motive such a proposal would be made.

But while it may not matter to anyone but a philologist what word is used to do what work, this does not apply to the work itself. There may be philosophical grounds for thinking that it is done badly or that it ought not to be done at all. Thus what looks like criticism of the choice of words may be a way of expressing dissatisfaction with the work that they perform. And I think that this is so in the case we are considering. The most important part of the work that is done by words like 'knowledge' and 'certainty' is to furnish guarantees of truth. To say that one knows something is to claim the right to be sure of it; to say that some one else knows something is to concede this right to him: to say that something is certain is to claim, or

5

allow, that it should not be doubted. Now the sceptic's position, as I interpret it, is that these concessions are made too lightly. This does not commit him to saying that we use the word 'know', or any other word, improperly. In one sense, we use such words correctly when we use them to claim or admit the appropriate guarantees. In another sense, we use them correctly when we apply them in accordance with the criteria which are ordinarily taken as warranting the guarantees. It is only in the second sense that dissatisfaction with the criteria can be interpreted as a wish to change the meaning of the words. The defect of this way of putting it is that it draws attention to an unimportant point, the fact that certain words are commonly used in the ways that they are, and away from the important point which is the consideration of the strength and nature of the backing which the guarantees require.

Not all sceptics would maintain outright that the backing with which we are normally contented is insufficient, that is, that our acknowledged criteria are not so stringent as they ought to be. But without denying that their satisfaction gives us the right to be sure one may still raise the question why it should. Such questions often take the form of asking how we know whatever it may be. And clearly to ask how we know something implies that we do know it. At the same time, the more difficult it is to see how something can be known the more one is tempted to conclude that it is not known after all. This is not to say that it is not true, or that there is not the conventional warrant for being convinced of its truth, but rather that even with this warrant we are not entitled to be sure. What happens is that failure to understand how we can in the circumstances be justified in making the claims we do leads to the suspicion that they are over-valued. Saying that we do not know what we think we know is a way of calling for a re-valuation.

Now to say that we over-value our evidence is to suggest that we might have better evidence than we do; but the peculiarity of the sceptic's position is that he rejects this suggestion. He wants to maintain both that a certain sort of evidence is in the circumstances the best that we could possibly have, and also that it is not good enough. It thus becomes for him a necessary fact that we have no sufficient guarantee of truth.

An illustration of this is provided by the problem of induction. In inductive reasoning we make the assumption that the future will, in the appropriate respects, resemble the past; or rather, since time is not in this case the important factor, that what has been found true in certain instances also holds good in further instances; in short, that there are fair samples in nature. As Hume saw, this assumption is not demonstrable; whatever measure of uniformity we ascribe to nature, there will be no self-contradiction in the denial that it holds. Neither, as Hume also saw, is it possible without circularity to show that this assumption is probable; for the only way of showing a hypothesis to be probable is to produce evidence which confirms it, and it is only if there are fair samples in nature that any evidence can be confirmatory. The same applies if we consider not some general assumption about the uniformity of nature, but any specific hypothesis or would-be natural law. Unless it is treated as a definition, in which case the problem is merely shifted on to that of making sure that anything satisfies the definition, such a proposition will not be demonstrable; the denial of it will not be self-contradictory. And once again to argue that it is probable is just to assume that inductive reasoning can be trusted. Attempts have indeed been made to find a backing for induction in the *a priori* theory of probability, but I do not think that they have been successful. It might even seem obvious that they could not be successful. For how from a purely mathematical calculus of chances could anything follow about what actually happens?

I think it may be granted that there is no way of turning induction into deduction: that is, that there is no device which will give to inductive arguments the formal validity that deductive arguments can have. Then those who raise the problem of induction are looking for an assurance that inductive reasoning, though not demonstrative, is nevertheless respectable. They want a proof that what we take to be good evidence really is good evidence. But what sort of proof could be forthcoming? Even if we could find some general principles, like Keynes's principle of limited independent variety, which would bestow at least the requisite probability upon the hypotheses that they covered, the validity of these principles themselves could still be questioned. They would not be demonstrable and any attempt to justify them on inductive grounds would be regarded as circular. We could claim that scientific procedure had served us well up to now, but to infer from this that we were right to trust it would again be to beg the question. But now it becomes clear that any answer that we can give is going either to be inadequate or else to beg the question. There can be no proof that what we take to be good evidence really is good evidence, because nothing is going to count as proof. And if it is to be held that without such proof all problematic reasoning is irrational, that all problematic reasoning is irrational will be a necessary fact.

Thus the sceptic proves his case. He successfully defies us by framing his challenge in such a way that it is impossible that it should be met. This still does not prevent a number of philosophers from trying to meet it, but for the most part it is now the custom to leave it alone. It is assumed that a demand for justification which there is no way of satisfying must be illegitimate. In current practice, justification gives way to analysis.

If the problem of induction has lost much of its sting, it is because the moves which lead to the sceptical impasse have become transparent. Once it is seen that there could be no court of superior jurisdiction, it becomes less troubling that inductive processes should be left, as it were, to act as justices in their own cause. There is, however, a class of cases in which the sceptic's arguments, though here too only underlining necessary facts, raise problems which it is not so easy to dismiss. These are the cases where the inference which is called in question is supposed not merely to extend our possessions within a given domain but to carry us from one domain to another. Examples are the passage from sense-data to physical objects, from the behaviour of other people to their inner thoughts and feelings, from the world of common-sense to the entities of science, from present to past. In all such instances we are supposed, at least for the purposes of the problem, to start with things that are accessible to our observation and to end with things that are not. The problem is to justify the transition. The sceptic sets the problem by arguing that it cannot be justified.

The first step in his argument is to establish that the objects to which we are inferring are not otherwise accessible to us. Thus it is maintained that while it may be correct in ordinary usage for us to speak of perceiving physical objects, we do not perceive them directly. They are not 'given' to us in the way that sense-data are. Similarly, one cannot observe another person's mind even in the way that one can observe his body; relatively to one's knowledge of their physical behaviour, one's knowledge of other people's thoughts and feelings is indirect. In the same way atoms and electrons, if they exist at all, are more heavily veiled from us than chairs and tables. The past enters into our knowledge only in so far as it is reflected in the present. In each case it is not just a mischance that we have at best to be content with indirect knowledge. It is logically impossible that it should be otherwise.

The second step in the argument is to show that no accumulation of the sort of evidence which is available to us can entail the conclusion which we wish to reach. There is no set of statements about sense-data, however long and complicated, from which it can be deduced that a physical object exists. Statements about people's inner thoughts and feelings do not follow from statements about their overt behaviour, nor statements about atoms and electrons from statements about scientific instruments or, more generally, from any set of statements about their so-called effects. However strong the present evidence for the existence of certain past events may be, it is not demonstrative. There would be no formal contradiction in admitting the existence of all the supposed records of the past, including our memory impressions, and yet denying that the corresponding past events had ever taken place.

But then, it is further argued, these inferences are not inductive either. Inductive reasoning is supposed to carry us, to echo Hume, from instances of which we have experience to those of which we have none. But setting aside the general problem of induction, it is essential that the instances of which we in fact have no experience should be such as we are capable of experiencing. From the fact that A's and B's have constantly been conjoined in our experience we infer when we come across an A that there is a B in the appropriate relation to it. But this inference to the existence of the unobserved B is here a substitute for the direct observation which for some practical reason we have not been able to make. Even allowing that this form of argument is justifiable, there is no warrant for extending it to cases where the things whose existence we are claiming to infer are such as not merely never have been observed but never could be. For what foundation could there then be for our inductive arguments and how could their success be tested? Some philosophers would go so far as to say that to infer the existence of something which was in principle unobservable was to reach a conclusion which was literally meaningless; and clearly no amount of inductive evidence can lead to a meaningless conclusion. But even if one does not go so far as this, it is plain, so the argument runs, that such conclusions can have no inductive backing. Experimental reasoning may carry us along at a given level, from actual to possible sense-data, from observation to prediction of overt behaviour: but it can never enable us to jump from one level to another.

It only remains to draw the conclusion that since these transitions cannot be justified either deductively or inductively, they cannot be justified at all. It would be a heroic sceptic who maintained that we had no right whatsoever to be sure, or even moderately confident, of anything concerning the existence of physical objects, or the minds of others, or the past. But even if he shrinks from carrying his argument to what appears to be its logical conclusion, he may still insist that it presents a question for us to answer. Perhaps we cannot be brought to doubt that we can come to know these things: but we have to explain how it is possible that we should.

It is this group of problems that provides the main subject-matter for what is called the theory of knowledge. They need not be treated as a single unit. A philosopher who will not be bothered with sense-data, and therefore sees no difficulty in the so-called problem of perception, may yet be disturbed by the sceptical arguments concerning other minds. One may be puzzled about the status of scientific entities while remaining indifferent to the argument which goes to show that we have no good reason for believing any statement about the past. But though the form of these arguments may be different in different cases, it is interesting to note that their pattern is the same.

There are various ways of meeting them. One is to deny the first step of all; to maintain that we do have direct access to what is here alleged to be inaccessible. This is the way of naïve realism. The position taken is that physical objects are perceived without any intermediary of sense-data, that one can by a form of intuition inspect the minds of others, that in memory one is directly acquainted with the past, that things like atoms and electrons are not in principle unobservable. Intuitionism in ethics supplies a further parallel. But of course it is possible to take up a naïve realist standpoint on any one of these issues, without being committed to it on the others.

Alternatively, one may deny the second step in the sceptic's argument. This is the way taken by those who pursue the policy of reduction. Physical objects are said by them to be logical constructions out of sense-data; the entities of science to be nothing over and above their so-called effects. The corresponding views in the other cases are that statements which appear to be about the minds of others are equivalent to statements about their bodies or about their actual and potential behaviour; and that statements which appear to be about the past are equivalent to statements about the present and future, that is to statements such as would normally be regarded as referring to records of past events, rather than to the past events themselves. Again, holding a reductionist view in one instance does not commit one to holding it in the others. Historically, there has been a sharp opposition between those who meet scepticism in this way and those who meet it in the first, but they have one important point in common. Both try to close the gap between evidence and conclusion through which the sceptic attacks. The naïve realist does so by bringing the evidence up to the level of the conclusion, the reductionist by bringing the conclusion down to the level of the evidence.

A third type of defence is to maintain that even though the gaps cannot be closed they can be bridged. Since the bridges are presented as the outcome of legitimate processes of inductive reasoning, this is a denial of the third step in the sceptic's argument. In some cases it is held that the objects of which our knowledge is in question, though not directly accessible to us in the straightforward way that the naïve realist supposes, are yet not in principle unobservable : they are unobservable given our situation, but our situation might logically be otherwise. This line may be taken with respect to the past and, less securely, with respect to other minds; when applied to other minds its point is to provide backing for the argument from analogy. In other cases it is admitted that the objects are unobservable but denied that this creates any special difficulty; with suitable safeguards, the introduction of unobservables is held to be legitimate. This attitude is most often assumed in dealing with the passage to scientific entities, but an example of it at a different level is to be found in the causal theory of perception. Since it is assumed that these unobservables are not reducible to their supposed effects, the problem of their status remains.

Finally, there is the course which may be described as that of taking the gap in one's stride. It is admitted that the step from evidence to conclusion is not deductive, and also that it is not inductive in the generally accepted sense. But this, it is held, does not condemn it. In each case, it is what it is. It can be analysed; we can, for example, show in what conditions we feel confident in ascribing certain thoughts or feelings to others; we can evaluate different types of record; we can distinguish the cases in which our memories or perceptions are taken to be reliable from those in which they are not. In short we can give a more or less detailed and enlightening account of the procedures that we actually follow. But no justification of these procedures is either necessary or possible. One can be called upon to justify a particular conclusion; one does so by appealing to the appropriate evidence. But no more in these cases than in the case of the problem of induction is it sensible to demand a proof that what we take to be good evidence really is so: there could be no such proof. On this view, the problems which the sceptic raises are insoluble because they are fictitious. It is the philosopher's task to exhibit the facts in such a light that the sceptic's logic leaves us unconcerned.

I cannot here attempt to discuss the validity of these various responses. This would require a detailed examination of each separate problem. There are, however, a few general comments which seem to me worth making. For instance, it may be said of the naïve realist position that it is not an answer to the sceptic's arguments so much as a refusal to consider them. The naïve realist escapes injury by remaining on the sidelines: he can be refuted only if he is lured into the game. Thus, if he can be got to maintain that sense-data are identical with the surfaces of physical objects or that memory images are identical with past experiences he can fairly easily be convicted of self-contradiction. But if, without bothering with sense-data or with memory images, he simply takes his stand on the fact that we perceive physical objects and remember past events, his position is secure. It has too in its favour the prestige of common sense: perception and memory are so much taken for granted that it seems perverse to make them the playthings of analysis. On the other hand, merely to say without further explanation that one has intuitive knowledge of the minds of others seems hardly adequate. To claim direct acquaintance with atoms and electrons would not even be correct, unless it were just a way of saying, again without explanation, that we do know certain scientific facts.

What is most objectionable about naïve realism is that it tries to disguise its empty-handedness. By invoking intuition, or direct acquaintance, it seems to be offering an account of the way in which things are known; but this account is spurious, or rather, it is no account at all. For example, to say that with memory one is in direct contact with the past may look as if it were an explanation of the way in which memory functions; but in fact the expression 'being in direct contact with the past' is intelligible in this context only if it is taken as a mere synonym for 'remembering'. In the same way, to say that physical objects are directly given is acceptable only if it is just a way of saying that we do perceive them. To say that one intuits the thoughts and feelings of others is false if it denies that one ever knows them by inference, but again acceptable if it merely stakes a claim to knowledge. It is in any case not an explanation. In general, to talk of intuition is in these contexts just a misleading way of insisting that we do know what we claim to know while dismissing the question how we know it. It is implied that no analysis is needed; perhaps even, what may very well be false, that no analysis is possible.

The naïve realist is happiest when the objects with which he has to deal hold a firm place in the ontology of common sense. The opposite is true of the reductionist. He most readily gains a hearing in the cases where we hesitate to say that the objects in question literally exist. The reductionist's hero is the average man who is patently a logical construction. There is no difficulty in translating the statements which are made about him into statements about men. But even in cases where a translation is not so easily forthcoming, the reductionist's approach still seems to be correct. I do not think that anyone has yet succeeded in laying down rules for translating statements about nations into statements about persons, but few of us would wish to say that nations were anything over and above the sets of persons who belonged to them. The example of the unconscious is perhaps less clear; but it is at least plausible to maintain that talking about people's unconscious thoughts and feelings must somehow or other be a way of talking about their behaviour. On the other hand, when it comes to the problem of other minds, there is great reluctance to consider that talking about the conscious mental states of others may be merely a way of talking about their behaviour: it seems sufficiently clear that one's own inner states are logically distinct from their outward manifestations, and one wishes to ascribe consciousness to others in exactly the same sense as one claims it for oneself. And if the reductionist's view of other minds is not very plausible, his treatment of the past is even less so. No one would be inclined on the face of it to identify past events with their present or future traces. If anyone takes this view it will be because some argument has convinced him that no other course is open.

In other cases it does not seem obvious either that the reductionist approach is right, or that it is wrong. There is nothing very shocking about the view that referring to atoms or electrons and other such theoretical entities is only a way of connecting the phenomena which they serve to explain. But so long as we fail to eliminate the expressions in which these entities are mentioned by providing translations in terms of the things to which they are supposed to be reduced, the claim that they are reducible remains rather empty. It seems to mark little more than a reluctance to say that these entities exist. What is required is an account of the way in which they enter into scientific theories and of the way in which these theories operate. Once this is achieved it may not very greatly matter whether we choose to say that they exist or not.

Much the same applies to phenomenalism in the usual sense; the thesis that the physical objects which we are commonly said to perceive are reducible to sense-data. Phenomenalism has been exposed to attack on the radical ground that the conception of sense-data is not precise or even clear: more seriously it has been argued that they are mythical entities imposed upon us through a philosophical confusion. I can only say here that I do not regard these arguments as conclusive. If an unobjectionable way of introducing sense-data can be found, there will at least be a case for saying that whenever we talk about physical objects we are in some way referring to sense-data. Even if sense-data are not admitted as entities, the same point may still be made in the form that things are nothing apart from, nothing over and above, what they seem. But here again the trouble is that the translations, the provision of which would validate this thesis, are not forthcoming: there are indeed good reasons for supposing that they can not be made. If he withdraws the claim that such translations are possible, the phenomenalist may have to be content with saying that physical objects are theoretical constructions which serve only to explain the occurrence of sense-data without being strictly reducible to them. This does not of course commit him, any more than the stronger version of phenomenalism, to saying that physical objects do not literally exist.

When it becomes so mild as this, the reductionist's method of answering the sceptic approaches the third of those that I listed, where an attempt is made not to close the gap between evidence and conclusion but only to bridge it. Neither is there any sharp distinction between the third method and the fourth. The difference is mainly one of emphasis. In the one case arguments are sought which will provide a justification for our closing the gap: in the other it is assumed that no such justification is required. But to the extent that the arguments simply rest upon showing how evidence and conclusion are related the two tend to coincide. It is, indeed, of little importance whether we regard the need for analysis as superseding the demand for justification or whether we make the justification consist in the analysis. In either case the analysis must be such that the sceptic's logic, when it cannot be shown to be faulty, must be made to seem innocuous. The question how this is to be achieved does not, I think, admit of any general answer. Though different in pattern, the problems which scepticism poses are different in detail; and in the cases where our defence is just to let the facts speak for themselves, it is the details that count.

MAIN PUBLICATIONS

Language, Truth and Logic. Gollancz. 1936 (Revised edition, 1946).
The Foundations of Empirical Knowledge. Macmillan. 1940.
Thinking and Meaning. Inaugural Lecture, H. K. Lewis. 1947.
Philosophical Essays. Macmillan. 1954.
Work Edited (with Raymond Winch), *British Empirical Philosophers*.
    Routledge and Kegan Paul. 1952.
Editor.   Pelican series of Philosophy Books.

ON SEEING AND HEARING

By WINSTON H. F. BARNES

Professor of Philosophy in the
University of Durham

ON SEEING AND HEARING

IN this paper I shall try to answer the question: What is it to see, hear, taste, smell or feel something? In one sense we all know. In another sense it is a matter for physiology. But in yet a third sense it is a philosophical question, the question whether when we speak of seeing something, for instance, we are referring to something existing or going on, some activity, process or state, distinct from all the physiological occurrences and everything which can properly be called 'bodily'.

The importance of the answer lies in its relevance to the more general controversy about the status of mind. Attempts to resolve the dualism of mind and matter in favour of matter are a recurring feature of philosophy. Materialism, with its notion of man as a machine, behaviourism with its conception of mind as something to be sought in the response of the organism as a whole to outside stimuli, and the more philosophical attempt of Professor Ryle in his *Concept of Mind*—all these allow no room, or seem to allow no room, for the experience of the senses, so far as we take this experience to imply the existence of goings-on fundamentally different from, no matter how closely related to, physical bodies with their qualities and their temporal and spatial relations.

A view commonly held by philosophers—so commonly held that one might almost call it the traditional view—is that seeing, hearing, tasting, smelling and feeling are 'operations of the mind': though they are private operations disclosed only to the person engaging in them. Locke, for example, refers to 'perception' as one of the operations of the mind which are disclosed by 'Reflection', in contrast with external things which are

65

disclosed by 'Sensation'. And he defines Reflection as 'that notice which the mind takes of its own operations, and the manner of them, by reason whereof there come to be ideas of these operations in the understanding'.[1] He explains: 'The term *operations* here, I use in a large sense, as comprehending not barely the actions of the mind about its ideas, but some sort of passions arising sometimes from them, such as is the satisfaction or uneasiness arising from any thought.'[2] Obviously he is not stressing very greatly the suggestion of activity in the term 'operation' since he is prepared to include pain and pleasure under this heading. He further says of Reflection: 'This source of ideas every man has wholly in himself';[3] and he clearly thinks that each man's Reflection acquaints him with those operations only which are performed in his own mind.

Substantially the same view is held by a modern philosopher, Professor G. E. Moore, who says that 'one of the chief things we mean, by saying we have *minds*, is, I think, this; namely, that we perform certain mental acts or acts of consciousness. That is to say, we see and hear and feel and remember and imagine and think and believe and desire and like and dislike and will and love and are angry and afraid, etc.'[4] It is also part of Moore's view that 'these acts are something very different from material objects'.[5]

In these passages from Locke and Moore there is one thing which seems to me to be wrong. It seems wrong to speak of seeing or hearing something as an '*operation* of the mind', as Locke does, and equally wrong to speak of it as an '*act* of consciousness', as Moore does. I hope to make clear the reasons for saying this later. But, in insisting that seeing and hearing are immaterial and private, these two authors seem to me to be correct. If we accept this we are committed to a belief in the existence of *something* non-material. Can we, must we, accept this conclusion? Or can we escape it?

Professor Ryle, in his *Concept of Mind*, boldly rejects any

[1]*An Essay concerning the Human Understanding*, II. i. 4.
[2]Ibid.   [3]Ibid.
[4]*Some Main Problems of Philosophy*, p. 4.   [5]Ibid.

such conclusion. Although on the traditional view seeing something is a mental act or operation, it is, he argues, a queer sort of activity, unobservable by others and apt to elude the scrutiny of the agent himself. Ryle holds that there is no such unobservable 'seeing' because there is no such activity as seeing. To have supposed that there is springs in part from a failure to distinguish between two types of verbs, task verbs and achievement verbs. To race is to do something, to undertake some task: to win is not. To have raced and won is not to have done two things but one with a certain upshot. The verb 'see' and others like it 'are not process words, experience words or activity words. They do not stand for perplexingly undetectable actions or reactions, any more than "win" stands for a perplexing undetectable bit of running.'[1] Of course, Ryle adds, there can be achievements not prefaced by task performances and he instances securing an appointment without applying for it.

Before considering this solution, which has the merit of great simplicity, we must distinguish, as Ryle fails to do, between speaking of an achievement and speaking simply of the upshot of a certain action. The same verb may signify either achievement or upshot. Suppose I aim to hit the bull's eye and thanks to my skill, I hit it; that is an achievement. If I aim to hit it and do so by a sheer fluke, that is doubtfully an achievement. If I snatch the rifle up, fire blindly and hit the bull's eye, that is not an achievement at all but it is an undeniable upshot. Everything that is achieved is an upshot but not every upshot is an achievement. In the case of the appointment which is secured without applying, this may or may not be an achievement. If I have moved heaven and earth to get my name considered without actually applying, it may be a very considerable achievement, though not perhaps to everyone's taste. If I have done absolutely nothing with this end in view, then it is not an achievement, though it may well be the upshot of work I did with other ends in view.[2]

---

[1] *The Concept of Mind*, p. 152.
[2] I can, of course, use *achieve* and *achievement* ironically, e.g. 'He achieved only disgrace by his action'.

The distinction required is somewhat different. The actions and processes of inanimate and animate nature result in a new position or state of affairs. A stone rolls down hill and comes to rest at the foot of the hill. There is its *action* in rolling and the final *state*, or how it ended up, viz. its resting at the foot of the hill. The lady in the music hall rhyme who wanted to go to Birmingham but was put down at Crewe did not achieve what she aimed to achieve by her travelling: but she engaged in travelling and her final state was being in Crewe. There are verbs which refer to activities and processes, such as *rolling* and *travelling*: there are ways of referring to states or positions such as *being at rest*, *being in Crewe*: and there are verbs which refer to a state or position resulting from a certain activity or process, such as *coming to rest*, *reaching Crewe*.

Now, of course, reaching Crewe and coming to rest are not 'perplexingly undetectable' bits of travelling or rolling. They are not bits of travelling or rolling; nor are they perplexingly undetectable. They can be detected with ease, viz. by observing the stone rolling and then observing it at rest and by observing the lady travelling and then observing her in Crewe. We have simply to observe a process or action followed by a state or position: and there is no difficulty whatever in doing this. Ryle— apart from his confusion about achievement words—has shown how to resolve the perplexity of some one who might complain that he had seen the stone rolling all the way down hill and had seen it at rest at the foot of the hill but had not seen it doing the peculiar action described as reaching the foot of the hill. Whether anybody has been, or is likely to be, perplexed in this way I should hesitate to say. Nothing in what Ryle has said throws any light on the problem presented by the 'perplexingly undetectable character' of seeing. For what state must we observe to follow the activity of looking in order to be convinced that seeing has taken place?

In his later book *Dilemmas*, Ryle lets off another volley at the notion that seeing is something which, while unobservable by any one, is somehow disclosed to the person seeing. He elaborates in detail a parallel between winning a race and seeing a tree. He admits that no one would be tempted to suppose that winning a race was an observable activity or state disclosed only to the runner, as we are in fact tempted to suppose that seeing a tree is: but he thinks that this is, in part, because we have been taught the rules governing verbs like 'win', whereas we have only picked up casually the rules governing verbs like 'see'. Unfortunately for Ryle's view there is a major difference in the way we *use* words like 'win' on the one hand and words like 'see' on the other. As we have seen there is no difficulty in seeing some one reach a certain point. Though the case is a little more complex, there is no difficulty in seeing some one, X, reach a point, P, before certain others, A, B, C, reach it. It is necessary simply to see X moving towards P, then at P, then beyond P and only afterwards see A, B, C do the same thing. For this reason there is no difficulty in speaking of seeing someone win a race: we say 'I saw Diabolus win the 2.30', whereas we do not, and cannot, say 'I saw Lord Lucifer see Diabolus' (though we do say 'I saw Lord Lucifer looking at Diabolus'). Nor have we any alternative expression such as 'I saw Diabolus in Lord Lucifer's sight'.[1]

Of course the matter is complicated when there are rules about cheating and proper entry and weight and even more so when there is a judge whose decision is final. In a straightforward race, in which no one is suspected of foul play or nonconformity with the rules, when I see Diabolus pass the post first I unhesitatingly say 'I saw Diabolus win the 2.30'. If Diabolus came in second and Faust which came in first was disqualified by the judges, then I still might say 'I sawDiabolus win the 2.30' once I knew the decision. Earlier I might have said 'I saw Faust win the 2.30'. I should have been wrong. One of the conditions of winning in this sort of race is that the judge should decide in favour. I cannot *see* him so decide: I have to *learn* of his decision. If I have seen the other conditions

---

[1] This last sentence is important because no one doubts that your having a hat on your head is observable, although we should never say 'I saw you have a hat on your head'. What we can say is 'I saw a hat on your head', and this is enough.

satisfied, I may say that I saw the horse win and if the judge's decision is in favour, what I said will be true, viz. that I saw the horse win, though I could not be sure that I had seen it win until I knew of the judge's decision. The fact that winning involves a complex of conditions, including a judge's decision which is not itself something I can observe, does not prevent one from speaking of seeing so and so win. Is winning in such cases something unobservable? No: but it includes an unobservable element, the judge's decision.

I think there can be little doubt that seeing a tree, hearing a bell, etc., are neither activities nor processes and are only in a partial way states. That they are not activities can be seen from the fact that we do not normally answer questions such as 'What are you doing?' or 'What did you do?' with 'I am seeing the moon rise' and 'I saw the moon rise'. The normal answers would be 'I am watching the moon rise' and 'I watched the moon rise'. The absence of the continuous tenses seems also to prove that seeing and hearing are not processes. We say 'I am sickening for something' or 'I am recovering from influenza' but not 'I am seeing a tree' or 'I am hearing a bell'. Of course, verbs such as *see* and *hear* can be used correctly in the continuous tenses. I can perfectly well say 'I am seeing a student at the moment' or 'I am seeing Judith into bed' or 'I was hearing Jane say her tables'. In these cases we are using these verbs to refer to activities, as is shown by the fact that we can replace 'seeing' by 'watching' and 'hearing' by 'listening to'; and watching and listening are activities. But this use, though quite correct, is not the normal use of verbs such as *see* and *hear*.

Are seeing and hearing states? They would have to be states in which people and animals could be. Now I can, of course, be in a certain physical state, e.g. filthy, sick, or in a mental state, e.g. depressed, hilarious, or in a state which it is difficult to classify as exclusively physical or mental, e.g. tense, exhausted. And there is also a looser use of 'state' in which when I have something wrong with a part of me I can be said to be in a certain state, e.g. when I have a headache or nausea. Seeing something is not very much like being in a state in any of these uses. But there is a class of verbs which refer not so much to a state in which I am as to a state of affairs in which I am central, e.g. *have, possess, own*. The activity or process of buying is followed by the state of ownership. The activity of getting is followed by the state of having. There seems to be a certain parallel between this sort of verb and verbs such as seeing and hearing. We do not normally use the continuous tense of verbs referring to this kind of state; we do not normally say 'I am having the pencil in my hand'. And these verbs of ownership further resemble verbs such as seeing and hearing in referring not so much to my state as to my situation *vis-à-vis* something else. But granting these resemblances we should not normally refer to seeing and hearing as states. If they are not activities, processes or states, what are they? The answer, I think, is that they are experiences. But this answer needs defence in view of Ryle's denial.

It seems to me that the composer of 'On Hearing the First Cuckoo in Spring' was, in his title, referring to an experience: and I don't think it will do to say that 'hearing' in this context must mean 'listening to'. In any event whether he merely caught the sound of the cuckoo's note or actively listened to it, there seems no reason to deny that he had an experience. What tends to raise doubts about the matter is that I can refer to experiences by using many other kinds of verb besides see, hear, etc. If asked to mention some interesting experiences I had had in the past I might mention not only seeing the Colosseum by moonlight but climbing Great Gable in mist and falling on the ice in 1947. If we consider these three experiences and the form in which they are referred to, we see that in each case a different kind of verb is used. Climbing is an activity, it is something I do. Falling is an accident, something that happens to me. Seeing is neither of these things. It is closely connected with the activity of looking; though on some occasions it seems more like something happening to me, e.g. when a particular scene unexpectedly strikes my eyes.

The accident, falling on the ice, might have happened to me while unconscious. I might then say: 'I had a dreadful experience. I lost consciousness and fell on the ice and only came to an hour later.' Here what I describe as an experience includes something that happened to me without my being aware of its happening at the time. It can be legitimately included because I was aware of what was happening to me before and after it happened. If I had never recovered consciousness after the accident, it would be permissible for some one to say 'That was a dreadful thing to happen to him' but not 'That was a dreadful experience he had'.

Consider now climbing Great Gable. We speak of ivy and creeper climbing; but we do not regard its climbing as an experience of the plant. But whereas falling is an experience if, and only if, I am aware of myself falling, i.e. see or feel myself falling, the activity of climbing is an experience by being differently related to my seeing, hearing, etc. I am not just aware of myself climbing as I might be aware of myself falling. I don't just see, or even watch, myself climbing. I have to watch my step in order to climb. Nevertheless, though the relation is different, I cannot climb without seeing or hearing or feeling, etc. If climbing is an experience, it is because I see or hear or feel in the course of the activity. It seems then that, though we use activity verbs such as *climb* and accident verbs such as *fall* to refer to experiences, they do so only if there is an implied reference to seeing, hearing, etc. Verbs such as *see* and *hear* are, in a nuclear sense, experience verbs. And henceforth I shall for convenience speak of these verbs as experience verbs. I have no wish to deny that activity verbs such as *climb* and accident verbs such as *fall* commonly refer to experiences, and many other activity verbs also, including a special class I am now going to discuss.

Corresponding to the experience verbs *see, hear, taste, smell, feel* are the activity verbs *look, listen, taste, sniff* (or *smell*), and *feel*. The relationship between the two corresponding verbs is not in all cases the same. I can be looking about merely, or looking for something or looking at something. These are three different but closely related activities. I am not doing any of these three things unless I see something. I can of course look for X without seeing X. But if I see nothing at all

I cannot be said to be looking. I can be said to be looking at X without seeing it. But, again, if I see nothing at all I cannot be said to be looking. If we want a verb which refers to the activity of looking without connoting seeing, we can speak of opening one's eyes. I might open my eyes and see nothing, if I were blind. This proleptic character is peculiar to the verb *look*. I can listen out for someone or something without hearing anything. I can taste something, i.e. sample it in the mouth, and taste nothing, i.e. get no taste from it. I can sniff or smell around and smell nothing. I can feel something, i.e. touch it, and feel nothing, i.e. get no sensation of touch from it. (Of course, in each of these last four cases my activity is an experience in virtue of the fact that I feel muscular sensations while listening, tasting, smelling, and feeling, and perhaps also see myself in a listening posture, etc.)

Let me try to make clear the precise relation between the activity of looking and the experience of seeing. Looking for my purse and at last seeing it *is* in some respects like making for a certain point and at last being there. In these cases seeing my purse and being at the desired point constitute an achievement if in the one case I see *what I was looking for* thanks to my assiduity and care in looking and if, in the other case, I am *at the desired point* as a result of similar effort. But I may run or walk without aiming to reach any particular point. And whether I run in order to reach a point, or whether I run aimlessly, at each moment I do in fact reach a certain point. This is true even if I suppose myself to be running towards X but am in fact running towards Y. It would be inappropriate, as we have already seen, to refer to this as an achievement. It is a result or upshot. With any kind of movement there is a continuous upshot, consisting in the fact that at every moment what is moving is at a different point in space. This is true whether the movement is something that simply happens, like a stone's rolling downhill, or whether it is a movement undertaken by a living being such as a rabbit's running about a field or a person walking about his garden. Looking about is a thing that I can do and it has as its continuous upshot seeing first one thing and then another. Looking at some particular thing has as its continuous upshot seeing first one feature of it and then another. Looking for some particular thing, e.g. a gentian, in so far as it involves looking about has as its continuous upshot seeing first one thing and then another: it is crowned by achievement only in so far as it has as an upshot seeing a gentian.

The difference between a verb like *find* and one like *see* seems to be as follows: When I search, and find the pen that I am searching for, there is a period of search during which I am without the object followed by a period during which I possess it. It would not be true to say 'I've found it' unless there were two such periods so ordered. Finding my pen does not refer to some activity that went on during either or both of these periods. 'I found it at noon' tells us, amongst other things, that the first period ended and the second began at noon: and we might, somewhat pedantically put it in another way by saying 'At noon my search was over and the pen was in my possession'. Now at noon I could have said 'I've found it' and later I can say 'I found it at noon'. Also at any time after noon I can say 'I still have it' but not 'I still find it' or 'I'm still finding it'. Compare seeing. I can say at noon 'I've seen it' or 'I see it' or 'I can see it'. (Note that I cannot say 'I find it' in the corresponding situation.) Instead of saying 'I saw it at noon' I need to say 'I *first* saw it at noon' or 'I caught sight of it at noon'. After noon I can say 'I still see it' or 'I can still see it'.

What conclusion follows from these linguistic facts? While looking for something is like searching for something in referring to an activity, seeing has a dual role, (*a*) like finding, which refers to the end of an activity and the beginning of a state of affairs, and (*b*) like possessing, which refers not to an activity but to a state of affairs. In sense (*a*) I may exclaim 'Ah! I see it now'. In this case it is plausible to say that seeing is 'detecting' or 'spotting'.[1] But if some one asks 'Do you see that

---

[1]But I am not always said to detect something when I first see it. I am said to detect something when there is at least some little difficulty about seeing, hearing, smelling it, etc. The same is true of 'spot' and to a lesser degree even of 'catch sight of'. When I enter my familiar study I see my desk but I do not detect it or spot it or even catch sight of it.

tree outside the window?' and I say 'Yes, I see it: I've been looking at it for some time', I am using *see* in sense (*b*) and it does not mean detect here. 'I still see it' and 'I still have it in sight' are like 'I still have it' and 'I still have it in my possession'. Now although we do not use the continuous tenses of a verb such as *possess*, this does not mean that the state of possession cannot have any duration. We say 'I had it all the time': and similarly 'I saw you all the time' or 'I could see you all the time'. The state, though it has duration, is complete at each moment of its duration. In Aristotelian language it is not a motion (κίνησις), i.e. an activity or process progressing towards an end but an actualized state (ἐνέργεια).

Let us consider more closely what is involved in seeing a bird. First, 'I see a bird' claims that there is a bird. Secondly, a blind man might successfully make this claim, but could not see a bird. If it is to be true that I see a bird I must be within a certain distance of the bird, looking in the direction of the bird (or in a suitably placed mirror), have eyes that function, are open, focused, etc. The bird and these conditions are observable. But lastly, there is a third factor which seems to me quite indispensable but very difficult to state satisfactorily. It is the fact that philosophers have sometimes expressed by saying that the tree must be present to my consciousness or that it must be 'presented' or that it must be in my visual field (as distinct from merely being in my field of vision : for I might not see it even though it was in my field of vision). I don't much like these ways of speaking but the fact which they attempt to pinpoint is enshrined in the word experience and can be brought out by considering the grammar of that word.

An experience such as seeing a tree is not a state in which I am nor is it an observable state of affairs in which I am involved, such as having something in my possession. In what sense then do I *have* experiences? First, let us notice that the verb experience is not a generic verb for see, hear, smell, taste and feel. Though I can speak of my experience of seeing the Colosseum by moonlight, I cannot speak of experiencing the Colosseum or of having an experience of the Colosseum. In the statement 'I had the

unforgettable experience of seeing the Colosseum by moonlight'
of may be taken to have the meaning *viz.*: in which case it
particularizes my experience as seeing the Colosseum; or the
verbal character of the noun experience may be stressed in
which case seeing the Colosseum is the experience which I experience. And this brings out that just as in one sense of *feel*
what I feel is a feeling, and in one use of *see* what I see is a sight,
so in the case of experience what I experience is an experience.
In all these cases we tend to replace the specific verb—*feel, see,
experience*—with the neutral verb *have*. ' I had a ticklish feeling',
'I had a sight of the ruin', 'I had a strange experience'. Note too
that, though I cannot speak of experiencing the Colosseum, I can
speak of experiencing a twinge of pain or a slight feeling of
nausea. Clearly the sense in which I have these things is neither
the sense in which I have things in my pocket or money in the
bank, since they are not possessions; nor is it the sense in which
I have a perforated eardrum or an ingrowing toenail, since they
are not bodily conditions. If they were either of these it would
follow that I could observe them, i.e. see, hear, smell, taste or
feel them (by contact).

About my sensations—the pains, itches, tinglings, etc.,
which I feel from time to time—one thing seems to me certain;
though they cannot be observed by any one (including myself) I am aware of them when I have them, and no one else
is. I want to draw attention to a *partial* parallel between having a
pain and having an experience such as seeing a tree or hearing a
bell. First, however, we must note the difference. Consider the
two remarks 'I see a bell' and 'I hear a bell'. What is common to
both is the claim that there is a bell. Unless there is a bell both
these assertions are untrue. Usually, when I make a statement of
this kind, I am as likely as any one to be right about there being
a bell. But of course I *may* be wrong: some one else may have
good reason to know that there is no bell and may say, when he
hears me say 'I see a bell', 'No, you don't: there is no bell'. Now
this brings out the difference between 'I see a bell' and 'I feel
an itch'. No one could have good reason to know that I had no
itch, and no one would take me up in this way.

But this is only half the story. The other half is equally important. 'I see a bell' and 'I hear a bell' refer to two different experiences. If I heard a bell and said 'I see a bell' my claim that there is a bell would be correct but my statement would not be true: because it does more than claim that there is a bell. 'Well, you must have been looking.' Perhaps I was looking and didn't see it. 'Well, you must have been looking at it.' There is an ambiguity here. There is a sense of *looking at* in which I might have been looking at it and yet failed to see it. This is not enough to make 'I see the bell' true. There is another sense in which *look* means (roughly) *inspect* and has as part of its meaning *see*. In this sense it is not necessary that I should have been looking at the bell in order that 'I see the bell' should be true. For I may have *caught sight of it* without looking at it. (I may see, notice, catch sight of one thing while looking at something else.) Now whereas I can observe (i.e. see or hear or . . .) you look at a bell, I cannot observe you see it. It may be objected: 'If I can see you look at a bell, and looking at a bell involves seeing the bell, then in seeing you look at the bell I must see you see it.' But this is not so, I can perfectly well see you sing, even though singing involves producing sounds which, obviously, I do not see. And I could still see you sing if I were deaf. What I cannot do is to see your singing, i.e. the song you sing, and if I am deaf I must depend on inference for my belief in its existence. But if my inference is correct, then I saw you sing. Any uncertainty attaching to the inference that sound was produced makes it uncertain whether or not I saw you sing: it does not make it impossible that I saw you sing. If, on second thoughts, I think it unlikely that sounds were produced I should say 'I thought I saw you sing'. Similarly, in the case of seeing you look at something, if I later came to think—perhaps because you told me—that you hadn't seen it, I should say 'I thought I saw you look at it' or (in this case there is an alternative) 'You looked right at it: I'm surprised you didn't see it'. In the latter event I use *look at* in such a way that it does *not* involve seeing.

To return now to seeing a bell. Assuming that there is in fact a bell and that I have my eyes open and am focusing them properly, then, if 'I see a bell' is to be true it is at least necessary that I should see a sight, and if 'I hear a bell' is to be true it is necessary that I should hear a sound. (I use *hear a sound* in a way corresponding to see a sight, i.e. in such a way that if I hear at all, then I hear a sound.) Now I am inclined to think that just as I can be quite certain that I have a pain, I can be quite certain that I see a sight or hear a sound. I do not have to make any observations to learn that I am seeing, for example, and not hearing. But though I am inclined to think this, it cannot be true, since I may think I see something when there is nothing there, or I may think I hear a sound when there is no sound. Still, thinking one 'sees something, when it isn't there' is an experience (a 'curious experience', we often say). Moreover, thinking one sees something is an experience that is very like seeing something in a respect in which it is unlike hearing something and thinking one hears something. We may say that they are both visual experiences. And I think we can at least say that when I have an experience, its character as visual or auditory or . . . is apparent to me without investigation: so that, whereas when I say 'I hear a bell' some one might reasonably say 'Are you sure it wasn't a piano?' it would be quite absurd of him to say 'Are you sure that you heard it and didn't rather see it?' or 'Perhaps you felt it and didn't hear it'.

Suppose I do in fact see a bell. The bell is a public, observable thing. I, who see it, am observable. If I am looking at the bell the direction in which my eyes are turned, their condition, their focusing, etc., all these are observable conditions. My seeing the bell is not some activity over and above my looking at it. It is the continuously renewed upshot of my training my eyes upon the bell. This upshot is not the sort of thing that could be observed. When the bell is seen by you, you are aware of its being seen by you: when the bell is seen by me, I am aware of its being seen by me. But I cannot observe you seeing it and you cannot observe me seeing it. Usually I have no doubt that I observe you looking at it because I observe you making those physical movements which people make when they are in fact looking and seeing. But there can arise cases where I do not know whether you in fact see something, though I observe you to be looking right at it. Suppose I am walking in a wood and I see someone, as I think, looking and listening intently. He calls out 'I see you over there', and points in my direction. Now suppose he is right about where I am. For all the observations I can make he may be lying: and he may have heard me and not seen me. Under questioning he may admit that nothing he saw suggested my presence to him but that he heard a whistle which he took to be mine. Supposing that the whistle was one that I uttered I can conclude that he heard me: but I now know *from what he has told me* that he had an experience of an auditory character and *from my own experience* that the claim he made on the basis of it is true. The fact that I have to ask him questions to establish the former fact is the best reason for thinking that I cannot establish it by observation. In the end Ryle comes very close to admitting that this is so. For he says that, though a man can reject the claim of people to have seen something happen if he knows that it didn't happen; if he knows that it did happen and 'that they could have seen it happen, the question whether they did see it happen is not one which he can decide without interrogating them'.[1] This seems to stultify the whole attack on the notion that seeings and hearings are 'inaccessible to observation'.[2] For we are compelled to resort to interrogation precisely where and when observation is out of place. Consider a parallel. You can ask me if my ankle is swollen. But you don't *have* to ask me, you can examine it yourself and see. But if it is a question whether my ankle is itching, you have to ask me. Turn the ankle this way and that, examine it as you will in this light or that, you will never observe it itching.

Given that our seeings and hearings are private, what sort of things are they? I have already insisted that they are not activities or operations. Are they physiological states? Obviously not, since they would be observable if they were. Are they, then, psychological states? This is very difficult to answer because we have no clear conventions as to what is a psychological state. Are they mental states? Or states of mind? I don't think so. A

[1] *Dilemmas*, p. 108.　　　　[2] Ibid.

man's mental state is described by words such as sane, insane, unbalanced, etc. His state of mind is described by words such as depressed, excited, hilarious. Are they states of consciousness? This seems to come closer to the mark. For I certainly cannot see or hear unless I am conscious; and equally I cannot be conscious unless I see or hear or taste or smell or feel something. But they are certainly odd kinds of states. When I pass from seeing one thing to seeing another, it seems a little strange to say that I pass from one state of consciousness to another. What I undoubtedly do is to pass from having one experience to having another. And, in fact, the word experience in this connection fulfils a function which it is very difficult to delegate to any other word. We ask people about their experiences. People tell us about their experiences. We never suppose that we can observe their experiences or that they can observe ours. Of course 'seeing a tree' is unobservable not in the sense that it is difficult or well-nigh impossible to observe it, nor in the sense that it eludes observation, as a mouse might, but in the sense that it is not the sort of thing that can be observed, i.e. seen, heard, tasted, smelt or felt (by contact). Nevertheless the person who sees a tree is aware that he is seeing and not, for example, hearing. Nor is there anything in the least remarkable in there being things of this kind. Neither those who have itches nor other people can observe the itches. But those who have them are aware of them.

In arguing that seeing and hearing are experiences and that, as such, they are private, I have said, I hope, only what is obvious on reflection. I have not said that what I see when I see a bell is really a *private image* or replica of a bell: nor have I said that seeing is a *peculiar activity* performed by minds as distinct from bodies. This is important as Ryle, for example, sometimes attacks different views on this matter without very clearly distinguishing them. At one point the contention under fire is that 'seeing, hearing and smelling belong where remembering, yearning and wondering belong, namely to the field or stream of consciousness'.[1] This contention is not so very wrong:

[1]*Dilemmas*, p. 101.

they have one leg in the stream. At another point the contention criticized is that 'what we see, hear or smell, cannot be, as we ordinarily suppose, things and happenings outside us, but are on the contrary, things or happenings inside us'.[1] This is a very different and much more surprising contention. I have tried to say something much less surprising than this. I have merely tried to bring out the simple and obvious feature about the senses which makes us feel, rightly, that each person is, by having senses, at once given access to a common world and at the same time possessed of a private one. Lamentation over the privacy is as misplaced as strenuous proclamations in favour of complete publicity.

MAIN PUBLICATION

The Philosophical Predicament. A. and C. Black. 1950.

[1]*Dilemmas*, p. 109.

SELF–ACTIVITY AND ITS MODES

By C. A. CAMPBELL

*Professor of Logic and Rhetoric in the
University of Glasgow*

SELF–ACTIVITY AND ITS MODES

I FANCY that other contributors to this volume besides myself may have been in one respect a trifle embarrassed—though in other respects much aided—by the Editor's invitation to bear in mind the directive concerning choice of subject that was addressed by his predecessor to the contributors to the 1924 volume. Ageing philosophers at any rate are likely already to have written a good deal about what they take to be 'the main problem of philosophy', and to have illustrated therein what is 'central in their own speculation upon it'. And it may well be that they feel doubtful whether they have much that is fresh to say on the subject. That, I fear, is to an appreciable extent my own case with regard to the two problems (I cannot easily distinguish between them in order of importance) which I personally should pick out as the key problems of philosophy; viz. the epistemological problem of 'the unit of cognition', and the metaphysico-moral problem of 'free will'. I judge it best, therefore not to write directly about either of them. It will, I trust, be sufficiently conformable with the general plan of this volume if I investigate instead what might be called a 'background' problem to the problem of free will—the problem of the general nature of that 'self-activity' of which, in my view, 'free will' is a particular mode. I welcome the opportunity of doing this, for it seems to me that the notion of activity has received much less than its due share of attention from contemporary British philosophers, and that insufficiently examined assumptions about it are apt to play an important part in the attitude one adopts towards the free will problem. In this paper I shall touch hardly at all upon the free will problem in a direct way;

but I venture to hope that, indirectly, the examination of the notion of activity which follows, inadequate though it will certainly be, may do something to reinforce the view of free will which I have tried to defend elsewhere.

'Activity' and its synonyms—agency, initiation, striving and the like—along with its correlative 'passivity' and its synonyms are expressions that we use every day of our lives. How, first of all, do we get the idea to which these expressions correspond?

On at least the general provenance of the idea we are fortunately able to count upon a very large measure of agreement. It is almost a philosophical common-place that we do not get the idea from observation of anything in the external world. There we may observe changes of various sorts, but nothing that could of itself even suggest the notion of an agency or activity that brings about the changes. We do come, indeed, rightly or wrongly, to ascribe agency to certain external things. But this ascription, it is agreed, is not based on direct observation of the things. What happens is that we read into these things a character derived from experience of our selves. It is from perception of the inner world of the mind, not from perception of the outer world of matter, that the notion of activity arises for us.

So much is more or less common ground. Immediately, however, we have to take notice of the fact that many philosophers declare that this idea is a 'fiction'.

Now this is, on the face of it, a somewhat puzzling pronouncement. Evidently it cannot be meant, in calling it a fiction, that there just *is* no idea for which the term 'activity' stands. That there is such an idea is a datum of the whole discussion. What then is meant when people tell us that the idea of activity is a fiction?

Roughly the first half of the present paper will be devoted to an examination of this question. If, as I believe, the outcome is to vindicate the objective validity of the idea in general, the way will be cleared for an attempt in the second half of the paper to reach a more precise understanding of activity by the discrimination of some of the main species within it.

I

It seems to me that there are, in principle, only two things that can with any plausibility be meant in calling the idea of activity a fiction. I shall deal with each in turn.

The first, and less important, is as follows. It may be urged that when we analyse the idea of activity with care, observing what precisely it is that we actually experience in those experiences which we are accustomed to speak of as experiences of 'activity', the constituents that are then disclosed turn out to be of such a character that we are no longer prepared, on reflection, to label the experience one of 'activity' at all. Our analysis reveals, perhaps, a certain complex of ideas and images and body-feelings—of cephalic tension, muscular innervation, and the like. But when we reflect upon this product of our analysis we realize that if, as seems to us to be the case, there is nothing *else* present in our experiences of 'activity' so-called, we have been deluded in supposing that such experiences have anything in them which entitles us to call them experiences of 'activity'.

I think that this is, at least sometimes, what is meant by calling 'activity' a 'fictitious' idea. But if so, surely the critic's logic is curiously perverse? For how can he judge that the constituents disclosed by his analysis of the experience are such that he is not really entitled to call the experience an experience of 'activity', except in the light of some *different* idea of activity already in his possession which he takes to be a *genuine* idea of activity, an idea of 'activity proper'? Otherwise he is using words without meaning when he says that the experience of these constituents (in conjunction) is not really an experience of 'activity'. And he will be in no better case if, belatedly discovering this implication of his procedure, he should now try to show that this 'different' idea of activity, which he had been using as criterion, is *itself* analysable into constituents which we can see not to warrant us in regarding it as 'really' activity. For he will only be able to condemn this *second* idea of activity in the light of a *further* idea of it in his possession which he takes to be genuine. And so on *ad infinitum*. The attempt to 'explain away' the idea of activity as fictitious always presupposes some other idea of activity which is assumed *not* to be fictitious. The idea of activity, it would seem, cannot be shown to be a fiction along these lines at any rate.

Nevertheless we can, I think, cordially agree with the critic of activity at least to this extent, that none of the sets of constituents into which analysts have so far resolved the experience of it does in fact give us anything that we feel satisfied, on reflection, to call 'activity'. Why should this be? Is it just that the analyses are bad analyses? In a sense, yes, and in another sense, no. They are (or may be) excellent analyses of *what we objectively experience* when we experience activity. But they are all of them very bad analyses, or rather they are not analyses at all, of what we *subjectively* experience when we experience activity. Herein, I suggest, lies the real root of the trouble. The critic cannot find anything deserving of the name of 'activity', because he seeks for it where it cannot possibly be found. For activity, if it is anything, is a function of the subject *qua* subject. It cannot be 'objectified'. To attempt to analyse the experience of activity from the standpoint of the external observer, ignoring the standpoint of the subject *qua* subject, the subject in its subjective functioning, is—if I may borrow Stout's apt adaptation of Berkeley's phrase—to blindfold ourselves and then complain that we cannot see. If the critic pursued what I suggest is the proper course of re-enacting, re-living, the subjective experience to which the name of 'activity' is commonly ascribed, he would, I think, find what he is looking for: and, by the same token, he would find that which he is himself unwittingly using as a criterion when he condemns as inadequate to anything one can properly mean by 'activity' the constituents he has analysed out from the standpoint of the external observer.

There are not, perhaps, many errors that bring in their train so extensive a series of philosophical disasters as that of supposing that 'experience' is reducible without remainder to consciousness of something *before* the mind, something *presented to* the subject. The error is in part explicable, no doubt, by the fact that it is not his subjective activity, but the objects to which it is directed, that commonly interests the experiencing subject, and that thus lies in the focus of his attention. The subject's consciousness of his own subjective functioning is, as a rule, very faint and inexplicit by comparison with his consciousness of his object. Yet it is a little surprising that the strenuous efforts of notable thinkers like Maine de Biran in the nineteenth century and Alexander, Pringle-Pattison, and Bowman in our own day, who have laboured to show that awareness of the subjective side is in some degree present in all experience, should have borne so very little fruit. Even if we are a little hesitant about endorsing their thesis in its full universality, still there do seem to be at least some experiences, for example, that of effortful willing, in which the direct awareness of subjective functioning can hardly be missed save by those who are determined on *a priori* grounds not to find it. When we have collated with meticulous care all the items 'objectively' apprehended in an experience of effortful volition, it remains perfectly clear that these items in their totality do not add up to what we in fact experience in 'making' the volition. There is missing what one might call, in Bradley's phrase, 'the felt out-going of the self from the self', the inner experience of the subject in its subjective functioning. To this experience we can at least attach a meaning; for we can reproduce it whenever we set ourselves to 'relive' a volition, although in the nature of the case it cannot be presented to us as an 'object'. It is thus, and thus alone, that activity in general is to be known: and I ought perhaps to give warning that a good deal of what I have to say in this paper will be incomprehensible to anyone unable to discover in his experience anything more than the presentation of 'objects' to a 'subject'.

I pass on to the second thing that might, I think, be meant by calling 'activity' a fictitious idea. Even if it be granted that there is an unique kind of experience which is called experience of 'activity', an experience not amenable to any internal analysis which might incline us, on reflection, to wish to withhold from it the name of 'activity' after all; still, it may be urged, there are

certain *external* facts which ought to persuade us that we are
mistaken in calling it an experience of 'activity'. For a man
cannot in strictness be said to be experiencing activity if he is
not *really* active. If there are facts which show that, in the given
situation, he is not really active, then his 'experience' or 'feeling'
of activity must be a delusion. And there *are* facts (it is alleged)
which very strongly suggest that a man may *feel* active and yet
not really *be* active. The man who wills to move his arm feels
active in so doing, even if in fact (as might occur through sudden
paralysis) his arm remains stationary. Is it not evident that here
at any rate his feeling of activity is illusory? His willing does not
in fact bring about anything. But if the feeling of activity is
illusory here, it is possible in principle that it is illusory everywhere. Perhaps even in normal cases where the bodily movement
does follow on the willing the man is deceived in supposing that
it is his activity in willing that brings this about. And has not
David Hume produced a formidable battery of arguments to
show that he *is* so deceived, and that there is no intrinsic
connection whatsoever discoverable between the act of willing
on the one hand, and, on the other hand, the bodily movement
which does in the ordinary run of things ensue?

Hume's arguments do not in fact seem to me so very formidable; but as it is far from evident where one is to find better
ones to the same purport, and as they have certainly exerted a
great deal of influence upon subsequent philosophy, we shall
be obliged to consider them at some length. There is, however,
one thing that can be said about them quite briefly, and at once.
In so far as they are directed to showing that activity of *any* kind
is unreal, they are invalid. The fact that the paralyzed man's arm
does not move when he wills it to move does not in the least
entail that he was wrong in his conviction that he was really
active. All that it entails is that he was wrong in his expectation
that his 'spiritual' activity in willing would produce a certain
bodily result—an entirely different thing. The failure to achieve
the end to which his activity was directed has no tendency to
disprove that he *was* active—spiritually active—*in trying to
achieve* that end. That the activity will achieve its 'objective'

(though only—if we may anticipate a little—in co-operation with other factors *not* under our control) is in the case of certain bodily movements our normal expectation. But even if this expectation were never fulfilled, the correct implication would be, not that our activity is *unreal*, but, at most, that it is *futile*.

In other words, on the question whether one is really active, in the sense of 'spiritually' active, the evidence of the subject's own direct experience is conclusive. Another man may *suggest* to me that I am not 'trying'—say, to move my palsied leg. But I, the subject, *know* whether or not I am trying. And if I do directly experience myself as trying, there can be no more point in asking whether I am really active, in the sense of 'spiritually' active, than there would be in asking whether, when I directly experience myself as in pain, I really am in pain.

It must be frankly admitted, however, that what we have gained so far (if we have gained it) against Hume is of only limited importance. Spiritual activity—'trying', 'willing'—is always directed to some objective. If there should be good reason to believe that this spiritual activity has no intrinsic connection with the coming to be of its objective, then even though its reality as such is established, it can hardly be regarded as a very valuable human possession. It is obviously something a great deal poorer than what we commonly mean when we think of ourselves as 'active' beings. We commonly think of our activity as an active *power*, capable of producing effects beyond itself. If in fact this supposed power is a myth, those who insist that 'activity' is a myth will not be so very far wrong after all.

And it is, of course, against activity in this sense of active *power* that Hume in his famous chapter in the *Enquiry* chiefly directs his attack. His discussion is conducted within the ambit of his search for the original of our idea of necessary connection. The suggestion naturally arises that perhaps the original is to be found in our experience of volition, where we seem to be directly aware of ourselves as actively producing that which we will; e.g. the movement of a limb. Is there in fact this *intrinsic* connection between the act of willing and the movement of the limb, or are we deceived in supposing that we directly discern it? Hume, of course, takes the latter view. 'We learn the influence of the will by experience alone.' We have no 'internal impression' of our will producing the bodily movement to which it is directed. And Hume thinks he can explain how the illusion that we do have such an impression comes about. What happens is that, after observing repeated instances of acts of will being followed by the bodily movements to which they are directed, 'the mind is caused by habit, upon appearance of the one event, to expect its usual attendant'. Hence 'a new sentiment or impression', a custom-bred expectation, that when we will a bodily movement that bodily movement will take place. This felt compulsion in our minds to pass from the one idea to the other is misinter-preted by us as a necessary connection between the things to which the ideas relate—here, the act of will and the bodily movement. Hence on the occasion of willing a bodily move-ment, we mistakenly suppose that we directly apprehend our volition bringing the bodily movement about.

That (very summarily stated) is how Hume thinks that the illusion comes about. But why is he so sure in the first place that it *is* an illusion?—so sure that we do *not* in volition discern an active power in ourselves? Hume advances a number of arguments. But it will suffice, for reasons that will appear shortly, if we concentrate upon one of them. I shall select the argument which is perhaps generally regarded as the most powerful.

The specific proposition which Hume is here out to disprove is that in willing a bodily movement we are directly conscious of our will actively producing the bodily movement. His disproof is based upon certain admitted physiological facts. It has been firmly established that when we will to move our leg (and succeed in doing so), the movement of the leg does not follow *immediately* upon our willing. What immediately follow are certain physio-logical changes. Intervening between our act of will and the bodily movement to which it is directed lies a whole series of cerebral, neural, and muscular movements. Now in the act of volition we have, normally, no consciousness whatsoever of these intermediary processes. We cannot, therefore, as we commonly suppose, directly discern the power of our will to move our leg, since this power, if it exists at all, is exercised only through intermediaries of which we are totally unaware. The causal relation, if any, between the act of willing and the movement of the leg is a *mediate* relation; and as we are unaware of the mediation, we clearly cannot be directly discerning that mediate relation. The causal relation as we *suppose* it to be, on the other hand, just isn't there; so we must be deluded in thinking that we directly discern it.

This argument of Hume's has often been attacked; and along very divergent lines. It seems to me, however, that none of the criticisms go quite to the heart of the matter. For, in my opinion, Hume and his critics alike assume a basic premise which, while it looks self-evident, is in fact false. This premise is that, when as we say, we 'will to move our leg', the *immediate* object of our will is the moving of our leg.

What I want to suggest is that the expression 'willing to move our leg' is in fact elliptical. If we attend carefully to what is actually in our minds when we 'will to move our leg' we find, it seems to me, that the *immediate* object of our willing is not the movement of our leg but certain kinaesthetic and other sensations upon which, we have learned from experience, the movement of our leg normally supervenes. No doubt this will appear at first sight a highly paradoxical suggestion; but I am inclined to think that anyone who makes the required introspective experiment with care will discover that it is none the less true. The ulterior object of my willing is the movement of my leg, but the proximate or immediate object is the producing of the appropriate sensations.

Perhaps the easiest way to satisfy one's self that this is the case is as follows. Everyone would agree, I take it, that there are certain sensations associated with the moving of one's leg, and also that, normally, we can produce an image of them at will. But now let us suppose that we have somehow forgotten what these specific sensations are—how far this is factually possible is beside the point. *Can* we, in such a predicament, *will* to move our leg? It seems clear to me that we can *not*—we just don't know how to set about it. We may, of course, *wish* to move our leg. But this is no more the *willing* to move our leg than the wish to move, say, our appendix is the willing to move our appendix. 'Willing' is always directed to something we conceive to be in our power. If we have forgotten the appropriate sensations, the wish to move our leg must remain a *mere* wish, totally impotent, incapable of passing into a 'willing' of the movement.

It might be objected, indeed, that our inability to will the bodily movement in the absence from our mind of the appropriate sensations does not formally establish the *priority* of the sensations to the bodily movement as object of our willing. Abstractedly considered, it might be the case that the bodily movement and the kinaesthetic sensations are inseparable for us, so that we cannot will the one without the other. But a very little reflection shows that this will not do. It seems perfectly possible to think of, and to will the occurrence of, the kinaesthetic sensations by themselves. In fact one can easily enough imagine a case in which, if a man wills the occurrence of the kinaesthetic sensations at all, he *must* will them by themselves. If a man has a foot amputated but still retains the sensations associated with its movement, then, provided he knows his foot is missing, he cannot *will* (though he may of course visualize, and want) the movement of it; yet he surely may (possibly from sheer curiosity about an interesting psycho-physiological phenomenon) will to produce the appropriate sensations.

I submit, then, that when we will a bodily movement the proximate or immediate object of our willing is the producing of the appropriate sensations, in the conviction—based ultimately on experience—that the ulterior object we have in view, the bodily movement, will thereby come to pass. But since it is only in abnormal situations, where the customary connection of sensations with bodily movement fails us, that the intermediary condition of the achievement of the latter tends to force itself upon our notice, we readily lose sight of this intermediary, and both speak and think as though the bodily movement were the immediate, and indeed the only, object of our willing.

Now when the basic premise of Hume and his critics is re-stated in this way, it puts a very different complexion on the whole matter.

We may readily admit, first of all, that between the move-ment of the limb and the appropriate sensations we discern no necessary connection. The connection is something that we learn solely from experience. We learn in infancy or in very early childhood, through what are at first instinctive or merely random movements of our body, that as a matter of brute fact certain sensations are usually associated with certain bodily movements. This purely factual information is the pre-condition of the stage at which we can *will* a body-movement. Hume is thus perfectly correct in so far as all that he wants to main-tain is that we do not in willing directly discern a necessary connection between our willing and the bodily movement willed. The contingent relationship between the (intermediate) kinaesthetic sensations and the bodily movement rules that out conclusively.

But what Hume requires to show, in order to prove that we do not directly discern real agency, active power, in our 'willing of a bodily movement' is, if our re-statement of the basic premise is sound, something very different. He has to show not just that there is no necessary connection discernible be-tween our willing and the bodily movement, but that there is none discernible between our willing and the appropriate kinaesthetic sensations. He has to show that the *latter* connec-tion is one that we *also* learn from experience. Hume, naturally enough, makes no attempt to show this. Nor, so far as I can see, is it possible to adapt any of the arguments he advances against the necessary connection of the volition with the bodily move-ment willed to support the different thesis that there is no necessary connection between the volition and the kinaesthetic sensations willed. Thus we could not, e.g. adapt the particular Humean argument with which we have been dealing, by pointing to unperceived intermediaries between the act of will and the occurrence of the kinaesthetic sensations willed. There is no psychological evidence of psychical intermediaries corresponding to the anatomical and physiological evidence of physical intermediaries that seems so decisive in the other case.

We have agreed that it is only by experience that we learn that specific kinaesthetic sensations are associated with specific movements of our body. The question at the moment is whether a plausible case may be made for the view that it is also from experience that we learn that there is a connection between willing these kinaesthetic sensations and their occurrence. I do not think that it can. Any such view presupposes that there is a stage at which we will these sensations without any expectation whatsoever that they will ensue. What, then, could possibly induce us to will them in the first instance? Do we, as it were, say to ourselves 'I should like to move my leg, and I have reason to believe from experience that if certain sensations occurred my leg would move. I should very much like, therefore, that these sensations would occur. What am I to do about it? Let's see whether "willing" them is any use—good gracious! Here they come!' This seems to me implausible in the last degree. I do not see how the 'experiment' of 'willing' a thing with a view to its coming into being could ever suggest itself to a mind which did not already regard willing as an act which tends to bring about that to which it is directed. Or do we perhaps discover the connection by sheer accident—*happening* to will these sensations, and then finding, to our surprise, that the sensations occur? But surely 'happening to will', or 'accidental willing', contradicts the very notion of willing. Willing is not the sort of thing we can do by accident; for the very essence of it is its *aim* to bring about a definite something. The earlier question therefore recurs, 'What makes us suppose that the act of willing will tend to bring the thing about if we do not already believe in the connection?' The notion that we could conceivably be *surprised* to find that willing produces what it aims to produce—a notion implied in the suggestion that we learn the connection from experience—seems really absurd. When we will X, we will it because, and only because, we believe that willing X tends to bring X about.

There is one further point that must be dealt with, however, if our answer to Hume is to be reasonably complete.

It is clear enough that if the active power of which we are directly conscious in willing to move a limb relates to the production of certain sensations, not to the movement of the limb, the mere fact that the limb may not be there does not raise any difficulty about accepting the reality of this active power. But suppose, now, a case in which, though the limb may be there, there is total anaesthesia with respect to it. If we are still able to image the kinaesthetic sensations, we can seek by willing to produce them; but they will fail in fact to ensue. Now there can be no doubt that in such a case, just as much as in 'successful' volition, we would seem to ourselves in the volition to be exerting an active power. But is it not evident that here at any rate we should be deceived, since nothing whatever is produced—not even the kinaesthetic sensations? And if we are deceived in supposing that we directly discern an active power in these unsuccessful volitions, must that not reflect back a doubt upon our supposed discernment of an active power in 'successful' volitions?

The difficulty is an instructive one; for the solution of it serves to bring out an important point about the nature of activity which we have not yet had occasion to notice.

It is undeniable, I think, that in the case cited we are deceived on one matter. We are deceived in our expectation that certain kinaesthetic sensations will ensue. But the fact that these sensations do not ensue does *not* imply that we are deceived in our belief that we are exerting an active power in relation to their production. For it is enough, in order for the volition to be an active *power*, that the exercise of it intrinsically *tends* to bring about the sensations willed; even though the co-operation of other factors, which may or may not be present, is required to ensure a successful issue. The lack of a successful issue is thus perfectly compatible with our being correct in supposing that we directly discern in the volition an active power in relation to the issue. The significance of these 'unsuccessful' cases of volition is to bring home to us that the co-operation of other factors *is* required if the end to which the active power of volition is directed is to be in fact achieved. Our being deceived in our 'expectation', in the case cited, is due simply to our being unaware that certain of the necessary co-operating factors are absent. Strictly speaking, the active power of volition seems best described in the terms used by Stout—'an active tendency towards its own fulfilment'. But no more than this is needed to enable us to maintain, as against Hume, that there is an intrinsic or necessary connection between volition and its 'object.'

But if volitional activity is no more than a *tendency* to its own fulfilment, is it really justifiable (it may be asked) to speak of a 'necessary' connection between volition and its object? When we speak of a 'necessary' connection between A and B, we usually mean that, given A, we *must* have B. Yet in the case before us it is admitted that, given the volition, we may not get its object.

It seems to me, however, that the point at issue here is at bottom verbal. The expression 'necessary connection' is no doubt most commonly used in the sense just mentioned. But it is also used on occasion merely to mark the contrast with *de facto* connection. It is in that wider sense of the term that we are claiming that the connection of volition with its immediate object is 'necessary'. And this is the sense specially relevant within the Humean context. For Hume, seeking to undermine the credentials of the idea of necessary connection, has been arguing that we do not really discern in volition an active power exerting influence upon the coming to be of the object; that the connection is purely *de facto*, not necessary. This is the position we were concerned to refute. Nevertheless I should agree that the common associations of the expression 'necessary connection' make it somewhat misleading in the present case, and that it would be preferable to speak of the connection between volition and its (immediate) object as 'intrinsic' only. There can, I think, be no objection on linguistic grounds to describing this connection as 'intrinsic', if it be true that the volition even 'tends' to bring about its object.

Space will not permit of our adding more than a word or two about Hume's criticism of the power of volition over *ideas*, which follows immediately upon his criticism of its power over bodily movements. But in truth there seems little need to say much. What Hume's arguments on this head boil down to is that we do not *understand how* our willing is connected with the coming to be of what is willed. We are not 'acquainted with the nature of the human soul and the nature of an idea, or the aptitude of the one to produce the other'.[1] The power of the will is 'unknown and incomprehensible'. But is there really anyone who holds the contrary? What is supposed to follow from this ignorance of the 'how'? To affirm that in volition we are directly conscious of an intrinsic connection between the act of willing and the coming to be of what we will does not in the least require us to affirm that in volition we *understand how* willing brings about, or tends to bring about, what it wills. For finite knowledge at any rate, there must be some things that just *are*; and the basic facts of our own nature may reasonably be supposed to fall into this category. We do not know *how* we are *what* we are. If it be conceded that we cannot will at all save in the conviction that our willing tends to bring about what we will, the intrinsic connection between willing and what we will may fairly be accepted as just an ultimate fact about our natures. After all, we do not understand how it is that we even *have* a will. But no one, I take it, supposes that we must wait until we know how it is that we have a will before we can justifiably believe that we do have a will.

II

It has seemed to me obligatory, the more so in the present state of philosophic opinion, to preface any attempt at a constructive account of activity by a rather extensive consideration of the prior question of whether there really is any fact to which the name 'activity' corresponds. I hope it may now be agreed,

---

[1] *An Enquiry concerning Human Understanding*, p. 68 (Selby-Bigge's edition).

even if only provisionally, that activity is some kind of a fact. On that assumption let us go on to enquire, as systematically as space will permit, into its diverse modes.

For its modes are, I think, highly diversified. There would appear to be several distinct species of activity, in each of which we recognize ourselves to be in a real sense 'active', and yet, on reflection, 'active' in irreducibly different ways. A fully systematic treatment would require to distinguish and relate to one another all of these several species. But to undertake so much within the confines of this paper would be palpably absurd, and we shall try to make our task manageable by narrowing our problem (as indeed our foreword indicated that we should) to that of placing in its proper perspective the specific mode of self-activity which is (or appears to be) involved in 'free-will'. We shall ignore here even so important a mode of activity as aesthetic imagining, since this would appear to have no special relevance for our present limited objective.

We may take our start from a seeming inconsistency in common ways of talking about activity. It is often said that the self is active, in some degree, throughout the whole course of its waking life. On the other hand, the self's activity in certain experiences—e.g. volition—is often sharply contrasted with its passivity in others—e.g. in suffering the onset of a sudden pain. *Prima facie* one of these two views must be mistaken. For how can the self be at times passive if it is always in some degree active?

The answer lies, I think, in recognizing a somewhat important, if obvious, distinction between activity *of* the self, which is 'self-activity' *proper*, and activities *within* the self, which can and frequently do go on even where the self regards itself as not *active* but *passive* in respect of them.

For evidence of this distinction there is no need to appeal to the shadowy realm of the 'sub-conscious'; e.g. to the now fairly well-attested phenomenon of sub-conscious intellectual processes which, in some happily endowed individuals seem able to function effectively while the conscious intellect is otherwise engaged, or even in complete abeyance, and to produce results at times which the conscious intellect would be proud to acknowledge as its own. To my regret, this enviable state of affairs, though I have no doubt of its enjoyment by many, is not one with which I have myself first-hand acquaintance. But in truth the *conscious* functioning of the intellect within the self, while the self itself remains inactive with respect to it, is a situation of which we have all had experience. For example. Often when we are trying to settle ourselves for sleep after a hard evening's brain work, ideas connected with the task we are struggling to lay aside keep surging up and 'milling about' in our minds. It is not to be denied that we have here 'activity' in some sense, and an 'activity' of a faculty which we recognize as in some sense belonging to the 'self'. But though we think of the activity as going on *in* the self, we do not regard our *self* as active in their regard. What our *self* is doing is trying to go to sleep, and it is with *this* endeavour that we naturally identify whatever self-activity proper there is in the situation. The intrusive activity of our intellectual consciousness, so far from being a phase of, or a secondary consequence of, the self's endeavour to settle for sleep, is experienced as offering resistance to that endeavour. Evidently, then, there can be activity of the intellectual consciousness within the self which we decisively distinguish from 'self-activity'.

That bodily activity also—even where it involves somewhat intricate physical manoeuvres—can be a merely functional activity within the self, is apparent at once. The practised pianist can play a familiar piece, and the expert juggler can accomplish at least the less dazzling feats in his repertoire, as it were 'automatically', with little or no 'engagement' of the self in their performance. Bodily activity is here undeniable, but *self-activity* in respect of it is near to vanishing point. In the sufferer from St. Vitus' Dance the vanishing-point of self-activity has been actually reached. The unfortunate victim certainly supposes his body to be undergoing a variety of lively muscular contractions, but he does not regard *himself* as active. On the contrary, he feels himself passive; patient, rather than agent,

in respect of the movements of his body. Evidently, then, bodily activity need not be an expression of self-activity; even though it is true that self-activity does exceedingly often find expression in bodily activity, just as it exceedingly often finds expression in intellectual activity.

Very obviously also the activities of our appetitive consciousness can be merely 'functional'. It is not necessary to elaborate the truism that desires are often felt as 'irruptions' within the self which *impede* the self in its active pursuit of its chosen end.

But in most obvious contrast of all with self-activity proper are the functional activities of our feeling-consciousness—pleasure and pain. Indeed pleasure and pain are so patently *not* manifestations of self-activity that they are sometimes taken as prime exemplars of pure passivity. Yet they should, I think, be placed in the category of 'functional *activity*'. We certainly do speak of pain, e.g. as present in different degrees of 'activity' (or 'quiescence'). If pain is present at all, we find it natural to speak of it as being in some measure 'active'. The inclination to regard these feelings as belonging to a merely passive side of our nature is not, however, surprising. For while the (functional) activities of our intellectual and appetitive consciousness resemble self-activity in having 'objectives', the 'activities' of pleasure and pain have no 'objectives'. Pleasure and pain may, of course, and normally do, *excite* self-activity towards objectives; usually the objectives of prolonging the pleasure or removing the pain. But in themselves they are directionless; and accordingly in much sharper contrast than intellectual and appetitive processes are with self-activity proper.

In the light of the above we may say, I think, that while it is difficult to suppose any experience of waking life in which activity in the sense of *functional* activity is not present, this is compatible with the complete absence, on occasion, of *self*-activity.

But although it is theoretically possible for activity *of* the self to be absent while functional activity *within* the self is present, this is, in practice, a somewhat rare phenomenon. Even in the type of case already alluded to, where intellectual or appetitive processes go on 'in despite of one's self', the self is almost always actively directing itself to *some* end; one may be active, e.g. in seeking to get to sleep, at the same time as one is passive in respect of the ideas which one's intellect may be 'churning out'. Nevertheless there are a few experiences in which it would be difficult to maintain that any trace of self-activity proper is discoverable. Upon the onset of a sudden, unexpected, and violent pain there seems to be an appreciable moment when the self is wholly absorbed by its feeling-consciousness; though almost at once self-activity is resumed in the conscious seeking for relief. Again, it is probably the case that a man can be so completely in the grip of some powerful emotion—paralyzed by fear, perhaps—that for a brief space his self is 'without aim or object'; self-activity is in absolute suspension. And 'action upon impulse', about which I shall be saying something shortly, is, I think, still another example.

Apart from these very occasional 'interruptions', however, it seems true that the self in its waking life is always active in pursuit of *some* end or other. Not, of course, that we are always explicitly conscious of pursuing an end. We may seem to ourselves, as we sit in the sunshine enjoying the sights and the sounds and the perfumed air of a summer's day, to be in a state of sheer quiescence, with no 'aim' in mind whatsoever. But we would not be enjoying these sensations if we were not consciously experiencing them; and we would not be consciously experiencing them if we were not *attending* to them; and we would not be attending to them if we were not *wanting* to attend to them. Our attention to them is the expression of our self-direction to the end of securing these enjoyable experiences. *Explicit* consciousness that we are directing ourselves to this end will probably only ensue if our agreeable state happens to suffer disturbance. Then we feel vexed because, as we have come to realize, it was our will, our aim, to go on enjoying the delights that nature was so bountifully providing. So far as sense-perception in general is concerned, it is safe to say that where there is in the self no active interest in what the senses may reveal the senses will reveal nothing. There will be a physical affection of the sense organs, but there will be no sense perception.

There would seem, then, to be a genuine form of self-activity which, if not absolutely all-pervasive of normal waking life, is next door to being so. It is essentially conative in character, a seeking to achieve ends more or less clearly conceived. Although this self-activity is conative, however, not everything which custom includes under the general heading of 'conation' is a mode of self-activity. Thus 'desire' is usually so included; but (as we have already noted) desire is often felt to be in actual opposition to the end to which self-activity is directed. And even when it is *not*, desire is never, strictly speaking, a *mode* of self-activity. There is a significant felt difference between desiring something and actively setting one's self to obtain it. Only in the latter case do we feel ourself to be 'active'. It is true, of course, that if we are in a state of desire towards X we normally go on to busy ourself to obtain X. But the two states are manifestly distinct. Desire normally engenders self-activity, but it is not itself a mode of it.

Nor can it be said that self-activity is invariably present even when our appetitions excite to definite 'action'. We have to take account here of the distinction between 'impulsive' action and 'willed' action. Purely impulsive action is no doubt rare in self-conscious beings, with 'the power to look before and after', but it can hardly be said never to occur. What distinguishes it from willed action is that in it action follows upon the impulse 'automatically', as it were, with no moment of intervention in which the self considers and endorses the end of the impulse. The self is not conscious of 'taking charge of' the situation. Its felt rôle is that of spectator rather than of agent. Hence we must say, I think, that self-activity is absent from the merely impulsive action. Willed action, on the other hand, differs from impulsive action precisely in the fact that in it the self does adopt the end of the impulse as its *own* end, and directs itself to its achievement. Here self-activity *is* always present.

Indeed this self-activity of willing or volition is identical with the self-activity we have just been discussing; that self-activity which, we claimed, is an all-but universal feature of our normal waking life. And if it seem a little odd, at first glance, to speak thus of volition as an all-but universal feature of normal waking life, that is doubtless because we are so apt to think of volition in terms of the deliberate choice between alternatives, which is of course *not* an activity that is pervasive of normal waking experience. But deliberate choice between alternatives is only one particular *species* of volition. The *genus* is the self's identification of itself with a conceived end; and this, though present in very varying degrees of explicitness, it is not paradoxical to regard as 'pervasive of normal waking experience'.

We have next to see, however, that this self-activity ingredient in volition, and characteristic of our normal waking life, is by no means the only kind even of *self*-activity. I want to draw attention now to a quite distinct, and (I think) uniquely important, kind. This is the self-activity which is exercised in what we can best call 'moral decision'. But as the term 'moral decision' has more than one usage even in philosophical contexts I must begin by explaining how I am using it here.

The two commonest usages are, I think, these. We may mean (1) the decision as to which of two or more courses, each of which has *prima facie* qualifications to be regarded as our duty, really *is* our duty. Moral decision here is primarily an intellectual matter. Or we may mean (2) not the decision as to *what is* our duty, but as to *whether we shall do* our duty. This is a decision which has to be taken in every situation in which there is for the agent a felt conflict between what he conceives to be his duty and what he most strongly desires; i.e. in the situation of 'moral temptation'. Moral decision here is wholly a moral matter, and may fairly be said to constitute the very core of the moral life. It is this sense of moral decision that is relevant to our present purpose. There is a distinctive kind of self-activity involved in moral decision so understood, and our business is to try to elucidate its nature.

A word first of all, however, about an alleged difficulty in the 'setting' of the situation of moral temptation as we have just described it—the conflict of 'strongest desire' with 'duty'.

It has sometimes been maintained that we can attach an intelligible meaning to the expression 'strongest desire' only after the event, when we know which course has actually been chosen; that there is no way of telling which of two or more competing desires is the strongest except by observing which of them finds expression in action. But this view is surely mistaken. We frequently know very well, in advance of our actual choice, that provided we allow our desiring nature *and nothing else* to dictate our choice, it is desire X and not desire Y or desire Z that will prevail. All we need do to measure the relative strength of competing desires is to ask ourselves, in the given situation, which of them would in fact issue in action if we allowed our desiring nature alone to determine our choice. Sometimes, of course, we shall find it difficult to return a confident answer. But the difficulty arises not because we have no valid principle of relative measurement to apply to the desires, but because when we do apply our principle to them we find that two or more of them are approximately equal.

Assuming then that the situation has been properly enough described, let us now directly examine it. The reader is requested (basically—or so it seems to me—there is no other way of proceeding, for we are trying to grasp what the mental act of moral decision is for the subject performing it) to imagine an experience of moral temptation and the taking of the moral decision between the rival ends that it presents; and he is further requested to consider whether he does not find that the following characteristics are unmistakably present in his moral decision as thus imaginatively experienced.

In the first place (I suggest) the agent experiences the decision as something which *he* makes. That is to say, it is for him a manifestation of *self*-activity. No demurrer to this deliverance of our practical consciousness is easily conceivable, and I pass on at once to the far more important, indeed crucial, characteristic which marks off this specific kind of self-activity from that which occurs in the ordinary choices where there is no felt conflict between duty and desire.

The decision whether or not to rise to duty (I suggest) is

experienced as something which, though (as we have seen) issuing from the self, does not issue from the self's *character* as so far formed. There is in every man at every stage of his life a developing, but relatively stable and relatively systematic, complex of emotive and conative dispositions which we call his 'character'. It is this inner system, this character, which determines what desires will emerge in response to a given situation, what will be the relative strength of these desires (if more than one emerge), and what, in consequence, will be his strongest desire. A man's strongest desire at any moment may in fact be regarded as a function of his character in relation to the given situation. But if that is so, moral decision cannot be experienced by the agent *as flowing from his character*. For it is of the very essence of the moral decision as experienced that it is a decision whether or not to combat his strongest desire, and hence to *oppose* his formed character; and presumably strongest desire or formed character cannot find expression in the decision whether or not to fight against itself. The self-activity of moral decision, then, as experienced, differs very significantly from the self-activity of ordinary choices in virtue of the fact that while in both cases it is the self that is active, in the former case it is not the self merely *qua* formed character that acts but the self as somehow transcending its own formed character.

Now I admit at once that this is a somewhat paradoxical deliverance of our practical consciousness. But the important thing is not whether it is paradoxical, but whether, as a reading of what we find ourselves believing, and unable not to believe, in the situation of moral temptation, it answers to our experience. To myself it seems clear that it does. And I am not wholly without hope that self-interrogation by the reader will lead him to the same result. Philosophers, it seems to me, have been somewhat too prone to reject as self-evidently absurd any view which implies that there is a distinction between the self and its 'character', without pausing to ask themselves whether in fact they do not themselves implicitly accept this distinction every time they make a moral decision between duty and strongest desire.

It is worth pointing out, moreover, that the alleged paradox is not really so paradoxical as it seems on the surface. It entails, admittedly, some limitation of the function of 'character' as a determinant of 'conduct'. But it leaves 'character' still an enormously important factor in the moral life. It is formed character, as we saw, that determines what in any given situation the relative strengths of the agent's desires will be; including, of course, in 'duty' situations, the strength of his desire for the end which enjoys the further, and quite different, recommendation of being conceived as his 'duty'. Now in all those practical choices—and they comprise perhaps 99 per cent. of the choices in most men's lives—in which there is *no* felt conflict of duty with desire, it seems clear that the determinant of choice can only be the agent's strongest desire. But if that is the case, then since it is a man's formed character that determines what his strongest desire will be, it is entirely conformable with acceptance of the distinction between self and character to hold that, over by far the greater part of the practical life, it is a man's character that determines his choices.

There will, I fancy, be some reluctance to accept our contention that, save where strongest desire is in conflict with what duty ordains, choice can only be in accordance with strongest desire. But I would ask, what possible motive *could* there be for a man to choose something different from that to which his desiring nature most strongly inclines him, except the fact that he deems this most strongly desired end to be somehow incompatible with his duty? No possible motive, surely, is conceivable. The implication may perhaps be unwelcome, but I do not see how it is to be escaped, that there are, in an important sense, no 'real' alternatives before the agent in those practical situations in which considerations of duty are present. Elsewhere choice follows strongest desire. On the other hand, this should not be supposed to entail that in the ordinary run of choices man is subject to a merely external determination. For a man's desires are not something external to his self. His 'strongest desire' at any moment is the expression, in relation to the given situation, of that developing, but relatively stable and relatively systematic, complex of conative and emotive tendencies which we call his 'character'. Moreover, willing or choosing involves on the part of the agent the formal act of *self*-identification with one of the competing ends. He must, in choosing, *accept* the end as his *own* end; and in that sense for what it is worth, his choice is always 'self-determining'.

There is, indeed, one practical situation which *looks* as though it constituted an exception to the rule that, save where there is conflict of desire with duty, choice follows strongest desire. Suppose I find in a given situation which raises no moral issues for me that my strongest desire is for X; and suppose that, irritated by philosophical theorists telling me that I have no option but to follow my strongest desire, I feel moved to vindicate my freedom to do otherwise by choosing the end of a weaker desire Y. Surely I *can* so choose? And surely, if so, this is incompatible with the thesis that (moral issues apart) choice follows strongest desire?

But a moment's reflection makes it clear that we are not really in this case choosing what we don't most strongly desire. All that has happened is that, under the stimulus of the philosopher's challenge to our freedom, our strongest desire is now directed to the vindication of that freedom, which is to be effected (we think) by choosing Y. So that here too, after all, our choice follows strongest desire.

It is worth observing, however, that what has just been said does not imply that, in believing himself to have real alternatives before him even in a *non*-moral practical situation, the agent is subject to mere illusion. When, e.g. he debates (without thought of anything but his own pleasure) whether he will read a book or watch the television programme, there is no reason to suppose him deluded in believing that he can choose *whichever* of these courses *he most strongly desires*. In *that* sense we can agree that there are 'real alternatives' open to him. He is mistaken only if he believes that he can choose either course *irrespective of* which he most strongly desires. In *this* sense the alternatives are not open. If he believes that they are, his belief is due, as I have tried to show, to a removable confusion.

It is not a belief *intrinsic to* the non-moral practical situation, as the belief that one can choose the course contrary to that to which strongest desire inclines is (I think) intrinsic to the situation of moral temptation.

Even on our view, then, formed character does determine conduct over by far the greater part of a man's life. But of course an element of paradox in the view inevitably remains. Unless moral decision is something quite different from what it is experienced as being, the self which makes the decision (we have to say) must be something 'beyond' its formed character. And it would be absurd to pretend that it is easy to make clear to one's self just how one ought to understand this 'something beyond'.

Strictly speaking, it does not fall within the scope of the present paper to attempt an answer to this last question. But I may perhaps be permitted to throw out, in passing, the suggestion that the difficulty we have in conceiving an act as at once the *self's* act and yet not flowing from the self's *character* is at bottom the difficulty—in one sense the impossibility—of understanding anything that is genuinely *creative*. If an act is 'creative', then nothing can determine it save the agent's doing of it. Hence we ought not to expect to 'understand' it, in the sense of seeing how it follows from determinate elements of the self's character; for then it would just not be a 'creative' act. We can expect to 'understand' it only in the sense of being able to 'attach meaning' to it. Now that, I submit, we clearly can do in the case of moral decision, *if* we approach it in the way appropriate to the apprehension of any genuine 'activity'; i.e. from the inside, from the stand-point of the agent *qua* acting. Unless the analysis given above of what moral decision involves for the experient of it is totally mistaken, the agent himself knows very well what it is to perform an act which is his own act and which is yet not determined by his formed character. From the stand-point of the external observer the creative act is, inevitably, sheer mystery, or worse than mystery. But it is vital to bear in mind that only from the stand-point of living experience *could* anything of the nature of creative activity be grasped if it existed.

And here, I am afraid, we must leave the matter so far as the present paper is concerned.

We have not done yet, however, with necessary distinctions within the general concept of activity. We had occasion first, it will be remembered, to distinguish 'functional activity' *within* the self from activity *of* the self—self-activity proper. We then went on to distinguish, as types of self-activity proper, what may be called the 'expressive' self-activity characteristic of ordinary willing, where our act is merely the expression of our character as so far formed, from the 'creative' self-activity involved in moral decision. We have now to draw attention to a further mode of creative self-activity. We shall call it 'moral-effort' activity.

This mode of self-activity is to be found in the sufficiently familiar experience which we commonly describe in some such terms as 'making an effort to overcome our inclinations and rise to duty'. The situation in which it is, or may be, evoked is the same as that in which moral decision is evoked, i.e. where strongest desire clashes with duty; and the reader must be asked, as before, to envisage such a situation and observe what he experiences when imaginatively engaged in it.

In this situation the agent is aware that if he lets his purely desiring nature have its way it is not X, his duty, but Y, the object of his strongest desire, that he will choose. But since the moral decision to be taken is between rising to duty or yielding to desire, it is plain that he believes that he *can* rise to duty, despite the contrary pressure of desire. He can rise to duty, however—or so it seems to him—only by exerting an *effort;* an effort quite distinct in kind from physical effort or intellectual effort (although either or both of these may be required consequentially, since the 'dutiful' course may obviously entail the exertion of physical effort or of intellectual effort or of both). This unique kind of effort may appropriately be named 'moral' effort; for its whole function is to enable us to resist the importunings of desire in obedience to duty.

Now this moral-effort activity has for the agent, I suggest—whether viewed by him in prospect or in actual performance—both of the characteristics noted in moral-decision activity. For the agent, it is *he himself* that makes the effort; and yet this effort is not, for him, determined by his character as so far formed, since he believes himself to be exerting it precisely in order to resist, in the given situation, the behaviour trend of his formed character; i.e. to enable him to act contrary to his strongest desire. Moral-effort activity, therefore, like moral-decision activity, is essentially creative, involving a causal discontinuity with formed character. But the discontinuity here is, in a sense, a sharper one. For while moral-decision activity *may* be exerted in favour of the end to which formed character inclines, moral-effort activity can in the nature of the case be exerted only in favour of what duty is deemed to ordain.

A further word is desirable on the relationship between the moral decision to rise to duty, the decision to make the moral effort, and the actual making of the moral effort.

So far as I can see, the decision to choose X, our duty, as against Y, which we most strongly desire, *is* the decision to put forth here and now the requisite moral effort. We cannot *really* decide to choose X unless we decide to make the moral effort; for we know, when we decide, that the choosing of X is possible only by our making the effort. Again, it seems to me clear that we cannot really 'decide' to make the effort and then in fact *not* make it. For moral decision (as we have agreed to use the expression) is the decision whether or not to make the effort to rise to duty *here and now*, in an actually present situation of moral temptation: and a supposed 'decision' to make a moral effort here and now, without in fact making it, seems to me something to which we can attach no meaning at all in terms of possible experience. Of course though we cannot 'decide', we can do that much weaker thing, 'resolve', to make an effort, and yet not make the effort; for mere 'resolve' may relate to action in the more or less distant future, in which case it costs us nothing now, and very possibly never will cost us anything. For example, we may resolve to make the effort to give up smoking, our resolve being made at a time when our craving for nicotine is temporarily sated, perhaps to the point of nausea, and immediate effort is not required. Tobacco is now, it may be, the object not of our strongest desire but of our strongest aversion. Perhaps this is the commonest kind of occasion upon which 'good resolutions' are made. But needless to say there is no difficulty whatever in conceiving ourselves failing to exert in fact the effort upon which we have earlier 'resolved'.

In the preamble to this paper I remarked that we should be engaged in investigating what might be called a 'background' problem to the problem of free will. The general relevance of what I have been saying to this latter problem will have been obvious. But let me now briefly point out the special relevance to it of the distinction we have drawn between, on the one hand, the two *creative* modes of self-activity—moral-decision activity and moral-effort activity—and, on the other hand, the *expressive* mode of self-activity present in ordinary acts of choice.

If it were the case that self-activity did not reach beyond what we have distinguished as 'expressive' self-activity, man's power of 'self-determination' could have only an extremely limited significance. His choices would, indeed, still be 'self-determining', in the sense that whatever end a self-conscious subject chooses he accepts as his *own* end. But such self-determination is formal rather than real, and is consistent with the *effective* determination of his choices coming from factors external to him. This becomes clear if we ask ourselves *why* a man comes to choose the particular ends he does choose in those situations—the ordinary run of situations—in which the *creative* self-activity of moral decision is not called for. The answer can only be that these are the things he most strongly desires. And if we then ask, what determines the relative strength of his desires, we are in the last resort forced back, it seems to me, upon the man's inherited nature and environmental nurture; that is to say, upon two factors outwith his own control. It is true that, proximately, a man's desires are the expression of his 'character'. But his character has been built up by past acts of choice which—if we still abstract from the creative self-activity or moral decision—are *themselves* in accordance with strongest desire. And when we finally ask (as we must) about these original acts of choice, before anything stable enough to be called a 'character' has emerged, I cannot see to what else we can point as determinant of the man's strongest desires (and accordingly of these choices) save the particular kind and degree of his congenital impulses *plus* the environmental situation by which they are in varying degrees fostered or discouraged.

In other words, it seems to me futile—as Sidgwick so clearly showed in his polemic against T. H. Green—to attempt to base an effective self-determinism upon the mere fact that a self-conscious being can be moved to act only for an end which he himself accepts or approves. If what he himself accepts or approves is a function of circumstances with which *he* has nothing to do; if in order to understand why he makes the specific choices he does make we must look in the last resort to the 'given' nature of the man and the kind of influences to which he has been subjected by his physical and social environment; then the 'self-determination' in the case is surely, as I have said, 'formal rather than real'.

But when, on the other hand, we turn to the *creative* types of self-activity in moral decision and moral effect, the whole situation is radically transformed. Here the self is revealed to itself as a being capable of *transcending* its own 'formed character', a being with a power, so far as these aspects of its conduct are concerned, of absolute self-origination. No man as actually engaged in making a moral decision between rising to duty or yielding to desire can possibly, I make bold to assert, regard that decision as determined by anything whatsoever save his own making of it here and now.

One final word. It will have been evident that throughout the greater part of this paper the propositions advanced depend for their verification upon an appeal to introspection. I have been describing what I seem to myself to find in and before my mind in certain experimental situations; and the implied assumption has been that, if I have described correctly, the reader who introspects carefully and without preconceptions will find that my reports hold good for his experience likewise. To some philosophers this may seem an assumption so large and so precarious as to vitiate the whole procedure; for introspection is, at the moment, much out of favour as an instrument of philosophical enquiry. Clearly I cannot now undertake a formal vindication of introspective method in philosophy, but I may be permitted to make one observation about its adoption in this paper. Recourse to the evidence of introspection may be undesirable where there is any effective substitute. But what if it is a case of 'Hobson's choice'? That, as I see it, is the situation so far as the investigation of 'activity' is concerned. If it be true, as it is generally admitted to be, that our idea of activity is got not from outer experience, but only from experience of our inner life, it is just not avoidable that we should have recourse to introspection for the appreciation of its character. Either we study activity through the medium of introspection, or we resign ourselves to not studying it at all. I cannot think that we should rest content with the latter alternative.

MAIN PUBLICATIONS

Scepticism and Construction. Allen and Unwin. 1931.
In Defence of Free Will. Inaugural Lecture, Glasgow. Jackson, Son, and Co. 1938.
Moral Intuition and the Principle of Self-realisation. Annual Philosophical Lecture to the British Academy. Oxford University Press. 1948.

PHILOSOPHICAL KNOWLEDGE

By FREDERICK C. COPLESTON

*Professor of Metaphysics in the doctorate course at the
Pontifical Gregorian University, Rome, and
of the History of Philosophy at
Heythrop College, Oxford.*

PHILOSOPHICAL KNOWLEDGE

IT is taken for granted, and with good reason, that astronomers, biologists, physicists, historians and so on possess a great deal of factual knowledge which other people do not possess. And it is possible to delimit with sufficient clarity the special field of knowledge of, for example, the astronomer or the historian. But it is not at all so clear what it is that the philosopher as philosopher knows or can know. Is it possible for him by philosophical reflection to attain factual knowledge about reality?[1] If so, are the propositions in which this knowledge is expressed capable of imparting fresh information about reality to at least some people? Or are they simply and always pompous ways of saying what everyone already knows? In the latter case we should have to say that the philosopher, unlike the astronomer, cannot increase our factual knowledge of reality. And we might then be inclined to say that philosophical knowledge, provided that we are willing to admit that there is such a thing, is concerned with the meaning of terms and propositions. Here, we may think, we are on safe ground. Even though we may abandon all claims that the philosopher can increase our factual knowledge about things, we can at least maintain the claim that he is capable of increasing our knowledge about the meaning of terms and propositions. 'Speculative' philosophy having been rejected, logical analysis or analysis of language still remains, and it is capable of resulting in what can properly be called philosophical knowledge.

[1]I use the word 'reality' in preference to the word 'world' because I do not wish to use a term which might appear to confine the scope of the question to material things.

Yet although it is easy to state that philosophical knowledge is concerned with the meaning of terms and propositions, it is not at all easy to say what is meant by this statement. Does it mean that the philosopher clarifies the meaning of terms and propositions for those who have been suffering from logical and linguistic confusion, so that it is only to these latter that information can be said to be imparted? Or does it mean that the philosopher can impart knowledge about the meaning of terms and propositions to those who have been suffering not from linguistic confusion but simply from ignorance? If so, the information imparted is presumably not simply the sort of information imparted by philologists and lexicographers. For if it were, we might prefer to turn directly to them for our information. There does not seem to be any adequate reason for supposing that the philosopher can do the philologist's work better than the philologist himself can do it. Is, therefore, the information provided by the philosopher information about the 'objective' meaning of terms and propositions? If it is, it would seem to be difficult to avoid the conclusion that the philosopher can in some sense at least impart information about reality. We might then be inclined to conclude that the statement that philosophical knowledge is concerned with the meaning of terms and propositions is a way of saying that though the philosopher cannot increase the number of contingent facts which we know, he can give us a better understanding of the facts which we come to know in other ways than by philosophical reflection. But the question then arises what is meant by this and how precisely the philosopher gives us this 'better understanding'. Further, if the philosopher can in some sense give us a better understanding of reality, is not the way reopened to 'speculative' philosophy? All that would then seem to be excluded would be the claim that the philosopher as philosopher can do the work either of the explorer or of the scientist.

The treatment of these questions seems to me to be complicated by the fact that the word 'philosophy' covers a variety of subjects and questions and discussions which have been traditionally grouped together under one heading.[1] It is possible for different people to recommend different definitions or descriptions of philosophy; and it is very difficult to find a formula which will fit all the branches of 'philosophy' in a wide understanding of the term. However, in this essay I wish to avoid discussion based on pre-selected definitions; and I do not pretend to offer any slick statement about the nature of philosophical knowledge. I intend to proceed in an empirical manner by selecting for examination certain discussions and inquiries which are generally thought of as pertaining to 'philosophy' with a view to seeing whether this examination throws any light on my main theme. If by doing this I succeed in making some slight contribution to the solution of the problem which I have raised, so much the better. But it may be, of course, that I shall merely succeed in illustrating the complexity of the problem. But this itself would not be an altogether despicable result. For simple solutions to problems are sometimes accompanied by failure to see the complexity of the problems at issue.

It seems to me to be true that certain philosophical discussions have resulted in the clarification of the meaning of terms and propositions for those who have been suffering from linguistic confusion. The discussion of the reference of universal terms is a fairly obvious case in point. Those who thought that to a universal term like 'man' there must correspond some sort of universal entity, whether a subsistent universal essence distinct from individual men or, as with some ultra-realists of the early Middle Ages, one essence existing simultaneously in different men under different accidental modifications,[2] can reasonably

[1] Bertrand Russell has remarked that philosophy is the No Man's Land between theology and science. The retort might be made, of course, that it is the philosopher's land. But there does seem to be some uncertainty about its frontiers.

[2] I have pointed out elsewhere that the early medieval ultra-realists were not victims simply of linguistic confusion as this is ordinarily understood. They were partly influenced by a mistaken notion of what was required in order to safeguard the theological doctrine of original sin and its transmission.

be said to have been suffering from linguistic confusion. They did not properly understand the meaning and function of universal terms. And those who, like Abelard, pointed out how the strange conclusions which follow from such theories can be avoided by means of a different analysis of the meaning of universal terms were engaged in clearing up a linguistic confusion in the minds of others. The latter can thus be said to have received information about the meaning and function of terms. Furthermore, they can be said, in some sense at least, to have received information about reality. For they were told that there are no such things as universal entities, that is, things existing independently of the mind. This does not mean that they were told simply that there is no empirical evidence in favour of the statement that there are universal entities, just as a man might be told that there is no adequate empirical evidence in favour of the statement that there are elves or fairies. For it was pointed out to them that a universal thing is intrinsically impossible. To say of anything that it is a thing is to say that it is an individual existent; and there can no more be an universal thing than there can be a round square. Hence they can be said to have received the information that reality is such that it cannot comprise universal entities.

But who received this information? Certainly not the ordinary man.[1] When Antisthenes remarked that he perceived horses but not horseness, he may have laid himself open to the retort that anyone who is not blind can perceive horses whereas it requires a mind to perceive horseness, but none the less he was speaking for the ordinary man. The latter would never dream of looking for universal horseness as an entity alongside individual horses. And the fact that it never occurs to the ordinary man to think that there are universal entities corresponding to universal terms seems to show that in some sense of the word 'know' he knows that there are no such things. In other words, the linguistic confusion which was dissipated by the opponents of ultra-realism was a confusion in the minds of philosophers,

[1] By the term 'ordinary man' I do not mean a moron; I mean simply the non-philosopher.

not in the mind of the ordinary man. Abelard cleared up a confusion in the mind of William of Champeaux, not in that of the contemporary man in the street. And the confusion was able to arise in the first place because philosophers are the sort of people who notice peculiarities about terms which the ordinary man does not notice. The latter uses universal terms correctly in the concrete propositions of everyday speech, but he does not reflect on them in an abstract manner. The ultra-realists, being philosophers, did so; and thus it was possible for them to fall into the confusion into which they did fall. And their opponents helped to dissipate a confusion in the minds of their colleagues, not in those of non-philosophers.

But though it can reasonably be said that the discussion about universal terms resulted in clearing up a linguistic confusion, it does not follow that the whole discussion can be accurately labelled as an example of the dissipation by some philosophers of confusion in the minds of other philosophers. In the first place the discussion does not necessarily begin with logical or linguistic confusion. To ask, for example, what is the meaning of the term 'beautiful' or what is objectively connoted by the term is not by itself a sign of linguistic confusion. To put such questions is, indeed, to ask for clarification; but the questions can very well precede any answers which might reasonably be regarded as the result of confusing one kind of term with another. If an answer is given which depends on or involves linguistic confusion, this confusion will have to be cleared up by further analysis. But though a question about the meaning of universal terms might be so formulated as to give evidence from the start of logical confusion, this is not necessarily the case.

In the second place, when any linguistic or logical confusion which may have occurred in the course of the discussion has been cleared up and the right answer, whatever it may be, has been given to the question raised, the philosopher does not find himself in precisely the same position as the ordinary man. The latter may use words like 'beautiful' and 'just' quite correctly in everyday speech, and in so far as he uses them correctly he can hardly be said to be altogether ignorant of their meaning; but it by no means follows that he can give an abstract analysis of the meanings of these terms. If he can do so, he is not an 'ordinary' man but a philosopher. If we suppose, therefore, that the philosopher can in principle give such an analysis, we can say that he can in principle attain knowledge which is not possessed by the ordinary man, even though this knowledge does not involve knowing entities which are unknown by the ordinary man. And in this case we can hardly reduce philosophy to the dissipation by some philosophers of linguistic or logical confusion in the minds of some of their colleagues, though this may very well be, as an empirical fact, one of the useful results of philosophical analysis.

To say, however, that philosophy cannot be reduced to the dissipation of linguistic confusion in the sense indicated above is not to say what it is that the philosopher knows or is capable of knowing that the ordinary man does not know. And in attempting to throw some light on this matter I take for consideration the philosophical analysis of causality.

We are all aware that there are causal relations, and this awareness finds expression in the concrete propositions of everyday speech. What the philosopher knows, as distinct from the ordinary man, is certainly not the fact that there are causal relations. Awareness of some concrete causal relation is presupposed by the philosopher when he sets about analysing the causal relation. Further, philosophical analysis of the causal relation cannot result in the discovery of hitherto unknown particular causes of particular events. We cannot, for example, discover the cause or causes of cancer of the lung by philosophical analysis.

This is, of course, one reason why philosophical analysis is often spoken of as linguistic analysis. In his analysis of causality the philosopher is not pursuing physical or chemical analysis: he is concerned with the meaning of a term. He does not pretend to discover that X caused Y, where X is a particular cause and Y a particular event: he asks rather what it means to say that

X is the cause of Y. In this sense he is concerned with language. And if theoretical, as distinct from practical, problems are problems of what to say rather than of what to do, we can say, if we like, that his problem is a problem of language.

At the same time this way of speaking can be misleading. For it may suggest that the philosopher is concerned with a problem of lexicography or of philology. And this is patently not the case. When he analyses the meaning of the term 'cause' or 'causality', he is concerned with the real or objective meaning of the term. That is to say, in the case of the proposition 'X is the cause of Y' he asks what is the relationship to which the proposition refers: he tries to state explicitly and abstractedly the meaning of the proposition in the light of the facts which the proposition purports to exhibit. He is concerned with language, but he is not concerned merely with words in the sense that he makes no reference to the facts exhibited by or described in the propositions in which the relevant terms occur.

Now, I have admitted that the ordinary man knows that there are causal relations. He may know very well that the banging of the door is caused by the wind. He doubtless knows very well how to stop the banging of the door. He requires no enlightenment from a philosopher on such matters. Nor, indeed, could the philosopher, as a philosopher, give him enlightenment about these matters. We must say, therefore, that the ordinary man knows, in some sense of the word 'know', what causality is. At the same time I have maintained that the philosopher, when he applies himself to the analysis of terms like 'cause' and 'causality', is concerned with the objective meaning of the terms. And this seems to imply that the analysis, if successful, yields a better understanding in some sense than the understanding of causality possessed by the ordinary man. But what is this 'better understanding'? What is it that the philosopher discovers or can discover by analysis which the ordinary man does not know?

We cannot legitimately say, I think, that the ordinary man is aware of some features of the causal relation and that the philosopher discovers other features, of which the ordinary man is unaware. An experienced diagnostician can frequently tell what is wrong with a patient by observing him, asking him questions, using a stethoscope and so on. But for the discovery of some maladies the use of X-rays or of some other comparatively exceptional means may be necessary. Again, while all can see some characteristics of an insect simply by using their eyes without the employment of any mechanical instrument, a microscope may be required for discovering other characteristics. But I do not think that the function of philosophical analysis is analogous to that of X-rays and microscopes in the cases just mentioned. It is not that the ordinary man has an explicit knowledge of some features of the causal relationship while the philosopher has explicit knowledge of other features. It seems to me that explicit knowledge of any of the features of the causal relationship considered as such, in abstraction, that is to say, from this or that particular causal relation, is philosophical knowledge. The ordinary man certainly experiences concrete causal relations. I am aware that I am now causing the typing of these words. But in so far as I am a non-philosopher I have no explicit and abstract knowledge of any features of the causal relation as such. And in so far as I possess a reflective and explicit awareness of any of these features I am a philosopher.

But this is not to say that the non-philosopher is completely ignorant of all the features of the causal relation. For awareness of concrete and particular causal relations comprises an implicit knowledge of all the features of the relation. This is shown by the fact, or what appears to me to be the fact, that we have only to reflect on our awareness of concrete particular causal relations in order to make explicit the peculiar features or characteristics of the causal relation considered as such. Indeed, on what else could we reflect in order to attain this explicit knowledge? And if explicit knowledge of the nature of the causal relation considered as such is obtained by reflective analysis on particular causal relations, it seems to follow that awareness of the latter comprises an implicit knowledge of the characteristics of the relation.

This suggests that philosophical analysis consists, in great part at least, in making explicit a knowledge already possessed implicitly by the ordinary man. The philosopher notices features of a situation, which the ordinary man does not notice but of which he cannot be said to be entirely ignorant. If someone returns from a journey of exploration and tells me of hitherto unknown butterflies which he has discovered, he gives me a fresh item of information which I could not have discovered by reflecting on the knowledge of butterflies which I may already happen to possess. But if a philosopher informs me that a, b and c are features of the causal relation, he is, if he is telling the truth, drawing my attention to and making me explicitly aware of true propositions which I could in principle have discovered for myself by reflecting on the knowledge which I already possess of concrete particular causal relations. Philosophical knowledge of the objective meaning of causality cannot be simply equated with awareness of particular causal relations. We can justifiably say that the knowledge attained by an adequate analysis is something different from the knowledge of particular causal relations possessed by the ordinary man. And if causal relations are features of reality and not simply mental constructions, we can justifiably say that an adequate analysis increases our knowledge of reality. At the same time it does not increase it by adding another item of factual information similar to the statement that delirium tremens is brought about by prolonged overindulgence in alcohol. It increases our knowledge by making explicit an awareness of the features of the causal relation as such which is implicitly comprised in awareness of particular causal relations. Or we can say that it increases our knowledge by drawing attention to features of a situation which are not 'noticed' by the ordinary man. It seems to me, therefore, that we can quite well admit that the philosopher as philosopher is neither an explorer nor an analytic chemist without being thereby compelled to say that there is no sense in which he knows, or can know, more than the ordinary man.

I have mentioned the activity of 'drawing attention to'. And I think that this activity has played and plays an important part in philosophy. We can see examples of it in political philosophy.

Consider, for instance, the organic theory of the State. It is, indeed, obvious that the State is not an organism in the sense in which a plant or an animal is an organism. But to call the State an organism might serve to draw attention to the facts that the State, in the sense of political society, is an organization in which different members co-operate for the fulfilment of a certain end or for certain ends, that it survives the death of individual members, that it possesses a continuity of tradition, language, and culture, and so on. Facts of this kind are not, of course, discovered by the political philosopher in the sense in which a scientist may discover hitherto unknown facts; but the political philosopher can draw attention to a certain set of facts which he has not discovered for the first time but which he underlines and so makes us notice. The analogy which he uses in describing the State helps to underline and draw attention to these facts.

The matter is not, of course, as simple as all that. If a political philosopher draws attention to certain features of the State, he presumably does so because he thinks that they are worth drawing attention to. And by the use of certain descriptive terms or analogies he endeavours to make the rest of us value what he values. A man who calls the State an 'organism' may very well wish to encourage in our minds a certain attitude of reverence towards the State as towards a quasi-transcendent entity to which individual human beings are subordinated and apart from which their lives and activities lose their significance. And the man who rejects the organism-analogy and substitutes some other descriptive term or analogy may do so because he regards this reverence towards the State as a quasi-transcendent entity as being highly undesirable and because he wishes to facilitate instead a view of the State as one among other forms of social organization, a form which possesses no pre-eminent sacredness. In his opinion the use of the organism-analogy encourages people to exalt the State 'beyond good and evil' and to neglect the value of the individual person.

In so far as terms and analogies are used to express a feeling about the State and to promote a similar feeling in others they can be said to have emotive and evocative functions. But we cannot justifiably conclude that a term which possesses an emotive function possesses no more than emotive significance. For its power to exercise an emotive function may depend on its power to draw attention to certain real features of political society. Thus the organism-analogy draws attention to certain real features of political society. At the same time, of course, it draws attention to certain features at the expense of others. Moreover, it may suggest features which are not in fact features of political society, or features which can be features of certain types of State but which many of us regard as undesirable. In the language of political theory descriptive and emotive functions may frequently go together and interpenetrate one another. And an important task of the clear-sighted political philosopher is to sort out and distinguish carefully these various functions. However, though I have mentioned the emotive function of terms like 'organism' when used in political theory because it is important not to forget it, my main point for present purposes is that terms used in political theory can also exercise the function of drawing attention to facts which the political philosopher is not the first to discover but which he wishes to underline and to make us notice.

Similar remarks can, I think, be made about the writings of a number of philosophers belonging to the 'existentialist' movement. If an existentialist writes, for example, of the radical insecurity and instability of human existence, he can hardly be said to be giving us fresh factual information of which we were hitherto completely ignorant. But it may very well be true that he draws attention to features of human existence on which we normally and for most of the time do not focus our attention. He may also think it important and desirable for various reasons that we should pay attention to these features of the human situation, and his language may be partially designed, by the selection of emotively-charged terms, to facilitate breaking through the so-called crowd-mentality and relating these features to oneself personally.

It may, indeed, appear that concepts like 'noticing', 'drawing attention to' and 'making explicit' are inapplicable to a form of philosophizing such as phenomenological analysis. If a philosopher, it may be asked, gives a phenomenological analysis of being-conscious-of, of perceiving, of loving or of awareness of values, does he only draw attention to what we already know? Does he not in some sense increase our knowledge?

We could hardly maintain successfully that the philosopher who gives a descriptive analysis of being-conscious-of opens up a new world in the same sense in which the European discoverers of America opened up a new world to their fellow Europeans. No doubt, even before the discovery of America some people thought that there was probably land 'out there' ; but this was not the same thing as knowing the existence of America. It scarcely needs saying that before its discovery both the existence and the natural features of the American continent were un-known by Europeans. Being-conscious-of was not, however, an unknown activity in this sense until a phenomenologist dis-covered it. All human beings are conscious of something at some time. Similarly, the philosopher who attempts to give a descrip-tive analysis of an activity like loving or hoping does not dis-cover love or hope in the sense in which Christopher Columbus discovered America.

Yet it is one thing to be conscious, attention being riveted on the object of consciousness, and it is another thing to reflect on being-conscious-of, attention being focused on this activity itself and not on the object. Similarly, it is one thing to love somebody, and it is another thing to reflect on the activity of loving. This bending-back of the mind on the activity itself, without the normal absorption in the particular concrete object of the activity, is obviously a necessary condition for a descrip-tive analysis of being-conscious-of or of loving or of perceiving. And if it is carried out, the structural features of an activity may be brought to light of which we were formerly not explicitly aware. In this sense our knowledge is increased; and to this extent we can speak of 'discovery'. But the new world which is opened up is simply the old world revealing itself to a mind which achieves the necessary change of direction in the focusing of attention. This enables the implicit to be made explicit.

When we read an adequate phenomenological analysis we 're-cognize' features of an already familiar activity, features which we had perhaps not previously noticed because our attention was directed towards the object of the activity rather than towards the activity itself. We are more in the position of a man who under the guidance of an art-expert appreciates hitherto unappreciated features of a familiar picture than in that of a man who listens to Professor Challenger telling him that he has discovered a living dinosaur in South America.

Another example. Let us suppose that a metaphysician concerns himself with beings as beings or with things as things and that he attempts to lay bare in explicit statement the fundamental and all-pervasive ontological structure of things. He must obviously start with reflection on the things with which we first become acquainted by other means than by philosophical reflection. And what he does is to focus his attention on what is in a sense most familiar, on what is so familiar that we normally do not notice it. And the results of this focusing of attention are propositions which are both familiar and unfamiliar. They are unfamiliar or strange because they state truths which we do not normally advert to in explicit, abstract and universal form. But once we understand the propositions we can see that they state in explicit, abstract and universal form truths which find implicit expression in the concrete particular propositions of everyday speech. Of course, a proposition which really does state an essential feature of a thing considered as a thing does not state a truth which could possibly be refuted. If, for example, a finite thing is essentially capable of change, it could never be true to say that there was a finite thing which was incapable of change. And in this respect a proposition which states any essential feature of a thing as a thing certainly differs from propositions like 'there are men on Mars' or 'all sheep on X's farm are white'. For even if these propositions were in fact true, they might conceivably be false. Nevertheless, a proposition about things as things can be informative in the sense that it states something of which we may not be explicitly aware in the abstract and universal form in which it is stated in the proposition in

10

question. Hence the proposition can be said to contribute to a clearer understanding of reality, and in this sense it increases knowledge.

I have maintained that there is a sense in which the philosopher can be said to increase our knowledge or understanding of reality, even though he does not play the part of the explorer. I have maintained, for example, that though we do not owe to the philosopher our knowledge that there are causal relations, the latter's analysis of what it means to say that one thing is the cause of another can increase our understanding of reality. The ordinary man's knowledge of causality may be called first-level knowledge. It is knowledge of particular causal relations without reflection on the causal relation as such. The philosopher's knowledge can be called second-level knowledge. It presupposes the ordinary man's awareness of particular causal relations and is the result of explicit reflection on the causal relation as such, the change from one level to the other being effected by a shift of attention. The philosopher has not at his disposal material which is not at the disposal of the ordinary man, but he adopts a different point of view. And the adoption of this point of view enables him to make explicit the metaphysic which is implicitly contained in the concrete propositions of everyday speech.

This last sentence should not be taken to mean that in my opinion the whole of what is customarily called logical or linguistic analysis can properly be called metaphysical analysis. But if I am right in thinking that the philosophical analyst, when he considers a theme such as the causal relation, is concerned with what I have called the objective or real meaning of terms and propositions, he appears to be engaged in the same sort of activity that many philosophers have regarded as metaphysical analysis. And when I speak about a metaphysic being implicitly contained in the concrete propositions of ordinary speech, I do not mean that by merely inspecting a set of words like 'Brown was killed by Jones' we can elicit a philosophical analysis of causality: the proposition has to be considered both in the light of the concrete relation referred to and from a particular point of view, a point of view which is not, for example, that of the detective. One can equally well talk about a metaphysic implicit in common experience. But inasmuch as this experience must be given verbal expression if we are to be able to discuss it, it is convenient to speak of a metaphysic implicit in the concrete propositions of everyday speech.

But if one believes, as I believe, that the philosopher can make positive affirmations about the human soul and about God, it is necessary to ask whether such affirmation can in any sense be considered as the result of making explicit what is implicitly contained in propositions of ordinary speech or in common experience. At first sight at least a claim that they can be so considered appears to lack even the slightest degree of plausibility. Nobody denies, for example, that there are causal relations. The point at issue is not whether there are causal relations or not but what the causal relationship is or what it means to say that X is the cause of Y, the demand being for a general definition and not for the act of pointing out a concrete example. But there are plenty of people who deny that there is any soul in man, at least if by 'soul' one means a spiritual principle; and there are many who doubt or deny the existence of a being possessing attributes which make it proper to call the being 'God'.

In spite of all that has been said to the contrary, it seems to me perfectly reasonable to claim that the ordinary man has an implicit awareness of the soul, which finds expression in everyday speech. I do not mean that either the philosopher or the non-philosopher enjoys a direct intuition of the soul. What I mean is this. On the one hand, the pronoun 'I' is used in such a way in ordinary speech that it cannot be taken to refer to an occult immaterial substance which happens to be situated in a certain body. I quite agree that an examination of ordinary language does not support the idea that man consists of an immaterial mind which happens to find itself in a body to which it has only an extrinsic relation. On the other hand, any attempt to substitute 'the body' in every case in which we use the pronoun 'I' would certainly appear forced and strange to the ordinary man. The latter would think it very odd if in sentences like 'I think that democracy is the most desirable form of political constitution' or 'I believe in God' or 'I consider that Tolstoy was a greater novelist than Edgar Wallace' we attempted to substitute for the pronoun 'I' exclusive reference to the body. We should have in any case to say, for instance, 'my body', a phrase which rather gives the show away. It is not unreasonable, therefore, to maintain that the ordinary man has an awareness of the self as something which neither excludes the body nor is simply identifiable with it without residue. This awareness is implicit in the sense that it finds expression in the concrete propositions of everyday speech, though the ordinary man does not focus his attention upon it or attempt to analyse it. And this implicit awareness forms the basis for philosophical reflection about the nature of the soul and about the relationship between soul and body. The philosopher does not enjoy privileged access to an occult entity; but he can reflect on the nature of man as revealed in human activities and in the concomitant awareness of those activities as 'mine'. He thus attempts to make explicit what is implicitly contained in the concrete propositions of everyday speech, provided that we add that the meaning of the propositions has to be interpreted in the light of the experiences to which they refer. I cannot within the compass of this essay discuss divergent explicit interpretations. The point which I wish to make is that positive affirmations about the human soul do not necessarily involve the philosopher in the claim that he is the privileged discoverer of an occult entity. The reflections of the philosophical psychologist who is neither a materialist nor a phenomenalist are not so remote from the level of everyday speech as they are sometimes depicted as being. By saying this I do not mean to suggest that the problem of man's psycho-physical constitution is an easy problem; for I do not think that it is anything of the kind. At the same time I do not consider that a solution is brought any nearer by insisting on the necessity for analysing the propositions of everyday speech and then interpreting them in a way which seems to me to make nonsense of what the ordinary man is accustomed to say about himself. It may be said that it is naïve and uncritical to take the ordinary man's utterances at their face value. But the question is whether these utterances are themselves naïve and uncritical in a pejorative sense. I do not think that they are.

Any view according to which there is a natural intuition of God seems to me untenable. For present purposes I use the word 'God' to mean a transcendent Being (identifiable neither with any finite thing nor with the aggregate of finite things) on which finite things are conceived as depending existentially. And I thus prescind from a more clearly Christian specification of the meaning of the term. But, even so, if one understands by 'intuition' a positive mental seeing, analogous to perception, of a present object, one cannot, I think, successfully maintain that there is a natural and universal intuition of God. Apart from the difficulty of adopting the heroic course of saying that atheists do in fact intuit what they declare that they do not intuit, I do not see, for epistemological and psychological reasons, how transcendent Being could be a direct natural object of the human mind. By saying this I do not mean to deny the possibility of mystical experience, nor its philosophical relevance. For though I do not think that mysticism is philosophy, one can philosophize about mysticism, as, for example, Bergson did. But the question which I am asking is what is the relation between ordinary common experience and the affirmation of God's existence, not between the latter and a comparatively exceptional experience.

It seems, however, to be true that some people[1] who are not philosophers at all in the academic sense of the word raise such questions as whether the complex of finite changing things which we call 'the world' is co-extensive with reality, whether human history is simply a chance episode in a physical cosmos which is

[1] I use the vague phrase 'some people' because I am obviously not in a position to say how many people raise questions of this sort. But some non-philosophers certainly do so.

synonymous with reality or whether it has some purpose and significance given it from outside. And to ask such questions is to raise the problem of the Transcendent. One can, indeed, try to interpret a question such as whether human history has a goal or purpose in such a way that it is capable of receiving, at least in principle, an empirically verifiable answer. For one can interpret the question as equivalent, for example, to the question what purposes or goals different individuals or groups have in point of fact set before themselves. But if it is interpreted in this way, it becomes a different question: it is no longer the question which was originally asked. For the questioner did not intend to ask what purposes human beings have as a matter of fact set before themselves, but what, if any, is the purpose of human existence and human history, whatever ideals different individuals and groups may have set before themselves. And to ask this question is necessarily to raise the problem of the Transcendent. For human existence and history can have no goal or purpose unless it is determined from outside, that is to say, by a Being which transcends history.

In my opinion these questions arise out of man's existential situation, not out of linguistic confusion on the part of philosophers. They are questions which any human being can raise simply because he is a human being. I do not say that every human being necessarily asks such questions; what I have asserted is that 'some people' who are not philosophers ask them. It is possible, for example, to become submerged in the everyday practical concerns of life. But it is a peculiarity of the human being, as distinct from other living things, that, though involved in the world and in the changing historical process, he is capable of standing-back, as it were, and of apprehending his involvement in the changing world of finite things. And it is in the context of this standing-back that the so-called ultimate questions arise as questions of vital concern to the questioner.

I have said that to raise these questions is to raise the problem of the Transcendent. At the same time the very questions themselves seem to imply some apprehension of the Transcendent, if, that is to say, they are seriously asked. If, for instance, I seriously ask whether the changing historical process (I do not refer here simply to human history) is co-extensive with reality, some marginal awareness of an undescribed background or ground of finite existence seems to be involved.[1] It appears to me that the focusing of attention on finitude and change produces an immediate inference to the Transcendent as the undefined and undescribed complement of the finite and changing. If, however, I speak of 'inference', I do not refer to syllogistic argument or, indeed, to any reflective argument at all. I use the word to show that I do not postulate any intuition of the divine being in itself or any direct apprehension of the Transcendent as a thing among things. Indeed, it is precisely because the Transcendent is not apprehended as a thing among things, an object among objects, that even when the questions of which I have been speaking have been seriously raised, agnosticism is still possible.

The questions are, I think, in some cases requests for a clear rational justification for this immediate inference or movement of the mind. And the traditional proofs of God's existence are so many attempts to meet this demand. The proof is an attempt to make explicit an implicit awareness which is involved in seeing the question as a real question. But it is sufficiently obvious that no such proof is an infallible instrument for compelling assent to God's existence. The metaphysician can help us to focus our attention on what in some sense is already familiar to us (finitude, for example, with all that it involves) and to see its significance; but he cannot compel us to do so. In other cases the questions are requests for light about the nature of the Transcendent. I cannot discuss this matter here. But it is perhaps worth while pointing out that 'speculative' metaphysicians have differed rather in their respective characterizations of ultimate reality than in their answer to the question whether finite things are co-extensive with reality.

[1] Many people perhaps simply ask themselves in a half-articulate manner some such question as, 'what is it all about?' But I think that the same observations apply even here.

And, without wishing to subscribe to agnosticism, I would add that this is only to be expected. The situation of the metaphysician can be said perhaps to prolong on the reflective level the situation of the ordinary man who has noticed and paid attention to those features of empirical reality with which the reflections of the metaphysician, as I conceive him, begin.

It might perhaps be reasonably expected that I should end this essay with a summary statement of what I take to be the nature of philosophical knowledge and of the way in which it is attained. But I doubt whether a single comprehensive formula can be found; and, even if it can, I do not pretend to have found it. However, some sort of a summary must, I think, be attempted.

In the first place, while admitting that one of the useful results of philosophical discussion can be, and sometimes has been, the dissipation by more clear-sighted philosophers of linguistic or logical confusion in the minds of their more muddled colleagues, I have argued that philosophy cannot be reduced to this activity, however beneficial the activity may be. For this dissipation of confusion may occur in the course of a philosophical inquiry which does not necessarily start with 'confusion', though it may be undertaken in response to a desire for clarification.

In the second place, that about which clarification is desired may often be the meaning of terms and propositions. And where this is the case philosophical knowledge can legitimately be said to consist in the knowledge of the meaning of terms and propositions. But I have argued that this should not be understood in a sense which is incompatible with saying that the philosopher aims at a better understanding of reality and that philosophical knowledge includes a clearer understanding of reality. For if there are, as I think there are, cases in which the philosopher can properly be said to be concerned with the real or objective meaning of terms and propositions, with what a term 'really' means or what we 'ought' to mean by it, reflection shows, in my opinion, that these are cases in which the philosopher is concerned, not with giving us new items of factual information of a kind which cannot be discovered by philosophical analysis, but with attaining a clearer understanding of the world already presented to us in experience and about which we speak in everyday discourse.

Thirdly, if one admits the truth of this contention, the way to metaphysics seems to me to be reopened. As I have already indicated, I should regard the analysis of causality, for instance, as a metaphysical inquiry. And those inquiries which are perhaps more commonly thought of as 'metaphysical' are due to the same desire for understanding which lies at the root of all philosophical inquiry. True, the questions raised will not meet with sympathetic consideration unless they are felt to be real questions. And it may well be that the more important ones will not be seen as real questions unless they are seen in the context of man's existential situation. But they are seen and raised as real questions before the philosopher applies himself to them. And I have suggested in the case of one particular problem at least that the very raising of the question implies an implicit awareness of the answer. The philosopher, therefore, tries to make the implicit explicit. But the fact that he is not in a position analogous to that of a privileged visitor to Mars helps to explain his limitations, which are indeed abundantly evident from the history of metaphysics.

A final remark. In this essay I have spoken of 'everyday speech' or 'discourse' or of 'ordinary language'. This is indeed a term, the meaning of which cannot be precisely determined. And its use may suggest a much sharper distinction between the 'philosopher' and the 'ordinary man' than I should wish to make. Nearly everyone philosophizes to some extent, even if it is only to the extent of from time to time asking himself philosophical questions. Metaphysics is not, I think, simply the hobby of a few eccentric individuals. The asking of metaphysical questions, at least of questions of vital concern to the questioner, is a widespread and sometimes very powerful tendency of the human mind. But my reason for using terms such as 'ordinary language' is my conviction that the philosopher in his reflections is confronted with the same world that is revealed to the non-philosopher or 'ordinary man' in his experience, an experience which, as expressible and communicable, forms the basis of philosophical reflection. How sharp one makes the distinction between the philosopher and the non-philosopher depends, of course, on the meanings one gives to the terms. In one sense comparatively few human beings are philosophers; in another sense a very great number can be said to philosophize from time to time.

MAIN PUBLICATIONS

Friedrich Nietsche, Philosopher of Culture. Burns, Oates and Washbourne. 1942.

Arthur Schopenhauer, Philosopher of Pessimism. Burns, Oates and Washbourne. 1946.

A History of Philosophy: Vol I, Greece and Rome, 1946 (revised, 1947); Vol. II, Augustine to Scotus (1950); Vol. III, Ockham to Suárez (1953). Burns, Oates and Washbourne.

Medieval Philosophy (Home Study Books). Methuen. 1952.

Aquinas. Penguin Books. 1955.

THE NECESSITY OF METAPHYSICS

By A. C. EWING

Reader in Philosophy in the
University of Cambridge

THE NECESSITY OF METAPHYSICS

THERE are two schools of thought for both of which I always have felt great sympathy, and an adequate combination of which, if that be possible, would constitute the high-water mark of philosophical achievement as far as I can conceive it. One is the idealist school which dominated Oxford towards the end of the last century and was still a fairly powerful influence, especially on undergraduate reading, in my student days there at the end of the First World War. The other is the Cambridge school of Moore and Broad as developed in the 'twenties or earlier. The sweep and richness of thought and profundity of the former appealed to me as did their faith in the rationality of the universe and their attempts at a comprehensive metaphysics, although I was not quite convinced by most of their central arguments including the one that the *esse* of physical objects necessarily involves reference to mind or experience. On the other hand, the Cambridge school had a far greater mastery of the linguistic tools of philosophy and a method of clear analysis which, I thought, was just what was needed to test whether the idealist claims were true or false or at least whether they had good reason or fallacies behind them. I felt that they were lacking in certain insights which the idealists possessed, but that they also escaped their vagueness, obscurities, and apparent confusions. They aimed at making philosophy as clear as the nature of the subject allows, and I have always thought that to try to do this is the first and one of the most neglected duties of the philosopher. Without committing themselves much to conclusions, they tried to develop the means by which any philosophy that is fully worthy of the subject must be built up.

Whether you are a positivist or a transcendent metaphysician, it is your duty to make what you have to say as clear as possible, showing just what, if anything, you hold to be self-evident or immediately known, and what your arguments precisely are, otherwise it is impossible for readers to know what they are up against and put your views to the test. And I have seen how often, when a particular problem is analysed into its constituent parts or alternative meanings and the ambiguities of the words in which it is expressed are revealed, it is already more than half solved. My idea was that the Cambridge school catered, roughly speaking, for the means, and the idealists for the end of philosophy, and I had the notion that one might use to rebuild a metaphysical system of idealism the tools forged under a quite different inspiration, or if not to build a system as a whole, at least to solve particular problems in philosophy on lines with which the originators of the technique would not have had much sympathy. However, every philosopher has his own way, and what I have adopted from the thinkers I have mentioned is hardly anything definite enough to be called a technique. I have never felt inclined to be a disciple of any philosopher, but I hope the spirit of both schools has entered deeply into me.

But I remember with less satisfaction the shock I had when in 1931, having spent my student days at Oxford and taught there and at Swansea for some years, I first came as a lecturer to Cambridge. I found dominant not the influence of Moore, Broad, or Russell, but the influence of Wittgenstein, and I must say that, no doubt partly through my own fault in misunderstanding him, the reaction his philosophy provoked in me was one of sharp antagonism. I have later realized that some of the views I attributed to Wittgenstein as dogmatic doctrines were not intended by him as such but as tentative suggestions not literally true, or rules of method, but I was not the only person to fall into this error; on the contrary it seemed at that time to be fairly general both among his followers and his opponents. The verification principle in particular seemed to me open to the strongest objection, and I was equally offended by the treatment of *a priori* principles as rules of language or arbitrary 'rules of the game'. Against these doctrines I advanced the argument among others that they were self-refuting, for the verification principle itself could not be verified by sense-experience[1] and the principle that there can be no synthetic *a priori* propositions must itself be synthetic *a priori* if it is to be known and to be of any interest.[2] To this it has been replied that the principles excluding any unverifiable synthetic propositions apply only to factual propositions and not to those prescribing rules, but still even prescriptive propositions require justification if they are to be asserted (and are not immediately known, as the ones I am discussing can hardly claim to be), and it remains extremely obscure how this justification could possibly be effected. However, Wittgenstein, at least in his later years, meant the verification principle not as a dogmatic proposition but as a methodological principle. It amounted to the rule—if you want to understand the meaning of a sentence, ask how it could be verified—a rule which does not necessarily, as it would in its dogmatic form, imply that all meaningful statements could be verified. And the saying that all *a priori* propositions are linguistic or 'rules of the game', we are told now, only brings out an analogy and is not to be taken as literally true. If so, however, it is at least important also to bring out the very big differences between what is described and what is taken as an analogy to describe it, and therefore I cannot regret having attacked the linguistic theory. And at any rate it must be realized that a rule of method cannot *prove* anything. People trying to dispose of metaphysics in such ways face the following dilemma—if the principle used is a true proposition, it is synthetic and yet cannot be verified by sense-experience; if it is not true but only a methodological assumption, it does not establish anything, for in order to prove a conclusion true, you need true premises.

In saying this, I do not mean to reject but to accept two of the main principles on which such modern philosophers insist: (1) that there are no affirmative existential *a priori* propositions, and that in consequence empirical premises are required for any

---

[1] *Mind*, 1937, pp. 347 ff.
[2] *Aristotelian Soc. Proceedings*, 1939-40, pp. 207 ff.

argument which is to establish positive facts about the real,
(2) that all content is derived from some experience, and that we
can have no idea of anything not given in or constructed from
experience. Only I should understand 'experience' far more
widely than 'sense-experience'. Seeing a logical connection and
appreciating values or obligations are experiences, and we cannot
at any rate rule out the possibility of veridical mystical or
religious experience. And I should insist also that propositions
constructed from empirical content might themselves not be
verifiable by experience, at least without the addition to experience of arguments that the verificationist would stigmatize as
metaphysical, e.g. propositions about physical objects realistically conceived, propositions about God. For we can conceive
qualities which we have experienced as also existing unexperi-
enced, and we can at least form some conception of qualities we
have experienced in a very limited form as existing in a vastly
purer form and higher degree.

Further, I was and still am much upset by the modern
tendency to treat philosophy as if it were just a discussion of
linguistics. I do not think common-sense to be verbally inspired,
and therefore I do not think that the arguments from the popular
usage of words are nearly so important as they are commonly
supposed to be. I well understand the Chinese student who
attended Cambridge philosophy lectures expecting to discover
truths about the nature of reality and found that what he did
learn were truths about the usage of the English language.[1] (Not
that the evil is confined to Cambridge or is more prevalent there
than at other universities today.) I have indeed emphasized the
importance of a careful attention to language in order to discover
ambiguities and analyse what is precisely signified by a statement, as a *means* to the successful prosecution of philosophy, but
I have relatively little interest in this study as an end in itself
and do not see why it should be called philosophy. To quote an
analogy the source of which I have forgotten, I sympathize with
the person who said that many contemporary philosophical

[1] Quoted by Professor Braithwaite in *Cambridge University Studies*,
ed. H. Wright, pp. 30-1.

discussions about language reminded him of a man sharpening and sharpening a knife with the greatest pleasure in his activity but never by any chance using the knife to cut anything.

The attack on metaphysics inflicted deep wounds which have by no means healed yet. Since the verification principle is itself unprovable, it could not disprove the possibility of metaphysics, but for all that its use, backed by a powerful mind and, to many people, very persuasive personality, somehow has done a very great deal to discredit metaphysics. The change of view in very wide circles shows itself in the following way. In the old days, metaphysics was regarded, like other sciences, as a discovery of new facts, though of course its method was radically different and the kind of facts supposed to be discovered were also very different. But they still were conceived as objective facts discoverable by the use of a reason which, even if it started from empirical premisses, went beyond these empirical facts to something not given empirically which they entailed or at least required as an explanation. This is now commonly assumed to be false or meaningless. It seems to be taken for granted even by the more moderate members of the school influenced by Wittgenstein that there cannot be any non-empirical facts, and consequently metaphysical statements are interpreted even by those who still have some sympathy with this subject as not asserting facts at all but expressing a new way of looking at empirically established facts so as to give a certain emotional aroma or something of this kind. What is left of metaphysics becomes in their hands something much more like an artistic creation than a study of what is true and what not. And even outside this inner circle the great majority of philosophers, in this country at least, have been rendered very reluctant to embark on metaphysical enterprises. There is a widespread feeling that metaphysics in the old sense has somehow been proved impossible, though one cannot lay a hand on the proof.

Under these circumstances it remains very important to insist that the denial of the possibility of asserting trans-empirical facts is an assumption for which, once we have admitted that the verification principle is not true, no evidence can be produced. The one argument for it left seems to be that the meaning of the words we have to use in asserting metaphysical propositions is derived from the context of common-sense and scientific language and that these words apart from this context lose all meaning. But this can be easily met by emphasizing the distinction between different degrees of meaning. The alternatives are not, on the one hand, a perfectly clear definite meaning and on the other no meaning whatever. In very few cases even in scientific language do our concepts attain the maximum of clarity and definiteness, and any theologian will admit that our idea of God is very far from being clear and adequate and yet insist that it is most worth while trying to form such an idea.

The effects of the assumption I am criticizing are particularly unfortunate when applied to the question of the existence of God, for the whole point of the emotional aroma here depends on an objective belief. Without the latter the religious person who derives peace from the thought of God would be like a student who should feel elated about his prospects in the examination just after his teacher had told him he was likely to fail. Religion is assuredly not a merely intellectual matter, but for it to be acceptable it must have an intellectual basis in a belief about objective reality, otherwise it means living in a fool's paradise.

There remains the old, old argument that metaphysicians disagree. But here we may call in the help of the very philosophers I have been criticizing. They have pointed out that, when two philosophers quarrel, what really happens is often this. One asserts the truth of p and the other the truth of q, p and q being apparently quite incompatible, but really neither 'p' nor 'q' is applicable, because some and only some of the criteria which justify the application of 'p' are fulfilled and some and only some of the criteria which justify the application of 'q'. Both sides may then be regarded as doing a valuable piece of work in supplementing each other, one pointing out the respects in which the situation differs from that usually expressed by 'p' and so giving the qualifications which must be added if 'p' is to be applied at all, and the other doing the same thing as regards 'q'. Each gives in fact part of the truth. In the final solution it will not then matter whether we say '*p*' or '*q*', provided we add the necessary reservations in either case, the arguments for *p* reappearing as reservations to be added if we say '*q*' and the arguments for *q* as reservations to be added if we say '*p*'. We can thus understand how philosophy may be regarded as progressing despite the perpetual disputes, because the solution will have to incorporate in itself the contribution of each side. As the pendulum swings now to one side, now to the other, the various contributions will be successively improved. This way of approach has been strongly emphasized by Wisdom himself as a means of dealing with disputes in critical philosophy, and I do not see why it should not also be used with disputes in metaphysical, speculative philosophy. I do not think indeed that all philosophical controversies can be treated exclusively in this fashion; there are such things as definite fallacies and definite contradictions between philosophers, but what I have said surely applies at least partially to a great many of the disputes between them. And we can well admit metaphysics without claiming for it absolute certainty or anything at all approaching that.

The more positive reasons for not condemning metaphysics may be prefaced by considering the question what is the metaphysics that it is proposed to exclude. Metaphysics has sometimes been defined as a general study of the nature of reality, but no one would deny a man the title of metaphysician because he did not profess to give an account of the whole of reality. In fact, what metaphysicians have done mainly is to produce studies of the general nature and relations of minds and physical things. But do modern philosophers really mean to exclude these from consideration? They certainly discuss them at very considerable length. It may be said that what they are doing is merely to analyse common-sense propositions about them, but can we do that without covertly doing metaphysics? Perhaps one might if all common-sense propositions were wholly false, but if, as is commonly supposed, they are true, to give an analysis of common-sense propositions about physical objects or minds is to lay down general non-scientific propositions about physical objects or minds which claim to be true, i.e. to do metaphysics. Even if the common-sense propositions are only partly true, we could hardly analyse them adequately without sorting out the true and false elements present in them, and so again doing metaphysics.

Metaphysics has also been defined as a study which goes beyond the realm of actual and possible human experience, and this is more in accordance with what modern positivistically inclined philosophers mean when they attack metaphysics. But what about physical objects? In the 'thirties the new anti-metaphysical philosophy was understood to involve the assertion of phenomenalism, but this is now usually repudiated. Yet the philosopher who denies phenomenalism is asserting the existence of objects which transcend human experience as much as is the theological philosopher who asserts the objective existence of God. If we are entitled to lay down true propositions about physical objects as they exist unperceived by human beings, in any except a hypothetical sense in which they are propositions about the experiences human beings *would* have under certain conditions, we are entitled to go beyond human experience, even though this involves making statements which are not even conceivably directly verifiable by us. And what about human minds other than my own? The solipsistic analysis of propositions about these in which Wittgenstein and Ayer at one time indulged would not now be defended, yet if we can make the transition to other human minds beyond our own experience, can the limit to permissible discourse be fixed where philosophers under these influences wish to fix it? Logically we are driven to make the transition because otherwise we could not give a satisfactory explanation of our own experience.[1] There is so much in it which can be explained and can only be explained by reference to minds other than our own. Yet, if this is a ground for asserting other human minds, may not similar grounds conceivably be found for going further? If we once recognize that in order to give a satisfactory account of my experience I must introduce existences not experienced by me,

[1] I do not say that this is the psychological cause.

I do not see what general principles I am now entitled to lay down in order to limit the metaphysician. We may of course refute or disapprove of particular arguments he uses, but we can no longer say that there cannot on principle be valid arguments which might lead us to metaphysics. Just as we have admitted that there is a valid transition from the experience of a single man to the existence of other men, so the realist urges that there is a valid transition to the existence of independent physical objects, often unperceived, and the philosophical theist that there is a valid transition to the existence of God. Other human beings have to be assumed to explain my experience, but so realists and philosophical theists will say that they only infer what is needed to explain human experience when they assert the existence of independent physical objects or of God. We cannot rule out all these arguments *en masse* at one fell stroke, whatever we may think of them in detail. Why are some 'transcendent' and therefore to be rejected, and not the others? Is it because the latter are scientific and the former not? But it would generally be held by philosophers that scientific arguments could not settle the issue between solipsism and its opposite or between realism and phenomenalism, thus implying that the arguments are philosophic, not scientific, after all. Perhaps the argument to minds other than our own may from its particular nature be immune to any criticisms such as those which threaten the other arguments, but to say this is to criticize the arguments in detail and not to lay down a principle which rules out all objective metaphysics.

If metaphysics cannot be ruled out on principle, it remains to say how I approach the subject and where I think metaphysical conclusions of importance to be positively indicated. For I imagine that it is in accordance with the intention of this volume for a philosopher to expound his general outlook, even though there is not space to give the detailed justification for it which would be needed and which he has tried to give in other writings. I assume that one of the things which can most profitably be done by a contributor is to bring together at least some of those thoughts which, as he formed a distinctive philosophical outlook, influenced him most. Now in so far as the modern type of philosopher can be said to have a metaphysics at all, it is one of a fundamentally irrationalist and pluralist character, and as such it stands in very sharp contrast to the philosophical views dominant at the end of the nineteenth century. Since causality is reduced on the objective side to regular sequence (perhaps with certain modifications which do not alter the principle), the real is regarded as a set of events not integrally connected but merely happening to follow one on another. Since logic is regarded as only a matter of language, there is no place for logical system or logical connection in reality. And there is no such thing as an explanation of facts in the sense of giving a reason as opposed to merely stating the antecedent facts. I sympathize much more with the earlier, rationalist view. I do not see how logic or mathematics can ever lead us to new conclusions, even relatively to our previous knowledge, if there is not a necessary connection between the content we had in mind at the beginning and different content which we have in mind at the end of the argument. And if both contents include properties of real things, these properties must surely be internally linked if our argument is to be a valid one. The linkage cannot be reduced to the mere containment of our conclusion in our premises. If the conclusion is merely part of the premises of an argument, it is a bad argument, and because it begs the question, does not prove anything. If it is said that the conclusion is 'implicitly' included in the premises, this either just means that the premises of a valid argument entail the conclusion, which everybody admits, or implies the false empirical proposition that the conclusion of a valid argument is always thought by us when we think the premises, though in a confused form. If it is said that for a perfect reasoner the conclusion would be so included, the answer is that, for it to be included, his premises would have to be different from ours, and therefore it would not be the same inference of which we are talking. There is not space to go into this matter at length here, but I shall just bring out what I mean by reference to a simple example, not drawn from the metaphysical but from the scientific sphere. Suppose we wish to measure the height of a mountain we cannot scale. We take a base, measure the distance from the base to the foot of the mountain, and the angle of projection of the top of the mountain from our base. We can then mathematically deduce the height of the mountain in question. The deduction is *a priori*, but because the premises are empirical it can be used to deduce an empirical fact. Now that the mountain is of such and such a height is surely an additional fact not forming part of the premises that the base is such and such a distance from the mountain and that the angle is such and such, yet it is certainly entailed by these premises. Therefore a fact can be logically entailed by a different fact. I do not see how the linguistic school can possibly get over this. Or, if the verbal objection is made that only propositions and not facts can 'entail', at least we must admit that the fact about the height of the mountain is determined *a priori* by, necessarily connected with, the other facts. Perhaps the linguistic philosophers did not really mean to deny anything that I have said, but if so I do not see how they can avoid accepting a conclusion which they certainly do not want to accept, namely, that there must be necessary connections in the real if we are to apply logic or mathematics to it at all. So I concluded that the numerical and spatial relations of things constitute a logical system not merely in our language or thought but objectively in the real world. (I do not mean that we know *a priori* that physical objects are in Euclidean space, but whatever space they occupy has a geometry with *a priori* relations.)

Since numerical and spatial relations in the physical world are all-pervasive, this reveals a very great deal in the way of logical connection and logical system in the real, but I think there are good grounds for going further still in this matter. Even if complete determinism is not true, we have to admit a great many causal connections both in the physical world and in mental life. Now what are causal connections? In dealing with these I have defended under the heading 'entailment theory'[1] a view which is by no means new—it was universally

[1]See *Idealism*, chap. iv, § 3.

assumed prior to Hume—but has now fallen on evil days so that its revival has struck many people as ridiculous or almost ridiculous. Yet it certainly cannot be said that the regularity view opposed to it gives anything like general satisfaction. On the other hand, I am now ready to admit that to say there is a relation of 'logical entailment' between cause and effect is somewhat misleading, and I should be prepared to substitute 'a relation closely analogous to logical entailment'. (Even when I first published the theory it was only after some hesitation that I adopted the former instead of the latter terminology.) I should have thought that, since we argue from cause to effect, it was difficult indeed to avoid admitting that, where our arguments are valid, there is a relation between cause and effect at least analogous to logical entailment, and the desperate contortions which modern inductive logicians have had to make in defence of induction indirectly support my contention. They have felt themselves obliged either to maintain that induction could not be justified at all, or to say that it could be justified only in a sense in which 'is justified' means simply 'is in agreement with what scientists actually think', or to commit the vicious circle of justifying the principles of induction by induction. If it is merely that what we regard as the effect has usually or always in fact succeeded the cause, what possible reason is there to suppose that it will succeed it in the future and not only in the past, for the unobserved and not only for the observed? But if the effect follows from the intrinsic nature of the cause, there is very good reason for supposing that it will do so. It seems to me plain that the original, natural conception of causation is that of an intrinsic connection between the causal conditions and their effects such that the nature of the former could not be fulfilled without giving rise to the latter, and that the reason why the quest for causes originally attracts men on intellectual and not merely practical grounds is because it is felt that to give the cause of something is to *explain* it, which it can only do if the cause not merely precedes the effect with regularity but has embedded in its internal nature a reason why the effect should follow. It is hardly a matter for surprise that inductive logicians are involved in difficulties when they forsake the original basis on which induction depended. It is true that we cannot discern any necessary connection between cause and effect in the physical world, and it is in consequence of this that we have to proceed inductively and not deductively or intuitively in trying to discover causal laws. It is true also that our causal inferences are not logically certain, as we might expect if they were *a priori*, but only probable in character, but this is because, even if the causal laws are really necessary, we ourselves cannot see their truth *a priori* but can only infer them by the indirect method of induction; and I contend that we should not be entitled to use inductive evidence at all for predicting the future even with probability if it did not point to necessary connections in nature but merely to *de facto* regularities. No doubt it is open to the sceptic to reply that, even if induction presupposes what I have said, my theory may still not be true; but even if this position cannot be strictly refuted, it does seem to me at least a strong argument against a view that it leads to the conclusion that there is no good reason for thinking it more likely that I shall die if I jump from the top window of a skyscraper tomorrow than if I continue sitting quietly in my study or that science is really in no better a position logically than the most groundless superstition. For, make no mistake, this is what follows if a logical presupposition necessary for induction be denied. Not that there is lacking in my mind besides this another argument both to support my view of causation and to justify induction, namely, the argument that the empirically observed occurrence of regularities to the extent to which they do occur calls out urgently for explanation and is only explicable on principle if there are necessary connections behind them. If there were nothing in the nature of A or in the nature of a third thing C to account for B following A regularly, the uniform sequence of B on A given in experience would, it seems to me, have the character of a coincidence antecedently no more likely than my having all the trumps in my hand in bridge ten times in succession. This to my mind is enough to show both that empirical evidence of sufficiently frequent sequences is good probable evidence for a law which will hold also in the future and that causal laws involve something analogous to entailment, for a regular sequence can only be redeemed from the status of a mere, highly improbable coincidence if there is involved a necessary law dependent on the nature of the things concerned.

If such a conception of causality as the one I have suggested is adopted, it will make a great difference to one's view of the world. Even if it be not true that everything is completely determined by causation, there is no real doubt that everything in the world is very much affected by it, and this on my view implies that everything is linked together in a logical system or something very like one. It further implies that there is a real reason for what happens to things in the nature of them and in that of other things. Without committing myself to the cosmological proof of the existence of God I might add that on the entailment theory the principle of causation becomes a principle of sufficient reason, a principle that everything must be explained by something else unless its nature is such as to make explanation by some other existent on principle impossible as in the case of the whole or of God and perhaps of free human volitions. Whether the physical world as causally connected is a self-sufficient system or whether it is essentially incomplete and depends on a transcendent being beyond itself is, however, a question which my argument for the entailment theory of causation is not intended to settle. The entailment view of itself neither implies nor excludes theism. Yet the question whether to adopt this view of causation or not remains an exceedingly important question for metaphysics. Not only does its acceptance much enlarge the sphere of rational logical or quasi-logical connection in the world, but it is highly relevant to the age-long issue between monism and pluralism. If a cause is just followed by its effect regularly, they may be regarded as essentially quite separate things with no organic, intrinsic connection whatever, but if the one is connected with the other in a way at all like logical entailment, can they be regarded as just different things? No, they are then internally linked so that the nature of the cause can only find fulfilment in the effect, and the nature of the effect can only be understood by reference to the cause. If C stands in any relation like logical entailment to E, it must be incomplete and internally incoherent without E. All things will then be by their very essence bound together, not directly indeed in most cases but indirectly through the system to which they belong. For everything is causally connected with everything else, directly or indirectly, though one might have to go back a long way to reach the causal connection.[1] A moderate monism seems to be indicated against the prevalent pluralism, moderate, I say, if only because the notion of causal laws itself implies very marked diversity in things and in events. What I have said certainly does not imply that reality has as high a degree of unity as is present in one substance or in one mind. This moderate monism is to my mind also supported by the impossibility of separating the qualities of a thing from its relations to other things.

I am not, however, prepared to say that the necessity of causation is just the same as that of logic or mathematics. It could not be, because the necessity of logic or mathematics is formal, while this necessity has to link content. There may well be various kinds of necessity. Another kind still arises in ethics. It is clear that in the case of anything which is good or bad intrinsically, or of any action which is right or wrong, its goodness or badness, rightness or wrongness, follows necessarily from its other factual characteristics. This is made clear by the fact that a person who was tempted to perform an act which he recognized to be wrong but other characteristics of which attracted him, could not compromise and perform an act otherwise the same but without the characteristic of wrongness, as he might alter a factual characteristic of a proposed act. But this necessity is not the necessity of formal logic nor is it causal.

All this has brought me much nearer than the vast majority of contemporary philosophers to the idealists, to whom I referred

[1]Even if the universe be expanding so rapidly that some parts can now never again causally affect others, they are still indirectly related by causation since their common causal ancestors affected each other causally.

at the beginning of this paper, when they make central in their epistemology and metaphysics the notion of a coherent system. I certainly never have swallowed their doctrines whole, and there are many points on which I should quarrel with them strongly, for example, their *definition* of truth as coherence, but I do attach a great deal of importance to their doctrine of coherence as a fundamental *criterion* of truth. I also attach much importance to it as a doctrine of the nature of the real. At the same time I am convinced that the epistemological theory in question must be amended to allow for various kinds of non-inferential cognition. Certainly, as the idealists themselves usually admitted in dealing with physical science and common-sense propositions about physical objects, it is not just coherence but coherence with our perceptual experience which we have to consider. Again, it seems quite clear that our memory judgements are not simply based on coherence. Nor could we build up an ethics on the coherence principle alone unless ethics were completely *a priori*, which practically nobody would maintain. We must fall back somewhere or other on immediate ethical judgements of good or bad, right or wrong, unless we take one of the naturalist or subjectivist views against which it has been in my ethical works one of my main aims to fight, and which would certainly be alien to the spirit of the idealists. There are also claims to non-inferential cognition in the sphere of religion which at the very least we are not entitled to rule out as *a priori* impossible. Nor would I exclude the possibility of seeing a logically self-evident proposition to be true in its own right. For these reasons, while adopting the coherence formula advocated by an earlier generation and now almost forgotten, I modify it and say 'coherence with non-inferential cognition'. This phrase will cover the various kinds of knowledge or reasonable belief which I have just mentioned as needed to supplement coherence. We may add that, for the coherence principle to work at all, we must be able sometimes to apprehend coherence itself immediately. The adherents of the theory are apt to say they exclude all self-evident propositions, but at least they will have to admit that it is sometimes self-evident that A coheres better than B with CD. We may invoke intermediate premisses to show coherence, but we cannot go on in this way *ad infinitum*.

My idea is that, while we are logically bound to fall back on immediate (non-inferential) cognition somewhere—the mediate implies the immediate—these immediate cognitions may be of all degrees of certainty, and where uncertain they need testing. But by what can they be tested save coherence with inferential beliefs and with other immediate cognitions? An advocate of the coherence theory will object to this view that the immediate cognitions could not be stated or understood by themselves without already bringing them into connection with other truths, so that we cannot recognize any immediately given data as separate from the system which we try to make coherent, and consequently have, after all, nothing to serve as a second criterion over and above coherence.[1] But still we must admit empirical content somewhere, if not as a self-sufficient datum, at any rate as an element in all our thought. You cannot have coherence without content to cohere. It is all very well saying that there are no sense-data or content apart from interpretation, but interpretation must be interpretation of something. Even if the phrase 'coherence with immediate cognition' suggests more self-sufficiency than we can allow to the contribution of bare experience, to say that the criterion was merely coherence would leave no place at all for the genuinely empirical element in human knowledge. The given must be present, if not as a set of facts apprehended separately from their coherence, at least as an element in thought.

By 'coherence' I do not of course mean merely logical consistency in the sense of not actually contradicting the other beliefs with which a belief is said to be coherent. The propositions that Delhi is the capital of India, that there are six chairs in this room, and that 'amo' is the Latin for 'I love', do not contradict each other, yet they would hardly be quoted as an example of a coherent system of propositions. By 'coherent' is meant rather fitting together into a system in which the

[1] A similar argument is fashionable today against sense-data.

different parts are in some way logically dependent on each other. At least this is the ideal. We cannot make of our different beliefs and items of knowledge a completely coherent system, but we should get as near to this as we can and the nearer we come to it the stronger the confirmation. Such an ideal is certainly very strongly operative in science. Observation is very important, but nothing that is put forward as a scientific theory can be completely proved or refuted by experience alone or even by experience plus a mathematical or logical argument. You can always escape from having to adopt an unwelcome theory if you are prepared to make sufficient arbitrary suppositions. Even the Ptolemaic hypothesis would be quite compatible with the observations even of today if we were allowed to make enough disconnected independent assumptions, but because the assumptions which were necessary for the maintenance of the Ptolemaic theory after the new observations which suggested its rejection did not fit into any at all coherent system, the theory was relatively soon abandoned. Of the numerous conceivable hypotheses which are logically possible and do not actually contradict experience the scientist will accept that which seems to come nearest to 'making sense of the world', nearest to giving us a rational system.

I know it is fashionable to say that the reason for preferring one scientific theory to another is only practical convenience, but to say this is either to abandon the claim of science to objective truth or to assume the very unlikely, anthropomorphic view that truth is measured by its convenience for human beings. Of two scientific hypotheses which both cover the facts one is more practically convenient than the other because it explains more, because it does more in the way of bringing them into a coherent system, and it seems to me vastly more plausible to say that the ultimate criterion is (apart from empirical or non-inferential cognition) logical coherence in a system than to say that it is practical convenience to us. And if coherence is freely used at least as a main criterion in all sorts of ordinary reasoning from physics to detective stories, why should we not be allowed also to use it in metaphysics in the absence of a successful special objection such as I have earlier in this article found the modern philosophers unable to bring against metaphysics?

Indeed, a consideration of the use of coherence as a criterion already itself seems to lead to a metaphysical conclusion of much importance, namely, that reality itself is a coherent system. If it were not, we should surely not be entitled to argue that a coherent ought to be preferred to an incoherent theory? Of course it may be replied that we are just wrong in using coherence as a criterion, but if so it will not be only metaphysics we shall have to drop. We shall have to give up at least most of science also, which to a modern philosopher is equivalent to throwing away the baby with the bath-water. We cannot get outside our thinking processes to prove the validity of their criteria by further, extraneous criteria; the only way of finding what the criteria are is to consider how we find ourselves constrained to think at our best when engaged in the various branches of study. If the criteria we find that we use have metaphysical implications, so much the worse for the anti-metaphysicians. I am well aware that in the opinion of the predominant school of philosophy to attribute rational coherence to the world is to suffer from a grave philosophical disease, but I cannot help holding the old-fashioned view that here Bradley and Bosanquet are nearer the truth than Russell or Wittgenstein. To speak thus may be to go against the main current today, but the tide does turn in philosophy as elsewhere, and it is antecedently very unlikely that a whole side of thought can be snuffed out as valueless. The present neglect of it only increases the importance of saying what is to be said on its behalf. At the same time I have no doubt that the doctrine that all our propositions are partly false applies at least to the propositions of metaphysics and that, when I am speaking of rational coherence, I am only speaking of one partial aspect of the whole.

Now, if we think of the real as coherent and of superior coherence as justifying the assertion of one view in preference to another, this certainly does open up the field for metaphysics. Metaphysical theories are, it cannot be denied, attempts to make coherent systems, at least of the part of the real with which we are in contact, and the main evidence cited in their favour has been constituted by their internal coherence and their coherence with our experience. In the absence of special grounds for excluding metaphysics it is a valid argument for a metaphysical theory that it takes us nearer to the goal of bringing all our experience into a coherent system, as it is a valid argument for a theory in science. I should say that the arguments for the existence of minds other than one's own and for the existence of physical objects themselves depend on the claim that these are needed to make anything at all like a coherent system of one's individual experience, thus showing that coherence may require the supplementation of an experience from outside by postulating entities beyond itself as explaining it, and this supplementation may be needed in other cases also, calling for more pretentious ventures of metaphysics as of science. Even the most metaphysical metaphysicians, though they may have appealed to supposed self-evident propositions too, have thought their metaphysics justified mainly as needed to explain and make a coherent system of what we find in experience.

There is one metaphysical problem of supreme practical and theoretical importance, the problem of the existence of God. I am far from holding that God's existence can be proved with logical certainty, and I am in sympathy with the present tendency in philosophy of religion outside Roman Catholic circles to base the justification of the belief in God more on intuition or, if you like, 'religious experience' than on argument. But this does not exclude its being *supported* by argument; and it certainly does seem that the notion of the world as a coherent system provides a much more promising background for theism than any philosophy which makes the world thoroughly irrational. There is at least much plausibility in maintaining that, provided the problem of evil cannot be seen to be on principle insoluble, the conception of the universe as the work of a perfectly wise mind with a perfectly good purpose comes nearer the coherence ideal, is therefore by the coherence criterion nearer the truth than a conception of it as the purposeless result of a conglomeration of atoms or indeed than any other conception of it that the human mind can frame. It is no doubt impossible for human beings to devise a theistic or any other metaphysical hypothesis which will rationalize the world completely, but it is surely reasonable to do as the scientist does and accept that hypothesis which will go furthest in the direction of systematizing and explaining, even if we cannot solve all problems or give a complete and ultimate explanation. It would certainly not be an adequate refutation of theism to point out that we cannot explain how God's purpose works in detail, mention for every evil a good to which it is a necessary means, or answer the question why God exists or exactly how he created the world. These are questions of which we could not possibly be expected to know the answer even if theism is true. In the absence of an answer we have not made the world a fully coherent system or given a full explanation, but it may still be argued that at least theism brings one nearer this goal. Thus the coherence principle opens up the possibility of defending a metaphysics congenial to the religious man, provided only the defenders of religion are prepared to link religion with rationality and not, as they have so often done, with the reverse. This presumption is strengthened when we reflect that our coherent system will have to be inclusive and not only internally coherent, for among the facts to be included are those of ethics and the ostensible intuitions of the mystics and of those who, while they could not claim to be mystics, still have some genuine more or less developed 'religious experience'. For one of the points where we must join issue with the positivist movement is in insisting that experience is not limited to sense-experience. Besides sense-experience there is the experience of having insight into non-verbal logical connections, the experience of ethics, the experience of aesthetics and the experience of religion. I have dwelt in my article on the quasi-logical character of the real, not because I regard this as the only aspect of reality worth consideration, but because one must concentrate on a limited field in writing such an article and it is the aspect most neglected today, yet it may well be that the experience which is metaphysically most illuminating and revealing is the experience of values and not the experience of seeing logical connections, still less the experience of causation.

MAIN PUBLICATIONS

Kant's Treatment of Causality. Routledge and Kegan Paul. 1924.
The Morality of Punishment. Routledge and Kegan Paul. 1929.
Idealism, a Critical Survey. Methuen. 1934.
A Short Commentary on Kant's Critique of Pure Reason. Methuen. 1938.
Reason and Intuition. Annual Philosophical Lecture to the British Academy. Oxford University Press. 1941.
The Individual, The State, and World Government. Macmillan. 1947.
The Definition of Good. Routledge and Kegan Paul. 1947.
The Fundamental Questions of Philosophy. Routledge and Kegan Paul. 1951.
Ethics. (Teach yourself Books). English Universities Press.

AN EXAMINATION OF TENSES

By J. N. FINDLAY

Professor of Philosophy in the University of London
(King's College)

AN EXAMINATION OF TENSES

MY philosophical history follows lines typical of the period through which I have lived: I have been through phases of Hegelianism, of Russellian realism, of Meinongian *Gegenstands-theorie* and Husserlian phenomenology. I was also deeply influenced by Wittgenstein. If my attitude to his teaching has become in some ways dissident, this does not mean that I am not immeasurably in debt to it.

I shall, in the first part of this article, attempt to give a brief, necessarily somewhat dogmatic-sounding account of what I as a philosopher believe myself to be doing, and of the procedures I follow in doing it. I shall also try to set out the assumptions that I think these procedures involve. I shall then, in the second longer part of my article, go on to give a specimen of my actual philosophical practice, by means of which its possible fertility (or sterility) may be assessed. This specimen will be an examination of the problems raised by our use of tenses, by our changing references to states of affairs as successively future, present and past. I shall try to come to reasoned decisions (not necessarily to the *only* such decisions that could be come to) in regard to these matters.

I

In my philosophizing I regard myself as concerned with 'concepts', with modes of conceiving, rather than with words or things. What I mean by a concept can be best elucidated by examples: thus I may have a concept of some thing (or things) as being numerous, or as being 587 in number, or as being to the left of something else, or as having ceased to exist many centuries ago, or as being *this* thing and no other, or as being twice as valuable as something else, or as being logically impossible, or as being alternative to this or that, or as having this or that as a consequence, and so on indefinitely. A concept is, on my usage, always an approach to or a dealing with 'things', though the 'things' with which it deals need not be actual but merely possible, and though they need not be confined to the common-or-garden things of one's daily dealings, but may be extended to cover those 'entities of reason' (classes, properties and the like) which are themselves the products of subtle changes in conception. But whatever 'things' one may admit, one must still distinguish between concepts, which involve the responses of an intelligent being, and the things conceived by their means. Quite plainly it is possible to conceive of the same things in varying manners (e.g. as differently grouped or related), and quite plainly it is largely arbitrary just how we conceive of them. Even the things of reason may be varyingly conceived, and there are, moreover, abstract aspects of objects to which no concepts correspond: thus we 'have no idea' of what song the Sirens sang, nor of the name of Hecuba's mother.

A concept is, moreover, on my usage, always an approach to something *as* being this or that, or *as* satisfying these or those conditions: it has, in other words, a 'content'. This mode of formulation must not, however, be taken as meaning that all conception is of necessity classificatory or predicative: we must, in fact, admit infinite variety in our modes of conceiving. Some of these must be said to credit things with characters, while others range them under kinds, in some of them we approach things singly, while others deal with them generally or collectively, some deal with things absolutely, while others treat them relatively or contextually, some show or point out their objects, while others deal with them much more distantly, in some features are treated abstractly and hypostatically, while others use them concretely and describingly, some conjoin and others disjoin, some posit, some question, others merely entertain, and some may be said to stand on their own legs, while others merely modify other modes of conceiving. It may at times be convenient to range all this variety of functions under a single predicative or classificatory model (as I myself have done in the examples above) but such a proceeding is both artificial and misleading.

To have a concept is, further, on my usage, to be ready to respond in an appropriate fashion in the right set of circumstances, but this appropriateness of response can be shown alike (*how* I shall not in detail here attempt to say) in the use of verbal expressions, in the performance of acts, and in the undergoing of inner-life occurrences. If the former has an undoubted priority in the 'pinning down' of our notions, and in enabling us to identify them, to communicate them and to talk about them, the second has a priority as being the complete fulfilment and exhibition of our understanding of anything, while the last has a priority for our own experience and enjoyment. Quite plainly, to have a concept is not merely to be able to use words correctly, even though this is by far the most definite way in which it is possible to have concepts, and even though there are many concepts, those, e.g. of a 'breach of promise' or of 'spiritual dryness', which it would be impossible to have in the absence of a settled use of words. We do not, however, wish to deny the possession of certain simple concepts to animals, nor to hold that they only have them in some strained or metaphorical fashion. And we also want to admit that there may be much in our use of words to which no important conceptual differences correspond, and we must therefore make appeal either to intuitions of meaning or to observations of behaviour, to determine *when* linguistic differences correspond to important conceptual distinctions and when they do not. If Platonizing philosophers have at times martyred the subtleties of linguistic usage on a Procrustean bed of simplifying conceptions, linguistic philosophers have as often martyred profound and pervasive unities of meaning on a set of Procrustean beds of linguistic triviality.

Having said that I as a philosopher feel obliged to deal with conceptions, I must now try to say *how* I feel obliged to deal with them. And I may here simply distinguish between a descriptive-analytic and a cathartic-reconstructive treatment of our notions. To embark on the former is to see 'how our notions stand', or to 'show how they work', in relation to other notions, and to the things to which such notions apply: it is to illustrate them, to see what more general notions they fall under, or what more specific notions fall under them, to bring out their closeness to, or remoteness from other conceptions, to consider the ways in which they may be combined with such other conceptions to form wholes of various kinds, to consider what other conceptions they entail, or exclude, or will tolerantly suffer. The *a priori* principles governing our judgements in various fields are the fruits of this sort of descriptive analysis. It is a patient, sober architectonic, not at all intent upon 'puzzles', such as Plato envisaged in his accounts of dialectic, and Husserl in his account of the 'eidetic sciences', and of which many philosophers from Aristotle to Moore have given interesting and valuable examples.

This straightforward descriptive analysis of our concepts is, however, always ready to pass over into a cathartic and reconstructive treatment. For notoriously a situation exists that may be described either by saying that our concepts sometimes *seem* to have applications, affinities, connections, exclusions, tolerances and so forth which they do not *really* have at all, and which conflict grievously with their normal employment, or, alternatively, by saying that many of our common concepts really *do* involve deep-set contradictions and obscurities, which demand their supersession by other clearer and more consistent notions. The former is, in the main, the sort of account that would be given by philosophers like Wittgenstein and Moore, who regard ordinary notions and ordinary usages as emphatically healthy, and who see the source of our philosophical confusions in a violent misconstruction, or an oversimplified misunderstanding, of their many subtle interrelations and workings. Whereas the other account would be one agreeable to the dialectical idealism of Hegel, which sees in our ordinary notions forces which, if fully developed, must necessarily push us on towards contradictory breakdowns, and which therefore also drive us on towards more harmonious, reconciling concepts. Thus, on the former view, our puzzlement in regard to the possibly illusory character of the whole external world is due merely to a sophisticated misunderstanding of the perfectly functioning commonsense notion of 'physical object', whereas, on the second view, it arises out of certain confused and self-contradictory notions of independence and externality which are inherent in that commonsense notion. I myself would prefer the latter to the former mode of conception. For it does justice to the fact that one may fall a victim to profound conceptual confusions even in cases where words play no important part at all—thus one may *feel* that one has lost one's personal identity, or that the whole world around one is illusory—and it also does justice to the importance of forming *new* philosophical concepts, which will bring out distinctions and connections that have passed unnoticed in ordinary talk and thought.

There remains one point, of great importance and obscurity, which must be touched on in this general preamble, and that is my belief in certain *non-arbitrary* standards of preference which determine how it is *best* for us to shape our concepts, and how in consequence it is best for us to do our philosophizing. To the type of conceptual realism which appeals to objective, eidetic relations on which valid conceptions must be founded, I see many grave objections. Quite plainly there are many alternative ways in which one's notions may be shaped in every field, among which there is not always any decisive advantage. Thus one cannot doubt that our mathematical notions might have been very differently shaped in a larger number of ways, and that some of these ways might have been as profitable and as legitimate as those which have been actually adopted. But what I cannot admit is that *everything* in our notions is a matter for arbitrary decision: to me decision is only possible, in this as in other fields, on a background of certain basic aims, in regard to which it would be *nonsense* to talk of deciding. Thus there are aims of consistency, clarity, continuity, communicability and the like which are plainly involved in the formation of all concepts whatever, and in terms of which some modes of conceiving are unhesitatingly to be preferred to others, while some are so perverse and outlandish as to call for something akin to moral condemnation. All this is conceded by those convention-alist philosophers who admit that some ways of speaking may be 'natural', 'convenient', 'tidy' and the like: what is wrong in their treatments is the suggestion that there is something trivial and dispensable in such qualities. Whereas it is on the firm foundations of the 'tidy' that, not only the uncertain edifices of metaphysics, but also the rules and principles of mathematics, and the canons of scientific method, repose. The whole subject of what may be called 'conceptual values' is, however, obscure: it is hard to enumerate *all* the features of concepts that would render them logically admirable, and to show, by something akin to a transcendental deduction, just why these and no other features of concepts must be necessarily pursued. I shall not, in this article, inquire further into these conceptual values: I shall be content to feel them and apply them.

II

I now pass from this programmatic preamble to the particu-lar concepts that I wish to examine. We have, it is plain, two very different ways of conceiving of what may be spoken of (in either case) as 'temporal position', of the *time* of the occur-rence or existence of objects and events. We have, on the one hand, a way of conceiving of such positions which may be said to be a conceiving of them *from* the standpoint of the conceiving individual, or, more strictly, from the standpoint of that actual conception in which that way of conceiving is being exercised. Thus a man may conceive of something as having happened a long time previously, or as being about to happen within the next few minutes, in either of which cases it would be correct to say that he is conceiving of such events from the standpoint of the actual occasion in which he now lives and thinks. This is so in the sense that *just how* he conceives of such events will depend on the precise relation—whether prior, posterior or contemporaneous—of the events conceived to his own act in conceiving of them: were that relation different, he would (if he conceived of them correctly) also conceive of them differently, and he *will* conceive of them differently when that relation is different. This mode of conceiving temporal position may be called the 'tensed mode', since the tenses of verbs are its primary and most natural expression. But it is, of course, also expressed in endlessly varying forms of behaviour and of inner experience, all those, in short, that would be said to bring out the difference between a retrospective, a prospective and what may be called (without fear of obscurity) a 'conspective' attitude.

There can, however, be another mode of conceiving temporal position in which the standpoint of the conceiving individual (or of his conception) plays no part at all, but in which a thing or event is taken as standing in some determinate or indeterminate temporal relation—some form of a relation involving temporal precedence, temporal subsequence or contemporaneity, relations which are, of course, exemplified in our simplest experiences—to a thing or event which has been chosen as a 'standard of reference', and which must, in the ideal case, be conceived of as being a *unique* case of some kind or character. Thus assuming that, once only in the course of history, a man such as we conceive Jesus to have been, will have been born in a place and manner such as we believe him to have been born in, we can place or date all objects and events of which we either know or surmise or suppose anything, in relation to such a 'Christian Era'. But we could just as well have made use of some less momentous standard of reference, or of a number of such standards having fixed relations to one another. This mode of conceiving position in time may be called the 'tenseless mode' since tenses are irrelevant to its effectiveness. It exists only in a contaminated and approximate form in the ordinary view of things, since we don't usually employ standards of reference, without also seeing them from the standpoint in which we actually live and think, and since we don't usually think of anything as coming before or after anything else, without also thinking of them either as having been, or as actually being, or as being about to be. It has been left to philosophers to abstract the mere relations of temporal precedence, subsequence and contemporaneity from the tenses which normally accompany them and to devise such forms of speech as the 'tenseless present', as well as various participial and gerundival constructions (e.g. 'Crowning of William at Westminster after defeat of Harold at Hastings'), in which the temporal relation of events to our thinking or uttering is entirely irrelevant. That such conceptions and expressions are artificial is not, however, a point in their disfavour: they have a foundation in ordinary notions and modes of expression, and their desirability or otherwise remains an open question.

A few important points must now be made in regard to what we have called the 'tensed' way of conceiving position in time. The first is that, while in the tensed mode of conceiving temporal position we may be said to conceive such position *from* the temporal standpoint of our actual conception, it would be incorrect to say that we conceived of such position *in relation* to this temporal standpoint, or that we used ourselves or our own acts of conceiving as a standard of reference. As remarked above, to say that we conceive temporal position *from* the standpoint of our own act of conception, is only to say that *how* we conceive of such position depends on where we are ourselves 'in time', in our relation to the things we think of, and that, were this relation different, we should conceive of such position differently. It does not mean that, in conceiving of things and happenings in tensed fashion, we must conceive of our own conceptions, and of where they are in time. In thinking of something as about to be, or as actually being, or as having been, we need not normally think of ourselves at all: we cannot therefore be *relating* what we think of to our own act in thinking of it. And we *could* relate whatever we are thinking of to our own act in thinking of it, without doing so in a tensed manner. Thus I can think of fighting as taking place at a site called Hastings 888 years before such fighting is written about in a paper called 'An Examination of Tenses', without thinking of the former as having taken place in the past, or of the latter as occurring now.

Those writers, therefore, are extremely misguided who speak of our tensed utterances as being 'token-reflexive', or as making covert reference to themselves as noises made on given occasions: one could at best call them '*quasi*-token-reflexive', since their form varies with their position in time, and their temporal relation to the things they speak of.

It is also interesting to point out that the tensed mode of conceiving temporal position permits of an indefinitely extensible *Einschachtelung* or Chinese-box complication: a thing or event may be placed in time, not merely from some actual standpoint of conceiving, but also from a secondary standpoint which is itself placed from that primary standpoint, or from a tertiary standpoint placed from a secondary standpoint, and so on indefinitely. Thus we may not only conceive of things as *having been* or as *about to be* (which is to regard them from our own actual standpoint of conception) but also as *being about to have been*, or as *having been about to be*, or as *having been about to have been about to have been*, to take only a few out of an infinity of examples. The more complex of these tense-combinations obviously require symbolic aids for their conception but this is not true of the simpler forms: it is, for instance, perfectly possible to *remember* one's anticipation that something would shortly be *over*. Some of these curious iterations of tenses are a source of special difficulties: thus we have many well-known puzzles in regard to events conceived in the past future, or as having been about to be. What is important to note, however, is the fact that the tensed mode of conception does not merely sort events into the two broad, and the one narrow category of the future, the past and the present: it also arranges them *within* those categories by relations of inexhaustible complexity.

The most important feature of the tensed mode of conceiving temporal position (and the feature which gives rise to most of its philosophical difficulty) is, however, the fact that this mode of conceiving *regularly and steadily changes*, as experience continues, and as our thought develops with it. Things thought and spoken of as about to be, must in the fullness of time (if our expectations are not mistaken) come to be thought and spoken of as actual and present, and it will then thereafter be always necessary to conceive and speak of them as *having been*. This steady change in first-order tenses will of course carry with it innumerable correlated changes in higher-order tenses, as well as constantly changing attributions of length and distance. We may note, further, that not only will these regular tense-changes take place in switching from one continuous tract of experience to another: they will also take place *within* the limits of a single tract of experience. Thus the beginning of the reading of this article by whoever is now reading it, might correctly have been conceived by him, no more than an hour ago, as *about* to take place in the future: it must now necessarily be conceived of as *having* taken place in the past. And we are often obliged, in situations of rapid change, to introduce such changes of tense within the limits of a single experience, or of the sentence which expresses it. There are experiences of which 'Coming, here, gone', or 'Going, going, gone' are the most natural expressions, and there are other experiences which can only be expressed in a running commentary, e.g. 'Now I think he's going to pass the ball to Jones, and now, yes, he has passed it to Jones, etc., etc.' Such running commentaries are of incalculable philosophical importance. For so obstinate is the determination of certain philosophers to think and discourse in an unchanging manner, that, feeling unable to do this in the longer segments of thought and utterance, they at least hope to achieve it within the limits of a single experience or expression. Here at least, they imagine, they will be able to seat themselves on a firm and stable perch, from which it will be possible to look out upon the rush and flux of things, while setting it at nought in their thought and discourse. But it is significant that, even on such a perch, they are by no means immune from the sawing tooth of time, and must in their talk adopt devices which resemble the moving finger of Cratylus. Only in a flash of thought and speech so brief as to admit of no discernible division whatever, could the tooth of time be evaded, and of such a flash it will unfortunately at once be true that 'le moment où je parle est déjà loin de moi'.

Having now explained these two distinct modes in which position in time may be conceived, I shall now make the point that both are entirely workable and legitimate. Philosophers have often questioned both this workability and this legitimacy, and have seen inadequacies and inner contradictions in one or other of the modes under examination. Thus it has been held, notoriously, at all periods in the history of philosophy, that there is something self-contradictory in attempting to think of the same state or object as being about to be, as actually being and as having been, and that, since this is the case, time and change must be in some sense 'unreal', and that we must therefore re-conceive the matters that we *mis*conceive in such terms in some other unchanging manner. On such difficulties I shall not here waste time: they are plainly cases of philosophical pathology admitting only of cathartic treatment. For our tensed modes of conceiving are such that it is only contradictory to conceive of one and the same matter in varying tenses, provided one does so in a single pulse of thought and experience: there is no contradiction, only admirable order, in the way in which our various tensed conceptions succeed one another systematically, as our experience develops and our thought proceeds. The appearance of contradiction only arises because we want our tensed conceptions to achieve an invariancy possible only for a tenseless mode of conceiving, for the quite wrong reason that invariancy is a mark of correctness in *other* fields of thought. Because correctly formed conceptions of the relations between the numbers 7, 5 and 12, never need to vary from one occasion, or from one person to another, and because all such conceptions either entail or are compatible with one another, we think there should be a like invariancy, and a like mutual entailment and compatibility among our various tensed conceptions. These requirements are, however, absurd: we are confusing the 'logic', the way of working, of one kind of notion with that of another. We are trying to achieve, in a mode of conception which is essentially changing, what can only be achieved in one that is essentially changeless. Such confusions lie at the root of the celebrated arguments of McTaggart, in which there is at once a determined attempt to retain the peculiarities of our tensed modes of conception, and an equally determined attempt to secure the advantages and observe the rules of a tenseless mode of conception, determinations which can only lead to an endless, unhappy oscillation between one mode of conceiving and the other. These difficulties have, however, been so thoroughly dealt with, and so elaborately seen through in past decades, that we need no more than mention them.

Many philosophers have, however, argued that, while there may be nothing self-contradictory in our tenses, they are none the less without relation to the *content* of our concepts, or, what is the same, to the *sense* of our linguistic expressions. To say in succession 'A garden party will be held', 'A garden party is being held', 'A garden party has been held' is not, it is argued, to conceive of the garden party in a really different light: it is merely to give an irrelevant indication of the temporal station from which one regards it, much as in certain societies it is customary for women, priests, and slaves to give an irrelevant indication of their social station by employing different verbal forms to describe precisely the same situation. If social or temporal station is to come out in our words, then it had better be explicitly referred to than covertly indicated, and this can, in the case of temporal station be done without a use of tenses (e.g. we can simply say 'Garden party contemporary with this utterance'). The use of tenses may no doubt express important differences in our own practical or emotional attitude towards things and events, which will plainly vary according as those things and events are thought of as coming before or after our utterances, or as doing so closely or remotely: it may also express an attempt to evoke such varying attitudes in our auditors. In neither case, however, will it express a genuine difference in *conception*. This line of objection is, however, profoundly question-begging: it refuses to admit, as entering into the content of our concepts, whatever might *change* from one occasion to another. Whereas, from the point of view of those who make use of tenses, the distinctions they draw seem to concern the things and events they speak of, to make, in fact, 'all the difference in the world' to them, and to concern themselves and their own acts of conceiving not otherwise than they concern any other thing or event. The position from which the user of tenses speaks and thinks seems to him to be not merely *his* but the world's: it is the 'actual state of the world', from which its other states must be placed and dated. And while the tenseless speaker may feel that he can do full justice to the sense of tensed statements in his tenseless language, the tensed speaker necessarily feels that there is something vital left out in the process: to say that a garden party comes after a given reference to it, is not to say whether either *is* happening now. We are here in a situation where we can only reflect on the complete futility of attempting to distinguish between what is 'merely part of our attitude' and what is 'genuinely part of the facts'—since this must necessarily vary from one mode of speaking or conceiving to another—or in trying to impose the notion of an identity of sense in the face of our own profound unwillingness to accept one way of speaking in complete exchange for another. We may note, further, that there is nothing incommunicable, whether from person to person or from occasion to occasion, in the sense of our various tenses, a notion that seems implicit in the objection under consideration. If you and I inhabit the same neighbourhood on a given occasion (as is common in linguistic intercourse), we can certainly *share* an experience of things expected turning into things actual and present, and of things actual and present turning into things merely remembered. And though we are obliged to change the tenses in communications received from the past, or to expect them changed in communications made to posterity, we none the less always know exactly 'what it would be like' to employ the tenses that others may use correctly. It is clear, further, that our tenseless modes of speaking and conceiving are all abstract outgrowths out of our tensed modes of doing the same, and can, in practice, only be imperfectly freed from the latter: there can therefore be nothing incommunicable, or for that reason non-significant, in our use of tenses.

There are also philosophers on the other side of the fence, who have held such things as that tenseless modes of conceiving

13

'falsify the nature of time', that they 'ignore or reject the reality of change', or that they 'freeze' change into something changeless, and so forth. These too are baseless contentions. For the mere fact that one talks and thinks in a manner which does not alter as things change and events pass, does not mean that one may not be talking or thinking *about* change and passage, any more than the fact that one talks and thinks in an extremely quiet and dispassionate manner means that one may not be talking and thinking about the most violent emotions. One may concern oneself with human passion in the passionless manner appropriate to lines, surfaces, and solids: one may likewise concern oneself with mutation and vicissitude in a manner which is exempt from either. It is plain, in fact, that one is dealing with precisely the same 'empirical material', whether one conceives in tenseless fashion of William as overcoming Harold at Hastings 888 years before the meeting of Mr. Dulles and Chou En-lai at Geneva, or whether one conceives, with an elaboration of tenses, that William first overcame Harold at Hastings, and that, when this had happened, something else happened after it, and that when that had happened, something else happened after *it*, until, after running through the content of the centuries in this fashion, one ends up by dealing in the present tense with Chou En-lai and Dulles at Geneva. Tenseless conceptions do not therefore deal with relations in some queer sort of spatialized or coexistent time: there are no such relations to be dealt with. They deal, even if in different fashion, with the same mobile, developing material as do tenseless conceptions.

All this being admitted, one may, however, still raise the question as to whether one or other of these modes of speaking and conceiving may not in some sense penetrate deeper, be more richly and truly revelatory of the nature of time than the other. For it does not follow that, because two modes of conceiving are alike workable and legitimate, that one may not have good reason for preferring the one to the other, or for wanting to *understand* the one in terms of the other. Now I myself incline to the view that we understand time more profoundly when we conceive of events in a tensed, rather than in a tenseless manner, and that we are very liable to misunderstand and to misconstrue our tenseless concepts if we are not always ready to pass over from them to the corresponding tensed modes of conceiving. I shall now be concerned, in the remainder of this paper, to give reasons for these statements.

My first reason for feeling that the tensed mode of conceiving temporal position is superior to the tenseless one, is that it does such abundant justice to the fact that we, *qua* speaking and thinking, always occupy a position in time, that we also continuously *change* that position, and that we must of necessity change it even within the bounds of a single thought or utterance. It does justice to the fact that it is impossible to talk and conceive from no standpoint at all (though we need not, of course, conceive of our standpoint), and that we can neither talk nor conceive from another temporal standpoint than the one that we in fact occupy, and that we cannot change that standpoint in another manner or direction than the continuous fashion which is the actual order of world-history. A tenseless mode of conceiving need not involve any of these nonsensical 'possibilities', but it certainly encourages one to conceive them, much as, perhaps, an artificially unpractical or unemotional treatment of moral questions (as is within limits possible) might encourage one to imagine that there would still be moral questions to consider in the absence of any emotional or practical attitudes on one's part. The very fact that we concern ourselves with the temporal relations of events without doing so from a particular standpoint might lead us to feel 'freely-ranging', 'transcendental', 'out of the picture': we might then feel as if we could alter our standpoint at will, or experience events in several orders or directions, or make discontinuous leaps in time, or arrest events and dwell in them at will. One may indeed *think* of events in what order one chooses, but one may not think of them, nor of one's experience of them, *as* existing or *as* occurring in any other than their actual order. There is not here some extraordinary bound set to our liberty of movement in time: our notions simply do not extend to such seeming 'possibilities'. We are only tempted to feel that we are being dragged in

reluctant fashion after time's slowly moving chariot, because
we have disjoined the events we experience from our own standpoint in experiencing them: we then feel as if there were some
liberty of movement open to *us* which is denied to *them*. Whereas, if we were always ready to pass over from a tenseless to a
tensed mode of conceiving things and events, we should be less
liable to such confusions. It would then cease to seem either a
hard dispensation or an inexplicable necessity that we should
'travel' in time at the 'rate', or in the manner and direction
that we do.

My second reason for preferring a tensed to a tenseless
manner of conceiving events is that I think it does better justice
to what has been called our 'immediate consciousness' or our
'immediate experience' of time. Or at least I think it does better
justice to *one* of the forms of that immediate consciousness, and
that the form which I regard as being the better and the more
interesting. Now it may seem odd to say that we have *two*
immediate consciousnesses of time: such seems, however, to be
undoubtedly the case. It is a duality reflected in the opposition
between two current models of the 'specious present', between
the 'saddle-back' model of James, which looks forward towards
the onrushing future as much as it looks backwards towards the
vanishing past, and the dry 'searchlight' of Broad, which can
only cast a momentary illumination over a narrow stretch of
temps perdu. I shall not here deal with all the intricate obscurities
of the specious present, but shall assume simply that there are
stretches of duration, of varying length and somewhat nebulous
boundary, which can in a pregnant sense be seen or shown or
experienced 'as wholes', and not merely collected afterwards in
piecemeal fashion. Now there is one way of showing a person a
stretch of enduring or successive data, which consists either in
producing, or in running through such data, and then saying,
at the *end* of the process: 'There you have a note lasting for
exactly one minute', or 'There you have a series of events
coming one after the other'. This must be the sort of ostension
practised by Broad, whose specious present always lies entirely
prior to the act which apprehends or refers to it. From this

mode of ostension no tensed conceptions arise. But there is an equally effective way of introducing someone to a stretch of succession or duration, and that is *to allow it to develop and to complete itself before him*, while accompanying such a development by a running commentary in which its successively unfolding phases are spoken of in changing tenses, e.g. 'Now Oriel I is nearing Balliol II and seems about to bump it, but Balliol II seems to be making an effort and drawing ahead, but now again it is losing its advantage, and now, yes, Balliol II has been bumped'. It would not be easy to make such a commentary run parallel with very rapid change, but with an improved symbolism it should at least be possible to talk as fast as one can perceive. Now in all such running commentaries the events described and the words used to describe them, may fitly be said to fall within the specious present, to enter into a continuous whole, and yet they are not merely gathered together retrospectively, but are added together *as they manifest themselves*. Our experience, in fact, in this kind of ostension, is a veritable microcosm of the whole of time. It contains an ever growing part of some developing event which is definite and which belongs to the past, and also an ever lessening segment which is indefinite and belongs to the future: it also contains a *minimum discernibile* of the narrowest presentness, an experiential rather than a mathematical knife-edge, which may be said to change its content throughout the whole happening ('Now this, now that, now that, etc.'). Now the sort of consciousness which develops with events, and which is led to conceive of them in ever changing tenses, is obviously a richer and a more interesting consciousness than the one which merely looks back upon things past in a manner which needs no tenses. For everything that is revealed to such a retrospective vision is also revealed to the developing mode of apprehension, which is as much retrospective as prospective. But this developing conception also turns its regard to what can only be called the *unfinished* or *growing* character of processes in time, from which the other type of conception turns resolutely away. Those thinkers, therefore, who have built up their accounts of time exclusively on a basis of the relations of *before* and *after*—

as has been done by many philosophers—may have developed an admirable way of talking and thinking about the past: they have not developed any adequate way of talking and thinking about the narrowly present or the future.

My most important reason, however, for preferring tensed to tenseless modes of conceiving position in time, is the fact that there are such deep and absolute differences between the way in which we think and deal with things past, and the way in which we think and deal with things future. There is, it is plain, a radical asymmetry between the past and the future, a fact whose full implications were brought out by the Austrian philosopher von Ehrenfels in his book *Cosmogony*. The basic point is simply that what *has* happened can be discovered or determined or inferred to an incomparably greater degree than what *will* happen: this fact seems to be so basic in the whole running of the universe, that our thought, language and practice have been shaped to meet it, so that we can scarcely talk or think of a situation in which this should be otherwise. The future is for us open, incompletely foreseeable, amenable to planning, to control, while the past, on the other hand, is beyond our altering, and is in principle completely knowable. These principles have a proverbial sanction, which might lead us to regard them contemptuously: we must none the less find out how they originate, and on what facts they are founded.

They have one foundation, of course, in our immediate consciousness of time. Thus I usually find, when I attend to such a temporal process as a successively unfolding tune or phrase, that there is a profound difference between the *declared*, *definite* character of the notes I *have* heard, and the as yet *open*, *undeclared* character of the notes I look forward to hearing. My whole experience of the tune or phrase is, in fact, one in which *more and more* becomes definite and declared, while *less and less* remains open and undeclared, until in the end the whole note or phrase hovers before me in its rounded completeness. There are of course exceptions to this general pattern. There are cases where I am very precisely prepared for what is to come, while I have lost the thread of what went before: such exceptions arise, however, on a background of cases in which the just past has firm outlines, while the just future is somewhat sketchy and nebulous. It is plain, further, that the asymmetry we have mentioned has a foundation in the fact that we have a developed, successfully functioning faculty of memory, whereas we have no such developed, successfully functioning faculty of 'precognition'. But the grounds of this radical asymmetry are by no means confined to ourselves and the make-up of our actual faculties: they plainly have a *cosmic* foundation. They are, in fact, so utterly deep-set and pervasive, that it is only with difficulty that we can think of them as altered.

We have, it is plain, a quite extraordinary difficulty in predicting the future which we never experience in retrodicting the past. We have, for instance, as von Ehrenfels points out, a highly circumstantial knowledge of human history during several past millennia, whereas we can predict nothing with comparable accuracy even within the next twenty years. And when we judge what *will* happen, we must always do so subject *to a proviso*: we must add an 'other things being equal', an 'if present trends continue', or an 'if nothing unforeseen interferes'. The point seems to be that prediction and retrodiction alike depend on the presence in our world of what have been called 'world-lines', long threads of continuity such as atoms, molecules, mountains, trees, persons, etc., which preserve their pattern and characteristic style of response over fairly long periods and in varying settings. Now it is an interesting fact that these world-lines preserve in their structure countless nicks, stains or traces of what has previously happened to them, of their manifold encounters and interweavings with other world-lines, whereas they seldom or never show any anticipatory marks in their structure from which their future encounters and interweavings may be inferred. Hence there is always an *if* in statements about the future which is only marginally present in statements about the past. Human memory is, in fact, no more than a special case of this cosmic asymmetry: our past encounters and performances have left marks on our neural structures, to which there is nothing comparable in the case of our future history.

Now can we conceive that this cosmic asymmetry should have been absent or reversed? Might we have been able to deal with the future as we now deal with the past, or with the past as we now deal with the future, so that the main point of our tensed modes of conception would be lost or altered? There is a sense in which we can conceive of these things, though our doing so would involve so complete a change in the working of all our notions, that it would be misleading to use the same words to express them. Our world has been seen to be asymmetrical in the direction earlier-to-later: to conceive of a world in which this asymmetry would be reversed, it is sufficient to conceive of states like the states in our world but running in a reverse direction (a supposition which is of course distinct from the nonsensical notion of a reversal of history or of the 'flow of time'). Now what would such a world be like? It would be a world in which there were numerous *anticipatory* signs of a coming event, just as there are at present many *surviving* traces of events that are past. These signs would at first be vague and indefinite, and would permit only of the most uncertain inferences: they would also be widely scattered throughout the universe. But, as time went on, they would assume even more definite outline, permitting of ever plainer prognoses: they would also converge from their scattered locations to a central zone of disturbance (just as events now diverge or radiate from such a zone). At last they would reach this centre, and would also achieve a limiting degree of definiteness: they would then pass over into the event that they had been so uniformly prefiguring. But once they had given rise to this event, they would forthwith utterly vanish from the scene, much as the Prophets and Sibyls ceased to function once our Saviour had appeared in the world. There would then be no clear indication that either they, or the event they had led up to, had ever been. Von Ehrenfels gives the example of ripples steadily converging to the centre of a pond, and increasing in strength and volume as they do so, until, when the last largest ripple reaches the centre, a stone emerges, leaving the water beneath it miraculously still.

In much the same way (in the world we are imagining) a man's mental history would start off with a state in which he enjoyed a fairly clear knowledge of the whole of his future life of which each part would assume more definite outlines as he drew nearer to it. But once he had been through a given part, of this fore-ordained programme, its outlines would at once become blurred and dubious: its content could at best be inferred by analogy from the foreseen future. In the end nothing would be clear beyond the manner of his death, unless, indeed, some form of adult education had succeeded in staving off the stupefying effects of experience. In this sort of world there could be no planning, nor any action in the sense in which we now understand them: it would not make sense to do A in order that B might come of it. One might indeed form the novel notion of doing A so that B might have preceded it: one could perform deeds that would lend support to a flattering picture of the past, a picture, be it noted, that would never need to stand up to future confirmation or refutation. It is vain to elaborate the picture further, nor could one do so with conviction. Enough has been said to show that a world in which the future had the degree of inferribility that we now attribute to the past, and in which precognition took the place of memory, would be a world so different from anything in our experience, that none of our notions would have a straightforward application to it, and that it is quite impossible, in practice, to avoid talking nonsense about it. It is plain, therefore, that there are important features of our cosmos and of human experience, which are better brought out by a tensed mode of conception, than by the tenseless notions favoured by certain philosophers.

MAIN PUBLICATION

Meinong's Theory of Objects. Oxford University Press. 1933.

IDENTIFICATION AND EXISTENCE

By STUART HAMPSHIRE

Fellow of All Souls College, Oxford

IDENTIFICATION AND EXISTENCE

I

WE inherit and develop many different forms of thought and statement. When we reflect in very general terms upon these forms of thought and statement, they may seem at various points inadequate to our experience or to our needs; if we criticize them, we are doing philosophy. We must have some standard of adequacy for the type of thought and statement criticized. The standard of adequacy must be found in some other type of thought and statement known to us. The criticism of any type of discourse therefore takes the form of a comparison with some other types of discourse which are taken as models of clearness and adequacy; in the extreme case all types of thought and statement are dismissed by philosophers as inadequate unless they approximate to some single standard of clarity, derived, for instance, from mathematics, or from singular categorical statements referring to our personal experience, or from these two taken together. The type of thought and statement taken as the model of clear thought and clear statement has varied from age to age and from philosopher to philosopher; a philosophical position can be defined by asking what type of statement is being taken as the standard and model of an adequate statement. But if there are different philosophical theories, it is natural to assume that almost all of them must be false and that at least one must be true, or very nearly true. Then the question arises: What grounds can be given for choosing one type of thought and statement rather than another as the standard? If it is in principle impossible to suggest any independently based criterion of adequacy, it is impossible to decide rationally between competing philosophical theories. If no one of the theories could ever be shown to be correct, there is no place for theories. We can come to understand the motives, historical and personal, for the various philosophical preferences of one type of discourse to another. But if there is no decision procedure there is no reason for constructing further theories; we need only notice and record, neutrally and without preference, the characteristic differences between different types of thought and statement, each of which has its own distinguishing type of clarity. This principle of tolerance has been the obvious feature of contemporary British philosophy; it is the new form of scepticism. It suggests that we cannot step outside the language which we use, and judge it from some ulterior and superior vantage-point. Every type of statement has its own kind of logic; we should in philosophy explore and record these differences, and not try to override them, or assimilate all discourse to a single type or closed set of types. Philosophy should be descriptive only, and not constructive.

There have been in the past two roughly distinguishable ways of criticizing established types of thought and statement, and of leading into metaphysical theory. The first way is through the so-called theory of knowledge: one may ask the question: 'Under what conditions can a statement be known with certainty to be true?' Since to understand a statement necessarily involves knowing under what conditions the statement in question could be known with certainty to be true or false, any direct answer to this entirely general question will involve assimilating all statements to a single type; for to state conditions of certainty which apply to *any* statement whatever is necessarily to take some one type of statement, with its appropriate conditions of certainty, as the model of what a statement should be. Nothing can count as an adequate statement which does not conform, in the conditions of its verification, to this single type. But we learn to distinguish different types of statement by learning to distinguish the different conditions under which certainty can properly be claimed in respect of them. It is for this reason that the theory of knowledge, which sets up some general standard of certainty, has always led directly into metaphysics. Since only statements which satisfy this *a priori* standard can be accepted as true statements, only the entities referred to in such statements can be said certainly to exist. By this argument Plato may prove that only timeless abstractions exist, since only timeless truths can be certain; or an empiricist may argue that, in the last analysis, only ideas and impressions exist, since we cannot be ideally certain of any statements of fact other than descriptions of our own sensations.

The second way to a philosophical theory lies through formal logic rather than through theories of knowledge. Logic, unlike the theory of knowledge, is not concerned with the general conditions of application for the vocabulary of a language. But the formalization of syntax, and prescription of rules of derivation between different syntactical forms, may also be used to restrict the variety of admissible forms of statement. The objections to this restriction are now widely recognized in British philosophy, and need no further discussion.

I am convinced that these two traditional ways of arriving at a metaphysical theory are invalid, and that it is always an error to look for some general criterion of knowledge and certainty, or to require that all significant statements should exemplify some single system of formal relationships. But I am still not convinced that philosophy either must be, or ought to be, confined to describing and discriminating the different types of thought and statement in actual use. I am not convinced that philosophy must be purely descriptive and unsystematic and that it cannot properly lead to any conclusions other than clarifications of established forms of discourse. On the contrary, I am convinced (1) that philosophy can be, and ought to be, systematic, as it generally has been in the past. By 'systematic philosophy' I mean a philosophy which tries to show the necessary relations and interrelations between those most general notions upon which all thought and language depend; outstanding among these most general notions are—existence, knowledge, identity, truth. It is the mark of these organizing notions that the conditions of their application must vary with every element of vocabulary with which they are combined. I think that all these notions are interconnected, in the sense that to fix the place and working of any one of them in our discourse necessarily involves fixing the place and working of most, if not all, of the others. One needs to see how the whole system of these organizing notions is to be fitted together, in their relations to each other, before one fully understands the place of any one of them. I therefore think that there is now more to be learnt from, for example, Leibniz, than from Hume; it seems to me that Leibniz asks the constructive philosophical questions which both need to be, and can be, answered, and that he tries to answer them in the only possible way, namely, systematically. (2) I am convinced that the actual established forms of thought and statement, which we may find in use in any particular language at any particular time, may carry existential implications which we may see grounds for repudiating, when we reflect upon them. And these grounds are found outside the particular conventions governing the particular types of thought and language considered; they must be found in some more general, and therefore philosophical, considerations about existence. These more general considerations about existence, of the kind considered by (for example) Spinoza, Leibniz, Kant, and Wittgenstein (in the *Tractatus Logico-Philosophicus*), are to be found in the organizing notions which necessarily enter into every type of discourse. Any particular established type of thought and statement may involve criteria of identity, or of knowledge, or of existence, which are either confused and undetermined, or so unlike those accepted in respect of closely analogous entities and expressions as to be unacceptable. On such grounds one may wish to reject some well established type of discourse as, in the last analysis, empty and void of content. (3) It follows that existential conclusions will emerge at the end of any attempt to systematize the organizing notions of thought and language. (4) But I must admit, what rationalist philosophers have generally not admitted, that there can be no way of *proving* that there is only one way in which the relation between these organizing notions can be correctly stated, and that any other systematic interrelation of them must be wrong. A philosopher can do no more than show the implications of accepting one systematic interrelation of them rather than another; the implications will be found in the type of familiar existential statement, or statement with existential implications, which is shown to be unclear, incomplete or radically misleading. To be blunt, one could not accept certain accounts of the relation between the criteria of identity and the criteria of existence, and at the same time believe that God exists; but this does not mean that one could *prove*, by a philosophical argument of this very general kind, that it is not true that God exists. It means only that peculiarly philosophical reasons might be given for doubting whether God exists; one may be presented with a choice between abandoning the philosophical position and abandoning belief in God.

II

It is evident that my argument must depend on a particular doctrine of existential statements, and of the existential implication of statements. I am assuming that we may be entirely clear about the meaning, and the established conditions of use, of a certain type of statement, and yet still be doubtful whether any statement of this type can be accepted as a contribution to knowledge; for while knowing what statements of this particular type are supposed to refer to, we may believe that nothing of the required kind actually exists. An atheist, for example, may know very well what a particular set of theological propositions means, and he may know by what tests true statements about the properties of God are conventionally distinguished from false statements; he may be able to describe the conventionally accepted criteria of application for theological expressions, and he may be able to explain what ordinarily counts as sufficient evidence that a theological statement of this type is true. But he may still believe that no statement of this type about God can be accepted as true, in the last analysis, on the grounds that the conventionally accepted criteria of application attached to the subject-term violate some more general requirements which any such criteria of application should satisfy. He may hold, for example, that it is illegitimate to refer to God as the subject of a statement in the manner required, since nothing would properly count as identifying God, and nothing would properly count as distinguishing him from other things; and he might hold that there is some universal and necessary connection between the possibility of identification and of individuation and a claim to existence. If this was the philosophical atheist's position, it would be incorrectly described by saying that he considered statements about the properties of God to be meaningless. His objection is not a matter of meaning, or of the correct use of words; in the normal sense of 'understand', he understands what is meant by the word 'God', and he knows how this word fits into the vocabulary and with what other expressions it is compatible and incompatible. Similarly, he may understand what is meant by 'the vast and impersonal forces at work in history', and he may know how this expression is logically related to other expressions in the vocabulary. But he may hold that anyone who uses the substantival expressions 'God', or 'the vast and impersonal forces at work in history', as subject-terms, is talking of something which cannot be identified, and which therefore cannot be said to exist; and therefore that first-order statements about the properties of God, or about the working of impersonal forces in history, cannot be accepted as true as they stand. The first-order statement which begins with an unqualified mention of God must be taken to imply that God actually exists; if God does not exist, the statement itself cannot be true as it stands, since the existential implication is false.

But it may still be argued that existential conclusions cannot emerge from a purely philosophical argument of the kind which I have mentioned, that is, from an argument showing some connection between the possibility of identification and individuation on the one hand and a claim to existence on the other; for we must distinguish between statements to the effect that something of a certain kind *could* not exist, as a matter of logic, and statements to the effect that something does not in fact exist. It is logically impossible that there should be an even number greater than two and less than four, and it is a matter of fact that there is no king of France. One may assume that there are only two possibilities: either (1) a descriptive phrase involves a contradiction: in which case it is logically impossible that anything should be found which satisfies the description; or (2) the descriptive phrase has clear and non-conflicting criteria of application, but, when these criteria are used, it is found by experiment that there in fact exists nothing which answers to the description. I am suggesting that there is a third possibility. The purely *a priori* grounds for denying that there are vast and impersonal forces at work in history are not necessarily of the same type as the grounds for denying that there is an even number greater than two and less than four. There may be no conflict or contradiction within the criteria of application of the subject-term considered, and there may be no doubt of how the subject-term is logically related to other expressions within the vocabulary; it is therefore not true that the subject-term is an impossible or meaningless expression, but rather that the accepted criteria of application of the expression are not of the kind which justifies its place as an unanalysed subject-term. The expression 'vast and impersonal forces in history' has its intelligible place in the language, but the conditions of its application are sufficient to show that, if the question is asked 'Do these forces actually exist in history?', the answer must be 'No'; for there are no means of identifying one of these forces, either directly or indirectly, and they cannot therefore be counted as something which actually exists. There are certain systematically related conditions which a meaningful expression must satisfy if it is to be taken as an expression which stands for something which can properly be said to exist; and these conditions are additional to the requirement that the expression itself must be meaningful as an element of the vocabulary, and that it must be possible to state its logical relations to other terms in the vocabulary. For, having determined the meaning of an expression, e.g. of 'gene' or 'image' or 'act of will' or 'subconscious wish', we may still argue about whether one can properly say that these expressions stand for something which actually exists. A purely philosophical argument of this kind is sometimes said to determine one's ontology. But this must not be taken to imply that these very general questions about existence are the luxury of philosophers, and are irrelevant to the ordinary claims to knowledge made in scientific and other kinds of discourse. On the contrary, a philosophical argument of this kind determines some order of priority among claims to knowledge. If the subject-terms of a particular type of discourse or branch of knowledge—for instance, Freudian psychology—cannot be said, in virtue of the conditions of their application, to stand for something which is plainly identifiable, then the statements held to be true within that type of discourse will not in the long run be accepted as genuine contributions to knowledge, unless their subject terms can be in some way defined in terms of other expressions which, in virtue of their conditions of application, can be said to stand for something plainly identifiable. In the familiar terminology of empiricism, we require that subject-terms, or substantival expressions, which cannot themselves be said to stand for something plainly identifiable, should be *reducible* to substantival expressions which do stand for something plainly identifiable. And the fact that we naturally use the word 'reduction', and that we have already a sense of the direction in which reduction must go, shows that we have in mind some criterion by which we distinguish within our vocabulary between substantival expressions which stand for something *directly* identifiable as existing, and substantival expressions which do not stand for something directly identifiable. We reject statements which have 'the vast and impersonal forces of history' as their subject-term, unless the mention of these forces is shown to involve some indirect allusion to something which actually exists, only because the conditions of application of this expression preclude it from being taken as standing for something directly identifiable. How then do we distinguish substantival expressions which stand for something directly identifiable? The thesis of empiricism, on which most British philosophy is founded, has generally at this point involved some imprecise allusion to the objects of perception and introspection. But this empiricist thesis cannot be sustained and made precise unless some relation between a perceptual claim on the one hand, and the twin notions of identity and existence on the other, is shown to be necessary in *any* use of language and in *any* type of discourse. I can only roughly indicate the relation here.

III

(1) 'That is Socrates' (2) 'That is a dagger' (3) 'It is yellow'. In (1) and (2) I am not describing; I am identifying; I am answering the question 'What, or Who, is that?'. In (3) I am describing, not identifying, whatever is referred to by 'that'. Aristotelian logic stressed the analogy between (1) and (2); contemporary empiricists, following Russell's logic, have so closely assimilated (2) and (3) as scarcely to mark any difference in function between them. The blanket term 'descriptive expression' is now often applied without distinction to '. . . is a dagger' and '. . . is yellow', as if Aristotle had no good reason for distinguishing Primary and Secondary Substance on the one hand from Quality and Relation on the other. This failure to underline what is involved in identifying a thing, and in answering the question 'What is that?', has confused the theory of perception on which empiricist philosophy has rested. In stating what it is that I see, hear or am touching, I may use any common noun or substantival expression which classifies the thing or event heard or touched as being a thing or an event of a certain kind; alternatively, I may use a proper name. I may put into my answer to the question 'What, or Who, is that?' anything which I know or believe to be true about the object or event referred to, whether or not the identification and classification is based upon the evidence of my senses at that particular moment. And it is a logical truth that there will always be an indefinite set of possible true answers to the question 'What is

that?'; there can be no unique classification, and on any particular occasion we select the identification which is relevant to
our particular interests at that particular time. The ordinary
vocabulary which we use in our identifications of kinds of
things is naturally a vocabulary which classifies by use and
origin: 'What is that?' is generally very near to 'What is that
used for?' or less commonly, to 'What is the origin of that?',
or to some combination of these two. If we have specified the
use and origin of the thing before us, we have generally specified
what kind of thing it is. We may be said, in using our senses, to
identify things by their appearance at that moment in conjunction with any other knowledge that we possess; but it is not
generally in virtue of some similarity of appearance that things
are classified as they are. I may correctly identify someone as a
general by the braid on his hat; but to say 'He is a general' is not
to say that he has braid on his hat or to say anything whatever
about his appearance. I may correctly identify the thing before
me as a dagger, rather than as a paper-knife, or rather than as a
shadow or an image projected by my imagination, by the look or
feel of the handle; but to say that it is a dagger is not to say anything about its look or feel. Similarly, I may identify my feeling
on a particular occasion as being a feeling of jealousy, or of envy
or of anger, by the quality of my particular sensation at that
moment, taken in conjunction with some other knowledge of
the situation: but in saying that it was jealousy, I am not trying
to describe the quality of just those particular sensations. A
statement of the type of 'This is a dagger' (or 'This is a case of
jealousy') cannot, as a matter of logic, be analysable in terms of
any description of the phenomena which enable the speaker to
make the identification on any particular occasion, or even in
terms of any description of phenomena which *might* enable
him to make the identification; and no description of the
speaker's visual experience, or of his sensations, is entailed by
any such identification, unless it is part of the meaning of the
classificatory term used that any object falling under it must
under all conditions have a certain appearance or produce
sensations of a certain describable quality. For these reasons

no set of descriptions of the look or feel of a thing will entail, or be entailed by, any identification of it as a thing of a certain kind; and an indefinite number of identifications are compatible with any particular look or 'feel', and any particular look or 'feel' is compatible with an indefinite number of identifications. But a description of the look of a thing often enters into an identifying statement when we are trying to make clear what we are referring to: 'That bright patch of light which you can see on the horizon is a large sailing boat'. Some philosophers, apparently confusing the 'is' of identity with the 'is a so-and-so' of identification, have interpreted these statements as self-contradictory in form; for how can the patch of light which I see *be* a large boat? They have argued that what I really see, *the* object of perception, must be the patch of light and that I do not, strictly speaking, see the boat. But compare the apparently similar form of statement: 'That sailing boat which you see on the horizon is a freighter'. The form of this statement should show that there is not, and cannot be, any answer to the question 'What is *the* object of perception?', since any number of statements of this form can be made whenever I am identifying what I see. The question 'What is that so-and-so which I see?' receives the answer 'That so-and-so that you see is a so-and-so'. Whatever fills in the place of either of the two 'So-and-so's' is a possible answer to the question 'What do you see?'

But it may still be argued that there is an important difference between the two statements 'That white spot which you can see on the horizon is a boat' and 'That boat is a freighter': namely, that there might be circumstances in which we would not wish to assert that there literally is a patch of light on the horizon in the same way that we would assert the literal existence of the boat which is a freighter. Therefore it may be said that there are two senses of 'see': the sense in which in saying that I see something of a certain kind, I imply the existence of something of that kind, and the sense of 'see' in which I do not imply existence. But this is a mistake; for we can only show that we do not wish to assert or imply the actual existence of the

patch of light on the horizon by amending the original statement
to: 'That thing which *looks like* a patch of light on the horizon
is a boat.' If the speaker does not accept this amended form of
his original statement, he is indeed committing himself to an
assertion of the actual existence of a patch of light on the horizon.
And this commitment is not a peculiarity of the verb 'see'; the
existential implication is contained simply in the unqualified use
of the substantival phrase, and will continue to hold whatever
ordinary transitive verb is substituted for 'see', provided that
it is not one of the verbs which are used specifically to cancel
or qualify the existential implication (e.g. 'That so-and-so which
I talked about does not in fact exist'). 'The stone I kicked', or
'I kicked a stone', so far imply the existence of a stone for
exactly the same reason that 'The stone I saw . . .' and 'I see a
stone' imply its existence. In both cases we can cancel the
existential implication by saying 'What looked (or felt) like a
stone' in place of 'a stone'. But a statement about what I see,
or have seen, is no more a statement about the momentary
look, or appearance, of the object seen than is a statement about
the object kicked.

What then is the relation between perception and existence
which is vaguely indicated in the empiricist thesis: 'Any knowledge outside mathematics must ultimately be derived from
perception and introspection'? The connection is to be found
in that fundamental form of statement 'This (That, It) is a
so-and-so', which is an identification made in the presence of
the object referred to.

One may use the pure referring expressions 'This' and
'That' and 'It' and others, absolutely without restriction, to
refer to anything of any category or type, whether existing or
non-existing. I know what you are referring to if I am in a
position to answer correctly the question 'What is he referring
to?'; and the answer might be 'He is referring to round squares',
or 'He is referring to the present king of France'. To know what
you are referring to, or speaking about, is not the same as to
know that there exists something to which you are referring;
you may not intend to refer to something which actually exists;

you may intend to refer to something fictitious, imaginary or logically impossible. The linguistic act of referring is the same in each case and is so far non-committal in respect of existence. Suppose that, pointing to the empty air, you say 'Is that a dagger?' and suppose it becomes plain that you intend to be taken as referring to something which actually exists, and that your reference is not a pretence or deceit, then I may say 'What are you referring to?'; for at this stage I still do not know what you are referring to, and I need a definite description to fix the reference. You, in this Macbeth situation, may provide any number of a variety of definite descriptions: e.g. 'That black shape I see over there' or 'That long black object pointing towards me'. I may then realize what you are referring to, namely, to something which you see and which looks like a black object, although I know that it cannot in fact be a black dagger. I may then say: 'I wonder what it is: for it is clear that you are seeing something'. And I may then come to the conclusion, using my eyes and also any other knowledge of the situation that I may possess, 'It is an image which is a projection of your imagination', or 'It is only a shadow'. To make a statement of this form (whether spoken, written, or said to oneself) *under these circumstances* is what I mean by 'identifying'. As regards the form of the statement, it is required that it should begin with one of the pure referring expressions 'This is . . .', 'That is a . . .', and end with a noun or substantival phrase, 'a so-and-so' or 'The so-and-so'. As regards the circumstances, it is required that the speaker should be in the presence of the object noticed and referred to when he makes his statement; and he can be said to be, in the required sense, in the presence of the object noticed and referred to, if and only if, any substantival phrase which he would use in explaining the reference of 'This' and 'That' would contain some reference to something noticed at the time of speaking. So 'That is a sailing boat' may be used to make an identification when it is said in the presence of the object, in the sense that the explication of the reference (i.e. the answer which the speaker would give to the question 'What are you referring to?' or

'What is?') is 'That thing which looks like a small white spot which can be seen on the horizon'. Any substantival phrase which could occur in such an identification, when the reference of the 'This' or 'That' is in this way an extra-linguistic reference, can be said to stand for something which is directly identifiable, and therefore to stand for something which actually exists. Anyone who wishes to maintain that there actually are vast and impersonal forces at work in history will be required to describe the circumstances in which the 'This' in 'This is one of the impersonal forces' would be used to refer extra-linguistically, that is, in such a way that the answer to the question 'What are you pointing to as being one of the impersonal forces?' would not be of the kind 'The so-and-so which has just been *mentioned*' but, 'That so-and-so which can be seen, felt or otherwise noticed there'. Because the conditions of application of the phrase 'The vast and impersonal forces' do not allow that there should be any circumstances in which the 'This' in 'This is one of the forces' should refer extra-linguistically, we require that, since these forces are not themselves directly identifiable, the expression should be somehow explained or analysed in terms of expressions which do satisfy this condition. And we may hesitate whether the substantival expressions 'gene' and 'subconscious mind' and 'act of will' can be said to stand for some thing which is directly identifiable and actually exists in so far as we hesitate whether there are circumstances in which we can say 'That is a gene', pointing with the 'That' to something extra-linguistic, or whether we can say 'This is an act of will which I feel myself making now'. And to decide whether we can make these direct identifications is to decide upon what I have called the conditions of application of these expressions. If we do allow 'This is an act of will which I am feeling now' as a direct identification, then, in specifying the conditions of the greatest possible certainty in the applica-tion of this expression, we will describe some typical circum-stances in which this identification could be made.

The logical connection between perception, in the widest sense, and existence can therefore be stated in the following way: it is a necessity of any thought and language that we should refer by the use of demonstrative expressions such as 'This' and 'That', and that we should identify something so referred to as a so-and-so; the notion of referring extra-linguistically, and in the presence of the object referred to, cannot be explained without some mention of what the speaker perceives or feels or otherwise notices at the time of speaking; it is a necessity that some reference should be extra-linguistic, and that therefore some identifications should be made directly and in the presence of the object referred to. The empiricist thesis: 'All knowledge, outside mathematics, must ultimately be derived from perception and introspection' expresses, misleadingly, the condition of any assertion (outside mathematics) of the existence of anything, and therefore expresses a condition of making any true first-order statement.

It is a further requirement that, attached to any substantival phrase which occurs in a direct identification, there should be some principle of individuation; for in answering the question 'What is that?', or 'What is that so-and-so?', the speaker must have some way of marking as a unit the object referred to. It follows in general that, if there is no principle of individuation attached to a noun or substantival phrase, one can infer that the noun or substantival phrase in question cannot enter into a direct identification; for one necessary condition of interpreting the extra-linguistic reference is lacking. It is important that formal concepts cannot for this reason enter into direct identifications; we cannot say 'That is a quality', 'That is a relation', 'That is a thing', 'That is an event', 'That is a cause', using the 'That' to refer extra-linguistically to something present and noticed; for when in these cases we are asked what we are referring to, we find that we always explain the reference by specifying some *expression* which we are identifying as being a relational expression or as standing for a quality. Connected with this fact, we find also that any principle of individuation associated with the application of the words 'quality', or 'relation', or 'thing' or 'event', or 'cause', mentions expressions; 'He has more than one good quality' seems to mean the same as

'More than one epithet of praise can be truly applied to him'. For this reason, if we ever have occasion to say, 'This is one quality and that is another', or 'This is one thing and that is another', we cannot give an extra-linguistic reference to 'This' and 'That'. And this is the ground from which much of traditional metaphysics can be, and has been, criticized. Determinism ('Every event has a cause') and doctrines about the totality of things, or of qualities, or of relations, can have no extra-linguistic reference. In this sense such doctrines cannot be interpreted as making informative statements about the world.

IV

But even if referring and identifying are connected with existential statements in the way that I have suggested, it may still be asked why substantival expressions, of the form 'a so-and-so' or 'the so-and-so', should have this peculiar place in correlating words and thoughts with reality, rather than, for example, colour adjectives or other epithets. When I am asked 'What is that thing which looks like a small white spot on the horizon?' and I answer 'It is a boat', I supply a noun, or a substantival phrase, as the appropriate kind of answer to a question of the form 'What is that?' Having made the identification, I can go on to refer to that particular boat and identify it as an armed merchantman or as a yacht; or I may also describe it as fast or well-built. There is a traditional test which distinguishes the identification of the thing or event from the further description of it, or from the description of its qualities, once it has been identified. If I have identified the thing before me as a boat, then the supposition 'Suppose it had not been a boat, but an aeroplane, we would have been in danger' is interpreted as equivalent to 'Suppose there had not been a boat there, but an aeroplane'. If we make a supposition of this kind, there is no point in preserving the constancy of reference to an identical subject; for there can be no point in supposing that this particular thing had been something of another kind, rather than supposing that there had existed something of another kind, occupying the place which this thing occupies. But one can in general suppose that a particular thing of a particular kind, to which reference has been made, might have possessed qualities different from those which it does in fact possess, without thereby abandoning the constancy of reference to the same particular thing. Certainly there is not, and cannot be, any precise rule prescribing the point at which, in a train of contrary-to-fact suppositions, constancy of reference to the same particular thing would altogether lose its point; the distinction between qualities and kinds, and between description and identification, is not a sharp dichotomy, and it must allow border line cases. But, given an appropriate common noun, I may deny that there are any so-and-so's by saying 'So-and-so's do not exist', or 'There is no such thing as a so-and-so'—'Fairies do not exist', 'There is no such thing as a fairy'. I cannot in the same way say 'There is no such quality as so-and-so'; for to say 'There is no such quality as unselfishness' is either to say that 'unselfish' is a word which has no definite sense, or to say 'There are no unselfish men'. I may explain what is meant by 'unselfish' by pointing to a standard specimen of unselfish human conduct, and saying 'That is a case of unselfishness, if anything is'. But if I am required to make the reference of the 'That' more precise, and am asked 'What are you referring to as a case of unselfishness?', I must make it clear that I am referring to a man, who is behaving in a particular way, and that I am describing him as being unselfish. When I identify an object before me as a man, it is incorrect to say that I only describe the object before me by attributing to it the complex of properties called 'human'; for in making the identification, I also pick out something which can be constantly referred to as the same man and which has that kind of continuity which determines what is meant by 'a man'. And it is a necessity of discourse that I should be able to pick out and to identify recurring things as the continuing subjects of discourse, attaching my statements to reality through this device of constancy of reference to the same thing. It is therefore a necessity that, in identifying objects, persons, or events perceived, or in identifying states of mind, I commit myself to a statement which has implications extending beyond any mere description of my experience, either at the time of making the statement or at any other moment of time; for, in identifying that patch of light which I see as a so-and-so, I open the possibility of further references to the so-and-so, and to the previous and subsequent history of this same thing, which must exhibit that particular kind of continuity which makes it the kind of thing it is.

The only restriction on the range of different types of thing or event which may be identified is imposed by the act of extra-linguistic referring itself, namely, that the reference ('This', 'That', 'He', 'She', 'It', etc.) must be understood, and, if necessary, explained, as a reference to something present and noticeable in the environment of the speaker, that is, as an extra linguistic reference. When this condition is not fulfilled, we cannot be said to have picked out something noticed in our experience as falling directly under a certain concept; and to identify something is precisely to pick out and to indicate something noticed in our experience as directly falling under a certain concept. And there can be no way, either of constructing, extending, or learning a vocabulary, which does not involve this procedure, if the vocabulary is to be applied in making true and testable statements about reality. In any sophisticated vocabulary there will be many theoretical and formal concepts which are applied in a manner which precludes them from entering into direct identifications. The difficulty is, and always has been, to draw a line, or rather a set of alternative lines, which mark off those substantival expressions about which we are prepared, on reflection, to say that they stand for identifiable things which really and indubitably exist, and this is the same as to mark off those concepts which are empirical concepts, in the sense that they enter into direct identifications, and that they are tied, by the act of referring outwards, to particular features of our experience at particular moments.

MAIN PUBLICATION

Spinoza. Penguin Books. 1951.

WHAT IS TO BECOME OF
PHILOSOPHICAL THEOLOGY?

By H. A. HODGES

Professor of Philosophy in the
University of Reading

WHAT IS TO BECOME OF
PHILOSOPHICAL THEOLOGY?

HISTORY shows that the development of philosophy has been continually stimulated by interests outside its own special field. There are three such interests whose influence can be traced through the whole history of philosophy. The first is an interest in the natural world and in the sciences which investigate it. The second is an interest in moral and political questions and standards of judgement. And the third is an interest in religion and in the chief object of religion, or God. If any of these three strands were removed, the fabric of philosophy would be very different from what it is.

In past times philosophy involved the construction of a body of reasoned conclusions about the nature of things, or 'metaphysics'. A metaphysical system was so constructed that all three of the above-mentioned lines of interest could find satisfaction through it. Questions about science and the natural world, about values and standards of conduct, and about God could all find answers in, or derive their answers from a metaphysical theory. The God-questions in particular found their answer in a discipline which has been called 'philosophical theology'.

Today the picture is different. An increasing number of philosophers disown metaphysics as a profitless pursuit, and reshape philosophy on very different lines. It is from this change in the pattern of philosophical thinking that the theme of this paper is derived. How did philosophical theology deal with the God-questions in the days when it was prevalent and generally respected? And, if religion continues in the future to be a serious factor in the intellectual life of mankind, and if among the new-style philosophers there are still some who find it an interesting subject of inquiry, what sort of questions are they likely to ask about it, and how will their standpoint be related to that of religion itself, or of the Church-theologians? Such is the theme of this paper, to be dealt with, I fear, all too sketchily.

I

By 'theology' in this paper I understand a form of methodical discourse relating to a being of the kind commonly spoken of in English as 'God'. By 'philosophical theology' I understand a theology which purports to establish its assertions on grounds of 'reason', that is on grounds which can be understood and assessed by any intelligent and mature person. If we can define 'religion' for the present purpose as the belief in the existence of God together with the pattern of behaviour which follows from that belief, theology will be the methodical statement and discussion of the belief-element in religion, and philosophical theology will be the attempt to isolate and treat critically that element which all possible theologies have in common.

Philosophical theology in the sense here defined has played a prominent part in philosophy from very early times. It has been one of the numerous components which together made up what was called 'metaphysics'. In times when metaphysics took the form of a systematic body of doctrine confidently claiming to expound the nature of things, philosophical theology formed the culminating point of the doctrine, to which all the rest led up and from which all the rest derived its deepest significance. As early as Aristotle the word θεολογία is used in this sense.

What was philosophical theology, in this its traditional form, essentially trying to do? Three things, I believe, two of which were in the proper sense metaphysical, while the third was logical and epistemological.

1. It was setting forth the 'proofs of the existence of God'. By this I do not mean merely that the philosophical theologian

was analysing and criticizing other people's grounds for believing in God, without committing himself to any conclusion
on the point. The philosophical theologian was *proving* the
existence of God, i.e. he was advancing grounds for that belief
which he himself found convincing and presented to the world
as such. He did not deal with all the possible grounds for believing in God. People have often held that belief because they
thought that God had somehow, by some special act at a
particular moment in history, revealed Himself to men. But
belief on grounds of revelation was not the concern of the
philosophical theologian. His claim was that there were
grounds for believing in the existence of God independently
of any self-revealing act on God's part—unless indeed the
giving of existence to the universe could be called a self-
revealing act.

2. People who have proved the existence of something may
be presumed to be able to describe that whose existence they
have proved. Philosophical theology was bound to explore
and state systematically what could be known of the attributes of God. On all essentials a solid agreement was reached
among all philosophers of the main European theist tradition, though there was room for dispute about various points
of detail.

3. Behind all these discussions the best informed philosophical theologians were conscious of a logical and epistemological problem. For the arguments which were held to prove
that God exists appeared also to prove that no description of
Him could ever be even partially accurate. All objects of human
experience are (to speak in ontological language) finite and
contingent beings, and, moreover, they are known to us in
terms of human thought and language. But it is of the essence
of the conception of God that He must be thought of as not
finite and not contingent, and that His nature is not describable
in terms of human thought and language. The theologian,
therefore, in undertaking to speak of God, is trying to make his
mind and tongue do what they never really can do, and if he is
a *philosophical* theologian he is aware that this is what he is

doing. Philosophical theology therefore came to include a serious discussion of the limitations under which it is possible to speak significantly about God at all, and the qualifications with which any sentence purporting to give information about God must be understood.

Although the traditional philosophical theology contained this logical and epistemological element, yet as a whole it was not a logical or epistemological enquiry. It was an ontological enquiry, purporting to give us information about a particular sphere of existence, and indeed indirectly about all existing things.

It has often been remarked how slowly and painfully the sciences disengaged themselves from philosophy; as if philosophy had been an oppressive power against which the sciences had gradually to assert themselves. It would perhaps be equally to the point to remark how slowly and painfully philosophy has disengaged itself from the sciences. In the earliest days the word φιλοσοφία seems to have been stretched to cover pretty well every methodical enquiry which was not ἱστορία, and though it was soon realized that one could be, for instance, an astronomer without having to be also a metaphysician, still it continued to be thought a natural thing that a metaphysician should have views on astronomy. He was the spectator of all time and all existence, and as such he contained all the special sciences implicit in himself. In the classical tradition therefore we find that physics is recognized as a section of philosophy. So also is psychology (the treatise *de anima*). At a higher degree of generality and abstraction than these we find τὰ μετὰ τὰ φυσικά, giving us the most general truths that it is possible to enunciate about the nature of the universe; and then finally on this foundation the structure of philosophical theology is erected. For it is found in physics and again in metaphysics that the components of the empirical world each and severally, and also that world itself taken as a whole, are such as to call for explanation in terms of something other than themselves. Philosophical theology is the finding of this explanation. So it and the sciences hang together as parts of a well-articulated whole, which whole is philosophy considered as a comprehensive survey of all that is.

Philosophical theology, so conceived, was a speculative science of natural reason. It was a science, that is it had a recognized method and terminology and it claimed to put its conclusions beyond reasonable doubt. It was a speculative science, that is, it established the existence and provided a description of its object without being able to observe that object, purely by inference from what is known of the objects of other sciences, although it asserted that its own object was very different from any of these. And it was a science of natural reason, that is it made no appeal to any divine authority or revelation, but claimed that its methods and principles were such as must carry conviction to any reasonable man.

Being thus independent of religious authority and yet reaching conclusions which were in substantial accord with religious belief, philosophical theology was of course a powerful support for religion. True, it did not go as far into detail as the religious systems do. It did not present a way of salvation or declare the whole counsel of God. Yet it established a foundation on which it could appear reasonable that God Himself should reveal these things, and so it could lead us to examine the rival 'revelations' which are in the world with a predisposition to find that one of them was genuine. If it is remembered that the traditional metaphysician claimed also to have established (in his treatise *de anima*) the immortality of the soul and (in his ethics) the moral law by which a righteous God would judge this soul, it will be seen how strong the support really was which religion received from the old-style philosophy.

Such then was philosophical theology in its original form: the finding of an ultimate explanation of things to round off a system of philosophy which was an exposition of the nature of things. And this was the prevailing conception of philosophy until about 250 years ago. In the eighteenth and nineteenth centuries, however, great changes began to take place. The old conception of philosophy was disturbed and the old conception of philosophical theology with it.

II

It was during the eighteenth and nineteenth centuries that the line between philosophy and natural science began to be more clearly drawn. This was done by accepting the principle that all questions of fact about the universe were matters for scientific investigation, while the proper business of philosophy was not to duplicate or rival science in its own field, nor yet to amplify it by opening up another field of reality, but to explore the quite different field of logic and epistemology, and to consider the principles and methods of science in the light of what it found there.

The line was not drawn with perfect clarity at first. For (a) it seemed as if epistemology and perhaps even logic required a basis of psychological analysis; while at the same time the methods of empirical science had not yet established their claim in the psychological field. So for several generations philosophers who had given up the idea of launching out into physical science were able to regard psychology as part of their own domain. Furthermore, (b) there was a persistent tendency for epistemology to be made a basis for speculative conclusions about the nature of things. Idealism in both its Berkeleian and its post-Kantian form is the great example of this; it begins with considerations about perception and thought, but by some strange twist of the argument it ends by drawing conclusions about reality and even about the Absolute Reality. Yet again, (c) throughout the eighteenth and nineteenth centuries and down to our own time (Alexander!, Whitehead!) there have continued to be philosophers who did not accept the new principle at all, but went on thinking of philosophy as primarily an exploration of the nature of things, differing from the sciences only in using a deeper analysis and taking a more comprehensive view.

Today at last the issue begins to be seen more clearly. Psychology has vindicated its right to be itself, and the philosopher for his part begins to see that his proper concern is not so much with the processes of perception as with the principles on which we interpret what we perceive and the linguistic formulae by which this interpretation is helped or hindered. Hence it is that the pattern of philosophical writing today shows three dominating features. (*a*) In the first place, more and more careful attention is paid to formal logic, and to the relations between it and mathematics on the one side and scientific induction on the other. (*b*) At the same time, logic broadens out to include a careful study of the functions of language and the principles on which languages are or can be constructed. And (*c*) more and more what used to be thought of as ontological problems are reinterpreted as problems about speech and solved by linguistic analysis. While this movement is not yet universally victorious, it is certainly one of the characteristic features of our time. For myself, I welcome it as speaking an important word, which yet is not the final word, about the methods, aims and functions of philosophy.

It is important to distinguish between this movement towards logical and linguistic analysis and the radical empiricism or positivism which is also a leading feature of philosophy in our time. The two have grown up together and the leading figures in both have been the same, so that in the public view they are hardly to be told apart. It is often assumed that if one sees philosophy as involving a study of language and approaches philosophical problems from a logical and linguistic point of view, one is committed to a positivist theory of meaning and to the iconoclastic form of analysis which that theory brings with it. It does not follow: and this will be of importance in the closing section of this paper.

If such is the way in which the relation between philosophy and science has unfolded itself, what follows for the relation between philosophy and religion, or between philosophy and theology, which is the methodological formulation of religious belief? We shall presumably try to make analogous changes here, to apply here also the principles which have been accepted elsewhere in philosophy. What will their application mean?

First of all it will mean recognizing that God is no more a philosopher's direct concern than matter and energy are, and that theology, the theory of God, is distinct from philosophy as physics is distinct from philosophy, however it may differ from physics in its own proper character. Theology grows up not out of the speculative ingenuities of metaphysicians, but out of men's commerce with God (or what they believe to be such commerce), just as physics grows up out of men's commerce with the material world. What philosophy has to do in this field is not to present itself as an additional source of theological information, but to explore the epistemology and logic of religious thinking and to comment on its principles and methods in the light of this exploration. (*a*) It must elicit the logical character of theological inferences; and this is harder than the corresponding task in respect of science, because religious thinking is apt to be more intuitive and formally elliptical, and its forms of expression are often imprecise. And (*b*) philosophy must look into the characteristics of religious and especially theological discourse, the linguistic conventions used and the types of signification employed here. And (*c*) finally, it must see what can be done by linguistic analysis to resolve particular problems and obscurities in this field.

Discussion today shows a tendency to centre, more than in the past, on questions of meaning. What kind of meaning are we to ascribe to sentences of the religious type, which mention God and the soul? In general a sentence can be said to have *meaning* if it can fulfil a function in relation to human purposes, and it has *logical meaning* if it can function as part of a system of discourse leading to the discovery of truth. A sentence has no meaning in any system of discourse to which it makes no contribution; e.g. statements about God make no contribution to physics, and so have no physical meaning. The question whether religious utterances have any meaning at all, and if so what kind of meaning they have, is therefore reducible to the question, whether religious discourse can be regarded as fulfilling a real purpose in human life, and in particular whether it can be regarded as leading to the discovery of some kind of truth.

The defender of theism usually proceeds by raising questions to which he offers his theism as an answer. They may be questions about the universe, or about human life and destiny, or about moral values, or about special kinds of experience which are known as 'religious experiences': in any case the theist presents an alleged fact, asks for an explanation of this fact, and offers God as the explanation. If he succeeds in making us feel that his questions are reasonable questions, and if at the same time we can think of no better answers than those which he offers, we shall be disposed to view his answers with favour. The trouble today, however, is that we are no longer as ready as we used to be to accept *any* interrogative sentence as a reasonable question, or *any* sentence beginning with 'because' as a reasonable explanation. We think there can be 'idle' questions, and before accepting a question as reasonable we require some indication of a possibility of answering it. At the same time too we have more rigorous standards than of old as to what *is* an answer and what is evidence for one. If we are not satisfied on these points, we may dismiss the question and its alleged answer as logically meaningless, i.e. as making no contribution to knowledge, whatever other purpose they may serve. Indeed, it is now a real possibility in our minds that religious utterances as a class may have only the kind of meaning which a dream has, or a poetic fantasy, satisfying deep needs of the soul but in no way describing real facts of the world.

I do not say that this is necessarily the right conclusion. The point is debatable. For on the one hand it is *prima facie* paradoxical to deny logical meaning to religious discourse, because people can talk to one another and understand one another and argue with one another in that medium. Their arguments have the appearance of being conducted soberly and carefully, in a recognized terminology and with recognized rules of method, as arguments should be; and the fact that religious discussions are so often inconclusive and religious disagreements inveterate is not a ground for denying logical significance to what is going on in them, unless we are prepared to rule out philosophy itself on similar grounds. And yet, on the other hand, *to some people* religious utterances really do seem to convey little or nothing. It is to be observed that even

among religious people and well-read theologians the language
of a tradition other than their own may be thus dead. Clearly,
therefore, an enquiry into the characteristics and meaning-
value of religious language is a task that must be undertaken.

If the question of meaning thus comes to the fore in current
discussion, that does not mean that the older question, the
question of the truth of religious statements and the evidence for
their truth, has lost its importance. On the contrary, I think it
has taken on a new urgency in modern times, as the weakness of
the answers so long accepted comes to be seen. For philosophical
theology in its traditional form made matters seem too easy.
It analysed, correctly as I believe, the principles which work in
the mind of the religious believer to maintain his conviction of
the existence of God. All the classical arguments, even the
ontological one rightly understood, do answer to something in
the religious way of looking at things. They formulate the
principles on which and the procedure by which all argument
in support of a theist position must move. But philosophical
theology failed to see what a gap there is between the standpoint of these arguments and the standpoint of everyday
empirical thinking or that of science. It talked rather as if there
were an easy and obvious bridge from the one to the other.
In Plato and Aristotle and their followers through the centuries,
ideas and principles which are really theological were read into
the theory of nature. Such were the all-pervading teleological
assumptions and the pre-scientific conceptions of causality.
Hence it was that the theological argument could appear to
arise naturally out of an attentive consideration of nature itself.
Today, with the methods, principles and governing concepts
of natural science more sharply defined, it becomes evident
that the central principle of the theological argument (the
principle that contingent beings must and can be accounted
for in terms of a being which is not contingent) is no part of the
logical apparatus of science, but belongs to a wholly different
realm of discourse; and we also see that such a principle cannot
be worked out to its consequences in terms of the concepts
which are current in science or in that part of philosophy which

analyses and interprets science, but requires its own concepts, which are hard to define. The logical explication of religious thinking is therefore a more subtle, complex and difficult operation than it has often been thought to be.

III

In an age when all branches of philosophy turn more and more towards linguistic analysis, there is no branch in which such analysis is more necessary than that which deals with religious ideas, because there is no form of language so complex, so powerful in its effects on some people and yet so baffling to the detached analyst, as religious language. This fact may be partly concealed from philosophers if they treat philosophical theology as a speculation of their own, an interesting philosopheme, in abstraction from the total context in which God-beliefs are at home. It becomes unmistakable when we look at the language actually spoken by religious people in religious contexts, when we listen to them preaching, praying or celebrating their liturgies. The language used in these activities is in constant need of interpretation and commentary, even for the faithful to whom it should be familiar. The language of systematic theology too, though its professed purpose is to clarify and co-ordinate, is in practice hardly less in need of explanation. If the philosopher lets himself go on this material he will not find himself at a loss for distinctions to draw, abstractions to make, or antinomies to wrestle with.

First of all we must draw the obvious distinction between utterances which are meant as statements of fact and utterances which are not so meant. A very great deal of religious speech is of the latter kind, and in it we can distinguish several sub-species. There is sheer exclamation. There is petition and thanksgiving. There are precepts, exhortations, aspirations, promises and vows. Here is a rich and varied material for analysis. It is, however, in one sense obviously of secondary importance. Petitions, promises and most of the other forms of speech mentioned here, though they are not in themselves statements of fact, make no sense unless certain statements of fact are presupposed.

All religious systems are based on certain beliefs as to matters of fact. These may be found stated in their sacred writings, in their preaching, and above all in their credal formulae and their systematic theology. But it is notorious that these statements are often made in language whose merits do not include precision. The standard devices of rhetoric are freely used, such as hyperbole and oxymoron. Metaphor is ubiquitous, and simile is developed into the peculiar form of the parable, which is widely used for the purpose of teaching. It can be pithy and pregnant with suggestion, and for some purposes this more than compensates for its lack of precision, but it leaves the analyst in despair. Moreover, all these oblique forms of statement can carry a heavy charge of emotion.

Worship and prayer are specialized forms of personal address, and the being to whom they are addressed is conceived in personal terms, i.e. as conscious, intelligent, purposeful, capable of entering into moral relationships. The religious man, in so far as he is religious, thinks of his God as a quasi-personal being with whom he is somehow in contact in every moment of his life, and the cultivation of the inner life which is characteristic of the religious devotee consists very largely of an attempt to make these personal relations with God more and more conscious and intimate. In creeds and systematic theologies this personal character of God is firmly asserted, and an attempt is made to analyse and formulate distinctly the various aspects of our relations with Him. The attempt is never wholly successful, because it never escapes from the figurative and parabolic language which is so characteristic of this world of discourse.

Since God (like other immaterial beings with whom religious people sometimes believe themselves to be in contact) is inaccessible to sense-perception and is not believed to operate (with certain exceptions) through the medium of a human body acting as human bodies normally do, it follows that our means of communication with Him must be of a kind unknown to common human experience, and there is therefore an inherent obscurity in all statements to the effect that God 'sees' or 'hears' or 'says' or 'does' anything. And since we have (ordinarily at any rate) no perceptual acquaintance with persons otherwise than as physical organisms possessed of intelligence, and we have therefore no empirical knowledge of how conscious, intellectual acts and processes could take place otherwise than as events in the history of such an organism, it follows that there is an inherent obscurity in anything that we may say by way of ascribing personal characteristics to God.

One might feel a passing temptation to seek escape by the phenomenalistic route, i.e. by saying that the real force and meaning of theological statements is in their use as a basis for constructing expectations. Thus, 'God exists' might mean 'there is a pattern of moral purpose in the course of events' or something of that kind. (The complete analysis would of course be much fuller than this.) The suggestion is superficially plausible, but it is no more acceptable here than it is in respect of our understanding of one another as human beings. The person to whom we acknowledge a duty, or whom we love, is not merely a complex of conditionally predictable behaviour-phenomena. He is a conscious centre which finds expression in these phenomena but is not exhausted in them. He is a self analogous in character to ourselves, knowing and enjoying what he does and suffers, and understanding us as we understand him. No one who takes the trouble to affirm the existence of God will agree to have his assertion interpreted otherwise than on this model.

It is noteworthy that, ever since philosophy took its rise and metaphysical systems began to be built up, there has been a tendency for elements of the vocabulary of metaphysics to be absorbed into that of religion. This has happened in more ways than one. Concepts like being, not-being, nothingness, with which some recent non-religious existentialists have made play, are also to be found in prayers and hymns and liturgies which are the forms of public and private devotion. More important, the metaphysical account of God as infinite, eternal, ontologically perfect, and the contrast in this respect between God and whatever is not God, is welcomed by religious writers and speakers and used and enforced on all levels of religious discourse. Abstract though they are, there can be no doubt that these metaphysical concepts mean something, and answer to something deeply rooted in the religious consciousness. But since they transcend the conditions of human experience, it is hard to see what their meaning can be.

None of the difficulties listed here were unknown to the makers of the great theological systems. They knew that in everything they said they were raising semantic problems, and they sought philosophical solutions for these problems. One such solution, perhaps the best known, is the theory of analogical predication, according to which no sentence describing God otherwise than negatively can be literally true. We have no material from which to construct concepts except the material of perception, and if we wish to describe something which is not a perceptible object we can only do so by saying that it is like a certain kind of perceptible object in certain respects, with due allowance for the fact that after all it is not a perceptible object. All descriptions of God must be understood as meaning that God is like perceptible objects in respect of the attributes mentioned in the description, but with due allowance for the difference between a finite and contingent being and an infinite and non-contingent one. It is obvious that unless we have some notion of what the infinite as contrasted with the finite actually is, this doctrine is an indirect way of saying that theological statements are unintelligible because of indefiniteness. But *how* have we a notion of what the metaphysically infinite actually is?

All in all, then, religious language is a very curious kind of language. It says and unsays, unsays and says, oscillating perpetually between yes and no. It is a way of talking which seems to come naturally to some people, while others can see little or no value in it. Used by one who has skill and experience in the delicate balancing of yes and no, it can attract by a certain suggestiveness which characterizes it, an impression that there is always more to be said than is being said, an invitation to look beyond the statements made to a meaning which transcends them. But it could be argued that though this may be a merit in poetry, and perhaps too in liturgical and devotional language, it is not so in theology or philosophy. In these spheres it may appear baffling and repellent. We understand easily why those whose logical and linguistic ideal is clarity and distinctness are not at home with religious language.

Can religious language, in spite of these frustrating characteristics, contrive to say significant and important things? That depends on the relation in which it stands to experience. Where in the empirical world shall we find the facts by reference to which religious words and symbols are to be interpreted? And in so far as religion goes beyond experience in what it says, from what launching base in experience shall we set out on the transcendent flight?

There is no doubt about the answer to the first question. Indeed, we have already given it. If in religion we suppose ourselves to be in quasi-personal relations with God, that means that God Himself is conceived on the analogy of a personal being, of the only kind of personal being with which we are acquainted in everyday life, i.e. of a human being. But of course the human body and those elements of human personality which are obviously bound up with the body are not brought into the analogy. When we speak of God as personal we mean intelligent, capable of knowledge and self-knowledge and intelligent will. Since in our own experience intelligence is the source of that peculiar kind of unity which is called apperceptive unity, and since the fuller development of intellectual understanding and intelligent purpose always brings with it a closer integration of the personality, it follows that God, being conceived as intelligent in a very high degree, is also conceived as possessing a very high degree of inner unity; and since human happiness, in the deepest sense of that word, springs from the unity of consciousness and the integration of personality, it follows that God is thought of as enjoying happiness in a very high degree, or as we say 'beatitude', while our own beatitude is declared, by the Platonic philosophy as well as by the great religions, to lie in assimilation to God. Aristotle put the essence of the matter clearly enough. 'If God is always as we are in our good moments, it is a marvellous thing, and if He is more so, it is still more marvellous; but such is the fact.'

It is worth noticing that the unity of God, so conceived, reacts upon our conception of the universe. For God is usually declared to be the maker and ruler of the universe. What 'making' and 'ruling' may mean in this context is indeed obscure; but at least they must be interpreted on the analogy of human making and ruling, where the thing made or ruled acquires a unity of structure, form, and purpose from the intelligent will of its maker or ruler. That the universe has such a unity as this is something which men have generally liked to believe, but which experimental science cannot verify. The assertion of the existence of God is also indirectly an assertion of this conception of the universe.

I have said that God is conceived as intelligent, integrated, and blessed 'in a very high degree'. So far we can go without departing from the recognized use of analogy. It is quite intelligible to take some empirical characteristic which can vary in degree, and postulate a higher degree of it than experience actually shows. But theism of course goes further than this and does something different in kind. It says that God possesses the attributes alluded to, and others, in an *absolute* or *unlimited* degree. Many of the more abstract and technical designations under which God has been referred to are alternative ways of expressing this notion of absoluteness. The Platonic ἐπέκεινα, Anselm's greatest thinkable, Duns' *actu existens infinitum* are examples of this. Others of the more recondite attributes of God are consequences of this one. Such are His aseity, His eternity, the identity of His essence with His existence, and so on. It is in speaking of this whole group of attributes that we take our decisive leap beyond the recognized range of analogy; for all experience is of things in relation, conditioned by the relations in which they stand, and here we are speaking of something not conditioned by anything at all, free from dependence or limitation. It is an old question in philosophy whether we can attach any positive meaning to phrases like these. Nor must we jump to the conclusion that the theologians at least will say we can. The best informed among them have long recognized and proclaimed the doctrine of the negative way, according to which the only true way to know God is to know Him to be different from anything that we can know. The intelligibility of the quasi-personal attributes of God is itself affected by this insistence on pushing them to infinity. Superhuman wisdom or goodness we can in a manner understand, even though we may not understand how a being possessing such attributes could really exist. But *infinite* wisdom and *infinite* goodness—what are these?

What we cannot understand from actual experience we may perhaps partly make out by reference to another aspect of our lives—our aspirations. For it is of the essence of aspiration that it looks beyond actual experience to something as yet not experienced, and the object of aspiration is always thought of as possessing some kind of excellence in a higher degree than we have yet experienced. Moreover, it is a common observation with a certain kind of writer that human aspirations are insatiable in terms of finite objects, and we may agree that this is actually true of some men, perhaps potentially true of all. Now, whatever else may be said about the words *infinite* and *absolute* in this theist context, it is certain that they are meant to signify the complete and lasting fulfilment of our aspirations: not merely this or that man's aspirations but those of all possible intelligent beings.

God as infinite or absolute being is, then, to be understood as a source of complete and final satisfaction. And He is this in two ways. God is himself in possession of beatitude; He is to Himself, in His own being, all that mind and will can require. At the same time our own beatitude, the repose of our mind and will, lies in the knowledge and love of Him. There is an experience called the 'vision of God' which is said to be available on certain conditions, to some extent in this life and to an incomparably greater extent hereafter. To this the adherents of at any rate some of the great religions are taught to aspire, and to make this aspiration the ruling principle of their lives.

Such is the experiential context in relation to which the meta-physical doctrine of God is to be interpreted.

IV

To analyse religious concepts and determine their place in relation to experience is a complex and difficult business. I have given no more than a hint of what it might involve. Yet in itself this analysis, however fully carried out, would not exhaust the questions which we ask ourselves in this field. For surely the most interesting and puzzling thing in connection with religious ideas is not their character as such, but the wide divergences which exist between the attitudes to them of different people. If the meaning of what is said in this field is somewhat elusive, the reasons which move some people to confident affirmation of what others equally confidently deny are no less hard to pin down. Why, in fact, do people make the subtle and equivocal constructions which we have just now analysed and confidently affirm that they contain truth? It is not impossible that the believer himself, in moments of detachment, should wonder at himself in this way. Can we help him to understand him-self? Can we isolate and express in neutral terms the belief-generating factor which is present in theists and absent in non-theists?

We can be sure of one thing: there is little to be gained by presenting theism as a quasi-scientific hypothesis, to be accepted as true because it explains certain facts of experience and because it can be verified in action. The attempt has some-times been made to present theist, or rather, Christian belief in this way, but it cannot stand up to examination. The facts and experiences to which theist or Christian apologists appeal are not comparable with real scientific observations or experiments. In this field we cannot create or control situations as we will, or isolate particular factors for study, or make a planned series of experiments; nay, so imprecise are our terms and so inadequate our analysis that we cannot predict or even report observations with the kind of precision which science expects. And on the other hand the conception of God, as we have just analysed it, is not easily to be accounted for on empirical inductive lines. It is the conception of something essentially mysterious and incommensurable with all objects of our experience, and these are attributes which it is hard to see as contributing to an explanatory hypothesis intended to account for particular facts. Yet it is just this mysterious character which makes God really God, which gives the specifically religious quality to the concept of Him. It is this which evokes the characteristically religious response of adoration.

Not only the content, but also the manner of religious belief is different from that of our belief in the truth of a scientific hypothesis. This latter kind of belief is built on an accumulation of evidence in the form of observations and experiments; it is the result of reflection on this evidence by experts in scientific research; and they put it forward and the layman accepts it from them, always as something provisional, open to revision in the light of fresh evidence which may at any time be found. There may be people in the world who accept the belief in the existence of God in this spirit, but they are probably few in number. Such is not genuine religious belief. Religious belief is not based on an accumulation of instances, but on a way of conceiving the structure of all that is; and it is held not as a theory which further evidence might modify, but as a fundamental and immutable truth. Nor again is it accepted on the authority of experts alone, but the individual believer often thinks and is often encouraged to think that he is competent to apprehend the force of the evidence for it, and to hold it as a matter of personal conviction, even though he may not be able to set it out in systematic form like a professional theologian. In a word, whether we like it or not, religious belief is treated by those who hold it as an ontological insight. This also explains the tenacity with which they retain it even in face of strong discouragement due to the difficulty of applying it on the empirical level.

Of this ontological insight (if such it be) the classic arguments of philosophical theology are an explication and analysis, incomplete no doubt, and made in the light of an old-fashioned logic, but still a true analysis as far as it goes.

This statement will of course be challenged on the ground that the real foundation of religious belief is not philosophical reasoning, but 'religious experience'. It is a contention which we have all heard advanced. For myself I should find it easier to discuss it if the meaning of the phrase 'religious experience' were more clearly defined than it often is. (*a*) It may mean that people believe in God because of events in the world's history, or in their own lives, which bring strongly home to them the conviction that here God is at work. But then it requires to be explained whence people obtain the notion of God in the first place. For it is not an empirical notion, as has been seen, and it cannot be extracted from particular events unless it has first been unconsciously read into them. The mind sees in particular events the hand of a God in whom it already believes, and if it is not already at least disposed to believe it will not see God's hand there at all. But it is the original source of the belief that we are seeking. If on the other hand (*b*) by 'religious experience' is meant a kind of compelling vision or intuitive realization of the reality of God and the dependence of all contingent things on Him, that is no other than the ontological insight of which I have spoken, and which the arguments explicate. In that case why not call it what we think it is?

It is no objection to say that in actual life religious convictions are often reached intuitively, the believer not being conscious of the reasons which have determined him; nor even that where the believer is conscious of his reasons, or thinks he is, he often denies having found his way to his belief by arguing it out along the classic lines. This last point has its importance, but not in the present context; for we are not now discussing the private ways, so various and indirect, by which people can come to the point of believing in God, but the structure and import of that belief when they have reached it and hold it. The believer may often be unable or unwilling to analyse the logical pattern of his belief, and may even fail to recognize the pattern when it is shown to him in abstract terms, which it may not be his business to understand. But this does nothing to show that the analysis is not correctly made by those whose business it is to make it.

'But Hume! But Kant! But Wittgenstein! . . .' Yes, I know. No one will listen to a metaphysical theology nowadays. We cannot speak of it without a curl of the lip. Even the theists are afraid to seem to depend on it, and talk about religious experience instead in the hope of being mistaken for empiricists. But why is this so? What have these modern writers done to discredit what used to be a well-regarded discipline? They have simply pointed out that it is not experimental or even truly empirical. From their own empiricist point of view they have laid down logical and linguistic tests, conditions as to methods of observation and verification, conditions as to the use of language, which they say any body of discourse must satisfy if it is to deserve to be recognized as a genuine branch of knowledge. Theology cannot satisfy these conditions, and therefore, they conclude, theology is not a genuine branch of knowledge.

The spread of views like these certainly brings theology under fire in a way that it never was under fire before. In the grand old days it was of course necessary for the theology of any particular religion to justify itself in face of criticism from the theologies of rival religions; but philosophical theology, which purported to contain the core of them all, had only to unfold its argument to command the assent of all honest and intelligent people. Or so it was thought. Today, however, when theology unfolds its argument it is at once challenged to show what right it has to talk in that way at all.

The challenge comes from the empiricist logic, and if the nature of theological discourse is what I have said it is, there can be no defence for it in terms of that logic. It follows that anyone in future who takes theology seriously in the sense in which theology claims to be taken seriously is committed thereby to rejecting important features of the empiricist logic; and in that case he must expect to be called upon to indicate what other logical doctrine, more favourable to the claims of theology, he puts in its place.

To some it may sound paradoxical to speak thus of confronting logic with logic; for the word 'logic' carries with it a suggestion of rigour and of certainty, and one feels that pronouncements in this field at least should be exempt from the possibility of challenge. But this applies to logic only in the sense of formal logic, which is not now in question. Logic in the broader sense in which one discusses such questions as truth, probability, verification, signification and the like, is by no means a rigorous science of that kind. And the fact is that people do not wholly agree as to what makes sense or what carries conviction. While there is of course much common ground, there is also a margin of difference on these points, and that difference, expressed in general formulae, results in differences of doctrine in logic. Such differences in logic are the expression of different views as to the functions which thought and language are able to perform, and the purposes for which they can rightly and properly be used. What is, in fact, the proper study of mankind? Does it or does it not include those metaphysical questions with which we have seen that theology is bound up?

I do not see how it is possible to take theology seriously as theology without raising this question and answering it in favour of the metaphysical mode of thought and speech.

How and on what grounds could the question be so answered? That is no small issue to raise, and I shall not attempt to deal with it in this paper. I will, however, make one observation about it. If logic, in the broader sense of the word 'logic', turns out in the end to involve questions of this kind, must we not conclude that it is, or at any rate leads on to, what can be described as an *ethic* of thinking and speaking? For the issue between the metaphysical and the empiricist thought-paradigm is not merely an issue between two ways of thinking; the different thought-paradigms are connected with different views of the proper aims and conduct of life in general, and the adoption of one thought-paradigm as against the other is therefore also implicitly a preference for the life-pattern which naturally goes with it. And when we come to balancing rival life-patterns against one another we are surely not far from ethical (or should I say existential?) questions.

Here, then, our present enquiry may properly pause, not because it has solved its problems, but because in investigating them it has brought us to the point where we see that another and a deeper and a more difficult enquiry might begin.

MAIN PUBLICATIONS

Wilhelm Dilthey, an Introduction. Routledge and Kegan Paul. 1944.
The Philosophy of Wilhelm Dilthey. Routledge and Kegan Paul. 1952.
Languages, Standpoints and Attitudes (Riddell Lectures). Oxford University Press. 1953.

THE PROVINCE OF LOGIC

By WILLIAM KNEALE

*Fellow and Tutor of Exeter College,
Oxford*

THE PROVINCE OF LOGIC

I

UNTIL recently logic has always been presented as the science of those common principles of reasoning which are valid for all possible studies, whatever their subject matter, and it is still conceived as such by mathematicians and other specialists who have most occasion to talk of logic in connection with their own work. It is therefore rather surprising to find in modern times two tendencies which are at variance with this conception.

On the one hand, it has become customary within the past forty years to present logic as a deductive science in which we have only one or two rules of inference but a host of asserted propositions, some introduced as axioms and the others derived from these in accordance with the rule or rules of inference. In antiquity already the principles of non-contradiction and excluded middle were allowed a special place as fundamental laws, and at a later date both Leibniz and Kant wrote sometimes as though the principle of non-contradiction were the sum of all truth in logical studies; but in general these laws have not been regarded as axioms from which the logician should derive theorems by deduction. The fashion of presenting logic as a deductive system in which all the asserted propositions have the same status as the so-called laws of thought is derived ultimately from Frege's *Begriffsschrift* of 1879, and it has probably been accepted in this century without much question because it is associated historically with a great enrichment of the science. Frege, indeed, said that he favoured the use of the *modus ponendo ponens* as sole rule of inference only because he thought this restriction made for greater rigour; and in his

Grundgesetze he allowed other patterns of inference for reasons of practical convenience. But he seems never to have questioned the need for some axioms. Presumably he thought he was committed to them by his programme of exhibiting arithmetic as an extension of logic.

On the other hand, there has arisen in British philosophy during the past twenty years a fashion for using the word 'logic' in a much wider sense, as though it meant the study of all interconnections of meaning between words. We find it said, for example, that a statement about the incompatibility of two colours belongs to the 'logic of colour words', that a philosophical enquiry about the status of minds is really a discussion of the 'logic of psychological verbs', and in general that philosophical questions are all problems of 'logical grammar' or, worse still, of 'logical geography'. The philosophers who talk and write in this way are usually not very much interested in the development of logic started by Frege (though their fondness for the word 'logic' may be due to the prestige which logic has acquired from that development), and their departure from traditional usage is quite different from that of mathematical logicians. With them 'logic' is no longer the name of a science concerned with the principles of inference common to all studies, but rather a name for any collection of rules in accordance with which we may argue in some context. One philosopher of this persuasion has even said that every kind of statement has its own logic. In such a welter of metaphor and epigram it is difficult to know what we are expected to take seriously; but it seems clear that this way of talking involves abandonment of the notion that logic is concerned with form as opposed to subject matter.

In this essay I shall try first to show how the restricted calculus of propositional functions can be presented satisfactorily without axioms. This result is not very important in itself, since it amounts only to a proof that this part of the systems of Frege and Russell can be derived from something simpler and nearer to the traditional conception of logic. But it is interesting because it suggests a reason for delimiting logic in such a way as to exclude not only Frege's talk about the reduction of arithmetic to logic, which led to the use of axioms in logic, but also modern talk about the logic of colour words. The attempt to work out this suggestion will occupy the last section of the essay.

II

We can dispense with axioms in logic if we can show that the propositions taken as axiomatic by Frege or his successors can all be derived from any propositions whatsoever by application of rules of inference valid for all subject matters. For to say that a proposition is necessary absolutely is surely the same as to say that it is necessary in relation to anything whatsoever, i.e. that no special premisses are required for the proof of it. But how in detail can we carry out this programme?

The author of the *Quaestiones Exactissimae in Universam Aristotelis Logicam,* formerly attributed to Duns Scotus, gives in *Quaestio* 10 on *Prior Analytics* i the following five remarks about *consequentiae:*

(1*a*) 'From any statement which contains a formal contradiction any statement whatsoever follows in a formal *consequentia,* e.g. from "Socrates exists and Socrates does not exist", which contains a formal contradiction, there follows "A man is an ass" or "The stick is standing in the corner".'

(2*a*) 'From any impossible statement any other statement whatsoever follows, not in a formal *consequentia,* but in a material *consequentia* good absolutely . . . e.g. "A man is an ass; therefore you are at Rome".'

(2*b*) 'From any statement whatsoever a necessary statement follows in a good absolute *consequentia.*'

(3*a*) 'From any false statement any other statement whatsoever follows in a material *consequentia* good circumstantially (*ut nunc*).'

(3*b*) 'Every true statement follows from any other statement in a material *consequentia* good circumstantially.'

Clearly the writer of this passage was a clever logician. Why, then, did he not formulate the principle which would be (1*b*) in my numbering, namely the principle that a formal truism such as 'Socrates exists or Socrates does not exist' follows formally from any statement whatsoever? I can only suggest that he found difficulty in proving (1*b*) with the patterns of formal *consequentia* he recognized. And this, if true, would not be surprising. For although (1*b*) corresponds to (1*a*) in an obvious fashion, it cannot be proved by any obvious adaptation of the argument that suffices to prove (1*a*).

The proof of (1*a*), given in *Quaestio* 3 on *Prior Analytics* ii, may be set out in modern symbolism as follows:

$$\frac{\dfrac{P \ \& \ \mathrm{T}P}{P}}{P \vee Q} \qquad \frac{P \ \& \ \mathrm{T}P}{\mathrm{T}P}$$
$$\frac{}{Q} \ .$$

Here the italic letters can be understood as abbreviations for any propositional *expressions* the reader may choose to consider. But just because the reader has free choice in interpretation, they may also be regarded as part of a simple device for talking about the patterns in which they appear. When I offer a scheme like that given above, leaving the reader to supply any interpretation he chooses for the several letters, it is clear that I commit myself to maintaining the *validity of the scheme*. For this reason italic letters occurring as above are sometimes called schematic letters.

When necessary, a *designation* for a proposition can be constructed by use of the sign '#' in front of the corresponding expression. Thus the schema set out above may be said to show how # Q, i.e. the proposition that Q, can be derived from # (P & TP). If the reader tries to show in similar style how # (P ∨ TP) can be derived from # Q, he will appreciate the difficulty that faced the author of the *Quaestiones Exactissimae*.

In their *Symbolic Logic* (p. 251) Lewis and Langford give a proof that may be summarized as follows:

$$\frac{\dfrac{Q}{(Q \ \& \ P) \vee (Q \ \& \ \mathrm{T}P)}}{Q \ \& \ (P \vee \mathrm{T}P)} \ .$$
$$\frac{}{P \vee \mathrm{T}P}$$

This is undoubtedly correct, but it is not so elegant as the proof of (1a) given above, since the principles of inference which it employs are not so simple and obvious as those used by the author of the *Quaestiones Exactissimae*. Would it not be just as useful to say that we derived the conclusion from the premiss in accordance with the inference schema $\dfrac{Q}{P \vee \neg P}$? In his *Logical Syntax of Language* of 1934 Carnap suggested in fact that we should regard the introduction of a logical axiom as the formulation of a rule of inference which allows us to infer the so-called axiom from the null class of premisses. This way of describing matters has the merit of showing that the question whether we should or should not have axioms in logic is not really one of basic principles, since the inclusion of axioms may be regarded as merely the use of somewhat curious rules of inference. But when this has been conceded, it is still interesting to ask what rules of inference are the simplest and most natural in the sense that they determine the meanings of our formal signs more directly than any others. And it may be expected that a full answer to the question will show why the author of the *Quaestiones Exactissimae* was unable to prove the paradoxical *consequentia* (1b).

In 1934 Gentzen produced a system of logic which contains only such rules of inference as he thought natural.[1] Apart from some small differences of symbolism, they are as follows:

(1) $\dfrac{P \quad Q}{P \mathbin{\&} Q}$ (2a) $\dfrac{P \mathbin{\&} Q}{P}$ (2b) $\dfrac{P \mathbin{\&} Q}{Q}$.

(3a) $\dfrac{P}{P \vee Q}$ (3b) $\dfrac{Q}{P \vee Q}$ (4) $\dfrac{P \vee Q \quad P/R \quad Q/R}{R}$

(5) $\dfrac{P/\dagger}{\neg P}$ (6) $\dfrac{P \quad \neg P}{\dagger}$

[1]'Untersuchungen über das logische Schliessen' in *Mathematische Zeitschrift*, vol. 39, pp. 176-210, 405-31.

(7) $\dfrac{P/Q}{P \supset Q}$ (8) $\dfrac{P \supset Q \quad P}{Q}$

(9) $\dfrac{Fx}{\forall xFx}$ (10) $\dfrac{\forall xFx}{Fa}$

(11) $\dfrac{Fa}{\exists xFx}$ (12) $\dfrac{\exists xFx \quad Fx/P}{P}$

Here each rule is presented by means of an inference schema, and those on the left are rules for the introduction of formal signs, while those on the right are rules for elimination. For the most part the rules are easy to understand, but there are some points that require comment.

The obelus in rules (5) and (6) stands for 'the false', and it gets this reference from a single additional rule standing outside the table of pairs, namely, $\dfrac{\dagger}{P}$. This can scarcely be described as a schema for possible inferences, since we never make inferences from what we know to be false; but the presentation of it may perhaps be taken as a statement to the effect that if the false were true everything would be true.

The 'a' in rules (10) and (11) is a schematic letter like the others in italic type, but the 'x' above the line in rule (9) and similarly the 'x' in 'Fx/P' of rule (12) are free variables whose scope does not extend across the horizontal line. Gentzen himself does not make this distinction explicitly, but it is essential for the correct use of his rules. Given a statement 'Fx' in which 'x' is a free variable expressing universality, we may pass to a statement '$\forall xFx$' in which universality is expressed by means of a quantifier; but we are certainly not entitled to pass from a singular statement 'Fa' to the universal statement '$\forall xFx$'. The 'a' of rules (10) and (11) may indeed be said to express universality, but only the universality of the thesis of the logician who offers the two schemata as valid for all possible interpretations of 'F' and 'a', not the universality of propositions appearing as premisses or conclusions in the arguments the logician studies.

The solidus which I have used in the formulation of rules (4), (5), (7), and (12) may be taken as an abbreviation for 'entails'. It is intended, of course, to suggest the horizontal line of an inference schema; but since it has the grammatical role of a verb, the signs to the left and the right of it must be understood as nouns, i.e. as designations for propositions. A full rendering of an entailment statement would therefore have the form '$\#P/\#Q$', rather than the form 'P/Q'; but it is convenient to adopt the convention that '$\#$' is absorbed by the solidus much as 'that' is absorbed by 'says' in the English sentence 'He says it is hot'. In either case we get simplification without ambiguity.

Gentzen, who uses the notation $\dfrac{[P]}{Q}$ instead of 'P/Q', speaks of $\#P$ as a supposition from which $\#Q$ may be derived. But the sense is the same; for what we sometimes call the derivation of a consequence from a supposition is really the process of convincing ourselves that the supposition entails the consequence.

Taken together, these rules are equivalent to the rules and axioms given by Heyting for intuitionist logic.[1] In order to obtain the classical system we must either introduce $\#(P \lor \daleth P)$ with the peculiar status of sole axiom pattern or allow for the elimination of the negation sign by the new schema

$$\frac{\daleth\daleth P}{P}.$$

In Gentzen's eyes it is one of the merits of this version of logic that it makes the classical system arise from the intuitionist by addition, rather than the intuitionist from the classical by omission. But he recognizes that the situation can be made to appear differently when logic is presented in a different fashion. I shall return to this point later.

It seems clear to me that Gentzen has in fact presented logic in a way more natural than that of Frege and Russell. It is true that the number of his rules is greater than the number of rules

---

[1]'Die formalen Regeln der intuitionistischen Logik' in *Sitzungsberichte der Preussischen Akademie, Phys-Math. Klasse,* 1930, pp. 42-56.

17

and axioms in *Principia Mathematica*, but here each sign is introduced separately and it is possible to prove the equivalences which are used in *Principia Mathematica* as definitions for the signs not taken as primitive. Furthermore, by a simple procedure like that which Chrysippus followed in the elaboration of his system of propositional logic the basic inference schemata can be made to yield others.[1] Thus we can prove that $P \& Q / P \lor Q$ by setting out the skeleton argument

$$\frac{\dfrac{P \& Q}{P} \; (2a)}{P \lor Q} \; (3a)$$

where the numerals at the ends of horizontal lines show which basic schemata have been used in the transitions. And when we wish, we can always derive a truistic statement pattern from any of our inference schemata, whether basic or derived, by application of rule (7), often called the principle of conditionalization.

Against all this, however, it must be admitted that there is something awkward in the system. Rules (4), (5), (7), and (12) all depend in a certain way on other rules. For what follows from a supposition must follow in accordance with some principle, and obviously this cannot be the principle formulated by means of the supposition. Why then did Gentzen find it necessary to introduce such a complication in just these places? The answer can be found from a comparison between the rules for conjunction and those for disjunction. It is well known that in the algebra of logic the conjunction and disjunction signs are dual to each other, and yet rule (4), which provides for elimination of the disjunction sign, does not correspond to rule (1), which provides for introduction of the conjunction sign, in the same way as (3a) and (3b), the rules for introducing the disjunction sign, correspond to (2a) and (2b), the rules for eliminating the conjunction sign. If we tried to write something which would correspond in the required way, we should get

$$\frac{P \lor Q}{P \quad Q},$$

[1]Sextus Empiricus, *Against the Logicians*, ii. 228 ff.

i.e. an arrangement of signs which cannot be interpreted as an inference schema since it has two propositional expressions below the line. There might, of course, be a convention whereby an arrangement of signs like that printed above could be taken as a conflation of two inference schemata, i.e. as a way of saying that each of the propositional expressions below the line could be inferred from that above. But this is not at all what we want, since it confuses $\#(P \vee Q)$ with $\#(P \,\&\, Q)$. In short, the curious features of Gentzen's system seem to be forced on him by the obvious fact that an inference cannot have more than one conclusion though it may have two or more premises. Probably it was this that prevented the author of the *Quaestiones Exactissimae* from completing his account of paradoxical *consequentiae* with a simple proof that a formally necessary proposition can be derived formally from any proposition.

III

If we wish to improve on Gentzen's result, we must consider derivation or inference as a special case of something I shall call development. Unfortunately there is no recognized terminology for talking about this, but it may be described metaphorically as setting out the field within which the truth must lie if certain premisses are to be accepted. When a man after consideration of certain premisses, say $\#P$ and $\#Q$, remarks that certain other propositions, say $\#R$ and $\#S$, cannot all be false if his premisses are all true, he may be said to be engaged in the development of those premisses. Neither $\#R$ nor $\#S$ is a conclusion of inference, but they may perhaps be called the limits of development up to date. Though for convenience we may suppose that they are expressed by sentences in the indicative mood, it must be understood that neither is asserted in the context of development. In order to make this clear we may, if we choose, write question marks after their expressions, but I do not think this will be necessary in what follows, because the formulae of unasserted limits will always be recognizable as such by their position in the tables of development which I construct.

The general pattern of a table of development is

$$\frac{P \quad Q}{R \quad S}$$

but between the initial formulae which express the premisses and the end formulae which express the limits there may be many intermediate expressions, i.e. expressions that occur both above and below lines. If a development has only one end formula, though this may be repeated many times at the bottom of different branches, it is a derivation of the proposition expressed by that end formula. Obviously a development that is not a derivation can always be continued in such a fashion that it becomes a derivation, namely, by the addition to each branch of a formula which is the disjunction of all the existing end formulae. If a derivation has no premisses, or, to speak more strictly, no premisses that cannot equally well be replaced by others, it is a demonstration. These relations will become clear when a few examples have been worked.

Just as a derivation is said to be valid if the premisses entail the conclusion, so a development may be said to be valid if the premisses *involve* the limits to which the development leads. Here I follow Carnap, who in his *Formalization of Logic* introduced the name 'logical involution' for the relation that holds between two sets of propositions when it is impossible that all of the first should be true and all of the second false. Entailment is then to be regarded as involution of a set containing only one member; and just as an assertion of entailment takes some such form as 'P, Q/R' so an assertion of involution other than entailment may take some such form as 'P, Q/R, S'.

The basic development schemata required for functional logic of the first order are as follows:

$$(1) \quad \frac{P \quad Q}{P \,\&\, Q} \qquad\qquad (2a) \quad \frac{P \,\&\, Q}{P} \quad (2b) \quad \frac{P \,\&\, Q}{Q}$$

$(3a)\ \dfrac{P}{P \lor Q}$ $(3b)\ \dfrac{Q}{P \lor Q}$ $(4)\ \dfrac{P \lor Q}{P \quad Q}$

$(5)\ \dfrac{\star}{P \quad \lnot P}$ $(6)\ \dfrac{P \quad \lnot P}{\star}$

$(7a)\ \dfrac{\star}{P \quad P \supset Q}$ $(7b)\ \dfrac{Q}{P \supset Q}$ $(8)\ \dfrac{P \supset Q \quad P}{Q}$

$(9)\ \dfrac{\{Fx\}}{\forall x Fx}$ $(10)\ \dfrac{\forall x Fx}{Fa}$

$(11)\ \dfrac{Fa}{\exists x Fx}$ $(12)\ \dfrac{\exists x Fx}{\{Fx\}}$

The asterisk in rules (5), (6), and (7a) indicates a place where we may put any propositional expression we please. It would have been possible to use a letter, say 'R', instead, but the asterisk serves the purpose of drawing attention to these rules, which are of special importance in demonstration. Apart from this usage, the only novelties here are the occurrence of two expressions below the line in rules (4), (5), and (7a) (i.e. in three of the places where Gentzen found it necessary to introduce suppositions) and the use of the sign '$\{Fx\}$' in rules (9) and (12) to represent the set of all possible values of the function $\neq Fx$. But these changes are enough to secure symmetry and allow for the introduction and elimination of each formal sign by the rules which seem most natural. Thus rules (5) and (6) are versions of the principles of excluded middle and non-contradiction, and with one exception the others are all obvious.

Rule (7a), which looks a little curious at first sight, is equivalent in effect to the principle that a material implication is entailed by the negation of its antecedent. If we wish we can easily get the latter as a derivative rule.

(13) $\lnot P / P \supset Q$

Proof. $\dfrac{\lnot P \quad \dfrac{\lnot P}{P}(6) \quad P \supset Q}{P \supset Q}(7a)$

But (7a) is preferable as a basic rule, because elegance requires that each formal sign should be introduced alone, i.e. that no basic rule should be concerned with more than one sign.

In general, a new development schema can always be derived from one already given by transferring a propositional expression to the other side of the horizontal line and adding or taking away a negation sign at the same time. Here, for example, is a new principle of development derivative from rule (4).

(14) $\urcorner Q/P, \urcorner(P \vee Q)$

$$\text{Proof.}\ \dfrac{\dfrac{\cfrac{\urcorner Q}{\dfrac{P \vee Q}{P\quad Q}(4)}\qquad \urcorner(P \vee Q)}{\urcorner}(5)}{P}\ (6)$$

The principle of conditionalization which occurred as a basic rule in the version of Gentzen's system given above can be proved within this new system quite easily. For it requires only that $\#(P \supset Q)$ shall be demonstrable if $\#P$ entails $\#Q$, and this is shown as follows:

(15) *If P/Q then* $\star/P \supset Q$

$$\text{Proof.}\ \dfrac{\dfrac{\cfrac{\star}{\dfrac{P}{Q}(\text{Hyp.})}\qquad P \supset Q}{P \supset Q}(7a)}{P \supset Q}(7b)$$

The consistency and independence of the new rules can be proved by adaptation of the arguments used for proving the consistency and independence of axioms for logic. For a proof of their completeness (in the sense of sufficiency for the demonstration of all validating patterns) it will be convenient to show how a basis that is already known to be complete can be established within our system.

First, we prove the equivalence of $\#(P \supset Q)$ and $\#(\urcorner P \vee Q)$, i.e. the equivalence that is used in *Principia Mathematica* for the definition of the material implication sign. This can be done by two derivations.

(16) $P \supset Q / \neg P \vee Q$

Proof.

$$\cfrac{P \supset Q \quad \cfrac{\cfrac{P \supset Q \quad P}{Q}(8)}{\neg P \vee Q}(3b)}{} \qquad \cfrac{\cfrac{P \supset Q}{\neg P}(5)}{\neg P \vee Q}(3a)$$

(17) $\neg P \vee Q / P \supset Q$

Proof.

$$\cfrac{\neg P \vee Q}{\cfrac{\neg P}{P \supset Q}(13) \quad \cfrac{Q}{P \supset Q}(7b)}(4)$$

Next, we check that we have the *modus ponendo ponens* as one of our basic rules, namely, (8). Thirdly, we construct demonstrations of the four independent axioms chosen by Whitehead and Russell for the calculus of propositions.

(18) $\star / (P \vee P) \supset P$

Proof.

$$\cfrac{\cfrac{\cfrac{\star}{P \vee P} \quad \cfrac{(P \vee P) \supset P}{P}(4)}{(P \vee P) \supset P}(7b) \quad \cfrac{P}{(P \vee P) \supset P}(7b)}{}(7a)$$

(19) $\star / P \supset (P \vee Q)$

Proof.

$$\cfrac{\cfrac{\cfrac{\star}{P} \quad P \supset (P \vee Q)}{P \vee Q}(3a)}{P \supset (P \vee Q)}(7b)(7a)$$

(20) $\star / (P \vee Q) \supset (Q \vee P)$

Proof.

$$\frac{\dfrac{\dfrac{P \vee Q}{P}\ (4)}{\dfrac{Q \vee P}{(P \vee Q) \supset (Q \vee P)}\ (3b)}\quad \dfrac{\dfrac{(P \vee Q) \supset (Q \vee P)}{Q}\ {}^{(7a)}}{\dfrac{Q \vee P}{(P \vee Q) \supset (Q \vee P)}\ (3a)}}{}\ (7b)$$

(21) $\star/(Q \supset R) \supset [(P \vee Q) \supset (P \vee R)]$

Proof.

$$\frac{\dfrac{Q \supset R}{\dfrac{R}{P \vee R}\ (3b)}\qquad (Q \supset R) \supset [(P \vee Q) \supset (P \vee R)]}{\dfrac{(P \vee Q) \supset (P \vee R)}{(Q \supset R) \supset [(P \vee Q) \supset (P \vee R)]}\ (7b)}\ (7b)$$

$$\frac{\neg Q}{}\ (16)$$

$$\frac{\dfrac{\dfrac{P}{P \vee R}\ (3a)}{(P \vee Q) \supset (P \vee R)}\ (7b)\qquad \dfrac{\dfrac{\neg(P \vee Q)}{(P \vee Q) \supset (P \vee R)}\ {}^{(14)}}{(Q \supset R) \supset [(P \vee Q) \supset (P \vee R)]}\ (13)}{(Q \supset R) \supset [(P \vee Q) \supset (P \vee R)]}\ (7b)$$

And finally we construct proofs for the additional axioms and two additional rules which Hilbert and Ackermann give for functional logic.

(22) $\star/\forall x F x \supset F a$

Proof.
$$\frac{\dfrac{\forall x F x}{Fa}\ (10)\qquad \forall x F x \supset F a\ {}^{(7a)}}{\forall x F \supset F a}\ (7b)$$

(23) $\star/Fa \supset \exists x\, Fx$

Proof.
$$\frac{\dfrac{Fa}{\exists x Fx}\ (11)\qquad\qquad Fa \supset \exists x Fx\ {}^{(7a)}}{Fa \supset \exists x Fx}\ (7b)$$

(24) *If the expression abbreviated by 'P' does not contain 'x'
free, then $P \supset Fx/P \supset \forall xFx$.*

Proof.

$$\cfrac{\cfrac{P \supset Fx \quad \cfrac{\cfrac{P \supset Fx}{P}\ (8) \quad P \supset \forall xFx}{}\ (7a)}{Fx}}{\cfrac{\forall xFx}{P \supset \forall xFx}\ (7b)}\ (9)$$

(25) *If the expression abbreviated by 'P' does not contain 'x'
free, then $Fx \supset P/\exists xFx \supset P$.*

Proof.

$$\cfrac{\cfrac{Fx \supset P \quad \cfrac{\cfrac{Fx \supset P}{\exists xFx}\ \cfrac{}{Fx}\ (12) \quad \exists xFx \supset P}{}\ (7a)}{P}\ (8)}{\exists xFx \supset P}\ (7b)$$

All the derivations are straight-forward, except those for
(24) and (25), which require some explanation.

When we enunciate rule (9) in the form $\dfrac{\{Fx\}}{\forall xFx}$ and rule (10)
in the form $\dfrac{\exists xFx}{\{Fx\}}$, we use the braces to make clear that we are
dealing with the class of all propositions that are values of the
function $\#Fx$, i.e. what we write are abbreviations for

$$\dfrac{Fx_1\ Fx_2\ Fx_3,\ \text{etc.}}{\forall xFx} \quad \text{and} \quad \dfrac{\exists xFx}{Fx_1\ Fx_2\ Fx_3,\ \text{etc.}} \quad \text{where } 'Fx_1', 'Fx_2', \text{ etc.}$$

are supposed to represent various values of the function. But it
is obviously impossible to construct tables of development with
more than a finite number of branches. How then can we ever
make use of our non-finite rules? Clearly the only possibility is to
prove something with complete generality of all the values of
$\#Fx$, using 'Fx' for this purpose *as though it were the expression
of such a value* rather than the expression of the function.
This is what we call reasoning with free variables, and it is such

use of 'x' that has led mathematicians to say sometimes that it denotes ambiguously all the various individuals whose names might be substituted for it. If we can show in this way that some proposition $\#P$ entails every value of $\#F$x, we can prove that $P/\forall$x Fx by the development

$$\frac{\dfrac{P}{Fx_1} \quad \dfrac{P}{Fx_2} \quad \dfrac{P}{Fx_3} \text{ etc.}}{\forall xFx}.$$

Similarly, if we can show in this way that every value of $\#F$x entails $\#P$, we can prove that $\exists$xFx$/P$ by the development

$$\frac{\exists xFx}{\dfrac{Fx_1}{P} \quad \dfrac{Fx_2}{P} \quad \dfrac{Fx_3}{P} \text{ etc.}}.$$

In either case it is essential, of course, that 'P' should be really the expression of a proposition and not an abbreviation for another expression containing 'x' in the same way as 'Fx'. All this is allowed for in the formulation of (24) and (25) above, with the result that these principles look a good deal more complicated than rules (9) and (12).

In his *Methods of Logic*, which is the latest attempt to improve the technique of logical investigation, Professor Quine uses a variant of the truth-table method for propositional logic but provides for the additional requirements of functional logic by four rules like those given in this section. In particular he gives a Rule of Universal Generalization and a Rule of Existential Instantiation which resemble respectively our rules (9) and (12) (except that they do not contain braces to indicate reference to all the values of the function) and lays down a drill for the use of free variables which is carefully designed to prevent illicit transitions such as that in the schema

$$\frac{\dfrac{\exists x\ Fx}{Fx}}{\forall xFx}.$$

When used together with a device of suppositions like that introduced by Gentzen, these rules undoubtedly simplify the construction of proofs. But Professor Quine himself talks of his procedure as the entry to a looking-glass world (p. 161); and so it must seem unless it is explained as a way of getting the advantages which are to be had at the earlier stage of logic from the construction of developments with many branches.

Although our system of rules of development has been obtained from Gentzen's system of rules of natural inference by a few small changes, the two are not equivalent. For Gentzen's is a version of intuitionist logic, while ours is a version of classical logic. The difference is not due, however, to the addition of any special axiom, nor yet to the provision of a new way of eliminating the negation sign, but to the alteration of rule (5) in a way that seems natural and almost inevitable when the notion of inference has been replaced by the wider notion of development. If anyone wishes for an intuitionist theory of development, he can have it by dropping our rule (5) and restoring Gentzen's in its place. But in this context Gentzen's (5) is obviously anomalous, since it does not introduce the negation sign in a straightforward way, corresponding to the way in which it is eliminated by rule (6), but employs the device of suppositions, which is no longer required for any other rule. In short Gentzen's success in making intuitionist logic look like something simpler and more basic than classical logic depends, as he himself admits, on the special forms of the rules he uses, and in particular on the requirement that they should all be rules of inference. If rules of development are allowed, the apparent advantage of the intuitionist system vanishes.

IV

I wish now to maintain that logic, as commonly understood, is the general theory of the relation which Carnap has called logical involution, i.e. the relation that holds between two sets of propositions when there is a valid development leading from the first set as premisses to the second set as limits, or in more familiar language, when it is impossible that all of the first set should be true without at least one of the second set being true also. This assertion may seem a little paradoxical, since logic is an old study, whereas no one had ever heard of involution until a few years ago; but my thesis is only a new attempt to give precision to an old idea.

It is often said that logic is concerned with the classification of propositions in respect of their forms and with the relations which hold between them in virtue of their forms. This is satisfactory, so long as we are content with an explanation of logical form by reference to examples. But how are we to decide whether or not an argument is *formally* valid when some logicians feel inclined by analogy to say that it is and others to say that it is not? Consider for instance the argument 'London is north of Paris, and Edinburgh is north of London; so Edinburgh is north of Paris'. In general, logicians have said that this, though certainly correct, is not valid in virtue of the forms of the propositions; but a few have tried to maintain that it has a formal justification which would become clear if we expressed all the propositions by means of a comparative phrase such as 'nearer to the North Pole'. In order to explain the notion of logical form and so delimit their field of study more exactly some logicians have suggested that logic is the theory of the notions expressed by a certain limited vocabulary, e.g. 'and', 'or', 'not', 'if', 'all', 'some'. This is undoubtedly an improvement, but it is open to an obvious objection. Why should we select just this vocabulary? Suppose, for example, that with Professor Quine we have reduced our list of primitives to Sheffer's stroke, the universal quantifier, and the epsilon of membership. Why should we now declare that these are the full menu of logic? Why should we not make the diet richer by throwing in a few other signs such as the '-er' of comparative adjectives or even the adjectives themselves? Clearly Professor Quine believes that he has some good reason for stopping where he does. Indeed he has suggested on various occasions that epsilon ought perhaps to be excluded.

It is a simple answer to these perplexities to say that formal (or logical) signs are those whose full sense can be given by laying down rules of development for the propositions expressed by their help. '&', 'v', '⌐', '⊃', '∀', and '∃' all pass this test, but '-er' and the epsilon of membership do not. The fact that signs of the first group all have their senses fixed by rules of development is fairly clear from the last section, but the contrast between these signs and all others may perhaps be made clearer by the explicit presentation of logic as the theory of involution statements. In this version we abandon the device of make-believe deduction, introduced by Chrysippus for the proof of derived rules, and exhibit the science as one in which involution statements are demonstrated by means of a few simple rules of the second order.

First we set out the following *general rules*, each in the form of an inference schema.

(i) $$\frac{\star}{P/P}$$

(ii) $$\frac{\Gamma, \Delta, \Theta, \Lambda/\Xi, \Pi, \Sigma, \Phi}{\Gamma, \Theta, \Delta, \Lambda/\Xi, \Sigma, \Pi, \Phi}$$

(iii) $$\frac{\Gamma/\Delta}{\Gamma, \Theta/\Delta, \Lambda}$$

(iv) $$\frac{\Gamma, P/\Delta \qquad \Theta/P, \Lambda}{\Gamma, \Theta/\Delta, \Lambda}$$

(vα) $$\frac{\star}{\{Fx\}/Fa}$$

(vβ) $$\frac{\star}{Fa/\{Fx\}}$$

(viα) $$\frac{\Gamma, \{Fx\}/\Delta \quad \{\Theta/Fx, \Lambda\}}{\Gamma, \Theta/\Delta, \Lambda}$$

(viβ) $$\frac{\{\Gamma, Fx/\Delta\} \quad \Theta/\{Fx\}, \Lambda}{\Gamma, \Theta/\Delta, \Lambda}$$

Here each Greek capital letter is to be understood as an abbreviated reference to any sequence of propositions the reader may choose, including under 'sequence' for this purpose sets with one member and even null sets. This use of Greek letters and even the substance of some of the rules is suggested by a later part of the work of Gentzen cited above, though the system which he elaborates there is different in kind from that considered here.

The first rule is no more than a licence to assert of any proposition that it cannot be true and also be false, and the effect of the next three is only to put on record the liberties we allowed ourselves tacitly when we followed the procedure of Chrysippus. Thus the second allows us to vary the order of initial formulae or end formulae just as we please, the third allows for additions at will either to the initial or to the end formulae of a valid development, and the fourth allows us to omit from our summary of a complex development any formula which occurs, like 'P' in the accompanying figure, neither as an initial nor as an end formula of the whole arrangement.

$$\Theta \quad \frac{\overline{\Gamma}}{P} \quad \Delta$$
$$\frac{}{\Lambda}$$

Together the second, third, and fourth allow for the elimination of redundancies before or after the solidus in an involution statement. As Leibniz said of one of his calculi, we take no account here of order or repetition. In general shape and also in purpose the two parts of the fifth resembles the first rule and the two parts of the sixth resemble the fourth rule; but the later rules are now complicated because they take account of possibly infinite sets of propositions. The braces used in the formulation of them have the same sense as those used in the rules of the last section, and so the set of propositions designated by the sign '$\{\Gamma/F\mathrm{x}, \Delta\}$' is that we should establish by proving that $\Gamma/F\mathrm{x}, \Delta$ with 'x' taken as a free variable.

Next we set out *special rules* for the various formal signs, namely, one principle of equivalence, or rule of substitution, to govern the use of each sign. These are adapted in part from rules of Professor Popper.[1]

[1] 'On the Theory of Deduction' in the *Proceedings of the Royal Netherlands Academy of Sciences*, vol li (1948).

$$\text{(vii)} \frac{\Gamma, P \,\&\, Q/\varDelta}{\Gamma, P, Q/\varDelta} \qquad\qquad \text{(viii)} \frac{\Gamma/P \vee Q, \varDelta}{\Gamma/P, Q, \varDelta}$$

$$\text{(ix)} \frac{\Gamma, \urcorner P/\varDelta}{\Gamma/P, \varDelta} \qquad\qquad \text{(x)} \frac{\Gamma/P \supset Q, \varDelta}{\Gamma, P/Q, \varDelta}$$

$$\text{(xi)} \frac{\Gamma, \forall \mathrm{x} F\mathrm{x}/\varDelta}{\Gamma, \{F\mathrm{x}\}/\varDelta} \qquad\qquad \text{(xii)} \frac{\Gamma/\exists \mathrm{x} F\mathrm{x}, \varDelta}{\Gamma/\{F\mathrm{x}\}, \varDelta}$$

Together the general and special rules suffice for the construction of the whole of the restricted calculus of propositional functions. Here, for example, is a demonstration of the demonstrability of one of the axioms in *Principia Mathematica*.

$$\frac{\displaystyle \frac{\overline{\star}}{Q \supset R/Q \supset R}\,\text{(i)}}{\dfrac{Q \supset R, Q/R}{Q \supset R, P \vee Q, Q/P, R}\,\text{(x)}}\text{(iii) (ii)} \qquad \frac{\displaystyle \frac{\overline{\star}}{P \vee Q/P \vee Q}\,\text{(i)}}{\dfrac{P \vee Q/P, Q}{Q \supset R, P \vee Q/Q, P, R}\,\text{(viii)}}\text{(iii) (ii)}$$

$$\frac{}{}\text{(iv)}$$

$$\frac{Q \supset R, P \vee Q/P, R}{\dfrac{Q \supset R, P \vee Q/P \vee R}{\dfrac{Q \supset R/(P \vee Q) \supset (P \vee)R}{\star/(Q \supset R) \supset [(P \vee Q) \supset (P \vee R)]}\text{(x)}}\text{(x)}}\text{(viii)}$$

It is interesting to notice that, while the rules which form the subject matter of this system are rules of involution, the second-order rules by means of which the proofs are constructed are rules of entailment.

The merit of this version of logic from our point of view is that it takes the notion of involution as fundamental and introduces the formal signs by means of rules which we can treat as definitions. Admittedly the special rules (vii)-(xii) do not by themselves allow for the elimination of the formal signs in all the contexts in which these may be used. But they determine the sense of the signs completely by fixing their roles in argument. No doubt the English word 'and' may have overtones of suggestion for which there is no allowance in rule (vii), but the logician's use of '&' is intended to convey just the sense allowed by that rule, neither more nor less, and similarly each of the other formal signs has precisely the sense allowed by its special rule. Although each such rule deals with the occurrence of a formal sign on one side of the solidus only, each rule is in fact sufficient with the general rules given earlier to provide for the introduction or elimination of its sign either before or after the solidus. Thus '$\Gamma/P \And Q, \Delta$' is equivalent in force to the pair of involution statements '$\Gamma/P, \Delta$' and '$\Gamma/Q, \Delta$'; and '$\Gamma/\forall x\, Fx, \Delta$' can be replaced by '$\{\Gamma/Fx, \Delta\}$'. In short, the formal signs are of special interest to the logician only because they can be used as auxiliaries for the presentation of the theory of involution.

Since there is a difference of the greatest importance between a set that can be specified by enumeration of its members and one that can be specified only by indication of some feature common to all its members, it is not surprising that functional logic, which deals with possibly infinite sets of propositions by reference to the functions of which the propositions are values, should prove to be a good deal more complicated than propositional logic, which deals only with finite sets of propositions. But the transition from propositional to functional logic does not take us outside the theory of involution, whereas the passage to the enlarged calculus of propositional functions brings us to a theory in which the notion of a thing's being so-and-so occurs *essentially*. The importance of this latter departure can be appreciated most easily when the enlarged calculus is presented as the theory of sets with epsilon as a new primitive sign. When Frege wrote, the difference between the enlarged and the restricted calculus of functions seemed to be of no great importance, but Gödel's theorem of 1931 shows that the enlarged calculus can never be completely axiomatized,[1] and it follows immediately from this that the epsilon of membership cannot be defined by any such rules as we have given for the connectives and the

[1] 'Über formal unentscheidbare Sätze der *Principia Mathematica* und verwandter Systeme' in *Monatshefte für Mathematik und Physik*, vol. 38, pp. 173-98.

quantifiers. In my opinion this is a good reason for deciding that the theory of sets should not be accounted part of logic.

If we come to the conclusion that the theory of sets should not be included in logic and so decide against Frege's programme of reducing arithmetic to logic, then *a fortiori* we must decide against talking of the logic of colour words, the logic of moral language, the logic of 'time', and so forth. For although the primitive notion of the theory of sets can never be characterized completely by axioms (i.e. by the formulation of *logical* conditions for the interpretation of the epsilon sign), membership is a relation of which every student of logic must undoubtedly have a concept, whereas the notions of colour, obligation, and time are in no way essential. There is indeed a sense in which the theory of sets is more fundamental than logic. For while logic is the common part of all theories, including the theory of sets, and capable of being presented without what is peculiar to the theory of sets, it is also itself the theory of a relation which holds between sets of propositions, and therefore a theory whose internal structure is determined by the distinction between finite and infinite sets. Furthermore, if we decide to say that mathematics is not reducible to logic, we shall have to admit that metalogic, or the theory of proof (i.e. the study in which we consider such questions as the possibility of establishing a decision procedure for a theory), belongs to that part of mathematics which is not logic. On the other hand, if men were all blind and therefore unable to formulate involution statements in which colour words occurred essentially, they would lack nothing required for the study of logic. For logic, as commonly understood, is not the collection of all true involution statements, but a science related to such statements in somewhat the same way as geometry is related to geography or arithmetic to bank accounts. No doubt a long continued fashion of abuse might make the word mean something different; for solecisms may become standard usages, just as rebels may become rulers. But the change could scarcely be a gain to philosophy, since it would involve the blurring of the important distinction between form and matter.

18

That talk of the logic of colour words is a strange novelty, can scarcely be doubted, since it puzzles well-educated men when they hear it for the first time. Why, then, has it been adopted by some philosophers in the past twenty years, and in particular by philosophers who pride themselves on their ability to detect dangerous departures from ordinary usage? It is difficult to answer this question, just as it is difficult to account for all the queer things that Hegel said about logic; but I think that the rise of the fashion may be connected with a change in the use of the technical term 'analytic'. In the usage of Kant and Frege a statement is analytic if, and only if, its truth is guaranteed by a principle of formal logic. But in recent times it has often been said that a statement is analytic if, and only if, its truth is guaranteed by the rules of usage for the words or other signs in which it is expressed. The second of these two definitions is so wide that it undoubtedly covers all truths known *a priori*. Unfortunately it suggests to many philosophers that all truths known *a priori* must be, as Hobbes said, 'Truths arbitrarily constituted by the Inventors of Speech'.[1] But that impression is due to a muddle about language which we cannot investigate here. For our present purpose the important thing is that failure to distinguish the two different senses of 'analytic' may lead philosophers to say that every statement which is certifiable *a priori* must be true on logical grounds. Some who feel a little bit worried by this novelty try to placate their linguistic consciences by drawing a distinction between formal and informal or non-formal logic. But this is only to make confusion worse. When we speak of formal logic, we do not mean a study that is formal in the sense in which dress or manners may be formal (though it may conveniently be *formalized* by the use of special symbolism), but rather that study of reasoning which concentrates attention on the forms of the propositions concerned as distinct from other studies of reasoning which have also sometimes been called logic but deal with psychological and epistemological considerations. There are of course many sound principles of reasoning which may be called non-formal because

[1]*De Corpore*, I. iii. 9.

they are concerned with special subject matters, but if logic is to contain all these it will be not the handmaid but the cannibal of the sciences.

MAIN PUBLICATION

Probability and Induction. Oxford University Press. 1949.

WORSHIP AND IDOLATRY

By H. D. LEWIS

*Professor of History and Philosophy of Religion in the
University of London*

WORSHIP AND IDOLATRY

THE main advances in religious thought today have been brought about by a better understanding of the nature of God's transcendence, an achievement which owes not a little to a finer appreciation of the teaching of some celebrated thinkers of the past. It has been made apparent, by eminent theologians as well as by philosophers, that God is somehow 'beyond' or 'other than' every finite reality. Our thought is directed to Him, not as a completion of the rational systems by which we explain other facts, but by a radical incompleteness in all such explanation which we do not hope to overcome. This is why the 'Being of God' is sometimes said to be bound up with the being of anything. It is also some divination of an absolute mystery at the limit of all explanation that has turned the attention of some philosophers today, in the pursuit of their ordinary secular aims, to the consideration of 'limit problems' and some express discussion of the meaning of 'transcendence'.

Indeed, I think I should hazard the suggestion that it is in being compelled to come to terms with some 'limit problems' in philosophy that the predominantly empiricist epistemology of today may be found to pass beyond itself and afford a means of absorbing its main achievements into a constructive view of our experience as a whole, thus rendering possible also kindred developments in ethics and other parts of philosophy. In that case the philosophy of religion may have a crucial role to play, not only in enabling us to achieve a new understanding of religion in a new cultural and social context, but also in respect of the general tasks of philosophy.

Some hint of this may be found in other contributions

to this volume. But I shall not pursue this matter further. For the aim of this paper will be to show how important it is that the better understanding of God's transcendence which we have achieved today should be combined with closer attention to certain features of religious experience; I hope thereby also to exhibit the enhancement of the importance of religious experience, as a means of knowing God, which is due to His transcendence.

I proceed to my proper task by repeating that what we most need to emphasize, in dealing with religion, is religious experience. As preachers and philosophers alike we need to be put in mind of its importance and to acquire a better understanding of the form of it which is appropriate today. The core of religion is religious experience. At the same time we need also to appreciate well that it is not possible to give an adequate account of religious experience solely in terms of the agent who has it or of his relations to his fellow men. The object of religious experience is God, and whatever else we may find it possible to say about God it is certain, as already indicated, that we must think of God as some reality complete and perfect in a way which is not possible for any other being or finite creature. He is the Creator, Himself uncreated, the Lord God before whom we bow in worship which it would be blasphemous to render to any other, blasphemous and a violation of our own nature. The sole object of genuine worship is a transcendent God.

The word 'transcendent' may not, however, be altogether a happy one here. For it is not always used in the same way. Some philosophers use it to denote 'the *a priori*' or to indicate 'non-natural' qualities in ethics. A recent debate on the limits of empiricism was given shape by the question 'How may experience be transcended?' Theologians sometimes concur in this usage to their own great confusion. For they wish also to mean more than has just been suggested by 'the transcendent'; they sometimes pass surreptitiously from positing one kind of transcendence to acceptance of another, blurring altogether the peculiar character of transcendence in the context of the notions with which this paper began. The ways of knowing this latter kind of transcendence, and the problems which attend it, are vastly different from the way we know the *a priori* or values, however we understand these and the problems to which they give rise. Philosophical discussions may likewise be confused by importation into certain logical or epistemological questions of religious associations of the term 'transcendence' which have no relevance to the point at issue. I suggest therefore that we should eschew the word 'transcendence' altogether in any reference other than a religious one and that in religious discussions it should be always reserved for the peculiar 'beyond-ness' or 'otherness' of God implied in the perfection or absolute completeness of His nature to which we have already drawn attention as distinguishing Him altogether from any of his creatures. It is of such a transcendent being that we claim to have experience in religion.

This will seem to many, however, to be much too comprehensive a claim. Religion, it will be argued, has not always had to do with the transcendent. Men have often worshipped merely natural objects—the sun or the moon, trees, mountains, rivers, animals. They have bowed down in worship before images which they have carved themselves. Then there are the gods of mythology, many and varied, and the semi-divine figures of early legends. Is there not even a notable religion, namely Buddhism, which, in its original and purest form, dispenses with God altogether? Have not men also worshipped the State or great political or national leaders and reformers? Are not communism and fascism often regarded as rival religions to Christianity? Indeed, may we not create a religion for ourselves out of very slight materials? Cricket or fishing seem to be their religion for some people, literature is full of misers who worshipped their gold and of other wretches who worshipped themselves or their power. Does not the lover adore his beloved and the film fan deem his star to be divine? Do we not find almost every lovely thing 'divine' or 'adorable' today?

Now the way we should deal with these examples differs considerably from one case to the other. The film fan, or the lady who 'worships her pet', are normally, though by no means invariably, abusing language or betraying the slovenly linguistic habits and imprecision of their age or set. They are not expressing a seriously religious attitude. But may they not sometimes do so? May there not be a perverted, idolatrous, but properly religious, worship of pets? I think there may and that crude idolatry is by no means a monopoly of primitive cultures. But we need also to draw careful distinctions, firstly between cases of mere loose use of language and cases of deep and persistent obsessions, and secondly between the latter and genuine idolatry. Not every total commitment is properly religious. A person may give his whole mind and devotion to a cause, possibly a trivial one like ministering to the whims of a pet or perhaps a high one like serving a party or a nation or promoting the advance of science or the cure of disease. But in no case should we straightway describe this as religion, genuine or perverted. It may be a wholly human activity, involving only human or sub-human matters. The resemblance it has to religion must not mislead us or induce us to use the same name for activities or attitudes of mind that are also radically different.

This point should be stressed before we say more about idolatry proper. Religion has suffered much from loose use of language, and in no case is this more evident than in the use of the word 'religion' itself. The adjective 'religiously' has become in common parlance a convenient word to describe any kind of thorough or wholehearted undertaking. One may clean one's boots, or tot up one's bills 'religiously'. No great harm comes of talking in this way, and no one is seriously misled; only the pedant could object. But once we pass from obviously trivial cases, the likelihood of serious confusion is only too plain. Sport, business, politics, art, science and kindred activities become at once religious; and it is not pedantic to object to this practice. For in this very loose usage of the term almost anyone will have a religion; most of us have some cause which we are prepared to support or some interest which tends to dominate others; if we extend the term a little further to include whatever happens to be a main interest, any purposive being will be religious by definition. This is, I believe, sometimes used as a way of showing that man is essentially religious, although he does not always have the 'true' religion. But it is an exceptionally Pyrrhic victory that is gained in this way, unless, as often happens, we proceed to load our conclusions with more than the premise warrants. Questions about the importance of religion or of the relation of religion to other activities are also confused by an undiscriminating use of the term 'religious'. So are questions about the place of authority in religion or the importance of dogma. Dogma in religion is not the same as dogma in politics or science, although there may be features common to dogma in all these cases. If we are to ask helpful questions about religion and deal with them effectively we must be more precise in our use of the term. Some reference to 'the supernatural' is at least required, and I suggest that by far the most helpful procedure will be to reserve the term 'religion' for activities or attitudes which involve some awareness of a transcendent Being.

This recommendation is not without disadvantages of which I am well aware. For it excludes, not only loose metaphorical uses of the term based on superficial affinities between religion and other activities, but also serious reference to 'ethical religions' or religions of humanity or religions with a 'finite God'. Nor can it be claimed that the latter exist only in books and theories. For ceremonies and ritual practices of various kinds have been suggested for them and sometimes adopted. A claim to be describing normal religious practice may also be made by theories, such as idealism, whose notion of transcendence is at any rate very different from that indicated above. For this reason I would not press my recommendation. But, on the whole, I think more would be gained than lost by its adoption. For I think it could be shown that in the practices or attitudes which are described in humanistic terms, such as 'ethical religion', there is in fact often a transcendent object of worship such as we normally find, I submit, in the practice of religion; and, secondly, even if common serious usage extends the term 'religious' to beliefs and practices which do not have a transcendent being as their object as well as to all which do, the difference between the latter and the former is so considerable that philosophical analysis may well be called in here to tidy up our linguistic habits in a way that may be much to the advantage of religion and of our understanding of it. This may become plainer if we look more closely now at allegedly religious practices which do not seem to have a transcendent God as their object.

Consider first the cases that may seem least ambiguous. I said earlier that there might be a genuine worship of pets. But I also suggested that this must mean more than excessive devotion to a pet or obsession with it. The latter may be perverse and unhealthy and present the moralist or the psychologist with a serious problem. It may reflect an unbalanced state of society or bad education, and it may thus call for sharp denunciation or satire. But however distressing such a disorder may be, and however grave the conditions which produce it, it may require nothing for its description beyond the terms normally available in morals or psychology. On the other hand a very similar state or practice may in fact also involve a great deal more. It may be a case of worshipping the pet. How does that happen?

It happens when a creature is invested with a significance that is dependent on some awareness of a transcendent reality and is made the centre of that significance. This is the opposite of religious symbolism. The religious symbol opens out to the transcendent, it refers away from itself. In idolatry the reverse happens, an attempt being made to hold on to a genuine sense of the transcendent but also to diminish it and contain it within the interest which some finite creature like ourselves, or inferior to ourselves, may have for us. Attitudes and feelings which it is appropriate for us to have only towards God are thus directed to His creatures. This is the most radical of all inconsistencies, the most revolting and the most devastating in its effects on our own natures and on our relations with others. It should not be equated at all with a mere obsession, however complete, or with any kindred psychological disorder. It is an essentially religious phenomenon, possible only where there is at least a spark of genuine religion. The practical importance of recognizing this is considerable. For an attempt to treat a religious disorder, in the clinic or elsewhere, in neglect of the religious factors involved, may be very ill-judged, it may aggravate the ill it sets out to remove or divert it to courses where it is less easily traced.

The best term to describe this peculiarly religious perversion seems to be 'daemonic'. A great deal has been written lately about 'daemonic powers', but not with much understanding or caution. Theologians, anxious to find support for traditional views, have turned to the manifestation of grave disorders in the life of society, especially those which lead to war and accentuate its grimness, for evidence of 'dark satanic forces' let loose in the world. Nervous disorders are also straightway interpreted in this way, the psycho-analyst in particular being often regarded by the theologian, but less often by himself, as a considerable ally of religion for this reason. This is usually bound up with highly questionable notions of sin and human corruption. These latter cannot be considered at the moment. But it is necessary to stress that, however we understand the upheavals and disorders of our time at the moral level or in respect to wickedness and guilt, the facts of social and moral disorder, even grave ones involving much unreason, do not of necessity call for some supernormal explanation in terms of 'satanic forces'. In great measure they can be ascribed to the social and economic complications consequent upon rapid scientific and industrial advances. It would be strange if recent changes in mode of life and culture did not require of us to weather such storms as we have met in our time. The cause of religion is thus weakened rather than strengthened if we quote in support of it matters susceptible of quite adequate explanations at their own level. Much recent theology has been crippled by that particular confession of failure.

At the same time the problems of the individual and of society may be drastically altered and accentuated by incursion into men's lives of truly daemonic elements, and it would not be surprising to find these coinciding with other ills and disorders. Such elements or forces, if we retain for a moment these common but somewhat vague terms, consist essentially in the proneness of men to contract their religious awareness in the way described and centre it on lesser objects than God himself. They involve a genuine awareness of God but an awareness which is in some fashion also repudiated or misconstrued, the misconstruction being more easy because we can know nothing of the transcendent except as mediated through a symbol. The symbol draws into itself the glory it should only be transmitting. How far the conditions of our time are conducive to idolatry of this kind is not easy to determine. But the following points may be borne in mind. There has been a general diminishing of religious awareness in Western countries as in other countries most open to the influence of the West, and a great secularization of life and culture; presumably this helps the debasing of religion to quasi-secular terms. The repudiation of overt religious beliefs and the criticism of religious dogmas, happening in situations where there lingers also the more radical religious awareness on which the former depend, encourage likewise the proneness to diminish religious significance and incapsulate it in the finite symbol. The misplacing of religious significance relieves it also of the control and direction to which it is subject in its proper form and allies it with other elements in our nature to which it is not native. The latter become over-charged and inflamed in consequence, a religious disorder which aggravates in turn such other disturbances of human character and society as are accentuated by the conditions of our time.

Detailed discussion of these matters would take us far afield. My concern at the moment is merely to note the way in which an awareness of the transcendent is involved in forms of religion which may at first appear to have some lesser reality as their object. But we shall not stray too far if we note two further points here.

The view is often held that daemonic influences involve the activity of malevolent creatures other than ourselves and not known to us in the normal ways, perhaps not known at all in some cases. The literature of this subject is vast and complicated, including much general literature as well as strictly religious writings; no attempt to sift it would be practicable here. But I should like to stress that little careful consideration has ever been paid to the question of the way in which the existence of such beings could be known. Is the knowledge based on some peculiarity of the events or experiences in which they are supposed to be operative? In that case it needs to be carefully described and its credentials scrutinized. I cannot myself imagine what it could be, but presumably the absence of normal conditions and influences and similar irregularities would come into the picture. So would more positive factors like voices or visions. Whether in themselves these would seriously upset our belief that, with completer knowledge of ourselves, we could ascribe the unusual phenomena in question to obscure conditions or occurrences in ourselves, seems to me very doubtful. The evidence would at least need to be exceptionally strong. A more likely possibility seems to be investigations similar to those which are sometimes alleged to establish communications with the dead. If some para-normal evidence of this kind were available, and especially if it could be correlated with cases of moral temptation, or similar situations, which present features suggesting a para-normal explanation, the case might be made. But there would also be need of large allowance for our proneness to indulge in personification and vivid imaginative presentation of our experiences. It is not enough that temptations, for example, should have an insistence and a repugnance to us or a novelty which seem like the whispering of another malignant being in our ears. For 'in a cool moment' the whispering will be found to admit of many other explanations. This will, I believe, apply to a great deal of the more specifically religious reasons and evidence alleged to support the belief in one or more evil spirits. I do not maintain that the existence of evil spirits other than men is inconceivable, although the idea does present difficulties of definition at least which are considerable. Nor is it inconceivable that such beings should influence us. Whether they do so, and can be known to do so, is quite another matter. But what I wish to stress mainly now is the substantial weakening of such arguments by the availability to us of a notion of daemonic powers which, without postulating other beings than ourselves, takes due heed of the truly religious character of the facts in question and does not reduce them to secular or humanistic terms. Such a notion seems to me to be provided in the account of the distortions in our own experience of the transcendent already outlined.

Account must be taken here also of what we may describe perhaps as negative religious disturbances. I mean this. If man is made for God, the absence of God in his life leaves a tremendous vacuum. This is apt to be filled by disproportionate developments of other interests, and in a predominantly secular age, disorders of this kind also may wreak havoc in the affairs of men and societies. They are quite different from the idolatrous perversions already noted, although they also have a religious origin, and they are less vile in themselves and presumably in their effects; but here again the more positive religious perversion may fuse with other disorders to produce a greater and more insidious total of disruptive power.

In asserting that there are idolatrous attitudes such as those described, and in insisting upon the difference between them and ordinary obsessions, the admission must be made that normal empirical evidence will not suffice here. For so long as we proceed on the basis of normal observation, the sort of objection adduced earlier against the belief in evil spirits confronts us again. Such peculiarities of some perverted preoccupations as may lend colour to the notion that they are quite different in nature from others would always be susceptible in principle of an explanation in humanistic terms. The recognition of idolatry for what it is must come in the first instance from within the religious consciousness itself, although that may in due course provide the basis of subsequent discriminations in terms of more incidental considerations.

It is not, however, in perverted or degraded forms of religion alone that we seem to find the worship of natural objects or of other creatures like ourselves. Early religion involves this also, but, in the first instance at least, in a way radically different and far less objectionable religiously. The questions that arise here are of course complicated and I know well that speculations about the origins of various forms of culture are notoriously uncertain. I do not wish to involve myself more than I can help in controversies about comparative religion and the history of religions which often require very specialized knowledge. But there are some observations on this subject which I must venture to make, although they cannot be properly defended here; and I hope it will not seem too presumptuous to do so.

Let me say then that there seems to me to be adequate reasons for maintaining that where religion as we know it exhibits continuity of form with certain early practices, there we shall also find continuity of substance. Prominent among such reasons are the parallel continuities in morality and art. Primitive morality may be very crude in many ways but it is recognizable as morality; early art is art, notwithstanding that it may be much else. Religion is also very closely related to our exercise of reason, although it cannot be wholly rationalized; it involves some apprehension of the limits of reason which, springing as it does from the exercise of reason itself and not from its range, does not require great rational advance or abstract formulation. There would be much in primitive life to awaken some sense of this ultimate mystery, as there would also be many situations in which the impact upon men of a supreme religious mystery would find concrete embodiment and specific forms. Indeed, part of our problem in religion today, very sheltered as most of us are in the normal round of our lives, is to find the civilized equivalents to early realism. In strains, tensions and perplexities of various kinds, and in their closeness to nature, the men of early times, who were after all rational creatures however limited, would become aware in some dim fashion of a transcendent reality other than themselves and the world about them. It is thus not surprising that so many words and practices come to us in the context of our civilized life today laden with a numinous meaning they acquired in very remote times. Anthropologists and students of comparative religion have taught us much about these matters of late and have adduced extensive other evidence (not merely in respect to exceptional phenomena like the worship of the 'high gods' of some early cultures, but generally) which tends to show how wide of the mark were the animistic and crudely polytheistic accounts of the origin of religion offered by the naturalistic theorists who held the field at one time. In suggesting that these new insights of the anthropologists themselves, together with the other considerations on which I am only able to touch briefly here, should be the basis of our approach to early religion, I think we may also stress here again that the religious person at least must view the evidence available to him from within his own religious consciousness. When we do this we shall find, I submit, that what seems outwardly centred on natural or secular objects has in fact much in common with the symbolism of mature religious life.

In addition, there is the belief, widely held by religious people, and especially by Christians, that our knowledge of God comes to us mainly, and on some views exclusively, through the special initiative of God in revealing Himself to us. Some adherents to this view hold that the revelation is confined to a specific tradition, the Judeo-Christian one; and, according to some theologians of renown today, revelation derives exclusively from certain notable central religious events. Those, however, who do not feel impelled to accept restrictions of this kind, but who find themselves persuaded to the view that God does intervene in men's lives and in the course of history to make Himself known to us, will find it hard not to believe also that it is God who is stirring men's hearts and inclining them towards Him in the practices which, in times and places remote from our own, have affinities or continuity with our own religious life.

To this the objection will perhaps be made that we can hardly associate with the God of Christianity or of other 'higher' religions certain barbaric and savage practices in which men have sometimes indulged under the promptings of their religion. That men's apprehension of God should be very incomplete and limited at certain stages of human development might, it will be argued, be compatible with God's progressive disclosure of Himself in all religions; but, the argument continues, we have to reckon also, not only with much backsliding and unevenness of religious development, but with cruel and repellent and polytheistic practices hard to ascribe to the intervention of the God we worship. Putting it at its very lowest, if the original motivation of religion, and its prime inspiration at all times, is some consciousness of a relation to a transcendent Being (or, if we wish to be even more noncommittal, Reality), how did this come to be so perverted and to expend itself in practices which are so hard to associate in any way with the One God of enlightened religion, much less be ascribed to His initiative or direct intervention? If man was made in the image of God, at least to the extent of having a genuine awareness of Him, how did the image come to be 'marred' or 'lost', to use the stock theological terms?

Traditional theology has a simple answer here, far too simple in my view. It is the doctrine of the Fall and original sin. Man was created innocent, his innocence consisting in right relation to God, albeit, according to some theorists, a somewhat restricted relation and a limited innocence. But something 'happened' to mar this original innocence and make man thereafter a creature alienated by his own sinfulness from his Creator and Lord. The evidence available of early forms of monotheism has not infrequently been avidly put in the service of this form of traditionalism by its upholders. But this doctrine seems to me open to the most serious objections, especially as normally propounded. It involves conceptions of guilt and sinfulness, as notions including certain ethical elements, which can in no wise be accommodated to the plainest deliverances of the moral consciousness. It also involves an assumption of human solidarity which will bear little scrutiny and which appears to leave totally out of account the independent ways in which human life has developed in various places and at different times. These objections will not be pressed here. But I want to suggest that an alternative explanation of the relevant phenomena, and one more consistent with religious experience as well as with ethical principles, may be found if we recur at this point to the observations already made above about idolatrous worship.

It was noted there that consciousness of the transcendent tends to set up some form of resistance to itself. The consolation afforded by the thought of our union with a supremely perfect reality, although it is the final source of contentment and peace to human beings, is also in one way disturbing and unwelcome. For it makes exacting demands upon us, not only through its effect on our moral and cultural standards, but more expressly and peculiarly by requiring certain mental or spiritual adjustments. It takes us out of the sort of securities on which we normally count and shows us the every-day world in which we are at home merging into a background which cannot be made familiar or mastered like our normal environment. This is all the more disconcerting because of its effect on normal experience; the ordinary certainties are called in question. But the shock is greatest when this ultimate mystery comes into human life with a positive power of its own, as also happens in religion. This not only constitutes a threat to man's own independence but is felt more positively as the impact of an alien power with which he is unable to cope, a power, indeed, by which he is apt to be crushed altogether. That is a well-known moment in religious experience, to which familiar religious utterances and the history of religion bear ample witness. The God of love is also the God of terror and wrath, and he is not the one, in the full religious sense, without the other. There is thus a sense in which men in turn are apt to resist God, to be in conflict with Him or try to escape Him, *just because he is God*. But they will not do this in the first instance by merely forgetting or disregarding God. For they are also drawn to Him and need Him. They will thus try to limit or restrict their own consciousness of God by containing it within the media and symbols which are needed for its articulation. This seems to me the essence and beginning of idolatry.

The process is, however, complicated by its affinities with other phenomena, cultural and ethical ones in particular. The more conscious a man becomes of God the more does he feel the horror of his guilt which he bears for his wrongful actions. He thus not only feels himself 'as dust', 'as nothing', but woefully unworthy, 'undone', and 'a man of unclean lips'. Nor does religious utterance always distinguish sharply between these moral reactions and the peculiarly religious element in religious experience, the relations between the two being so close; they are usually merged in one general expression of destitution and despairing unworthiness. This is one further reason for the superficial plausibility of traditionalist theories of sin. The latter seem to chime in well with notable prophetic utterances whose worth and authenticity it would be hard to doubt, and they have been made much of by upholders of traditionalism. But these are not subjects which can be investigated closely here. All that we need to note at the moment is that if man's sense of moral unworthiness is intensified by religion, this affords an additional inducement to limit the power of religion upon him, in other words to fly from the judgement under which he feels in the presence of God by containing the God to whom he is so irresistibly drawn within forms more amenable to his own imperfections and waywardness.

Such idolatry may take one peculiarly insidious form. It may coalesce with moral evil. The essence of immorality is that a man puts his own aims before the greater claims of others, he puts himself 'at the centre'. And in putting himself thus at the centre he is also apt to draw into himself the religious overtones of his experience which he is trying to enclose in a finite symbol. The contraction of his religion is in the expansion of his own importance, and he finds the media of religious perversion in himself and in the excessive assertion of his own aspirations. This intertwining of moral evil with properly religious perversions is a most significant characteristic of religion; it presents us with two strands in the history of religion which we need to distinguish and consider carefully in their relations to one another—in distinction from the common practice of taking the religious utterances which reflect these two strands in the web of the religious life as relating to one indiscriminate whole. By pursuing the course suggested we shall find many matters clarified for us and we shall more easily avoid those strange aberrations of traditional theology which lead to pronouncements completely opposed to our most elementary moral convictions.

The history of the higher religions bears out these matters well. For the progress of religion has been far from even, and the back-slidings and lapses into idolatry from which certain peoples had been emancipated, the Hebrews in particular, throws a peculiarly interesting light on paganism which helps us to understand it better in all its forms. The idolatry we read of in the Bible is not only, for the most part, condemned expressly as the lapse of people who have known the true God and forsaken Him, but seems to call for peculiarly violent denunciation because it is in this way a perversion seen very clearly as such and abhorred with exceptional intensity by the prophets in the white heat of their own religious experience. No doubt the detestation of corrupt moral practices comes into this also, but who can fail to detect even there the peculiarly religious horror at the investment of these practices with the false values of a perverted relation to the living God? This does not prove that idolatry has always taken the same form essentially, but it creates an additional presumption in favour of that explanation which the detection of parallel cases elsewhere may strengthen.

Significant also is the common reaction of Christian converts to their former religion. In many cases they do not merely deplore it for its limitations or stupidity or for barbarous practices which it may have prompted or sanctioned, but detest it actively as the worship of idols—that is what was wrong most of all with their old religion—the worship of idols. It is doubtful whether such violence could be engendered did not the idolatry in question contain some element in common with the new religion, something which is now seen to be peculiarly abhorrent in its old perverted form, as a discord to the musician who might not be unduly worried by mere noise. Here also then we have a strong suggestion that idolatry and 'true religion' have the affinities suggested.

But we have also to remember how much religion requires certain rites and ceremonial practices of various kinds for its perpetuation. These are apt to acquire a momentum of their own, especially as they are the habits of societies and not, as a rule, of men in more individual capacities, societies in many cases moreover of a very conservative temper. It has often been remarked by historians and anthropologists that the reasons for many practices of primitive people, sometimes practices to which great importance is attached, are beyond recovery except in the form of wild conjecture, and not always that. One need not therefore be surprised if religious practices were also in many instances continued when the real motivation which made them properly significant has been lost. This would be peculiarly likely to happen where the interest and prestige of a privileged elite was involved. A priesthood has some vested interest in religious rites, and it is apt to become narrowly devoted to the institutions and customs it serves on their own account as part of a way of life and an attitude that have become habitual to them and are deeply rooted in the traditions of which they are bearers. To suppose that a priestly elite deliberately exploits its position, and even does this when its own belief is weak or lacking, is, in most cases, far too great a simplification, although we are not without evidence of cunning and naked deception of that kind. But there are many other subtler ways in which a body vested with certain responsibilities, such as usually falls to a priesthood, would be inclined to perpetuate religious practices when the true religious life has gone out of them.

I much doubt, however, whether this would in fact be a permanent state of affairs. For not only are there the normal occasions and promptings of religious experience already noted, but it is hard to believe that the life would die out altogether from the ceremonials which have become religiously enervated, or that it would not flicker again and revive from time to time. The rites would themselves have an initial appropriateness to their purpose and their perpetuation would carry with it associations which would live as part of the common culture of the community. The history of religion is not usually the history of an alternation of live and dead religion, but of religion glowing with various degrees of intensity. But the fact that the forms in which religious life is expressed, and by which it is cultivated, can be continued in a nexus of social custom when their true purport has been dimmed or lost, makes it easier to understand how there could be seemingly religious practices in the absence at least of the consciousness of the one transcendent God which, I have suggested, is the origin and motivation of religion and the main source of its life at all times.

A peculiarly sinister consequence of this perpetuation of empty forms is that, as the life of religion rarely dies out altogether but only flickers feebly, these forms readily yield themselves to the more radical inherently religious types of corruption I have also noted. As the life of religion returns these become inflamed into daemonic worship of a ritual, a creed or a book. Of this, most unhappily, we are not without some manifestations today. It is a sobering thought that our own adherence to a doctrine or our regard for the Bible may become themselves a vile form of idolatry. Few things have more horror in them than such distortions of Christianity, most of all when they unmask themselves in violent denunciation of morality and avail themselves of enlightenment to darken counsel.

Note was taken earlier also of another form of religious perversion, one not so insidious in itself or at the properly religious level, but fraught with grave consequences. When the consciousness of God is dim or absent there is created in human personality a vacuum which is apt to be filled by distortion of other interests developed beyond their proper place in human personality. To the extent that this has happened in the past, and especially where there has supervened upon this malformation the properly daemonic perversion of truly religious factors of experience also described, it can well be understood again that there would be initiated and perpetuated many ugly practices which we would never associate directly with religion as we know it, and of which the enlightened religious sense is the first and most fierce censor, but which nonetheless are not unrelated to religion understood in terms of the consciousness of the one God.

Finally, account must be taken of the context within which religious experience is formed. Religious experience does not happen in a vacuum. For while it is true, as I have stressed especially, that any object may prompt the consciousness of some absolute transcendent source of all things, this knowledge remains formal and bleak unless it is linked, as it almost invariably is in actual fact, with some divination of a special relation in which an individual stands at a special juncture in his own life to this Supreme Reality. The knowledge of the being of God is bound up for us with the transmutation of some particular experience, perhaps that in which the thought of God's existence comes vividly home to us, into a specific embodiment of God's relation to us. If this can be shown to be true of all religious experience, then one can also see how religion is conditioned by the social and cultural media in which it finds this embodiment. If the latter are crude and undeveloped, these crudities cannot but reflect themselves in the completer religious experience which is so organic to them. Crudities in religious life must, therefore, be largely ascribed to undiscriminating ethical or aesthetic reactions, to ignorant and erroneous beliefs about the world around us, and to the imperfections of the first attempts of men to understand their religion and formulate some kind of cosmological system. The problem of the existence of mistaken and inadequate notions of this kind, and of the distressing consequences to which they lead, does not directly concern us now. It is part of the general problem of evil and the gradual evolution of higher forms of life out of lower ones. But it can at least be seen that there is nothing peculiarly discreditable to religion itself in its suffering certain defects and limitations from its involvement in other human defects and limitations, once we find that the latter do not in themselves present insuperable obstacles to religion.

I think we shall find that many of the practices of unenlightened religion which would at first give us pause in maintaining that the God of the higher religions is present in the former too and making Himself known to men in the manner appropriate to their condition, are due to the conditions on which religious life supervenes, and only indirectly to religion itself. But we have also to remember that much which may seem superficial and unintelligible to us with a certain knowledge of the world and a special religious background may have much significance in another cultural context which it is not in our power to understand. Those who merely laughed at the 'superstitious' savage for bowing to his carven image or offering it food and sacrifice seem certainly to have failed to appreciate certain reasons which the savage himself had for doing this. It was not *qua* stone, *qua* merely natural object that the image, or whatever it may have been, elicited these attentions; and it is now widely agreed, in consequence especially of the studies of R. R. Marrett, that it is not as the habitation of some spirit that inanimate objects are reverenced and worshipped. It seems to me thus very likely that intimations of God's dealings with men came to man in early stages of human development, and still come to backward peoples, in ways whose considerable religious worth can not be gauged at all from superficial inspection of its outward forms and accompaniments. Thus, what we might describe as idolatry is not always false; nor is it inevitably corrupt, it may only be immature and incipient. This is why a Christian, for example, may find sympathetic responses in himself when he enters imaginatively into the atmosphere of certain pagan religions. Is not the reader of Pater's *Marius the Epicurean*, if he reads at all appreciatively, gently stirred into a genuine religious glow as he enters into the description of pagan ceremonies in the opening pages or later when presented with Christian practices which he would not adopt or find meaningful for himself today? This happens independently of one's own particular religious persuasion, because there is something deeper than the overt practices which animates these and has varying measures of affinity with the substance of our own religion.

But while we may regard paganism as, in some degree, an anticipation of the religion we consider to be true or an incipient form of it, we must not ignore its darker side, which is partly due to general limitations affecting the setting in which religion comes to birth and partly due to the various forms of corruption we have noted. The task of maintaining and developing true religion is thus two-fold, on the one hand to maintain the integrity of the specific religious factors in religious experience, and, on the other, to refine the material which is indispensable for it in such a way as to lead to better cultivation of the whole religious life. The history of religion must be approached on a similar basis. All these matters call for much amplification. But my purpose at the moment is to remove what may have seemed a grave objection to the suggestion that religion should always be regarded as involving some conscious relation to a transcendent reality. I have said nothing about high religions which do not come into the class of idolatrous worship with which I have been largely concerned. But I think it could be shown that religions like Buddhism or Confucianism which are sometimes said to be atheistic do in fact depend much on the consciousness of the One God of other religions, as they also exhibit much the same distortions of it in their history. This will, I believe, be much plainer and the confusions which surround controversies on such matters much dispelled, when we learn better how to think of God in human experience. I have no space to comment on allegedly humanist religions, and must be content with noting that humanism as a religion seems to be largely the invention of intellectuals and has rarely thrived as a religion proper. To the extent that it has thrived, as 'ethical religion' for example, it has been largely parasitic on other religions, borrowing from them emotional attitudes and habits which it could not properly generate itself and which soon reveal their hollowness and irrelevance in this artificial setting. This is also largely true of the panthea of gods of some of the civilizations of antiquity. When they ceased to be living symbols of a genuine reality, they lived on in men's minds and practices through some social significance which they retained or on account of their place in literature and art. Here also, then, I suggest that the deities in question took their place in a living religion because the worship of them in some way referred beyond itself, not perhaps in ways fully appreciated by their votaries, to a more mysterious and absolute reality which found symbolical expression in them. These are not, however, topics that I can pursue further now, and, in concluding, I must add that, even if I am wrong in suggesting that the practices which we generally describe as religious do involve a reference to the same transcendent object of worship as is claimed for 'true religion', and if I had for this reason to abandon the recommendation to reserve the word 'religion' for worship of that kind, one problem would still remain paramount, namely, granted that, in some religions at least, there is a conscious relation to a transcendent reality, how does this come about and what can we say about the specific experiences in which it happens? This seems to me to be the crucial problem for religious thought; and in the growing and inevitable sophistication of contemporary culture our success in dealing with this problem will have more to do than we usually realize with the actual maintenance of religion.

MAIN PUBLICATIONS

Morals and the New Theology. Gollancz. 1947.
Morals and Revelation. Allen and Unwin. 1950.
Gwybod am Dduw. University of Wales Press Board. 1952.
Editor. Muirhead Library of Philosophy. Allen and Unwin.

FREEWILL AND PUNISHMENT

By J. D. MABBOTT

*Fellow and Tutor of St. John's College,
Oxford*

FREEWILL AND PUNISHMENT

'To understand punishment is to understand responsibility' (Bradley)

I. *Introduction*

THE present state of philosophical thought on these two subjects is, and has been for over fifty years, thoroughly deterministic. The only exceptions known to me are the views of N. Hartmann, C. A. Campbell, and H. D. Lewis. In the theory of punishment, retribution has been defended by no philosopher of note except Bradley. Reform and deterrence are the theories accepted in principle and increasingly influential in practice. On freewill the most thorough recent analysis, that of Professor Broad, is typical.[1] His characteristically patient and acute argument leads him to two conclusions. It is an illusion to believe that on any occasion I could have acted otherwise than I did (everything in the state of the universe immediately before my action being the same). It follows that it is equally an illusion to believe that I ought to have acted otherwise than I did, except in the sense that if I had been a better man I would necessarily have done better than I did.

The older debates tended to assume that, while reason and science pointed to determinism, moral obligation required indeterminism. This latter connection is confirmed by Broad's linking of his two conclusions noted above. Recent discussions have, however, rejected and indeed reversed this connection. They have argued that responsibility requires determinism, and they have linked this argument with deterministic theories of

[1] *Determinism, Indeterminism, and Libertarianism* (1934). Reprinted in *Ethics and the History of Philosophy* (1952), pp. 195 ff.

punishment. It is with these recent tendencies that this paper will be mainly concerned.

II. *Freewill and Science*

First, however, I shall refer briefly to the older type of determinism resting on science. Science works on the assumption that all observable events are subject to causal law. It is inconceivable that one set of events on a minor planet, the actions of men, should escape this network of causal determination.

But this argument has been greatly weakened by changes in the conception of what science and causality are. There is now little talk in science of irresistible forces or indeed of any forces at all. Science reveals no compulsions and establishes no necessities. All that is observed is regular conjunction. Scientific laws are only probable, and the measurements on which they rest are only approximate. No scientist would now claim that, given sufficient evidence, he could in principle predict with exactness and certainty the behaviour of any physical object. Thus the head-on collision between science and freewill is avoided.

But there are further special reasons which make even the cautious type of prediction characteristic of modern science inapplicable to human conduct. There are three features of scientific method which are essential for any approximation to accurate prediction. The first is measurement. When a scientific law is used to predict the behaviour of a particular object, the special features of the object are represented as quantitative values of the variables in the law. But many of the psychological factors involved in the empirical study of human conduct are not measurable. States such as pain or grief, motives such as hope and fear, the 'instincts' of the older textbooks such as sex and self-assertion, the complexes and censors of their more recent successors—none of these can be given numerical values.

The other two features of scientific method which render it inapplicable in its full rigour to human conduct are analysis and generalization. By 'analysis' I mean the assumption that, for any specific piece of explanation, some features of the object are irrelevant (chemical constitution when gravity is being studied, mass when spectroscopic behaviour is under examination). The irrelevant features are assumed to make no difference to the operation of the features the special enquiry concerns. There are good grounds for holding that the elements of a human personality are not related in this way. The aspects of a man's character, his desires, etc., are so interconnected that none of them would be what it is without the others. Those who write testimonials know this problem, especially if they are asked by government departments or American employers to describe their subject under, say, twenty-nine headings: intelligence, imagination, orderliness of mind, industry, conscientiousness, reliability, social tact, savoir faire, sense of humour, etc. The writer is baffled. He wants to say everything under each heading. What would the man's intelligence be without his imagination, his industry without his conscientiousness, his social tact without his sense of humour and so on? The human personality defies such dissection.

The third essential feature of scientific prediction is generalization, the assumption that the behaviour of some members of a species is good evidence for the behaviour of others. But human personalities are unique. Again in writing a testimonial, one feels that all these general words—lively, alert, solid, sensible—miss the essential flavour of the man; and the better one knows him the more abjectly they fail.

These arguments have been frequently urged before,[1] and there is no need to expand them here. I shall illustrate them by showing how two authorities in special fields have held that the uniqueness of human personality makes scientific method misleading. T. E. Lawrence had studied the 'science of war' in

[1] Cf. H. Bergson, *Les Données Immédiates de la Conscience*, chaps. ii, iii (English trans., *Time and Freewill*, especially pp. 89, 159-69). F. H. Bradley, *Ethical Studies*, chap. i, especially (2nd edn.), pp. 19-26, 34-40. L. J. Russell, 'Ought Implies Can', *Proceedings of the Aristotelian Society*, vol. xxxvi (1935-36), pp. 157-62.

Clausewitz and Foch, but found its conclusions unsatisfactory in practice. 'A line of variability, Man, persisted like a leaven through its estimates making them irregular. The components were sensitive and illogical. . . . Nine-tenths of tactics were certain enough to be teachable in schools, but the irrational tenth was like the kingfisher flashing across the pool, and in it lay the test of generals.'[1] A. E. Housman had seen the 'science of textual criticism' in its German professors and found it also inadequate in practice. 'Textual criticism is not a branch of mathematics nor indeed an exact science at all. It deals with a matter not rigid and constant like lines and numbers, but fluid and variable; namely, the frailties and aberrations of the human mind and of its insubordinate servants, the human fingers. It therefore is not susceptible of hard-and-fast rules. It would be much easier if it were; and that is why people try to pretend that it is, or at least behave as if they thought so. Of course you can have hard-and-fast rules if you like, but then you will have false rules and they will lead you wrong, because their simplicity is inapplicable to problems which are not simple but complicated by the play of personality.'[2]

III. *Self-determinism*

Some recent arguments maintain that moral responsibility requires not freedom (as usually supposed) but determinism; a determinism relying not on impersonal laws or scientific analysis, but on a necessary causal connection between the action and the self whose action it is. Bradley was the first to make a powerful case for this view.[3] If it is possible for my self to do alternative actions then which action it does must have no connection with my self but be a matter of chance. A man does not mind his action being predicted from knowledge of his character. When those who know him well say 'We knew you

---

[1] *Seven Pillars of Wisdom*, 1940 edn., pp. 198-9.
[2] 'Textual Criticism', *Proceedings of the Classical Association*, 1921, p. 68.
[3] *Ethical Studies*, pp. 12-16, 52-4.

would never do that', when they call him 'reliable' and 'trust-worthy', these predictions do not offend him or seem to him to menace his freedom. This argument is weak in two ways. It is true that we do not mind such predictions, but that is because they predict our good deeds. It is praise and not prediction which we welcome. If anyone said 'I knew you well enough to be sure you would let us down' or 'Knowing you as I do, I told the others you were certain to be late' we should not be so satisfied. The second weakness is exposed by Bradley himself. In Note B,[1] he points out that prediction from character is reliable only so far as character does not alter. But character is alterable and alterable by a man's own acts. Is he responsible for these acts? Bradley gives no answer and moves on to another difficulty in prediction from character. Character is the system of formed and relatively permanent dispositions. But there are elements in my self which are not part of my character because not so systematized, e.g. desires which I have never experienced before. Is an act springing from such a desire voluntary and free? Bradley seems to admit that it is. 'The volition results not merely from the habituated or principled self, but from that plus a new force; and, if the volition were a "resultant" only, the result *must* be different. As it is, all we can say is that it *may* be.'[2] Given the habituated self and the new force (i.e. given *all* the factors) the action is still not necessitated. But this is surely to accept indeterminism not self-determinism.

Another set of arguments to show that self-determinism is implied by moral responsibility is that put forward by R. E. Hobart.[3] The indeterminist maintains that praise and blame are impossible unless the subject could have done otherwise than he did. Hobart reverses this position. For, he says, we do not praise and blame actions we praise and blame *people* for their actions. 'What a brave man!' 'That was the act of a coward.' The act is taken to arise necessarily from the self. 'By their fruits shall ye know them.' Similarly with remorse. Remorse does not require

[1]Op. cit. pp. 50 ff.   [2]Op. cit. p. 54 (italics original).
[3]'Freewill as involving Determinism', *Mind*, vol. xliii (1934), pp. 1 ff.

that I could have done otherwise; quite the contrary. For remorse is self-reproach. I say 'How selfish I was, how thoughtless,
how unkind'.

It is true that all these ways of talking are normal usage.
They all imply that we praise or blame the self for its acts.
But the weakness lies in the question of time. A quotation from
Sidgwick will illustrate this point. 'Is my voluntary act at any
moment completely determined by (1) my character as it has
been partly inherited, partly formed by my past actions and
feelings and (2) my circumstances at the moment? or not? Could
the volition I am just about to originate be certainly calculated
by anyone who knew my character at this moment and the forces
acting upon me?'[1] At first glance these two questions seem to be
the same. But, in the first, the words 'at any moment' and 'at the
moment' clearly refer to the same moment; while in the second
sentence the action I am 'just about to originate' is the effect
of my character 'at this moment'. The questions are quite different. Is it my self as it is now or my self as it was immediately
before the action which is to be regarded as its cause? It is clear
that the first alternative is that required by Hobart's argument
about praise and blame. When I praise a man for a brave deed,
I am not saying 'What a brave man you were just before you
did that!' But the relation between a man's self *now* and his act
now is not a causal relation. The courage, loyalty, etc., which we
commend are dispositions and the relation between a disposition
and its actualizations is not causal. Moreover, we cannot limit
the reference to the self to dispositions. As Bradley admitted, a
man may act on a new desire or in such a way as to alter his
character. To cover all these cases we must reformulate our
question. 'Given the state of myself as it is now and the circumstances as they are now, are two alternative actions possible
now?' The answer is clearly 'No'; for my act now *is* the state of
myself as it is now. If anyone asks me 'What are you doing now?'
I reply 'Thinking about freewill'. If he asks instead 'What is the
state of your self now?' I shall reply, 'I am thinking about
freewill'. The relation between the self and its acts is like the

[1] *The Methods of Ethics*, p. 46.

relation between a body and its shape. The question 'could a body be in exactly the state in which it is now and not have the shape it has now?' must be answered in the negative; but a body is not the cause of its shape. Hobart should have seen this when he wrote 'Can I try to turn on the light *at the very moment when* I am not trying to do so?' and says this would be a contradiction in terms.[1] But later he changes the time reference and says 'The one essential fact is that the nature should *precede* the act'.[2] The fallacy here is the fallacy Locke committed, that of thinking of substance as something lurking behind its attributes and causing them to exist. I conclude that the argument so persuasively put by Hobart for determinism as required by praise and blame breaks down.

IV. *Determinism, Blame, and Punishment*

The most interesting recent development in the freewill controversy has been the presentation of a view originally put forward by Schlick and fully worked out by P. H. Nowell-Smith[3] and F. Ebersole.[4] This view maintains that punishment and blame cannot be justified on retributive grounds. They are awarded in order to influence future action. A man should not be punished or blamed unless he could have acted otherwise. The problem of finding a criterion for responsibility is answered by saying that those acts are free which can be brought about or inhibited by punishment. A schoolboy is not punished for stupidity because punishing him will not make him less stupid. He is punished for laziness because punishment will make him less idle. To say that idleness is a moral failing and one which the boy 'could help' is just to say that it is amenable

---

[1]Op. cit. p. 21 (my italics).   [2]Op. cit. p. 21 (my italics).

[3]'Freewill and Moral Responsibility', *Mind*, vol. lvii (January 1948). 'Ethics' (Pelican Edition), chaps. 19, 20. 'Determinists and Libertarians', *Mind*, vol. lxiii (July 1954). (Referred to below as FMR, E, and DL respectively.)

[4]'Free Choice and the Demands of Morals'. *Mind*, vol. lxi (April 1952). (Referred to below as FDM.) Italics in quotations from all the above sources are mine throughout.

to punishment. Thus we do not have to establish independently that a criminal was responsible, or that a boy could help doing what he did, in order to justify punishment or blame. 'If it is true that praise and blame are means employed to bring about good events and prevent bad ones, they are appropriate not to all good and bad events but only to those they can in fact bring about or prevent. Since a moral action is one that can fittingly be praised or blamed, it follows that a moral action is one that can be brought about or prevented by these means.'[1] Moral traits 'can be strengthened or weakened by fear of punishment or of an adverse verdict. And when we remember that the purpose of moral verdicts and of punishment is to strengthen or weaken certain traits of character, it is not difficult to see that this feature so far from being synthetically connected with the notion of a moral characteristic, a virtue or a vice, is just what constitutes it . . . moral character is just that set of dispositions which can be moulded by these means.'[2]

The first problem in this view concerns the effects of punishment and blame. Sometimes Nowell-Smith says that an act is free and the agent is responsible for it only if the act can be *prevented* by punishment. (Cf. quotation above. Or again, moral characteristics are 'those which can be strengthened or *inhibited* by praise and blame'.[3] 'Rewards and punishments are means of varying the causal antecedents of actions so that those we desire will occur and those we wish to *prevent will not occur*.'[4] And 'prevent' must mean prevent from recurring at any future time.) Now obviously this goes too far and at other times Nowell-Smith has a milder view.[5] 'Fear of punishment will *affect* the future behaviour of the thief . . . there will be a motive *tending* to make him refrain'.[5] 'The point of blame is to strengthen some motives and *weaken* others'.[6] Here blame or punishment is justified if its infliction makes it *less likely* that the wrong act will be done. But now the criterion ceases to acquit the kleptomaniac, for kleptomaniacs do not steal when they see a policeman or shop assistant watching them and do take ingenious steps to

---

[1]FMR, p. 55. [2]E, pp. 303-4. [3]FMR, p. 36.
[4]FMR, p. 59. [5]FMR, p. 60. [6]E, p. 296.

avoid detection. Their behaviour therefore is 'affected' by fear of punishment. The reason for regarding them as irresponsible is not that this fear has no effect but that they show independent signs of motiveless irrationality. They steal vast numbers of silk stockings or suspenders, which they then proceed to hoard and not to resell.

Ebersole, unlike Nowell-Smith, sticks firmly to the view that punishment is justified only if it *prevents* crime. 'We must be able to know that condemnation *will reform*. It must fulfil its intention to *prevent* repetition of the wrong for which the person is punished.'[1] But he goes on to say 'In the strong sense of "justification" which I have been using, punishment is never justified. We are forced to take action on the best knowledge available; attempted reform more often than not does not come off.'[2] But surely a 'justification' which never justifies any actual punishment cannot be worth discussing.

(It is a weakness both of Nowell-Smith and of Ebersole that they call the effect of punishment 'reform' or 'change of character'. But a man who abstains from crime from fear of punishment is not reformed. Punishment may deter but does not reform.)

The view under examination holds that a trait is moral if it is inducible by punishment, whereas non-moral traits are not so inducible. My ability to write legibly is not a moral trait, yet it was certainly induced by punishment. My technique of scale-playing is not a moral characteristic, yet it owes what effectiveness it has to the knuckle-rappings and apple-withholdings practised by my music-master.

A further difficulty is that, as my quotations have shown, it is sometimes punishment or reward which are said to dissuade or prevent a man from acting wrongly. At other times and more accurately it is fear of punishment and hope of reward. 'The addict or compulsive will respond neither to *threats* nor to encouragement.'[3] Thus the analytic link, if there is one, is between responsibility and threats or fears, not between responsibility and punishment or blame. There is also here an

[1]FDM, p. 256.   [2]FDM, p. 257.   [3]E, p. 306.

unnoticed asymmetry. A reward system working perfectly requires actual rewards, but a punishment system (that is, a threat system) working perfectly (i.e. when the threats succeed) requires no actual punishments.

Moreover, the act which is affected by blame or punishment is not the act *for which* the blame or punishment is awarded, since the one follows and the other precedes the award. This is not always clear in Nowell-Smith. (Cf. quotation above, 'Since a moral action is one that can fittingly be praised or blamed, it follows that a moral action is one that can be brought about or prevented by these means'.) Ebersole is clear on this. We tend to think that blame or punishment is justified by the past sin or crime committed. But 'our only justifiable concern is with the person as he has been made by the result of his wrong choice. Our concern with his former self is justifiable only because without enquiring what he was like before the condemned action we do not have any way of knowing what he is like after the condemned action.'[1] The only relevance of the act 'for which' (as we inaccurately say) he is punished is *evidential*; it shows us what sort of a man we have to deal with and we can deal with him accordingly. Ebersole says, wrongly, that previous commission of the wrong is the only evidence we can have. But we sometimes know that a man was stopped from committing a crime by external circumstances; and in that case Ebersole would have to say that punishment was equally in order. He admits this in an extreme and imaginary example. 'If we possessed a sensitive brain-wave machine which would predict whether a person would commit a crime and what sort of censure or punishment would prevent it, then we would have no need to be concerned with a person's past.'[2] This is surely the *reductio ad absurdum* of the view we are examining, as it is of all reform theories of punishment when consistently carried through. It is impossible to justify punishing or blaming people who have done no wrong.

It might be said that this is a verbal criticism. We do not *call* reformatory treatment 'punishment' or 'blame' unless there is

[1] FDM, p. 252.   [2] FDM, p. 255.

a past act which is our 'evidence' that our victim needs reform. But the justification of the treatment is the same whether there is a past act or not. But this is obviously not the case. As we shall see, serious questions of status arise when we ask who has a right to blame or punish. These questions are quite different and much more difficult when a man has done no wrong, and we ask who has the right to reform him.

Moreover, if it is admitted that it is fear of punishment and not punishment itself which deters or 'reforms' the bad man, there is no reason why other fears may not do this too. Fear of physical consequences have kept men chaste and fear of unpopularity have kept them honest. There seems no reason to limit 'moral' and 'responsible' to those traits and actions which one type of fear can affect.

Ebersole regards a particular infliction of punishment as justified solely by its effect on the person punished; and in his earlier article Nowell-Smith appeared to share this view, though this may have been because his example of punishment was that of punishing a schoolboy for idleness. Punishment, however, is mainly a legal question. Even here it is often held that a punishment is justified only if it reforms the criminal and deters him and others. But this is completely mistaken, as I have argued at length elsewhere.[1] Men can be deterred by the punishment of an innocent scapegoat and punishment itself never reforms a criminal. The effect of punishment on the criminal is wholly irrelevant to its justification (though measures additional to the punishment—publicity and prison chaplains—are properly employed to achieve these extraneous ends). The justification of punishment is that a law has been broken; the justification of law is quite another matter. The legislator may be utilitarian, the judge may not. In *Ethics* Nowell-Smith fully accepts this view.[2] Punishment is justified by reference to law. Laws and the legal system are justified on utilitarian grounds. But this breaks the neat logic of the connections responsibility-wrong-punishment.

[1]'Punishment', *Mind*, vol. xlviii (April, 1939).
[2]E, pp. 271-2.

A final criticism may be added. This line of argument depends on connecting 'ought' and 'moral' with blame and punishment. But what of acts which are immoral and yet ought not to be punished? Punishing requires a status. No one has a duty or even a right to punish me for any immoral act as such. I must first break a law, and then the punisher must be an authority responsible for the law or to the society whose law it is. Blaming people too—that is, expressing adverse verdicts on them—requires a status. Nowell-Smith says 'If a man deserves blame, someone would be justified in blaming him. Not necessarily you; for you may be in no position to cast the first stone or indeed any stone at all.'[1] I should say 'not necessarily anyone'— and indeed the scripture Nowell-Smith quotes carries this conclusion. 'Let him that is without sin among you. . . .' Blame is here shown to require moral superiority; if not that (and especially if its aim is reform) it seems to require some special relationship of authority (parental, pedagogic, tutorial).

There are acts then which are immoral and responsible, yet for which neither blame nor punishment is justified. Here it may be replied that 'he was responsible' means that blame or punishment would have deterred him, had they been justified, which they were not. 'A free action', says Nowell-Smith, 'is not an uncaused action but one caused by characteristics that *can be* strengthened or inhibited by praise and blame'.[2] Not that they ought to be. But this is another serious weakening of the whole nexus ought-moral-free-blame-punishment on which the theory depends.

A similar point comes out in Ebersole. His four 'judgements'—(*a*) Jones ought not to have done that, (*b*) Jones is to blame, (*c*) Jones is responsible, (*d*) Jones ought to be punished— are confused by him with actual verdicts passed on sinners by their judges or moral tutors. If I say *to Jones* 'You acted wrongly; you are much to blame; you were responsible', I may well be attempting to affect his future action (as well as passing judgement on his past). But if I say '*Jones* did wrong; he was to blame'; etc., it is unplausible to hold that these judgements are aimed at reforming Jones. Ebersole sees the difficulty and replies 'In order to be effective such judgements need not be directed to the wrongdoer. They may be spoken to others; even so they are justified because they influence the guilty person indirectly by surrounding him with a "social atmosphere" such that he and others are less likely to commit the condemned crime.'[1] But obviously this solution will not explain condemnations of Nero or of Mr. McCarthy—that is, any judgement which is incapable of influencing the subject about whom it is made. Since 'ought' and 'moral' and 'responsible' must surely have the same meaning irrespectively of the time or space references in the sentences containing them, it seems impossible to regard their use as reformative, since the number of people whom we can reform by using them is minute compared with the number of those we cannot.

For all these reasons I am not satisfied by this latest attempt to connect determinism with responsibility. I remain convinced that moral responsibility requires that a man should be able to choose alternative actions, everything in the universe prior to the act, including his self, being the same. Nowell-Smith adopts as his analysis of 'he could have done otherwise' that he would necessarily have done otherwise if he had been a different man and this difference could have been brought about by punishment or blame. 'When we say A could have done the sum correctly had he so chosen, we do not imply that he could on that occasion have so chosen. But we do imply that A is such that, under certain circumstances, he will choose to act correctly; and that these circumstances can be brought about.'[2] It seems clear to me that we do not mean this when we say 'A could have got the sum right'. When Nowell-Smith says 'these circumstances *can* be brought about' (i.e. by punishment or blame) the same analysis of 'can' must apply, namely that my rulers or teachers or parents would have punished me if *they* had been adequately punished. The regress is unavoidable.

I do not see how anything clearer can be said than that we seriously mean 'he could have done otherwise' categorically.

[1]FDM, p. 251.   [2]FMR, p. 59.

If analysis fails to do justice to this, so much the worse for analysis. If we are asked for criteria of responsibility, we have to do as the lawyers do. Here is our conception of freedom. It is 'defeasible'—that is, we can accept certain evidence as evidence that it is absent but there can be no evidence that it is present in a given case. For this reason too the defence of freewill must always be (as this chapter has been so far) an attempt to refute deterministic arguments rather than a positive argument itself.

V. *Indeterminism and Punishment*

Recent discussions have made it clear that indeterminism presents great logical difficulties. If our analysis of 'free' involves a categorical 'could' and not merely a hypothetical 'would if', we should expect that instances of freedom should be directly observed. Yet I agree entirely with Nowell-Smith's rejection of Professor C. A. Campbell's view that we are directly aware in certain cases that our choice is undetermined. I agree with him also in rejecting Campbell's restriction of freewill to cases of moral effort and his consequent treatment of non-moral decisions as mechanistically determined. The most effective answers to the difficulties of indeterminism are in my view those given by N. Hartmann in his *Ethics* (vol. iii). There cannot be a criterion of free action, for a criterion would inevitably be deterministic. The evidence for freedom lies not in a direct awareness of instances of it but in its link with moral responsibility. But this does not mean that only moral or immoral actions are free. It means that, if there were no moral choices, it would be an open question whether other choices are free or not. Moral responsibility is not an illusion; it is unintelligible how such an illusion could arise. Hate and fear might cause us to blame others without justification but not to blame ourselves. There can be no biological utility in the load of guilt which men carry.

I shall not expand these points further, but try to show what difference indeterminism makes to our views on punishment. Punishment, on the Nowell-Smith and Ebersole view, is a determining cause in a psychologically determined situation. Men must do what their natures prompt, and punishment alters their natures. It is often thought that this view of punishment, the reform theory, is modern and humane compared with the retributive theory, which is primitive and barbaric. But the essential point about retributive punishment is that it treats the criminal as a man. A law is not, as the determinists would hold, a particular kind of cause (on a level with a drug or hypnosis or psychiatric treatment). It is not a cause at all, because it presents a choice and assumes freedom and responsibility. Retribution is the agent's own act. The law can *threaten;* but there is only one thing that can justify a punishment and that is something the legislator cannot bring about, namely, a free choice by the subject. Hegel put this clearly. 'By being punished the criminal is honoured as a rational being . . . his punishment is derived from his own act.'[1] To be punished for reform reasons is to be treated like a dog. A sane adult demands to be held responsible for his actions. He rejects as an intolerable insult the well-meaning exculpations of the sympathetic scientist, whether presented on social or psychological grounds. Retributive punishment closes the account, reformative punishment opens it. The points I have been making are well illustrated by Christopher Isherwood's description of the Garcia Moreno prison in Ecuador.

A U.S. or British prison-inspector would condemn the Garcia Moreno from the ground up. No doubt the food is poor, the accommodation inadequate and the sanitation primitive. No doubt the official approach to the problems of criminal psychology and social rehabilitation is hopelessly unscientific. And yet, strangely enough, I didn't feel nearly so ashamed and depressed as I usually do in such institutions. It sounds sentimental and reactionary to write this, but I keep remembering the look on those men's faces. Nobody had tried even with the best intentions to understand them. Nobody had studied them. Nobody had made them feel, however tactfully, that they were misfits or types or cases. Nobody had even told them that their crimes were the expression of certain social conditions, bad economic environment. . . . Each of those prisoners had killed one or more human beings. Perhaps

[1] *Philosophy of Right,* § 100, trans. T. M. Knox, p. 71.

some were sorry, perhaps some weren't. But all of them looked like intact individuals, not criminals, not humiliated. . . . Certainly the Garcia Moreno is pretty bad. But I am afraid there are many cleaner, kinder, infinitely more terrible places in which men are forced to spend a quarter of their lives.[1]

VI. *Philosophy as Linguistic Analysis*

I hesitated to accept the editor's invitation to contribute this chapter to *Contemporary British Philosophy*. For I am well aware how far from contemporary the line I have followed will appear. Philosophy nowadays claims to be concerned wholly with the analysis of language. But almost everywhere the analysis has resulted not in an account of how words are used, but in legislation about how they ought to be used—legislation which contravenes the normal usage. Moreover, since this legislation cannot be linguistically justified, it is justified by reference to the facts or the experiences described, and commits the legislator to one theory about these facts rather than another. In 1939 I wrote about punishment partly because I found it a good test case for the controversy then appearing between utilitarian and deontological theories of ethics. I have written about it again on the present occasion because I find it once more a test case for the whole procedure and method of philosophy.

How do the recent theories of punishment and responsibility which I have been criticizing, stand as analyses of language? Nowell-Smith maintains that his account of responsibility exhibits what the ordinary man means by 'could have done otherwise'. Both he and Ebersole, however, admit that there are retributive elements in the ordinary use of 'punishment', which their theories do not fit; though they both think these elements are dying, and Nowell-Smith tries to explain them as survivals from a primitive theology. Ebersole, however, goes much further in his admissions. He allows that the accounts he gives of 'ought' and 'moral' and 'free' involve a complete break with ordinary usage. But if so these arguments cannot be an analysis of language.

[1]*The Condor and the Cows*, p. 77.

There are many other instances of this difficulty, which I may briefly mention. The basic positivist principle was that the meaning of a proposition was the method of its verification and that any proposition not verifiable (or probabilifiable) by sense-experience was meaningless. It was early objected that this principle must itself be meaningless since it is not verifiable by sense-experience. The positivists then retreated to the view that their principle was not a proposition at all, and was therefore neither true nor false; it was a rule exhibiting the use of the word 'meaning'. But it is obvious that this 'rule' recommends a use of 'meaning' which no one not a positivist has ever followed. In the theory of perception analytical philosophy has usually accepted phenomenalism, or anyhow rejected a 'continuant' or 'substance' theory of physical objects. The theory it rejects is the one enshrined in the usage of ordinary language. In moral (and aesthetic) theory, analysis accepts subjectivism in one form or another. Again this is to take sides in a dispute between rival theories; and the side it rejects is that which expresses the ordinary usage of words like 'good' and 'right'. Subjectivism may be a defensible theory of morals, but it cannot claim to be an analysis of linguistic usage. Analysis gives a behaviouristic account of the feelings of other people. To say a man is feeling pain is to say that he is wincing or shrinking or crying aloud. And then two alternative analyses (both equally unconvincing) are open for 'I feel pain'. On the first, 'I feel pain' will be explained behaviouristically too (as by the James-Lange theory) to mean merely that I am frowning, wincing, shrinking, etc. There may be reasons for accepting behaviourism, but it is absurd to maintain that it is an analysis of the normal usage of 'feel pain'; and the 'reasons' cannot therefore draw on language for their support. The alternative account of 'I feel pain' would be to admit this is an introspective report of a private feeling. But this would involve that 'feel pain' has a different meaning when used by me or about me by somebody else. And again language would give no support to this difference.

All these examples show the common pattern I described above. The analysts claim to be giving rules of linguistic usage. They adopt, in each case, one of the two rival meta-physical theories which disputed each field between them before linguistic philosophy was heard of. In each case the theory they adopt is the opposite of the one which in fact the rules of language embody. It is then clear that they are legislating for a reform in language and laying down rules which no non-philosopher would accept as the rules in accordance with which he uses the word 'meaning' or 'free' or 'right' or 'thing' or 'pain'. The reasons they have for this cannot be linguistic; and they are in fact mainly the old-fashioned reasons for determinism, phenomenalism, subjectivism, or behaviourism, along with the empiricist bias of their analytic method towards accepting science as their model both in method and result. What is happening is a return to metaphysics. Much useful clarification of minor issues has certainly been achieved by linguistic analysis; and a major achievement of the linguistic approach is its recognition of the 'open texture' of ordinary language. But the belief that the linguistic approach can dissolve the major age-long philosophical controversies (such as those noted above) seems to break down at every turn.

I have suggested that it is mistaken to regard behaviourism, subjectivism, phenomenalism, determinism as analyses of linguistic usage. But the rules of linguistic usage may well so change as to make these theories coincide with usage. In the case of behaviourism this is clearly impossible, unless and until human beings cease to feel pain; and, when pins are stuck into them, twitch and squeak and grimace in a reflex way. It is unlikely that the ordinary man's language will ever become phenomenalist, because of the practical direction of his interest. In aesthetics, however, the situation seems to me to be fluid. Some ordinary men do use 'beautiful' in accordance with subjectivist rules which make it equivalent to 'I enjoy and approve'. For example, they expect and are not at all worried by divergence and changes of taste. They do not condemn other people whose taste differs from theirs as poseurs or perverted or blind. The reasons which have brought about this change include some of those which have made philosophers

subjectivists (variations of taste, the absence of any formal verification procedure when tastes differ, the discovery that those
who differ from them are sincere and consistent and, in other
ways, adult and intelligent people). They do not include the
logical reasons which in addition have influenced philosophers
(the rejection of *a priori* synthetic propositions, the equation of
verification with sense-experience, the identification of thought
with natural science). It is unlikely that subjectivism will
advance as rapidly in moral as in aesthetic language. For it is
possible to live with a man whose aesthetic tastes differ from
our own but not if his moral standards differ. Morality has to
be sustained by conviction and conviction is a great objectifier.
(Even in aesthetics a committed life has this effect. I doubt
whether any practising artist or critic will ever use aesthetic
words according to subjectivist rules. It is the outsider, who
'knows what he likes', who tends to be subjectivist.)

How do matters stand with regard to blame and punishment?
I have argued that usage is here indeterminist and retributivist.
A change of usage would not be merely linguistic; it would not
represent a triumph of philosophers in persuading men to use
language in a way more fitted to the unchanging facts. If
language changed it would be because the facts changed; since
the facts in question are men's actions and attitudes. If the
deterministic and reform language were adopted, it would be
because men no longer felt guilt and remorse, but only regret
for past sins—or rather for past mistakes. Men would no longer
blame but pity the wrongdoer. They would say 'to know all is
to pardon all' and they would pardon all; or rather pardon like
forgiveness would disappear (as I do not even pardon or forgive
a man for what he does under drugs or hypnosis).

I admitted that, in regard to punishment, reform and deterrence views hold the field in theory and are increasingly
dominant in practice. Does not the latter admission mean that
the rules for the use of punishment have changed? There are
tendencies in this direction, and in some circles (those most
influenced by psychiatry) they have gone far. It is also true that
among those concerned with actual punishment (magistrates,

21

police, the Home Office) the treatment of juvenile offenders has changed its character and now tends to follow a straightforward utilitarian pattern. But the word 'punishment' when applied to children (compare 'chastisement') has always tended to follow special rules. There are, however, few traces of a general change in the ordinary man's attitude to the punishment of sane adults or in the procedure of the courts in normal adult cases. The ordinary man regards psychiatrists with deep suspicion. After any brutal murder or assault one hears on all hands 'Now I suppose they'll say he was mad and couldn't help it, poor thing'. The courts assume responsibility unless the defence can prove the presence of disease. They do not, like some psychologists, regard the commission of a crime as itself adequate evidence of disease and consequently of the need for treatment.

What would happen if this change occurred? If throughout our courts and in our common language determinism and its allied theories of punishment prevailed? My quotation from Isherwood indicates what this would mean in our attitude to criminals and in its effect on criminals themselves. What is more menacing and often forgotten is that it would result in a tyranny which would be as dehumanizing for the rulers as for their victims. These things begin with scientific treatment of the criminal classes. But the question 'who is a criminal?' is itself determined by government; and the belief that men can be cured of anti-social tendencies by punishment leads irresistibly towards 'Brave New World' and '1984'. What is shocking to most people about these Utopias (and about the confession, stage-trial, and brainwashing techniques which are their actual counterparts) is not the cruelty (for there need be none), nor the falsity of the creeds thus imposed, but the degradation and violation of human personality. What is often forgotten and is still more shocking is that, towering over these ordinary citizens, who are no longer men but material-for-moulding, are other men—'Big Brothers'—men who have usurped the throne of God. Again what is fundamental is not that they are sadists or power maniacs, nor that their creeds are superstition and their economics rotten; it is that they have adopted as human beings a role which their own treatment of human beings makes monstrous. They have put themselves beyond the pale of society, for society has become their clay and their creation. That is why the fall of a régime like Hitler's, or in a lesser degree of an individual like Beria, has the marks of a nemesis without parallel in history. The Greek tyrant never pretended to possess men's souls; the Roman emperor said 'Let them hate provided that they fear'. The modern master of men would remove the chance of hate and the need of fear. At the moment at which our punishment language becomes determinist in its rules, we shall have set our feet on a path which degrades our criminals to a sub-human level, as those horror Utopias degraded all their citizens, and which will promote our rulers to a superhuman level which would reduce to a pale shadow the Divine Right of Kings.

MAIN PUBLICATIONS

The State and the Citizen. Hutchinson's University Library. 1948.
Moral Rules. Annual Philosophical Lecture to the British Academy. 1953. Oxford University Press.

ETHICAL INTUITION

By DONALD M. MACKINNON

Regius Professor of Moral Philosophy
in the University of Aberdeen

ETHICAL INTUITION

THE arguments against intuitionism in ethics are well-known, and the matter might be thought closed. Yet philosophical doctrines sometimes take a very long time to die even when they are formally pronounced extinct; indeed it has been truly remarked by some that this obstinacy is a very important fact about their peculiar character. If they could more easily be put to sleep, that would be because they were not expressions of philosophical perplexity and insight, but, for instance, scientific hypotheses. In this essay I want briefly to review some of the traditional arguments for intuitionism in some of its different forms, and then to indicate the arguments which have been offered against them; from there I shall pass to what I am really concerned to do, namely, to discuss the controversy between the intuitionists and their critics. I say controversy in the singular; but it will appear that as a matter of fact there are several issues at stake, even though, in my view, one of these is central.

As I understand his position, the philosophical intuitionist is concerned to argue, in some way, for the view that fundamental principles of morality or of value are self-evident and irreducible. To say that they are self-evident is, of course, to say something of the way in which we claim to know them, or in which it is said that if we reflect, we will find that we do know them. To say that the principles are irreducible, however, is to say something about the relation of these principles to other principles from which philosophers have claimed that the principles of morality or value can be derived, or with which they are somehow connected. Thus, if I say that I know that I am morally bound to do what I have promised to do in the same way in which I know that a straight line is the shortest distance between two points, I am saying something about the way in which I know the two matters to be so, and suggesting, for instance, that my knowledge of my obligation to fulfil my undertakings is of the same order as my insight into the necessary properties of a straight line in Euclidean space. This is, of course, to make a very important, and a highly disputable claim. But it is to make a claim of a quite different order from the claim which I make when I say that such a principle as that I ought to do what I have promised to do is irreducible; for when I say that it is irreducible, I am not saying anything of the way in which I come to know it (at least not directly), but simply something concerning the relation of this principle to other principles, for instance to my concern as a human being for the welfare of my fellows. In setting out the contentions of intuitionists, it may be helpful to get this distinction clear at the outset; for it seems sometimes as if the intuitionists were much more anxious to maintain something about the status of the moral obligations of which we are conscious, or of the claims that we make for certain states of affairs as of intrinsic worth, than to maintain a particular epistemological doctrine. It may, indeed, be said that the very looseness of our common use of the expression 'moral consciousness' shows how tightly the two issues which I am venturing to distinguish are tied up in our thinking. But for purposes of exposition, the distinction is perhaps worth making, and in what immediately follows I am anxious to clarify first of all what exactly it is that intuitionists are asserting concerning obligation and worth.

To say that moral obligation is irreducible is, of course, to claim for it a certain uniqueness. I say a certain uniqueness; for when the claim is made in one context, it assumes a certain difference of force from that which it assumes in another. Thus Butler argues in his *Dissertation* against those who would make benevolence the whole of virtue; he also argues in his *Sermons* against those who would derive morality from the 'abstract relations of things'. It is a commonplace to say that when he argues against Shaftesbury in the *Dissertation*, he is writing like an intuitionist; but it is less commonly remarked how similar his style is when, for instance, in the 15th Sermon he defends the primacy of practical reason against those who would somehow subordinate the practice of virtue to metaphysical insight, making the fulfilment by human beings of their duty wait on their penetration of the hidden secrets of creation. Yet the underlying attitude is the same in both places. The utilitarian who says that benevolence is the whole of virtue, is ironing out the actual complexity of human nature in the interest of a principle for which he claims an almost metaphysical universality and necessity; while the metaphysician is distracted from the familiar effort to follow conscience by his conviction that the place of morality in the scheme of things must first be shown him. If the utilitarian argues for the sovereignty over our inherently complex nature of a principle of benevolence which is too narrow for that nature's manifold diversity, the metaphysically minded moralist is too inclined to flee from the achnowledgement of that nature's claims upon him as something which supplies its own justification. It is important to note the similarity in style of Butler's arguments in these two places; in both alike he is loyal to the principles he has formulated in the Preface to his *Sermons*. He is attending to human nature as he finds it, and eschewing the hazard of generalization; he is acting as an empiricist in the sense in which continental thinkers continually accuse writers in these islands of doing!

For the purposes, however, of this study he is admirably illustrating the intuitionist procedure in ethics. For he is refusing to iron out complexity in the interests of a spurious unity, or to seek at the cost of honesty, avoidance of an element of pluralism. We have diverse obligations, this because, for Butler, our nature is inherently complex. In his *Sermons* he gives us a picture of that nature, writing of it not as a modern psychologist might seek to lay bare the springs of its behaviour, but rather in something of the manner of a novelist to whom we attribute deep psychological insight. He shows how, for instance, sympathy without 'resentment' can easily topple over into sentimentality; but that if a proper feeling for the demands of retributive justice is not balanced by a readiness to forgive, the result is a merciless inhumanity. His argument against Hobbes' reduction of sympathy to a form of fear is famous; it is indeed a classical example of the appeal to 'ordinary language'. But throughout his *Sermons* Butler is making analogous appeals to what our sense of the facts of our complex nature, as that sense has been formed by tradition and experience, compels us to accept concerning ourselves.

No doubt, if pressed, Butler would have said that it was conscience which thus compelled us to reckon with ourselves as we found ourselves. It was against this authoritative element in our nature that we were acting when, for instance, we made benevolence the whole of virtue. Yet his argument contains much that seems capable, or almost capable, of standing apart from his peculiar doctrine of conscience, even to derive its weight from its fidelity to the actual logic of traditional moral discourse.

Benevolence is the whole of virtue, only within the bounds of justice and veracity. So Butler argues and insists that if men ignore the qualifications and suggest that benevolence is unconditionally the whole of virtue, they are ready, implicitly if not actually, to justify thereby 'some of the most shocking instances of injustice, adultery, murder, perjury, and even of persecution'. Such a readiness is the logical consequence of what they say in thus abandoning qualification in their assent to the thesis that benevolence is the whole of virtue. If they refuse to admit this, it is because they have carried over into their new and unconditional use of the term benevolence, some of what belongs to it from its other more familiar and duly qualified employments. They have not noticed that when it is said of this disposition that it is the whole of virtue, by that claim alone the content of the disposition is subtly changed. Butler need do no more than appeal to accepted use to establish this. He obviously thinks it enough to discredit the thesis that benevolence is the whole of virtue to point out that if we say this, then we must say that in certain circumstances, courses of action are justified, which we would regard as involving the breach of principles of no less authority than that of concern for the general good. Indeed, we have only, he implies, to ask ourselves how we conceive that good to realize that it is something whose very form and content alike are defined for us by the absence of such evils as I have catalogued in my quotation from him. To take away from the notion of a general good, and of the disposition in the agent to seek it, this context of recognized restraints from which it in part, at least, derives its sense, is absent-mindedly to transform the notion itself.

Indeed, a certain sort of philosopher might well be tempted to suggest that what we mean when we say that people have consciences, is no more than that they do argue in this way, or are in some way compelled to recognize the special sort of cogency belonging to this kind of argument. It might even be maintained that conscience is no more than a 'logical construction' out of the fact that people do argue in this way. If, of course, this seems a plausible account of the matter, we must say that when Butler regarded his claim that benevolence was not the whole of virtue as something guaranteed by conscience, he was simply insisting that the arguments on which his view rested belonged to a particular class of arguments: viz. those arguments out of which we say that conscience is a 'logical construction'.

But perhaps this is too sophisticated for the present stage of the discussion. Yet what I am trying to bring out is the fact that the irreducibility of ethical principles in which intuitionists claim to believe is something with which we best get to grips when we see the claim as a move, or even as a set of moves, in argument rather than as something capable of dogmatic exposition. It is when we are told that as a matter of fact *all* there is to morality is the devising of sets of rules whereby human beings can be constrained to live together in such a way that the greatest amount of happiness for all may ensue, that we tend to make the sort of moves that intuitionists make; it is the suggestion that 'that is really all there is to it', which sets our teeth on edge. It is the confident finality which marks the iconoclast's reduction of the complex to simples in relation, which compels our 'Yes, but surely—'.

Hitherto we have largely concentrated on the implications of Butler's classical criticism of utilitarianism. But it should, of course, never be forgotten that the same sort of moves must frequently occur, as Butler obviously realized, when we are dealing with the more pretentious efforts to rest morality on some metaphysical foundation. Maybe few today will believe, or openly avow their belief, in some general principles concerning the structure of being, as such, which constrain a particular policy of life on human individuals. But we are not wanting examples of suggestions that human responsibility is an illusion and that we must behave in this way or that because history demands it of us; nor, and this is crucial for my argument, do we want examples of the most vigorous protest against this sort of insistence. What can we say of the logic of such protests? Or, if a more Kantian idiom is preferred, what assumptions are transcendentally presupposed in the making of them? That, as a matter of fact, such protests have been made we know; we need only refer to Mr. Isaiah Berlin's recent passionate philosophical prophesying. Such a fervent defence of the 'freedom of open possibilities', of the simple truth that 'men could have done otherwise', and that 'men can do otherwise', is an impressive example of the tenacity of intuitionist style of language. Perhaps Mr. Berlin's writing is not philosophy but itself the matter of a philosophical or logical analysis. That does not affect, indeed it even strengthens, the point I am making; there would be no problem there at all if the facts concerning ethical discourse to which the intuitionist is insisting that we attend, were not deeply embedded in crucial examples of that sort of language.

In such writing as Mr. Berlin's it is claimed that we are free, in some sense the authors of what we do. The claim is made in strong protest against the thesis that some impersonal absolute called historical necessity, can be charged with being the supreme, sovereign, indisputable source of all that happens and all that is done. The word that evokes protest is the word 'must'. It is not true that we *must* do all that we do do; we are more sure, so it is insisted, that we are responsible for what we do than that there is a destiny shaping our end and our actions to ineluctable purposes of its own. No doubt this sense of our responsibility for what we do, this belief that we are in some sense first causes (as Kant seems to have thought) is very difficult indeed to reconcile with much else that we believe. But we do believe, and this we clearly recognize, when we seriously attend to the consequences of denying it in the name of some supposedly sovereign historical necessity.

Thus, to take an obviously crucial contemporary example, we are told we must in these islands, accept the necessity of developing the hydrogen bomb. The phrase inevitably suggests a kind of inescapable burden that we must take upon our backs, or even some sort of movement of the world-spirit, with which we must identify ourselves. Yet we would not, I think, in our saner moments, accept this sort of thing for an instant. Necessity is not the name of something to be accepted; there is rather a choice to be made, a Yes or a No to be said, a tragic Yes or No maybe as the Yes and No of Creon and Antigone were tragic.

We are even prepared to welcome the frankly metaphysical language of 'open possibilities' to give us sharper purchase here on the content of our belief. Of course, to repeat myself, such a welcome has to be seen as a move in a game. To understand what is the content of the claim for freedom in the sense of being able to do otherwise, I must look at the context in which such a claim is made. But seen in that context, it is surely not unfairly represented as another claim for the irreducibility of the ethical, and as I had implied in my reference to the *Antigone*, for the possibility of the tragic. We are insisting by the almost poetic violence of our language, that the very status which we attribute to our actions in calling them free, should not be gainsaid; and we are demanding that the freedom which we claim for what we do should be interpreted quite simply and unsophisticatedly. Above all, it must not be given a sense which obviously erodes, in some way or other, what we commit ourselves to when we say that our actions are freely chosen.

To some the implication of this discussion may be that I am reducing the claim of the intuitionist to a claim that we are justified in using language in a particular way, or in keeping for a certain sort of language, a special kind of logical autonomy. Later in this essay I shall want to discuss this point at much greater length. For the time being, I would just suggest that because the business of the world of men is so largely 'carried on in words', a plea for the irreducibility of a certain dimension of human existence (to use a very different almost discreditably existentialist idiom) may very well take the shape of insisting that a particular sort of discourse is autonomous. Thus, if I deny that mathematics is reducible to logic, what I may be doing is simply denying that propositions about numbers can be treated as compendious shorthands for propositions about classes, etc. Similarly, if I say that morality cannot be reduced to expediency, I may be saying no more than that there is a special sort of discourse which we call moral, and which is somehow not completely describable in terms of the devising and criticizing of means to be taken to achieve ends universally accepted as desirable. Yet, of course, this notion of autonomous discourse is one that is full of difficulties and we must, I think, allow that the doctrine of ethical intuition in the narrow sense, has been an effort to meet them.

The very title of their doctrine makes clear how important the belief in ethical intuition was for the moralists whose work we are considering. It is important only to be on guard, however, against the way in which the labels of philosophical schools, even when accepted as badges by their supposed members, are misleading. What matters is that we should get behind the pigeonholing to the actual philosophical issues that have driven people to speak in terms of an intuitive morality.

We may safely begin by acknowledging that to regard a certain range of facts as irreducible occasions the temptation of supposing that to that range there must correspond a particular sort of knowing. We argue in a certain way, we obstinately continue doing so, giving to certain definitions of the terms in which we argue, what I will call a preclusive force; we will not allow these definitions to be altered. Rather than accept such alteration, we will jettison theories. If we are told that freedom is knowledge of necessity, when we draw the consequences from that proposition, we see that we are logically compelled to say things that we are simply not prepared to say. We experience a kind of jam, analogous to that which we experience when (to use a famous example), we draw out the consequences of supposing time to be unreal; if time is unreal there are no temporal facts and then when we say that we had tea an hour ago and will have supper in four hours time, we are saying nothing at all. But we are quite sure that when we indicate the interval between tea and supper, we are saying something. It is surely in some way the same where freedom is concerned; when we say that we are the authors of what we do, we are sure that we are saying something. But on what does this conviction rest? Or, to use an older language, whence do we derive this notion of our moral causality? Or, what is the exact status of our belief that we are responsible agents, what the logical justification of our refusal to accept as descriptive of our situation, the implicates of metaphysical theories which deny our freedom? To answer that our refusal is based intuitively, comes perilously near simply inventing a new idiom for insisting on the uniqueness which is the point at issue, a new idiom which makes matters more difficult by seeming to invent an esoteric faculty called intuition. Of course it was easier as long as it could be supposed that the axioms of Euclidean geometry were synthetic *a priori* truths and as long as that discipline could be regarded as a system of non-inductively established propositions concerning the properties of configurations in actual space; the existence of such a body of supposed truths seemed to support the claim that apart from the ordinary routes of perception and induction the mind had access to the necessary forms of the spatial as such. Thus it was tempting to suggest that when we knew that we ought to do what we had promised to do, we were knowing something analogous to what we knew when we knew that two straight lines could not enclose a space. Both truths alike were universal and necessary; both gave us immediate access to what showed its necessary character in its own right; and it was even added sometimes that the immediate grasping of such first principles was the most exalted activity of intellect as such.

But recent changes in the understanding of the distinction between pure and applied geometry and their relation, as well as advances more recent still, in that of the way necessary propositions 'work', have made this view quite inadmissible; for if we are still told that to understand ethical intuition, we should think of our grasp of the necessary properties of a straight line as such, we can only reply that what is supposed to illuminate difficulty and set perplexity at rest, is itself nothing more than the expression of confusion. The 'grasping of the necessary properties of a straight line as such' is not the name of any easily recognizable intellectual act or operation.

Moreover, even if we had been conservative in our understanding of geometry, we might have wondered whether as a matter of fact we did actually think of our duties as if they were points, or our rights as if they were straight lines. We might have been vaguely unhappy at the suggestion that there was no phenomenological difference between Euclidean points and straight lines on the one hand and, let us say, promises and injustices on the other. The apologetic advantage gained by treating supposed geometrical and ethical intuition as co-ordinate species of a genus could only be slight; more would be needed to make an 'honest woman' out of the latter. If, however, it was said simply that after all there was a thing called intuition at the basis of geometry; why therefore should there not be something given the same name at the basis of ethics?, the reply might well come that if the two types of intuition were utterly diverse, the existence of the one was no argument whatsoever for the existence of the other.

There is no doubt that one of the things which intuitionists hoped to gain by the admission of something called ethical intuition, was an immediacy in the basic source of ethical knowledge which would be a proper counterpart to the irreducibility of what in such knowledge, we knew. What is irreducible is underived, and it was insisted that the absence of derivation must be epistemic as well as ontological. And it may indeed be argued that with the advent of modern linguistic methods, this sort of artificial to and fro between what we know and the way in which we know it, has been abolished; something of this sort may seem to have been admitted in the earlier paragraphs of this essay, where the notion of irreducibility was analysed in terms of the way in which we argue. Some might actually go as far as to suggest that such phrases as 'we know directly', 'we are certain', occurring in ethical contexts, simply conveyed emphasis, adding nothing in content of assertion, but simply advertising the speaker's temper of adherence to what he said. Yet I suspect, that however confused their idiom, the intuitionists were calling attention to something important by their anxiety to speak about the manner of our knowing as well as concerning the status of what we know.

As I have said earlier, this something may perhaps be seen if we ask ourselves more about what I have called our obstinacy in refusing redefinitions of basic ethical notions. *In Logik gibt es keine Moral;* thus Dr. Rudolf Carnap. But the very fact that Dr. Carnap uses this language to enunciate a fundamental thesis in his philosophy of logic, suggests the hostility between the ethical and the arbitrary. To say that logic has nothing to do with morality is worth saying because it brings out in an arresting way the arbitrariness of the conventions on which, if Dr. Carnap is right, logically necessary truths depend. We are extremely unwilling to surrender the sort of principles we have mentioned earlier in this paper. Even at the cost of seeming inconsistency (Kant's word for this was antinomy), we go on using two contradictory styles of language in talking of our behaviour; and what is more we refuse the tempting offers of erosion (the logical empiricist's panacea) or 'higher synthesis' (the metaphysician's *gnosis*).

Now, in recognizing this obstinacy in continuing to talk in a particular way, we are calling attention to something that we know in our own experience. If the matter of our obstinacy can be set out in terms of a persistent fidelity to certain definitions, what we are thus expounding is something that we

22

ourselves do under a special sort of compulsion. We do not sit light by such things. When we admit this, we are admitting a fact about ourselves which seems somehow of a different order from our recognition that we have a certain I.Q., or a certain chronic inability to understand the higher mathematics. It is of course abundantly true that the intuitionist usually fails to bring out that what (in his language) we immediately knew when we knew an ethical fact, was something about ourselves; Butler and Kant were both very much wiser here. They saw in different ways that ethical knowledge was in some sense a special sort of self-estimation; Kant's preoccupation in his ethics with freedom made it impossible for him to escape from bringing this out with an almost overwhelming clarity. Had it, however, been more continually recognized, the actual nature of what the intuitionists were trying to bring out could have been discussed without *some* of the attendant myth-making and myth-destroying.

At the risk of repetition, may I try to make clearer what it is that seems to me to be the crux of the matter? When we look at what happens when we argue about conduct, we do find 'with our ears and our eyes' (in Professor Wisdom's phrase) that as a matter of fact the discussion does jam at certain places, that we do seem to be operating in terms of conceptual horizons which present a determinateness, an inflexibility, a rigidity to which there is no precise parallel. What the theory of ethical intuition is trying to do is to find a way of bringing out the subjective aspect of such experience. Such language as that of immediacy is simply a way towards capturing the character which belongs to it. It may be that behind and beneath the problem of ethical intuition, we shall find the perennial difficulties concerning self-knowledge, concerning the status we can assign to what we find ourselves compelled to say about ourselves. Maybe even what lies at the bottom of this problem is the problem of the status of the language of Kant's antinomies, the language in which we do speak to ourselves of a predicament in which we are certainly involved. Has this language justification? Is it sound and fury signifying nothing? Is the fact that we are prepared to say we are compelled to talk it in any sense justification of such language? Are there indeed styles of language that are somehow their own justification? What would it be like indeed for a language to be its own justification?

To speak of a language as its own justification is perhaps to use a forced, and even violent, form of expression; and it may seem to some that it is paradoxical to write in this way after speaking of the obstinacy displayed in the refusal to accept certain conceptual redefinitions. The notion of a language as its own justification may indeed suggest to some the sort of activity Kant believed to be the prerogative of an intuitive understanding, which created its own objects by thinking them. To say that the idiom of an immediately discerned moral universe is its own justification, seems to mean, if it means anything, that by speaking such a language, we create the state of affairs to which it refers.

Yet I would argue that this is not nearly so shocking as it sounds; certainly not if we give its proper status to the notion of freedom or if a metaphysically-flavoured word be permitted, of creativity. Language may be the instrument whereby we bring a world into being; certainly if the business of the human world is indeed largely carried on in words, this will be no more than what we should expect. After all, we are surely all of us familiar with the notion of linguistic 'performance' (to use Professor Austin's expression). We are alive to the peculiarity of such words as 'vow' and 'promise', 'threat' and 'warning'. Is there not something analogous in, for instance, the very greeting of another person as a responsible agent? May we not even venture the paradox that freedom is something created by language? Certainly we must never forget how vast a field of different activities is covered by the word 'language'; how diverse and complex the fabric of relationships it brings into being and sustains.

But what of the obstinacies of which I have spoken? Certainly we seem to advance a little in understanding by treating moral discourse as creative; it is somehow liberating not to find ourselves looking all the time for the facts to which it refers, but to see them almost evoked by its use. But this creativity is something limited; there are things ruled out as inadmissible. We know that in some types of religion great emphasis is laid on the efficaciousness of sacramental words and actions to achieve a height and a depth of worship outwith the reach of the individual, to create, if you like, for him the very possibility of worship (the Catholic Eucharist could be regarded as a *locus classicus* of the 'performatory' use of language). Yet what to the religious man such creative acts and utterances further, or make possible, is adoration, an activity inward and outward at the same time, but wholly directed upon something other than itself. The language of religion is, in the end, *realist;* so too is the language of ethics, at least in respect of what I may call loosely its background. No doubt by behaviour and by our speech, we bring into being, or fail to bring into being, a 'realm of ends'. Yet we cannot represent that realm, however it may depend on the rational activity of will, as something that we may, or may not, affirm at choice. The integrity involved in its affirmation is an imperative; there is nothing here allowing us for a moment to suppose that our individual caprice can justify a refusal of acceptance. It is paradoxical to speak of bringing into being what we accept, representing what we create somehow as already real. Yet it is to the necessity of this paradoxical stretching of our language that the intuitionists are inviting our attention. In morality we are active and bring into being a moral universe by our actions; yet even as we do this we are constrained to represent that universe as something in some sense, already *there*, and commanding us to embody its pattern in our daily dealings.

Of course this language is metaphorical; yet even the rigorously formalist Kant was compelled to metaphor and image in the end. Thus, when in the *Tugendlehre* he writes of love, he uses with great effect, the picture of a gravitational field, thus conveying the role in human relations of affection and reverence by the image of attraction and repulsion in the universe of forces.

The difficulty of intuitionism is not lifted by the deeper understanding of ethical language that follows minute attention to its creative role and character. Certainly our understanding of the moral consciousness is enormously advanced when we look at the way language works in the building of the human world. But still the idiom of the language we use in building that world leaves us with its problem; for there is a sense in which we have to regard it as neither of our own absolute making, nor as something forced upon us by the nature of observable facts we would describe by its means. It is something certainly fashioned, achieved, created. Yet it is also in some sense, found and thrust upon us, even if we need in the end the resources of metaphor to convey the character of that thrusting. Butler and Kant, in different ways, would say that it was the constants of our nature that imposed the pattern of speech we thus experienced as thrust upon us; indeed they would, in different ways, represent that speech as a coming to terms with our nature. In this they may, I suspect, be right; but whatever view we may take on that matter, it is this inescapable element of finding, not making, this element of what we can only call 'realism' in the conventional sense in moral awareness that leaves us with the problem of ethical intuition.

It must be admitted that it is on this last point that the shrewdest critics of intuitionism have fastened; this suggestion of a mysterious finding, this language of realism. This criticism is made with special clarity by the classical utilitarians, the apostles of a rational moral objectivism. No greater mistake could be made than that of supposing that the strict utilitarian is, in any sense, the defender of a subjective ethic. He is rather concerned to offer a criterion by which the moral quality of an act can be as exactly measured as the temperature of a room. That, admittedly, is, of course, the paradigm, the ideal standard; but by means of loyalty to it, the utilitarians are able effectively to turn aside from the metaphysical quagmires in which, in their judgement, intuitionists get bogged down. It is a mistake, of course, simply to construe their attitude in terms of a purely theoretical hostility to metaphysics; it has also a markedly practical direction. The claim to intuition is seen not simply as the claim to some mysterious faculty, or source of knowledge;

it is judged also to be a way whereby prejudice, tradition and the rest, are subtly immunized against rational scrutiny and justification.

Perhaps the very difficulty we had experienced in setting out the character of the intuitionist's claim makes the earthiness of the utilitarian peculiarly satisfying. His view is down to earth; it also possesses the characters of economy, of simplicity, and of radicalism. No longer, as in the religiously inspired ethic of Butler, need we attend to the subtle complexity of human nature. We are under the sovereignty of two recognizable masters, pleasure and pain. Differences of quality of satisfaction are of no import. The other issues which elude settlement by combination of measurement with observation,—they can be ignored; better so, for attention to them can easily distract our attention from adjusting our standards so as to advance our journey towards the unquestionably acceptable human goal of happiness.

Paradoxical though it may seem, the utilitarian is ready to challenge the authority of 'ordinary language' in the name of his humanly acknowledgeable sovereigns, pleasure and pain. If 'ordinary language' seems to authorize attention to complexity, even by the way we use it, to encourage acknowledgement of obstinacies, then it is 'ordinary language' that must go, 'commonsense' that must be dismissed as a smoke screen concealing from us the proper, valid sanction of our behaviour. Simplicity is the ally of a proper radicalism, of a proper readiness to ignore conservative hesitancy, which may seek to sell itself to the unwary as a true empiricism (as, of course, classically in the political writings of Edmund Burke).

The world of 'ought' is the servant of the world of 'is'. To speak of ethical facts is to speak of what is chimerical; to create for oneself the illusion of a world that is somehow represented as the superior counterpart of that world of fact wherein statements are verified and hypotheses confirmed, is to invite needless trouble. We may say, of course, that the creation of such a world is only a moment in discourse, something to be understood in terms of what we are trying to bring out by means of it; we are not for a moment supposing that our idiom of finding suggests anything in the way of a geographical exploration of the transcendent. It is simply a way in which we have to talk in order to represent what compels representation. But what is this compulsion? Is it not neurotic, fantastic, something without rational justification? Is it not fantasy, distracting men from the real business of living, much as a fantastic projection of childish conflicts into adult situations pulls asunder the life of the full-grown human being?

Yet Mill said, 'it is better to be Socrates dissatisfied than a fool satisfied', and wrote in his *Essay on Liberty* in similar temper. What is it like to know such a fact as that? Or rather . . . can we explain to ourselves what it is to know such facts? For we know that we do know them. The knowledge is certainly not only a recognition of something as being the case, like the emptying of a 'bus, or the departure of a train. In saying that such things are so, we do something to ourselves. Sooner or later in serious discussion of ethical intuition we face the problem of self-knowledge, the problem, I might dare to say, of our presence to ourselves.

What is it for one man to be better than another, what is it for one way of living to be higher than another? What is it to know such facts? It is to the credit of the intuitionist (and perhaps no one brought out the underlying problem better than Mill) that he has never let us forget the strangeness and yet the persistence of these questions. If he has been a metaphysician, for the most part the intuitionist has limited his attention to the metaphysical questionings and gropings that are raised within the compass of a human life. If he has been prepared to speak of the transcendent, the speech has been made in order to remark something men avow in their actions and in their life, even perhaps in the way in which men keep the problems of their own existence before them.

This last formula might, I think, be used as a description of what Kant achieved in his discussion of the antinomy between freedom and causality. His own language is strange enough in all conscience; we are, according to him, empirically determined and noümenally free; of course his exact meaning is determined by the context of this part of his argument in the close unity of the whole Kritik. To expound its precise sense one would have to attend to the Aesthetic and the Analytic as well as to its immediate context in the Dialectic. But is it altogether to do violence to a proper interpretation to suggest that what Kant is offering is almost a method of learning how to keep hold of one's proper situation in being? We are in language that is nakedly metaphorical, citizens of two worlds; we look on ourselves in two ways. We are always tempted to escape this dualism. What Kant would have us learn is to see such temptation for what it is, an impulse of escapism; it will continually assail us, and the lesson which Kant is trying to teach in this part of the Kritik is not one learned once for all. It is rather a precarious perception requiring often to be renewed; for the kind of self-knowledge of which it is perhaps a crucial expression, is not something easy for men.

To explain this a little less cryptically I will use the idiom of roles. We are all of us used to playing various roles in life, some of them similar enough to require a painful disentanglement in order that we may play them for what they are. A man may lie one day on the psychiatrist's couch, and by a process of free association, seek to trace the source of his present disordered life in unacknowledged past conflict; the same man may also kneel and speak of the same disorders in very different language to a priest in the confessional. 'Mea culpa, mea culpa, mea maxima culpa'. He is the same person, talking all the while and listening a little: by his speech he creates, or helps to create, two worlds, and by what he does and what is said to him, he is in two ways remade. Or so he may believe. Maybe to run away from the confessional and its peculiar styles of self-abasement, would seem to some likely to hasten the pace of human recovery; but it could also subtly, for some at least, lead to a profound human impoverishment. For to quit that world altogether would be a denial of responsibility; yet paradoxical though it may seem, that responsibility must be affirmed in relation to, not out of relation from, the other realm, the realm whose symbol is the couch.

For we are men, a point to which Kant in his strange idiom, was painfully trying to call attention.

There is an analogy between the antinomy of freedom and causality and the opposition between the utilitarian and the intuitionist approaches to ethics (I am here using the word intuitionist in a sense defined by the clarification of the notion in the earlier parts of this essay; I am thinking of an intuitionist as one who stresses the uniqueness of the moral consciousness in the way in which I have indicated).[1] The utilitarian, as I have insisted, is down to earth, deeply concerned with the observable betterment of human lot; he is extroverted, conscious of happiness as an obtainable goal provided proper means are taken to achieve it. Whereas the intuitionist is pressed, is unable to avoid a much more deeply introspective vision of the human situation. This must be admitted, especially in a study conducted from the point of view of a deep sympathy with the intuitionist attitude. There is a sense in which 'intuitionism is not enough' just as 'libertarianism is not enough'. As I made out earlier both alike are moves in a game; and there is a sense in which it is the game that matters.

One can carry this point further, and in doing so, maybe illuminate a little the traditional problem of the conflict of duties. It was the utilitarian's claim, among other things, to provide a means of deciding when one or more of our traditionally accepted duties conflicted. The 'greatest happiness' principle provided a court of appeal in such cases; the claim with the greater or greatest stringency, could be assessed by reference to the promotion of this universal human end. It is a commonplace of the textbooks to insist that intuitionists refuse this way of dealing with the problem; there is no single court of appeal; our duties form a plurality, and must be reckoned irreducibly as such. With the analysis carried out in this essay in mind, it is possible to comment on this refusal. One might say, unkindly, that the intuitionist has almost a

---

[1] It will be clear from this that in terms of traditional language I am allowing the intuitionist to be, in the end, the exponent of a *Gesinnungsethik* contrasted with the utilitarian *Erfolgsethik*.

vested interest in the conflict of duties. For if that conflict is a permanent element in human life, it is a partial vindication of his argument that in morality we are reckoning with the stuff of a predicament, with what is perhaps problem, or even mystery, rather than solution.

It is one of the great benefits conferred by the recent revival of linguistic self-consciousness among philosophers, that phrases like 'conflict of duties' have been rescued from their pigeon-holes in the textbooks, and viewed again in the context of their living use. It is almost a revelation to be reminded that it is the tragedians, like Sophocles in the *Antigone*, who have written most profoundly of the conflict of duties, who have used the phrase to best advantage and with surest understanding of its peculiar grammar. It is, in my judgement, perhaps the supreme strength of the intuitionist approach to ethics that it insists that such conflict as that shall be in the last resort more than sound and fury signifying nothing. How is tragedy possible? Under what conditions can we have genuinely tragic situations? It is some of those conditions, at least where the moral con-sciousness is concerned, that the intuitionists have tried to uncover. As I said earlier, their work must be seen as a move in a game.

May I add one last comment? I have admitted writing this essay in considerable sympathy with the underlying impulses of intuitionism. May I therefore say that I recognize the incompleteness of their standpoint? There is a sense in which, as Dilthey so well brought out, one's philosophical standpoint does reflect and express a general set of mind and will. The intuitionism that I have defended is, itself, a defence of the rights, of the peculiar status of self-knowledge, if you like, of the peculiar dignity of spiritual experience. But it is, and must be recognized as, only a move in a game. It is the substance of tragedy that men are the prisoners, not of their weakness, but of their achievement; to understand can be a source of blindness. Philosophy is not tragedy, nor is it life; and therefore in philo-sophy where one describes moves in a game, moves with which one has great sympathy, one at the same time remembers

something at least of the game. Therefore this essay must end
with acknowledging that maybe the order of the curriculum in
many Scottish ordinary classes of moral philosophy is right in
beginning with the utilitarians, but certainly very wrong if it
forgets them at the end. Nothing is resolved in a higher
synthesis!

MAIN PUBLICATIONS

On the Notion of a Philosophy of History. L. T. Hobhouse Memorial
    Trust Lecture. Oxford University Press. 1954.
Work Edited. *Christian Faith and Communist Faith.* Macmillan. 1953.

FIFTY YEARS OF PHILOSOPHY

by H. J. PATON

*Emeritus Professor of Moral Philosophy in the
University of Oxford*

FIFTY YEARS OF PHILOSOPHY

I

WHEN Professor Lewis, in the exercise of his editorial office, urged me to give my impressions of philosophy during the last fifty years—a suggestion I had casually thrown out, along with some others, in a too light-hearted spirit—I received something of a shock; for as soon as I began to take the proposal seriously, I saw at once how subjective any such impressions of mine must be. To attempt a balanced and dispassionate estimate would require five to ten years of solid work. Hence it has seemed to me less misleading, and in the last resort more modest, to cast my impressions in an unashamedly autobiographical form. This may throw less light on philosophical progress than on personal limitations of no interest to any one except myself. Yet in a way perhaps I may hope to represent, however inadequately, what has sometimes been called 'the lost generation'—the many scholars whose lives were sacrificed in the early years of the First War because generals had not then discovered that brains may have a greater military value than can be displayed in trench warfare by platoon commanders. The loss of these men—and of their sons—has contributed to the melancholy mediocrity of the subsequent period in so many walks of life, but especially in politics. In philosophy it has helped to make development more abrupt, and perhaps less balanced, than it would other- wise have been.

Even the few of that generation who were lucky enough to survive, in most instances because of some infirmity of body or character, have been hampered by the troubled conditions of the present century. One war is a serious, if temporary, disturbance to reflexion at a time when a man's philosophy is being formed; but two wars, together with the anxieties and pre-occupations that come before and after them, constitute something more like a permanent laming, if they have been taken seriously. In my own case the present essay might have shown a wider sympathy if ten precious years spent in the service of the Admiralty and the Foreign Office could have been devoted instead to the intricacies of mathematical logic and the many ramifications of the modern linguistic movement.

II

Although I am almost bound to write from a too narrowly Oxford point of view, my philosophical studies began before I had the good fortune to become a member of that university. As a Scotsman and a son of the manse I was early introduced to theological thinking, which is no bad preparation for philosophy; and one of my schoolboy recollections is a protracted argument with my witty friend Robert Gibson, who later became a Fellow of Balliol and was killed in 1915. The subject of our debate was whether Adam could have been free in eating the apple if God had known from all eternity the precise moment of the Fall. Our discussion may have been less profound than one in which I recently took part on the possibility of reconciling scientific prediction with human freedom; but the topic was the same, and it certainly gave us no less fun.

It was, however, at the University of Glasgow that I received my official philosophical baptism. Although reading for a degree in Classics, I was able, in accordance with the admirable practice of the Scottish universities, to do a considerable amount of work at Logic and Moral Philosophy as well as at Mathematics and English—my one regret is that I did not also take the class of Natural Philosophy at a time when elementary physics would have come to me easily. The philosophical teaching was perhaps less original than it had been in the latter half of the previous century; and Sir Henry Jones, who was something of a prophet, contrived to give me the impression that after ages of confusion and error the truth, as expounded by Hegel and clarified by T. H. Green and Edward Caird, had at last been discovered so that little remained to be done in philosophy except to elaborate some further details. I was agreeably surprised to find I had been born at so happy a stage in the development of human thought, and I had hopes of adding a few bricks to the final edifice.

It was all very exciting, and I enjoyed even the traditional manipulations of *Barbara, Celarent.* In those days every new idea was a challenge, and for a short time I was almost obsessed with mathematics. But perhaps my greatest experience, apart from some intense private thinking of my own, was reading Bishop Berkeley for the first time. His arguments fully persuaded me that matter was non-existent. A jolt of this kind is salutary if we are to awake from dogmatic slumber; but it was a great relief when in Oxford I began to believe once more that a tree was a solid and permanent body which continued to exist even if no one was looking at it.

Another benefit I took away from Glasgow was a fondness for the give and take of argument when seasoned with wit and tempered by good humour.

III

The University of Oxford offered a more varied landscape, as is indeed almost inevitable because of the great number of its philosophical teachers. Yet this very richness tends to produce a self-sufficient society exposed to the risks of complacency and parochialism. Although I believe, with Walter de la Mare, that there is an inner core of personality which remains identical through the whole of an individual's life, it is a humbling reflexion to think how differently I might have written this essay if I had attended the University of Cambridge.

It is true that the existence of Cambridge, if of no other place, was recognized, at least as a source of errors. Even a few years ago a friend of mine, not himself a professional philosopher, could burst out with the remark, 'The difference between an

23

Oxford and a Cambridge man is greater than that between any two European nationalities'. This difference has been expressed in the epigram that an Oxford man knows less and less about more and more till he knows nothing about everything; a Cambridge man knows more and more about less and less till he knows everything about nothing. In philosophy the difference would, I suppose, be regarded from a Cambridge point of view as one between clear analysis and cloudy synopsis. If we leave out the adjectives, both processes would seem to be necessary for a sound philosophy. The former isolation of the two universities was a misfortune, and the credit of being the first to break through the iron curtain belongs, unless I am mistaken, to Professor Price.

The philosophical fare offered to Oxford undergraduates before the First War ranged from an almost orthodox Hegelianism to the pragmatism of Schiller, who, although he had a few camp-followers—if this term may be used without disrespect—seemed to have every man's hand against his. Yet amidst all the differences there was a great deal of common doctrine based mainly on the study of Plato and Aristotle, which seems to me, though I have heard this denied, to have been pursued more widely and intensively than it is at the present time. In my own case it was Plato who became an absorbing interest; and I was on the way to becoming a Platonic scholar when our leisurely world was suddenly shattered by war. After the war had worn bloodily to its end I felt, as probably others did also, that I must concern myself with problems more closely germane to the present time.

Interest in Greek thought was only part of a wider interest in the history of philosophy, which was considered to be a necessary safeguard against the revival of exploded errors. We were perhaps too ready to believe that no one who had failed to master Plato and Aristotle and Kant and Hegel, not to mention other thinkers, was qualified to construct a philosophy of his own. This modesty was better than the bland assumption that philosophy began somewhere about the year 1900; but it may have led some of us to accept too easily doctrines that were really obscure in the hope that they would become more comprehensible with further knowledge. Philosophy is an adventure in which a man should risk making a fool of himself when he is young: he can do it so much more gracefully then than later. A creative thinker cannot afford to spend too much time on the study of history, which, although it is a valuable discipline, is by no means fool proof, since we are all apt to concentrate on the past doctrines which support our present prejudices. On the other hand, it is absurd to imagine that we are thinking philosophically when we wrestle with the problems of Whitehead or Wittgenstein, but are mere historians when we struggle with those of Aristotle or Hegel.

Although in the period before 1914 there was a common background such that everybody was able to understand everybody else, there were also lively subjects of dispute. Absolute idealism, as it was called—that is, Hegelianism modified by Anglo-Saxon caution—was still in the ascendant: to say that it was already on the wane would be, I think, to judge by hindsight rather than to express the feeling of the time. What can be said with certainty is that a kind of realism was also in the air. Its chief spokesman was Professor Cook Wilson.

The balance of such a dispute is seen very imperfectly through the eyes of an undergraduate or even of a very young don. I first became clearly aware of it through my good luck, which was shared by a few other Balliol men, in having J. A. Smith as a tutor in my final year, although he had at that time already become a professor. My relations with him continued to be very close after I became a don, and indeed lasted till his death many years later. He had been bitten by the new realistic doctrines and was endeavouring to work them out in detail, although—as I remember him saying in a lecture—'with ever increasin' difficulty'. The difficulty may have been caused partly by an enthusiasm for Benedetto Croce which was already growing upon him and was later extended to Giovanni Gentile. Although he wrote little and seemed to regret that he had abandoned philology, 'his first love', for philosophy, he was not only a man of great learning and of almost excessive ingenuity, but also by far the best teacher I have known. He had a wonderful gift for entering into the mind of others; and although he could be naughty enough when cornered in an argument and became in his later years rather misty and rhetorical, he treated the most feeble reflexions of his pupils with unfailing courtesy, and indeed with an exaggerated and sometimes embarrassing respect. It was a rare privilege to be introduced to two such diverse lines of thought under his guidance.

As for the wider scene, this was marked by the contrast between Oxford and Cambridge, both of them with outposts in other parts of the country. St. Andrews was distinguished by the notable group of Stout and Burnet and A. E. Taylor, while in Edinburgh Pringle-Pattison expounded a personal idealism of his own. When we look back on it, all these thinkers and many others were, in spite of their real differences, very much in the same line of country. It is hard to get the whole situation into perspective and not to distort it in the light of subsequent knowledge. Some modern writers are apt to speak as if a band of pygmies had been dominated by the gigantic figures of G. E. Moore and Bertrand Russell. This may have been so in the eyes of God; it may even have been so in the eyes of Cambridge, although there too, I imagine, men like McTaggart and James Ward were still regarded as outstanding thinkers; but it was not so in the eyes of the philosophical world as a whole. Moore was certainly treated everywhere with respect; his views had a certain kinship with the realism of Cook Wilson and Prichard, though any connexion would probably have been repudiated by both sides; and it was not unknown even for Oxford undergraduates to claim that the difficulties of moral philosophy vanished as soon as good was recognized to be an unanalysable quality like yellow. Russell, as I remember it, was commonly regarded as a brilliant but quite unaccountable character, for ever producing bright new, although manifestly impossible, theories—a sort of Bernard Shaw who had strayed into philosophy; and even his mathematical researches were, I fear, too often considered as amiable eccentricities or wrong-headed attempts to develop a line of enquiry already proved to be fruitless. For philosophers generally, at least outside Cambridge, Bradley and, in a lesser degree, Bosanquet were the dominant figures even to those who opposed them. It is a complete falsification of history to describe them (I take this from my note of a review in a popular journal) as smallish men or—still worse—as fascists whom the British people were unable to stomach. They were not indeed to be ranked among the great creative thinkers of all time; but in their day and generation they were big men, and they had quite a long run for their money. The vulgarity of fascism would have been wholly beyond their comprehension, as it would to any liberal-minded Victorian gentleman.

In those days although the spatial, if not the temporal, horizon may have been too restricted, an occasional comet from abroad might flash for a time above it and shine among our local stars. I have already mentioned Croce, but perhaps the brightest luminary was the French philosopher Bergson, a man as modest as he was gifted. He too has faded, but it is always possible that some of these comets may return.

IV

When I came back to Oxford after the Peace Conference of Paris, I had to serve almost immediately as Junior Proctor so that it was not till 1921 that I could settle down again comfortably to philosophy. Apart from the hideous gaps wrought by the War the scene was outwardly almost unchanged. In the background were the venerable figures of Cook Wilson and J. A. Stewart; and Bradley himself, although a recluse, was still very much alive. Yet, while there were many able teachers (I need mention only such men as Webb, Carritt, Ross, and Stocks), the dominant influence was exercised by the Big Three, J. A. Smith, Joseph, and Prichard—or by the Big Four, if we take in Joachim, who was slightly detached and less given to the cut and thrust of debate. He was the only one wholly committed to the tradition of absolute idealism, and his book on *The Nature of Truth* was to me the most illuminating exposition of that philosophy. All these thinkers were highly distinctive individuals as well as fine scholars and accomplished dialecticians. With J. A. Smith and also with Joachim, whom I knew less well, I always felt that philosophy was a co-operative task. I felt this less with the other two. Although in some respects I shared many of Joseph's views, his remarkable combination of critical acuteness and extreme complexity—no doubt through my own fault— used to paralyse rather than stimulate my reflexions. As to Prichard, while I always enjoyed the care and zeal with which he pursued his own line of thought, he seemed to me curiously unable to understand the thinking of anybody else, as can indeed be seen from his book on Kant.

It is easy to be wise after the event, but all the intellectual ferment of that time had far less lasting effect than might reasonably have been expected. I put this down partly to the Oxford tutorial system, which for all its merits makes too great a demand on the physical and mental energy even of the most robust—the amount of teaching done, for example, by Joseph bordered on the fabulous. It also encourages the belief that philosophy lives in the intercourse of mind with mind rather than in books and systems. This doctrine, though not without its truth, may lead to a dangerous dissipation of effort. It is far too easy for a body of clever men, if they share the same pre-suppositions, to arrive after discussion at some conclusion which they take to be final. But no such conclusions can influence the world unless they are worked out into a system and committed to the permanence of cold print. It is a pernicious habit, dating at least as far back as Cook Wilson, to publish little during one's life-time and pass on to one's successors the duty of editing a mass of material which is no longer sufficiently relevant to the questions of the day. The practice of dialectic may also become too gladiatorial and may produce in the timid a fear of pub-lication which naturally increases with advance in years and in local repute. Whatever be the explanation, there was left a literary gap to be filled by less inhibited, and perhaps less over-burdened, writers from Cambridge. Even in the safer field of scholarship the vast amount of Aristotelian knowledge which was distributed over so many would have been almost entirely forgotten if Sir David Ross had not proved himself an exception to the rule.

A more serious defect was the general ignorance of science. At a time when physics was undergoing a revolution there was no one competent to learn the lessons of the new discoveries; and although the new mathematical logic was universally condemned, no serious attempt was made to refute it, and nothing whatever was offered in its place. As to psychology, every hackle was up at the mere mention of its name—Bradley was alone in showing a wider sympathy—and the prevailing attitude was mirrored in the well-known story of the examinee who finished a not too impressive answer by saying, 'Here Logic ends and Piscology and Error begin'. In all this Cambridge occupied a privileged position; and C. D. Broad, an exact contemporary of my own, was capable of expounding even the mysteries of Einstein with his customary lucidity.

In Oxford Collingwood and I were the only representatives of our generation—a slender bridge between predecessors at least ten years older and successors at least ten years younger. We had much in common, including at that time an interest in Italian philosophy, though he seemed to me too ready to slur over its difficulties. He was a supremely clever man, sometimes rather too quick in claiming all knowledge as his portion, an expert historian as well as philosopher, a writer of remarkable fluency and elegance. Unfortunately he worked himself too hard, alike in teaching and in research, till his health suffered and ultimately his judgement. The stream of books he poured out in his later years became a gallant race against death; but he has won by them a greater influence than he had while he was alive.

Apart from Russell, whose influence—outside Oxford— was steadily increasing, the most original writers of this period were Alexander, Whitehead, and Wittgenstein. Each propounded a new philosophy, but—if this is not too harsh a judgement—they all suffered, though in very different ways, from a failure to master the art of communication. An indolent man will want to be very sure that they were working on the right lines before he can feel justified in expending the time and energy necessary to absorb their doctrines. Of the three, Wittgenstein has had incomparably the greatest influence, and it is to be hoped that some of his able disciples will make his meaning clearer to the world. For myself I am ashamed to say that, being allergic to logical atomism in any form, I took the *Tractatus* at the time of its publication to be reasoning most obscurely from mistaken premises to impossible conclusions. By this I missed what to many has been a great experience; and although I have considerable sympathy for much of his later work, I am naturally not sufficiently excited by his candid rejection of previous errors which I have never shared.

All of this was taken calmly by Oxford in its stride. The man who succeeded in fluttering the dovecots for the first time was A. J. Ayer in his *Language, Truth and Logic*, and this was not published till as late as 1936. Perhaps the flutter was only a mild one, but I should hesitate to repeat in print some of the things said about him at the time. Whoever may have failed in the art of communication, he certainly did not. He exposed the nature of Logical Positivism, if I may so express myself, in all its naked horror, and he did so with a plausibility worthy of John Stuart Mill at his best. His doctrine, as I imagine he would now agree, was rather too simple; but it was a great achievement, especially at his age, to sum up a whole trend of thought (however mistaken) in brief compass and so to produce a philosophical classic which marks a milestone in modern thinking. I do not mean that I regarded it at the time as other than brilliantly wrong-headed, but it forced us all to realise what we were up against.

During the early twenties I was lecturing on Plato and Croce as well as on more general subjects. I collected a good deal of material for a book on the Italian philosopher; but although I continued to be influenced by him, at least in aesthetics and ethics, his system as a whole began to seem rather thin and unsatisfying. In 1925-6 I spent a sabbatical year happily in California, where I profited, I hope, by the change of intellectual climate, if not as much as I ought—I was mainly occupied with writing a book on ethics in too great haste and consequently at too great length. Although I should express myself differently today, it contains many doctrines which I still hold. The prevailing ethical theories appeared to me to be too intellectualistic, whether they rested on intuitions of duty or of good; and I have never been able to understand why intelligence should be supposed to be shown only in thought and not in action. Hence I attempted to interpret moral value in terms of rational or reasonable willing and of teleological rather than logical coherence; but at that time I drew my inspiration more from Plato and Aristotle and Croce and the Oxford idealists than from Kant, with whose writings I was still imperfectly acquainted.

The terms 'realism' and 'idealism' are now generally abandoned, on the whole not unwisely, but my own brand of idealism was a cautious one, not unmixed with some realism in regard to physical objects. While I have always distrusted over-bold assertions about the Whole, I have never ceased to believe that in philosophy analysis is only a means to synopsis. The idealist doctrine that our so-called knowledge is at best provisional and imperfect still seems to me to offer a healthy mean between dogmatism on the one hand and scepticism on the other. It also induces sympathy for attempts to develop any hypothesis in detail, because of the hope that they will bring out its errors and lead on to something better. As against this, the realism of the period, so far as it claimed infallible knowledge or unquestionable intuitions or a right to rule out other lines of investigation from the start, seemed to me to spring more from confidence of temperament than from depth of insight.

V

When suddenly translated in 1927 to the comparative peace of the Chair of Logic in Glasgow I hoped to find time for the study both of mathematical logic and of Kant's philosophy. During his sojourn in Oxford G. F. Hardy, the Cambridge mathematician, had aroused interest (including my own) in the former subject even if he had made no converts. The tradition of Adamson and Edward Caird on which I now entered placed me almost under an obligation to start lecturing at once on *The Critique of Pure Reason*. This latter task turned out to require the bulk of my energies during the next ten years, and other interests had to be neglected. I still wish I could have managed both subjects, but one must submit to the limitations of human life; and it would not be a good thing if all the philosophers of a period combined to explore a single avenue and left the grass to grow on all the others.

It was not, I think, purely the accident of a tradition that drove me to the study of Kant. I had always accepted the assumption that a firm grip on his doctrines was the necessary preliminary to further advance; and by this time I was convinced that there was some flaw in the idealist doctrines, which could be corrected only by going back to the fountain-head. But there was more to it than that. Though I did not profess to understand his work—on my first reading of the *Critique* I had to stop at the chapter on Schematism on the ground that nobody could possibly make head or tail of it—I had always felt drawn to him, chiefly perhaps because I saw that he was trying to work out the implications of a human experience which must develop in time. The *Critique* was one of the books I had to read yearly in preparation for my tutorials; and, although often baffled, I used to speak of him with an enthusiasm which, on looking back, seems to have been based on some natural sympathy rather than on exact knowledge.

In my innocence I had imagined that I could make his doctrines clear to myself in a couple of years given up to intensive study. The task proved far more formidable than I had expected. From the beginning I knew that the difficulties arose from the honesty and subtlety of his mind and not from muddle or confusion. I never had any use for the patchwork theory popular at that time, which supposed his work to be a mass of contradictions: if this were true, intelligent study of him would be useless, not to say impossible. It was a great pleasure when I first discovered a concentrated version of this strange error in Vaihinger's short essay on *The Transcendental Deduction of the*

Categories; for the argument there is as clear as it is clearly fallacious. Although it may sound arrogant to say so, the plain truth is that I found the commentators, both English and German, more misleading than helpful—their main effect after weary hours of labour was to make me feel that Kant was neither understandable nor worth understanding; yet when I returned to the original, I seemed, like Goethe, to be entering a lighted room. If I could have studied with Ebbinghaus of Marburg at that time, I should have saved myself an immense waste of effort; but I did not then even know his name, and the works of Klaus Reich and de Vleeschauwer, who is to me only less illuminating, were still unpublished. As it was, I had to struggle on as best I could against a mass of established errors. Year after year I produced a new version of my lectures, meeting with apparently unsurmountable difficulties and talking a great deal of nonsense in the process. In the end I believe I got clear enough at least to help others to make further advances, although I was not equipped to adjust Kant's thought to modern discoveries in mathematics and physics. It is my hope that a promised book by Reich may do something to supply this deficiency, and that a new injection of Kant's philosophy may stimulate thinking in the present age as it has done so often in the past.

During this period it was my good fortune to have close contacts with many Scottish philosophers, especially with my colleague A. A. Bowman, whose fertile mind and gift of utterance might have won him a more than local reputation if his work had not been cut short by an untimely death, which was hastened, I fear, by his devotion to good causes, particularly to the League of Nations, and by his incessant struggle to help a host of correspondents in the solution of their personal problems.

VI

By the time of my return to Oxford in 1937 the philosophical climate was already greatly altered. Although many of my seniors still survived to receive well-merited veneration, they no longer dominated the scene. Collingwood and I had become the last comparatively young representatives of the pre-War world with its different approach to philosophy; and although he struggled on manfully, his health was already impaired. It was a time for new men and new ideas. The change was the more obvious to me because of my ten years' absence, and the transition, which I should like to have seen at close quarters, had no doubt been gradual. Because of the direct personal connexion between teacher and pupil there is in the old universities of England a real continuity under surface differences; and men like H. H. Price —*anima naturaliter Kantiana*, if I may call him so—W. C. Kneale, J. D. Mabbott, and Gilbert Ryle appeared to be equally at home in the old world and the new. But the Cam was flowing into the Isis, and it seemed to me that a fresh era had begun.

It began under evil auspices. Just as my first two years of teaching as an Oxford tutor had ended with the First War, so my first two years of teaching as an Oxford professor ended with the Second. Indeed the second time was much worse, for in this case coming events cast their shadow well in advance and were preceded by the year of anxiety and shame which culminated in Munich and made serious thinking impossible. During the Second War I could only use my spare time in trying to do for Kant's ethics what I had already done for his metaphysic of experience. This was an easier task, and I believe I was able to show by reasoned argument that many of the traditional interpretations are absurd. Perhaps the time may come when they will no longer be dogmatically repeated without any attempt to answer the case against them.

VII

Whatever may be thought of post-War philosophy, there can be no doubt that it is very much alive. Its missionaries have gone out to the ends of the earth, some of them with almost too much evangelical zeal. Critics have found it narrow and inhuman, as if it had become at the best a game and at the worst a logomachy. Against such views may be set the almost lyrical remark once made to me by Richard Robinson in the Turl at Oxford on a summer's day, 'Never has there been such a blooming of philosophy in the whole history of the world.' This assessment receives at least external support from the sheer numbers both of those who teach and of those who study the subject in that ancient university, to say nothing of others. I should find some difficulty in agreeing with the lady who, whether seriously or in jest, began an argument by saying 'Now that we have escaped from the age of error'—this reminds me too much of my own youth—but I am sure that discussions today are as lively and intelligent as they ever were, and certainly no less co-operative. In spite of an increased burden of teaching, at least in my own parish of Oxford, there is a greater willingness to hazard the risks of publication. Articles may take a bigger place than they did in the past, but the number of good books is surprisingly great, and literary style has on the whole improved in clarity, if not always in elegance. There is a whole galaxy of brilliant young men who have already made their mark as a likely source of future illumination.

Although the Hegelian tradition has been worthily carried on by writers like G. R. G. Mure and T. M. Knox, the present age is as much dominated by the linguistic movement as the beginning of the century was by idealism, and it would be absurd to pass judgement on either in a couple of paragraphs. It is, however, obvious that the philosophical study of language is in itself of great value and interest—it ought to be extended, with the aid of philologists, to languages other than English, and also, with the aid of literary critics and even of a philosophical critic like Croce, to the language of poetry: it was at first too closely confined to that of mathematics and science; and its association with logical atomism and with behaviourism is little more than a historical accident. It is equally obvious that a new method has been developed for dealing with philosophical problems generally, although to claim that this is the only legitimate method is a sample of the exaggerations that often accompany a recent advance. In my opinion it is a mistake to suppose— if I may allow myself to exaggerate a tendency which rarely proceeds to such extremes—that any language, whether home-baked or dehydrated, can be used as a standard to which philosophical thinking must conform. But we should be blind not to see that the original dogmatism and narrowness are being gradually dispelled—that the whole movement is becoming more mellow and more flexible, and that the traditional questions of philosophy, at one time arrogantly swept aside, are again beginning to be considered, let us hope with deeper insight. Some doctrines familiar to veterans like myself from our philosophical infancy are emerging hesitantly as fresh discoveries. Even external criticism is better informed and more adequately equipped than it was at first. There is also a closer contact with America; and in spite of indifference to modern European philosophy outside one period in Vienna we have gained not a little from foreign scholars driven to our shores in their search for freedom.

If I were asked to state in one word the main impulse to all this new thinking, and particularly to the whole logical and linguistic movement of this century, I should take the question literally and say simply that it was science (including mathematics). The flaw in the idealist movement was a lack of interest in scientific thinking, a lack wholly alien to the Critical Philosophy from which it sprang. If it is not too parochial to say so here, I have never ceased to regret that a scheme for combining philosophy and science in the Oxford curriculum was rejected after the First War, mainly because Joseph suffered metaphysical qualms at the last moment. Even after the Second War similar proposals languished through lack of adequate support, but it is now possible at least to combine philosophy with psychology, and steps have been taken to provide teaching in the philosophy of science.

Indifference to science tends to pass over, as if at the behest of Hegel, into indifference to everything except science as a proper subject for philosophical study: ethics and aesthetics and political philosophy seemed to suffer a temporary eclipse at the very moment when they were most needed. But these tendencies may be ascribed both to the uncertainty of the times and to the ever mounting prestige of science, which—in spite of some confused thinking to the contrary—cannot but be ethically and aesthetically neutral. So great is this prestige that some philosophers seem almost to identify philosophic thinking with scientific, and to suppose that any non-scientific thinking must be mere emotive utterance. Even reputable philosophers have made assertions which in the past would have been regarded as showing either a congenital incapacity for the subject or a lack of the necessary education. But philosophical thinking about science is to be sharply distinguished from science itself, since it is concerned with the nature and validity of the principles on which scientific thinking proceeds. If this difference is admitted, there is no reason why philosophy should not similarly concern itself with the principles of art and morality and politics and history and religion. Even if it were confined to the study of language, the use of which is only one of the human activities in which rational principles are manifested, it would still be arbitrary to concentrate on the language of science and ignore all the others.

This more catholic view is, it seems to me, gradually winning acceptance. Unless it does so, I should fear even in this sober country a lapse into existentialism, which is one way of reacting against an over-emphasis on science and against a narrow intellectualism which confuses reasoning with rationality. It is always easy to predict events after they have happened, but one lesson to be drawn from the history of the last fifty years is that no one is likely to foretell in what direction philosophy will move next. My hope is that the wider sympathies of recent years will lead to more comprehensive and more synoptic philosophies; for although we are all agreed that one task of philosophy is to clear up particular muddles, I cannot believe that this is enough.

This excursion has turned out to be even more egotistical and more parochial that I expected at the outset, and it has explored the archaeological remains of the parish rather than its more modern buildings. I am particularly conscious that I have not done justice to the Cambridge thinkers, like C. D. Broad, from whom I have learned much, although not so much as I ought. I have not even mentioned John Wisdom, whose generous commendation of a linguistic suggestion that to me seemed obvious was a source of gratification many years ago. But if I had written of all whose thinking I respect, this article would have become a list of names, while if I had tried to express my debts adequately, it would have become a book. When I reflect on how much I could have said about how many even of those whom I have passed over in silence, I am almost tempted to accept the verdict that never—well, hardly ever—can there have been such a blooming of philosophy in the whole history of the world.

MAIN PUBLICATIONS

The Good Will. Allen and Unwin. 1927.
Kant's Metaphysic of Experience. Allen and Unwin. 1936.
The Categorical Imperative. Hutchinson's University Library. 1947.
The Moral Law. Hutchinson's University Library. 1948.
In Defence of Reason. Hutchinson's University Library. 1951.
An Alleged Right to Lie. Kant-Studien, Vol. 45, 1953/4
The Modern Predicament. Allen and Unwin. 1955.

WORKS EDITED

Philosophy and History (with Professor Klibansky). The Clarendon Press. 1936.
The Philosophical Series in Hutchinson's University Library.

THREE VIEWS CONCERNING
HUMAN KNOWLEDGE

By KARL R. POPPER

Professor of Logic and Scientific Method
in the University of London

THREE VIEWS CONCERNING
HUMAN KNOWLEDGE

I. *The Ultimate Betrayal of Galilean Science*

ONCE upon a time there was a famous scientist whose name was Galileo Galilei. He was tried by the Inquisition, and forced to recant his teaching. This caused a great stir; and for well over two hundred and fifty years the case continued to arouse indignation and excitement—long after public opinion had won its victory, and the Church had become tolerant of science.

But this is by now a very old story, and I fear it has lost its interest. For Galilean science has no enemies left, it seems: its life hereafter is secure. The victory won long ago was final, and all is now quiet on this front. So we take a detached view of the affair nowadays, having learned to think historically at last, and to understand both sides to a dispute. And nobody cares to listen to the bore who can't forget an old grievance.

What, after all, was this old case about? It was about the status of the Copernican 'System of the World' which, besides other things, explained the diurnal motion of the sun as only apparent, and as due to the rotation of our own earth.[1] The Church was very ready to admit that the new system was simpler

[1] I emphasize here the diurnal as opposed to the annual motion of the sun because it was the theory of the diurnal motion which clashed with Joshua 10, 12f., and because the explanation of the diurnal motion of the sun by the motion of the earth will be one of my main examples in what follows. (This explanation is, of course, much older than Copernicus—older even that Aristarchus—and had been repeatedly re-discovered; for example, by Oresme.)

than the old one: that it was a more convenient *instrument* for astronomical calculations, and for predictions. And Pope Gregory's reform of the calendar made full practical use of it. There was no objection to Galileo's teaching the mathematical theory, so long as he made it clear that its value was *instrumental* only; that it was nothing but a 'supposition', as Cardinal Bellarmino put it,[1] or a 'mathematical hypothesis'—a kind of mathematical trick, 'invented and assumed in order to abbreviate and ease the calculations'.[2] In other words, there were no objections so long as Galileo was ready to fall into line with Andreas Osiander who had said in his preface to Copernicus's *De revolutionibus:* 'There is no need for these hypotheses to be true, or even to be at all like the truth; rather, one thing is sufficient for them—that they should yield a calculus which agrees with the observations.'

Galileo himself, of course, was very ready to stress the superiority of the Copernican system as an *instrument of calculation.* But at the same time he conjectured, and even believed, that it was *a true description of the world;* and for him (as for the Church) this was by far the most important aspect of the matter. He had, indeed, some good reasons for believing in the truth of the theory. He had seen in his telescope that Jupiter and his moons formed a miniature model of the Copernican solar system (according to which the planets were moons of the sun). Moreover, if Copernicus was right, the inner planets (and they alone) should, when observed from the earth, show phases like the moon; and Galileo had seen in his telescope the phases of Venus.

---

[1]'. . . Galileo will act prudently', wrote Cardinal Bellarmino (who had been one of the inquisitors in the case **against** Giordano Bruno) '. . . if he will speak hypothetically, *ex suppositione* . . .: to say that we give a better account of the appearances, by supposing the earth to be moving and the sun at rest, than we could if we used excentrics and epicycles, is to speak properly; there is no danger in that, and it is all that the mathematician needs.' Cf. H. Grisar, *Galileistudien,* 1882, App. ix.

[2]The quotation is from Bacon's criticism of Copernicus in the *Novum Organum,* ii, 36.

The Church was unwilling to contemplate the truth of a New System of the World which seemed to contradict a passage in the Old Testament. But this was hardly its only reason. A deeper reason was clearly stated by Bishop Berkeley, about a hundred years later, in his criticism of Newton.

In Berkeley's time, the Copernican System of the World had developed into Newton's Theory of Gravity, and Berkeley saw in it a serious competitor of religion. He was convinced that a decline of religious faith and of religious authority would result from the new science if its interpretation by the 'free-thinkers' was correct; for they saw in its success a proof of *the power of the human intellect, unaided by divine revelation, to uncover the secrets of our world*—the reality hidden behind its appearance.

This, Berkeley felt, was to misinterpret the new science. He analysed Newton's theory with complete candour and great philosophical acumen; and a critical survey of Newton's concepts[1] convinced him that this theory could not possibly be anything but a 'mathematical hypothesis', that is, a convenient *instrument* for the calculation and prediction of phenomena or appearances; that it could not possibly be taken as a true description of anything real.

Berkeley's criticism was hardly noticed by the physicists; but it was taken up by philosophers, sceptical as well as religious. As a weapon it turned out to be a boomerang. In Hume's hands it became a threat to all belief—to all knowledge, whether human or revealed. In the hands of Kant, who firmly believed both in God and in the truth of Newtonian science, it developed into the doctrine that theoretical knowledge of God is impossible, and that Newtonian science must pay for the admission of its claim to truth by the renunciation of its claim to have discovered a real world behind the world of appearance: it was a true science of nature, but *nature* was precisely the world of mere phenomena, the world as it appeared to our assimilating minds. Later certain Pragmatists based their whole philosophy upon the view that the idea of 'pure' knowledge was a mistake; that

[1] See my 'Note on Berkeley as a Precursor of Mach', *Brit. Jour. Phil. Sci.*, vol. iv, pp. 26 ff.

there could be no knowledge in any other sense but in the sense of instrumental knowledge; that knowledge was power, and that truth was usefulness.

Physicists (with a few brilliant exceptions[1]) kept aloof from all these philosophical debates which remained completely in-conclusive. Faithful to the tradition created by Galileo they de-voted themselves to the search for truth, as he had understood it.

Or so they did until very recently. For all this is now past history. Today, the view of physical science founded[2] by Cardinal Bellarmino and Bishop Berkeley has won the battle without another shot being fired. Without any further debate over the philosophical issue, without producing any new argument, the *instrumentalist view* (as I shall call it) has become an accepted dogma. It may well be called now the 'official view' of physical theory since it is accepted by most of our leading theorists of physics (although neither by Einstein nor by Schrödinger). And it has become part of the current teaching of physics.

II. *The Issue at Stake*

All this looks like a great victory of philosophical critical thought over the 'naïve realism' of the physicists. But I doubt whether this interpretation is right.

Few if any of the physicists who have now accepted the instrumentalist view of Cardinal Bellarmino and Bishop Berkeley realize that they have accepted a philosophical theory. Nor do they realize that they have broken with the Galilean

[1]The most important of them are Mach, Kirchhoff, Duhem, Poincaré, Bridgman, and Eddington—all instrumentalists in various ways.

[2]Duhem claimed a greater number of philosophers and scientists as instrumentalists than I consider justifiable, although he has been followed in this by other historians of science. It must be admitted, however, that Euxodus (as it appears from Simplicius' commentary) set himself the task of evolving a system of rotating spheres, in order to deduce the observable phenomena of planetary motion, *without attri-buting physical reality to his spheres.*

tradition. On the contrary, most of them think that they have kept clear of philosophy; and most of them no longer care anyway. What they now care about, as physicists, is (a) *mastery of the mathematical formalism*, i.e. of the instrument, and (b) *its applications;* and they care for nothing else. And they think that by thus excluding everything else, they have finally got rid of all philosophical nonsense. This very attitude of being tough and not standing any nonsense prevents them from considering seriously the philosophical arguments for and against the Galilean view of science (though they will no doubt have heard of Mach[1]). Thus the victory of the instrumentalist philosophy is hardly due to the soundness of its arguments.

How then did it come about? As far as I can see, through the coincidence of two factors, (a) difficulties in the interpretation of the formalism of the Quantum Theory, and (b) the spectacular practical success of its applications.

(a) In 1927, Niels Bohr, one of the greatest thinkers in the field of atomic physics, introduced the so-called *principle of complementarity* into atomic physics, which amounted to a 'renunciation' of the attempt to interpret atomic theory as a description of anything. Bohr pointed out that we could avoid certain contradictions (which threatened to arise between the formalism and its various interpretations) only by reminding ourselves that the formalism as such was self-consistent, and that each single case of its application (or each kind of case) remained consistent with it. The contradictions only arose through the attempt to comprise, within *one* interpretation, the formalism together with more than one case, or kind of case, of its experimental application. But, as Bohr pointed out, any two of these conflicting applications were physically incapable of ever being combined in one experiment. Thus the result of *every single* experiment was consistent with the theory, and unambiguously laid down by it. This, he said, was all we could get. The claim to get more, and even the hope of ever getting

[1] But they seem to have forgotten that Mach was led by his instrumentalism to object to atomic theory—a typical example of *the obscurantism of instrumentalism* which is the topic of section V, below.

more, we must renounce; physics remains consistent only if we do not try to interpret, or to understand, its theories beyond (*a*) mastering the formalism, and (*b*) relating them to each of their actually realizable cases of application separately.[1]

Thus the instrumentalist philosophy was used here *ad hoc* in order to provide an escape for the theory from certain contradictions by which it was threatened. It was used in a defensive mood—to rescue the existing theory; and the principle of complementarity has (I believe for this reason) remained completely sterile within physics. In twenty-seven years it has produced nothing except some philosophical discussions, and some arguments for the confounding of critics (especially Einstein).

I do not believe that physicists would have accepted such an *ad hoc* principle had they understood that it was *ad hoc*, or that it was a philosophical principle—part of Bellarmino's and Berkeley's instrumentalist philosophy of physics. But they remembered Bohr's earlier and extremely fruitful 'principle of correspondence' and hoped (in vain) for similar results.

(*b*) Instead of results due to the principle of complementarity, other and more practical results of atomic theory were obtained; some of them with a sensational big bang. No doubt physicists were right in interpreting these successful applications as confirmations of their theories. But strangely enough, they took them as confirming the instrumentalist creed.

Now this was an obvious mistake. The instrumentalist view asserts that theories are *nothing but* instruments, while the Galilean view was that they are not only instruments but also (and mainly) descriptions of the world, or of certain aspects of the world. It is clear that, in this disagreement, even a proof showing that theories are instruments could not seriously be

[1] I have explained Bohr's 'Principle of Complementarity' as I understand it after many years of effort. No doubt I shall be told that my formulation of it is unsatisfactory. But if so, I am in good company; for Einstein refers to it as 'Bohr's principle of complementarity, the sharp formulation of which . . . I have been unable to achieve despite much effort which I have expended on it.' Cf. *Albert Einstein: Philosopher-Scientist*, ed. by P. A. Schilpp, 1949, p. 674.

claimed to support either of the two parties to the debate, since both were agreed on this point.

If I am right, or even roughly right, in my account of the situation, then philosophers, even instrumentalist philosophers, have no reason to take pride in their victory. On the contrary, they should examine their arguments again. For at least in the eyes of those who, like myself, do not accept the instrumentalist view, there is much at stake over this issue.

The issue, as I see it, is this.

One of the most important ingredients of our western civilization is what I may call the 'rationalist tradition' which we have inherited from the Greeks. It is the tradition of critical discussion—not for its own sake, but in the interests of the search for truth. Greek science, like Greek philosophy, was one of the products of this tradition,[1] and of the urge to understand the world in which we live; and the tradition founded by Galileo was its renaissance.

Within this rationalist tradition, science is valued, admittedly, for its practical achievements; but it is even more highly valued for its informative content, and for its ability to free our minds from old beliefs, old prejudices, and old certainties, and to offer us in their stead new conjectures and daring hypotheses. Science is valued for its liberalizing influence—as one of the greatest of the forces that make for human freedom.

According to the view of science which I am trying to defend here, this is due to the fact that scientists have dared (since Thales, Democritus, Plato's *Timaeus*, and Aristarchus) to create myths, or conjectures, or theories, which are in striking contrast to the everyday world of common experience, yet able to explain some aspects of this world of common experience. Galileo pays homage to Aristarchus and Copernicus precisely because they dared to go beyond this known world of our senses: 'I cannot', he writes,[2] 'express strongly enough my unbounded

[1]See my paper 'Towards a Rational Theory of Tradition', *Rationalist Annual*, 1949.

[2]Salviati says so several times, with hardly a verbal variation, on the Third Day of *The two Principal Systems*.

admiration for the greatness of mind of these men who conceived [the heliocentric system] and held it to be true . . . , in violent opposition to the evidence of their own senses. . . .' This is Galileo's testimony to the liberalizing force of science. Such theories would be important even if they were no more than exercises for our imagination. But they are more than this, as can be seen from the fact that we submit them to severe tests, by trying to deduce from them some of the regularities of the known world of common experience—i.e. by trying to *explain* these regularities. And these attempts to *explain the known by the unknown* (as I have described them elsewhere[1]) have immeasurably extended the realm of the known. They have added to the facts of our everyday world the invisible air, the antipodes, the circulation of the blood, the worlds of the telescope and the microscope, of electricity, and of tracer atoms showing us in detail the movements of matter within living bodies. All these things are far from being mere instruments: they witness to the intellectual conquest of our world by our minds.

But there is another way of looking at these matters. For some, science is still nothing but glorified plumbing, glorified gadget-making—'mechanics'; very useful, but a danger to true culture, threatening us with the domination of the near-illiterate (of Shakespeare's 'mechanicals'). It should never be mentioned in the same breath as literature, or the arts, or philosophy. Its professed discoveries are mere mechanical inventions, its theories are instruments—gadgets again, or perhaps super-gadgets. It cannot and does not reveal to us new worlds behind our everyday world of appearance; for the physical world is just surface: it has no depth. *The world is just what it appears to be. Only the scientific theories are not what they appear to be.* A scientific theory neither explains nor describes the world; it is nothing but an instrument.

I do not present this as a complete picture of modern instrumentalism, although it is a fair sketch, I think, of part of its original philosophical background. Today a much more

[1]See my paper 'The Nature of Philosophical Problems and Their Roots in Science', *Brit. Jour. Phil. Sci.*, vol. iii, pp. 124 ff.

important part of it is, I am well aware, the rise, and the self-assertion, of the modern 'mechanic' or engineer.[1] Still, I believe that the issue should be seen to lie between a critical and adventurous rationalism—the spirit of discovery—and a narrow and defensive creed according to which we cannot and need not learn and understand more about our world than we know already. A creed, moreover, which is incompatible with the appreciation of science as one of the greatest achievements of the human spirit.

Such are the reasons why I shall try, in this paper, to uphold at least part of the Galilean view of science against the instrumentalist view. But I cannot uphold all of it. There is a part of it which, I believe, the instrumentalists were right to attack. I mean the view that, in science, we can aim at, and obtain, *an ultimate explanation by essences*. It is in its opposition to this Aristotelian view (which I have called[2] 'essentialism') that the strength and the philosophical interest of instrumentalism lies. Thus I shall have to discuss and criticize two views of human knowledge—*essentialism* and *instrumentalism*. And I shall oppose to them what I shall call *the third view*—what remains of Galileo's view after the elimination of essentialism, or more precisely, after allowance has been made for what was justified in the instrumentalist attack.

III. *The First View: Ultimate Explanation by Essences*

Essentialism, the first of the three views of scientific theory to be discussed, is part of the Galilean philosophy of science. Within this philosophy, three elements or doctrines which concern us here may be distinguished. Essentialism (our 'first

[1] The realization that science is not indubitable *epistēmē* (*scientia*) has led to the view that it is *technē* (technique, art, technology); but the proper view, I believe, is that it consists of *doxai* (*opinions, conjectures*), controlled by critical discussion as well as by experimental *technē*. Cf. my 'Humanism and Reason', *Philosophical Quarterly*, April 1952.

[2] See section 10 of my 'Poverty of Historicism', part i, *Economica*, vol. xi, pp. 86 ff., and my *Open Society and its Enemies*, vol. i, chap. 3, § vi, and vol. ii, chap. 11, §§ i and ii.

view') is that part of the Galilean philosophy which I do not wish to uphold. It consists of a combination of the doctrines (2) and (3). These are the three doctrines:

(1) *The scientist aims at finding a true theory or description of the world* (and especially of its regularities or 'laws'), *which shall also be an explanation of the observable facts.* (This means that a description of these facts must be deducible from the theory in conjunction with certain statements, the so-called 'initial conditions'.)

This is the view I wish to uphold. It is a part of our 'third view'.

(2) *The scientist can succeed in finally establishing the truth of such theories, beyond all reasonable doubt.*

This second doctrine, I think, needs correction. All the scientist can do, in my opinion, is to test his theories, and to eliminate all those that do not stand up to the most severe tests he can design. But he can never be quite sure whether new tests (or even a new theoretical discussion) may not lead him to modify, or even to discard, a theory. In this sense, all theories are, and remain, hypotheses—conjectures (*doxai*) as opposed to indubitable knowledge (*epistēmē*).

(3) *The best, the truly scientific theories describe the 'essences' or the 'essential natures' of things—the realities which lie behind all the appearances.* Such theories are neither in need of, nor susceptible of, further explanation: they are *ultimate explanations*, and to find them is the ultimate aim of the scientist.

This third doctrine (in connection with the second) is the one I have called 'essentialism'. I believe that, like the second doctrine, it is mistaken.

Now what the instrumentalist philosophers of science, from Berkeley to Mach, Duhem, and Poincaré, have in common is this. They all assert that explanation is not an aim of physical science, since physical science cannot discover 'the hidden essences of things'. The argument shows that what they have in mind is what I call *ultimate* explanation.[1] Some of them, such

[1]The issue has been confused, at times, owing to the fact that the instrumentalist criticism of (ultimate) explanation was expressed by

as Mach and Berkeley, hold this view because they don't believe that there is such a thing as an essence of anything physical: Mach, because he does not believe in essences at all; Berkeley, because he believes only in spiritual essences, and thinks that the only essential explanation of the world is God. Duhem seems to think (on lines reminiscent of Kant[1]) that there are essences but that they are undiscoverable by human science (though we may, somehow, move towards them); like Berkeley he thinks that they can be revealed by religion. But all these philosophers agree that (ultimate) scientific explanation is impossible. And from the absence of a hidden essence which scientific theories could describe, they conclude that these theories (which clearly do not describe our ordinary world of common experience) describe nothing at all. Thus they are mere instruments.[2]

The instrumentalist philosophers therefore reject the third doctrine, i.e. the doctrine of essences. (I reject it too, but for somewhat different reasons.) At the same time, they reject, and are bound to reject, the second doctrine; for if a theory is an instrument, then it cannot be true (but only convenient, simple, economical, powerful, etc.). They even frequently call the theories 'hypotheses'; but they do not, of course, mean by this what I mean: that a theory is *conjectured to be true*, that it is a descriptive though possibly a false statement; although they do mean to say that theories are uncertain: 'And as to the usefulness of hypotheses,' Osiander writes (at the end of his preface), 'nobody should expect anything certain to emerge from astronomy, for nothing of the kind can ever come out

some with the help of the formula: the aim of science is *description rather than explanation*. But what was here meant by 'description' was the description *of the ordinary empirical world;* and what the formula expressed, indirectly, was that those theories which do not describe *in this sense* do not explain either, but are nothing but convenient instruments to help us in the description of ordinary phenomena.

[1]Cf. Kant's letter to Reinhold, 12.5.1789, in which the 'real essence' or 'nature' of a thing (e.g. of matter) is said to be inaccessible to human knowledge.

[2]See my 'Note on Berkeley, etc.', referred to above.

of it.' I agree with the view that there is no certainty about theories and that they may be improved; and even with the view that they are instruments, although I do not agree that this is the reason why there can be no certainty about theories. (The correct reason, I believe, is simply that our tests can never be exhaustive.) There is thus a considerable amount of agreement between my instrumentalist opponents and myself over the second and third doctrines. But over the first doctrine, there is complete disagreement.

To this disagreement I shall return later. In the present section, I shall try to criticize (3), or the essentialist view of science, on lines which are somewhat different from those of the instrumentalist criticism. For I cannot accept this criticism. Its argument that there can be no 'hidden essences' is based upon its conviction that *there can be nothing hidden* (or at least that what is hidden can only be known by divine revelation). From what I said in the last section, it will be clear that I cannot accept an argument that must lead to the rejection of the claim of science to have discovered the rotation of the earth; or atomic nuclei; or cosmic radiation; or the 'radio stars'.

I therefore readily concede to essentialism that much is hidden from us, and that much of what is hidden may be discovered. (I disagree profoundly with the spirit of Wittgenstein's dictum 'The riddle does not exist'.) And I do not even intend to criticize those who try to understand the 'essence of the world'. The essentialist doctrine I am contesting is solely *the doctrine that science aims at ultimate explanation;* that is to say, an explanation which (essentially, or by its very nature) cannot be further explained, and which is not in need of any further explanation.

Thus my criticism of essentialism does not aim at establishing the non-existence of essences; it merely aims at showing the obscurantist character of the rôle played by the idea of essences in the Galilean philosophy of science (down to Maxwell who was inclined to believe in them but whose work destroyed this belief). In other words, my criticism tries to show that, whether essences exist or not, the belief in them does not help us in any way and indeed is likely to hamper us; so that there is no reason why the scientist should *assume* their existence.[1]

This, I think, can be best shown with the help of a simple example—*the Newtonian theory of gravity*.

The essentialist interpretation of Newtonian theory is due to Roger Cotes.[2] According to him, Newton discovered that every particle of matter was endowed with *gravity*, i.e. with an inherent power or force to attract other matter. It was, also, endowed with *inertia*—an inherent power to resist a change in its state of motion (or to retain the direction and velocity of its motion). Since both gravity and inertia inhere in each particle of matter, it follows that both must be strictly proportional to the amount of matter in a body, and therefore to each other; hence the law of proportionality of inert and gravitating mass. Since gravity radiates from each particle, we obtain the square law of attraction. In other words, Newton's laws of motion simply describe, in mathematical language, the state of affairs due to the inherent properties of matter: they describe the *essential nature of matter*.

[1]This criticism of mine is thus frankly utilitarian, and it might be described as instrumentalist; but I am concerned here with a *problem of method* which is always a problem of the fitness of means to ends.

My attacks upon *essentialism*—i.e. upon the *doctrine of ultimate explanation*—have sometimes been countered by the remark that I myself operate (perhaps unconsciously) with the idea of an *essence of science* (or an *essence of human knowledge*), so that my argument, if made explicit, would run: 'It is of the essence or of the nature of human science (or human knowledge) that we cannot know, or search for, such things as essences or natures.' I have, however, answered, by implication, this particular objection at some length in my *Logic of Scientific Discovery* (sections 9 and 10, 'The Naturalist View of Method') and I did so before it was ever raised—in fact before I ever came to describe, and to attack, essentialism. Moreover, one might adopt the view that certain *things of our own making*—such as clocks—may well be said to have 'essences', viz. their 'purposes' (and what makes them serve these 'purposes'). And science, as a human, purposeful activity (or a method) *might* therefore be claimed, by some, to have an 'essence', even if they deny that natural objects have essences. (This denial is not, however, implied in my criticism of essentialism.)

[2]R. Cotes' Preface to the second edition of Newton's *Principia*.

Since Newton's theory describes, in this way, the essential nature of matter, he could explain the behaviour of matter with its help, by mathematical deduction. But Newton's theory, in its turn, is neither capable of, nor in need of, further explanation, according to Cotes, at least not within physics. (The only possible further explanation was that God has endowed matter with these essential properties.[1])

This essentialist view of Newton's theory was, by and large, the accepted view down to the last decades of the nineteenth century. That it was obscurantist is clear: *it prevented fruitful questions from being raised*, such as 'What is the cause of gravity?' or more fully, 'Can we perhaps explain gravity by deducing Newton's theory, or a good approximation of it, from a more general theory (which should be independently testable)?'

Now it is very illuminating to see that Newton himself had not considered *gravity* as an essential property of matter (although he considered *inertia* to be essential, and also, with Descartes, *extension*). It appears that he had taken over from Descartes the view that the essence of a thing must be a true or absolute property of the thing (i.e. a property which does not depend on the existence of other things) such as extension, or the power to resist a change in its state of motion, and not a relational property, i.e. a property which, like gravity, determines the relations (interactions in space) between one body and other bodies. Accordingly, he strongly felt the incompleteness of his theory, and the need to explain gravity. 'That gravity', he wrote,[2] ' should be innate, inherent, and essential to matter, so that one body may act upon another at a distance . . . is to me so great an absurdity that I believe no man who has in philosophical matters a competent faculty of thinking can ever fall into it.'

It is interesting to see that Newton condemned here, in anticipation, the bulk of his followers. To them, one is tempted

[1] There is an essentialist theory of Time and Space (similar to this theory of matter) which is due to Newton himself.
[2] Letter to Richard Bentley, February 25th, 1692-93 (i.e. 1693); cf. also the letter of January 17th.

to remark, the properties of which they had learned in school appeared to be essential (and even self-evident), although to Newton, with his Cartesian background, the same properties had appeared to be in need of explanation (and indeed to be almost paradoxical).

Yet Newton himself was an essentialist. He had tried hard to find an acceptable ultimate explanation of gravity, by trying to deduce the square law from the assumption of a mechanical push —the only kind of causal action which Descartes had permitted, since only push could be explained by the essential property of all bodies: that of extension.[1] But he failed. Had he succeeded, we can be certain that he would have thought that his problem was finally solved—that he had found the ultimate explanation of gravity.[2] But in this he would have been mistaken. The question 'Why can bodies push one another?' *can* be asked (as Leibniz first saw), and it is even an extremely fruitful question. (We now believe that they push one another because of certain repulsive electric forces.) But the Cartesian and Newtonian essentialism, especially if Newton had been successful in his attempted explanation of gravity, would most likely have prevented such a question from ever being raised.

These examples, I think, make it clear that the belief in essences (whether true or false) is liable to create obstacles to

[1]This Cartesian theory of causality is of decisive importance for the whole history of physics. It led to the principle of action by contact, and later to the more abstract 'principle of *action at vanishing distances*' (as I may call it), of an action propagated from each point to its immediate vicinity; i.e. to the principle of differential equations.

[2]Newton was an essentialist for whom gravity was not acceptable as an ultimate explanation, but he was unsuccessful in his attempts to explain it further mathematically. Descartes, in such a situation, would have postulated the existence of some push-mechanism: he would have proposed what he called a 'hypothesis'. But Newton, with a critical allusion to Descartes, said that, in this situation, he was not going to invent arbitrary *ad hoc* hypotheses (*hypotheses non fingo*). Of course, he could not but operate constantly with hypotheses (e.g. with an atomistic theory of light 'rays'); but this saying of his has been interpreted as an authoritative criticism of the method of hypotheses, or (by Duhem) as a declaration of his instrumentalism.

25

thought—to the posing of new and fruitful problems. Moreover, it cannot be part of science (for even if we should, by a lucky chance, hit upon a theory describing essences, we could never be sure of it). But a creed which is likely to lead to obscurantism is certainly not one of those extra-scientific beliefs (such as a faith in the power of critical discussion) which a scientist need accept.

This concludes my criticism of essentialism.

IV. *The Second View: Theories as Instruments*

The instrumentalist view has great attractions. It is modest, and it is very simple, especially if compared with essentialism.

According to essentialism, we must distinguish between (i) the universe of essential reality, (ii) the universe of observable phenomena, and (iii) the universe of descriptive language or of symbolic representation. I will take each of these to be represented by a square.

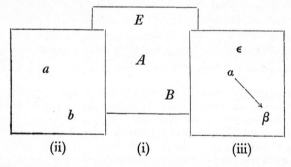

The function of a theory may here be described as follows.

a, b are phenomena; A, B are the corresponding realities behind these appearances; and α, β the descriptions or symbolic representations of these realities. E are the essential properties of A, B, and ϵ is the theory describing E. Now from ϵ and α we can deduce β; this means that we can explain, with the help of our theory, why a leads to, or is the cause of, b.

A representation of instrumentalism can be obtained from

this schema simply by omitting (i), i.e. the universe of the realities behind the various appearances. α then directly describes a, and β directly describes b; and ϵ describes nothing—it is merely an instrument which helps us to deduce β from α. (This may be expressed by saying—as Schlick did, following Wittgenstein—that a universal law or a theory is not a proper statement but rather 'a rule, or a set of instructions, for the derivation of singular statements from other singular statements'.[1])

This is the instrumentalist view. In order to understand it better, we may again take Newtonian dynamics as an example. a and b may be taken, for example, to be two positions of two spots of light (or two positions of the planet Mars); α and β are the corresponding formulae of the formalism; and ϵ is the theory strengthened by a general description of the solar system (or by a 'model' of the solar system). Nothing corresponds to ϵ in the world (in the universe ii): there simply are no such things as attractive forces, for example. Newtonian forces are not entities which determine the acceleration of bodies: they are nothing but mathematical tools whose function is to allow us to deduce β from α.

No doubt we have here an attractive simplification, a radical application of Ockham's razor. But although this simplicity has converted many to instrumentalism (for example, Mach), it is by no means the strongest argument in its favour.

Berkeley's strongest argument for instrumentalism was based upon his nominalistic philosophy of language. According to this philosophy, the expression 'force of attraction' must be a meaningless expression, since forces of attraction can never be observed. What can be observed are movements, not their hidden alleged 'causes'. This is sufficient, on Berkeley's view of

[1]See, for an analysis and criticism of this view my *Logic of Scientific Discovery*, 1956 (1935) especially note 7 to § 4, and my *Open Society*, note 51 to chap. 11. The idea that universal statements may function in this way can be found in Mill's *Logic*, book ii, chap. iii, 3: 'All inference is from particulars to particulars.' See also G. Ryle, *The Concept of Mind* (1949), chap. v, pp. 121 ff., for a more careful and critical formulation of the same view.

language, to show that Newton's theory cannot have an informative or descriptive content.

Now this argument of Berkeley's may perhaps be criticized for the intolerably narrow theory of meaning which it implies. For if consistently applied, it amounts to the thesis that all dispositional words are without meaning. Not only would Newtonian 'attractive forces' be without meaning, but also such ordinary dispositional words and expressions as 'breakable' (as opposed to 'broken'), or 'capable of conducting electricity' (as opposed to 'conducting electricity'). These are not names of anything observable, and they would therefore have to be treated on a par with Newtonian forces. But it would be awkward to classify all these expressions as meaningless, and *from the point of view of instrumentalism* it is quite unnecessary to do so: all that is needed is an analysis of the meaning of dispositional terms and dispositional statements. This will reveal that they have meaning. But from the point of view of instrumentalism, they do not have a descriptive meaning (like non-dispositional terms and statements). Their function is not to report events, or occurrences, or 'incidents', in the world, or to describe facts. Rather, their meaning exhausts itself in the permission or licence which they give us to draw inferences, or to argue, from some matters of fact to other matters of fact. Non-dispositional statements which describe observable matters of fact ('this leg is broken') have cash value, as it were; dispositional statements, to which belong the laws of science, are not like cash, but rather like legal *'instruments'* creating rights to cash.

One need only proceed one step further in the same direction, it appears, in order to arrive at an instrumentalist argument which it is extremely difficult, if not impossible, to criticize; for our whole question—whether science is descriptive or instrumental—is here exposed as a pseudo-problem.[1]

[1] I have not so far encountered in the literature this particular form of the instrumentalist argument; but if we remember the parallelism between problems concerning the *meaning* of an expression and problems concerning the *truth* of a statement, then we see that this argument closely corresponds to William James's definition of 'truth' as 'usefulness'.

The step in question consists, simply, in not only allowing meaning—an instrumental meaning—to dispositional terms, but also a kind of *descriptive meaning*. Dispositional words such as 'breakable', it may be said, certainly describe something; for to say of a thing that it is breakable is to describe it as a thing that can be broken. But to say of a thing that it is breakable, or soluble, is to describe it in a different way, and by a different method, from saying that it is broken or dissolved; otherwise we should not use the suffix 'able'. The difference is just this— that we describe, by using dispositional words, what may happen to a thing (in certain circumstances). Accordingly, dispositional descriptions *are* descriptions, but they have nevertheless a purely instrumental function. In their case, knowledge *is* power (the power to foresee). When Galileo said of the earth 'and yet, it moves', then he did, no doubt, assert a descriptive statement. But the function or meaning of this statement turns out, nevertheless, to be purely instrumental: it exhausts itself in the help it renders in deducing certain non-dispositional statements.

Thus the attempt to show that theories have a descriptive meaning *besides* their instrumental meaning is misconceived, according to this argument; and the whole problem—the issue between Galileo and the Church—turns out to be a pseudo-problem.

In support of the view that Galileo suffered for the sake of a pseudo-problem, it has been asserted that in the light of a logically more advanced system of physics, Galileo's problem has in fact dissolved into nothing. Einstein's general principle, one often hears, makes it quite clear that it is meaningless to speak of absolute motion, even in the case of rotation; for we can freely choose whatever system we wish to be (relatively) at rest. Thus Galileo's problem vanishes. Moreover, it vanishes precisely for the reasons given above. Astronomical knowledge can be nothing but knowledge of how the stars behave; thus it cannot be anything but the power to describe and predict our observations; and since these must be independent of our free choice of a co-ordinate system, we now see more clearly why Galileo's problem could not possibly be real.

I shall not, in this section, criticize instrumentalism, or reply to its arguments, except the very last one—the argument from general relativity. This argument is based on a mistake. From the point of view of general relativity, there is very good sense—even an absolute sense—in saying that the earth rotates; it rotates in precisely the same sense in which a bicycle wheel rotates. It rotates, that is to say, with respect to *all* local inertial systems. Indeed, relativity describes the solar system in such a way that, from this description, we can deduce that *any* observer situated on *any* sufficiently distant freely moving physical body (such as our moon, or another planet, or a star outside the system) would see the earth rotating, and could deduce, from this observation, that for its inhabitants, there would be an apparent diurnal motion of the sun. But it is clear that this is precisely the sense of the word 'it moves' which was at issue; for part of the issue was whether the solar system was a system like that of Jupiter and his moons, only bigger; and whether it would look like this system, if seen from outside. In all these questions, Einstein unambiguously supports Galileo. Nor should my argument be interpreted as an admission that the whole question reduces to one of observations, or of possible observations. Admittedly, both Galileo and Einstein intend, among other things, to deduce what an observer, or a possible observer, would see. But this is not their main problem. Both investigate physical systems and their movements. It is only the instrumentalist philosopher who asserts that what they discussed, or 'really meant' to discuss, were not physical systems but *only* the results of possible observations; and that their so-called 'physical systems' which *appeared* to be objects of study, were, *in reality*, only instruments for predicting observations.

V. *Criticism of the Instrumentalist View*

Berkeley's argument, we have seen, depends upon the adoption of a certain philosophy of language, convincing perhaps at first, but not necessarily true. Moreover, it hinges on the *problem of meaning*,[1] notorious for its vagueness and hardly offering a hope of a solution. The position becomes even more hopeless if we consider the more recent development of Berkeley's arguments, briefly sketched in the last section. I shall try, therefore, to force a clear decision of our problem by a different approach—by way of an analysis of science rather than an analysis of language.

My proposed criticism of the instrumentalist view of scientific theories can be summarized as follows.

Instrumentalism can be formulated as the thesis that scientific theories—the theories of the so-called 'pure' sciences—are nothing but computation rules (or inference rules), fundamentally of the same character as the computation rules of the so-called 'applied' sciences. (One might even formulate it as the thesis that 'pure' science is a misnomer, and that all science is 'applied'.)

Now my reply to instrumentalism consists in showing that there are profound differences between 'pure' theories and technological computation rules, and that instrumentalism can give a perfect description of these rules but is quite unable to account for the difference between them and the theories. Thus instrumentalism collapses.

The analysis of the many functional differences between computation rules (for navigation, say) and scientific theories (such as Newton's) is a very interesting task, but a short list of results must suffice here. The logical relations which may hold between theories and computation rules are not symmetrical; and they are different from those which may hold between various theories, and also from those which may hold between various computation rules. The way in which computation rules are *tried out* is different from the way in which theories are *tested*; and the skill which the application of computation rules demands is quite different from that needed for their (theoretical) discussion, and for the (theoretical)

[1]See, for this problem, my two books mentioned here in the footnote on p. 373, and my paper 'Self-Reference and Meaning in Ordinary Language', *Mind*, vol. 63, N.S., pp. 162 ff.

determination of the limits of their applicability. These are only a few hints, but they may be sufficient to indicate the direction and the force of the argument.

I am now going to explain just one of these points a little more fully, because it gives rise to an argument somewhat similar to the one I have used against essentialism. What I wish to discuss is the fact that theories are tested by *attempts to refute them* (attempts from which we learn a great deal), while there is nothing strictly corresponding to this in the case of technological rules of computation or calculation.

A theory is tested not merely by applying it, or by trying it out, but by applying it to very special cases—cases for which it yields results different from what we should have expected without the theory, or in the light of other theories. In other words, we try to select for our tests those crucial cases in which we should expect the theory to fail if it were not true. Such cases are 'crucial' in Bacon's sense; they indicate the cross roads between *two* (or more) theories. For to say that, without the theory in question, we should have expected a different result, implies that our expectation was the result of some other (perhaps an older) theory, however dimly we may have been aware of this fact. But while Bacon believed that a crucial experiment may establish or verify a theory, we shall have to say that it can, at most, refute or falsify a theory.[1] It is an attempt to refute it; and if it does not succeed in refuting the theory in question— if, rather, the theory is successful with its unexpected prediction —then we say that it is confirmed by the experiment. (It is the better confirmed[2] the less expected, or the less probable, the result of the experiment has been.)

---

[1] Duhem, in his famous criticism of crucial experiments (in his *Aim and Structure of Physical Theory*), discusses only the fact that crucial experiments can never *establish* a theory. He fails completely to discuss the question whether, and to what extent, they can *refute* it.

[2] The degree of confirmation will therefore increase with the improbability (or the content) of the confirming cases. See my 'Degree of Confirmation', *Brit. Jour. Phil. Sci.*, vol. v, pp. 143 ff.

Against the view here developed one might be tempted to object (following Duhem[1]) that in every test, it is not only the theory under investigation which is involved, but always the whole system of our theories and assumptions—in fact, more or less the whole of our knowledge—so that we can never be certain which of all these assumptions is refuted. But this criticism overlooks the fact that, if we take the two theories (between which the crucial experiment is to decide), each *together* with all this background knowledge, as indeed we must, then we decide between two systems which differ *only* over those two theories which are at stake. It further overlooks the fact that we do not assert the refutation of the theory as such, but of the theory *together* with that background knowledge; parts of which, if other crucial experiments can be designed, may indeed one day be rejected as responsible for the failure. (Thus we may even characterize a *theory under investigation* as that part of a vast system for which we have, if vaguely, an alternative in mind, and for which we try to design crucial tests.)

Now nothing sufficiently similar to such tests exists in the case of instruments, or rules of computation. An instrument may break down, to be sure, or it may become outmoded. But it hardly makes sense to say that we submit an instrument to the most severe tests we can design, in order to reject it if it does not stand up to them: an air frame, for example, can be 'tested to destruction', but this severe test is undertaken, not in order to reject the frame when it is destroyed, but to obtain information about the frame (i.e. to test a theory about it), so that it may be used *within the limits of its applicability* (or safety).

For instrumental purposes of practical application, a theory may continue to be used *even after its refutation*, within the limits of its applicability: an astronomer who believes that Newton's theory has turned out to be false will not hesitate to apply its formalism within the limits of its applicability.

We may sometimes be disappointed to find that the range of applicability of an instrument is smaller than we expected at first; but this does not make us discard the instrument *qua*

[1]See n. 1, p. 378.

instrument—whether it is a theory or anything else. On the other hand, a disappointment of this kind means that we have obtained new *information*, through refuting a *theory*—the theory that the instrument was applicable over a wider range.

Instruments, even theories *so far as they are instruments*, cannot be refuted, as we have seen. The instrumentalist interpretation will therefore be unable to account for real tests, which are attempted refutations, and will not get beyond the assertion that *different theories have different ranges of application*. But then it cannot possibly account for scientific progress. Instead of saying (as I should) that Newton's theory was falsified by crucial experiments which failed to falsify Einstein's, and that Einstein's theory is therefore better than Newton's, the consistent instrumentalist will have to say, with reference to his 'new' point of view, like Heisenberg: 'It follows that we do not say any longer: Newton's mechanics is false. . . . Rather, we now use the following formulation: Classical mechanics . . . is everywhere exactly "right" where its concepts can be applied.'[1]

Since 'right' here means 'applicable', this assertion amounts precisely to saying 'Classical mechanics is applicable where its concepts can be applied'—which is not saying much. But be this as it may, the point is that *by neglecting falsification, and stressing application, instrumentalism proves to be as obscurantist a philosophy as essentialism.* For it is only in searching for refutations that science can hope to learn and to advance. It is only in considering how its various theories stand up to tests that it can distinguish between better and worse theories and so find a criterion of progress.

Thus a mere instrument for prediction cannot be falsified. What may appear to us at first as its falsification turns out to be no more than a rider cautioning us as to its limited application.

[1] See W. Heisenberg in *Dialectica*, vol. 2, p. 333 f. Heisenberg's own instrumentalism is far from consistent, and he has many anti-instrumentalist remarks to his credit. But this article here quoted may be described as a consistent attempt to prove that his quantum theory leads of necessity to an instrumentalist philosophy, and thereby to the result that physical theory can never be unified, or even made consistent.

This is why the instrumentalist view may be used *ad hoc* for rescuing a physical theory which is threatened by contradictions, as was done by Bohr (if I am right in my interpretation, given in section ii, of his principle of complementarity). If theories are mere instruments of prediction, we need not discard any particular theory even though we believe that no consistent physical interpretation of its formalism exists.

Summing up we may say that instrumentalism is unable to account for the importance, to pure science, of severely testing even the most remote implications of its theories, since it is unable to account for the pure scientist's interest in truth and falsity. In contrast to the highly critical attitude requisite in the pure scientist, the attitude of instrumentalism (like that of applied science) is one of complacency at the success of applications. Thus it may well be responsible for the recent stagnation in theoretical physics.

VI. *The Third View: Conjectures, Truth, and Reality*

Neither Bacon nor Berkeley believed that the earth rotates, but nowadays everybody believes it, including the physicists. Instrumentalism is embraced by Bohr and Heisenberg only as a way out of the special difficulties which have arisen in quantum theory.

The motive is hardly sufficient. There is always a difficulty in interpreting the latest theories, and sometimes they perplex even their own creators, as we have seen in the case of Newton. Maxwell at first inclined towards an essentialist interpretation of his theory; a theory which ultimately contributed more than any other to the decline of essentialism. And Einstein inclined at first to an instrumentalist interpretation of relativity, giving a kind of operational analysis of the concept of simultaneity which contributed more to the present vogue of instrumentalism than anything else; but later he repented.[1]

[1]*Note added to the proofs.* When this paper went to press, Albert Einstein was still alive; and I intended to send him my paper as soon as printed. My remark referred to a conversation we had on the subject

I trust that the physicists will soon realize that the principle of complementarity is *ad hoc*, and (what is more important) that it only has the function of averting criticism and preventing the discussion of physical interpretations; though criticism and discussion are urgently needed for reforming any theory. They will then no longer believe that instrumentalism is forced upon them by the structure of contemporary physical theory.

Anyway, instrumentalism is, as I have tried to show, no more acceptable than essentialism. Nor is there any need to accept either of them, for there is a third view.[1]

The third view is not very startling or even surprising, I think. It preserves the Galilean doctrine that the scientist aims at a true description of the world, or of some of its aspects, and at a true explanation of observable facts ; and it combines this doctrine with the non-Galilean view that though this remains the aim of the scientist, he can never know for certain whether his findings are true, although he may sometimes establish with reasonable certainty that a theory is false.[2]

One may formulate this ' third view ' of scientific theories briefly by saying that they are *genuine conjectures*—highly informative guesses about the world which, although not verifiable (i.e. capable of being shown to be true) can be submitted to severe critical tests. They are serious attempts to discover the truth. In this respect, scientific hypotheses are exactly like Goldbach's famous conjecture in the theory of numbers. Goldbach thought that it might possibly be true; and it may well be true in fact, even though *we do not know, and may, perhaps, never know, whether it is true or not.*

I shall confine myself to mentioning only a few aspects of the 'third view', and only such aspects as distinguish it from essentialism and instrumentalism; and I shall take essentialism first.

---

[1] Cf. § 5 of my 'Note on Berkeley, etc.', referred to above.

[2] Cf. the discussion of this point in § v, above, and my *Logic of Scientific Discovery* (*passim*); also my paper 'Philosophy of Science: a Personal Report', in *British Philosophy in the Mid-Century*, edited by C. A. Mace; Allen and Unwin, London, 1956.

Essentialism looks upon our ordinary world as mere appearance behind which it discovers the real world. This view has to be discarded once we become conscious of the fact that the world of each of our theories may be explained, in its turn, by further worlds which are described by further theories—theories of a higher level of abstraction, of universality, and of testability. The doctrine of an *essential or ultimate reality* collapses together with that of ultimate explanation.

Since according to our third view the new scientific theories are, like the old ones, genuine conjectures, they are genuine attempts to describe these further worlds. Thus we are led to take all these worlds, including our ordinary world, as equally real; or better, perhaps, as equally real aspects, or sides, or layers, of the real world. (If looking through a microscope we change its magnification, then we may see various completely different aspects or layers of the same thing, all equally real.) It is thus mistaken to say that my piano, as I know it, is real, while its alleged molecules and atoms are mere 'logical constructions' (or whatever else may be indicative of their unreality); just as mistaken as it is to say that atomic theory shows that the piano of my everyday world is an appearance only—a doctrine which is clearly unsatisfactory once we see that the atoms in their turn may perhaps be explained as disturbances, or structures of disturbances, in a quantised field of forces (or perhaps of probabilities). All these theories are equal, in their claims to describe reality, although some of them are more conjectural than others.

Thus we shall not, for example, describe the so-called 'primary qualities' of a body (such as its geometrical shape) as real, and contrast them with its merely apparent 'secondary qualities' (such as colour), as the essentialists once did. For the extension and even the shape of a body have since become *objects of explanation*, in terms of theories of a higher level; of theories describing a further and deeper layer of reality—forces, and fields of forces—which are related to the primary qualities in the same way as these were believed, by the essentialists, to be related to the secondary ones. From our point of view, both kinds of qualities are equally real, and so are forces, and fields of forces—in spite of their undoubted hypothetical or conjectural character.

But is not just this conjectural or hypothetical character of our theories the reason why we should not ascribe reality to the worlds described by them? Should we not (even if we find Berkeley's 'to be is to be perceived' too narrow) *call only those states of affairs 'real' which are described by true statements*, rather than by conjectures which may turn out to be false? With these questions, we turn to the discussion of the instrumentalist doctrine which, with its assertion that theories are mere instruments, intends to deny the claim that anything like a world is described by them.

I accept the view (implicit in the classical or correspondence theory of truth[1]) that we should call a state of affairs 'real' if, and only if, the statement describing it is true. But it would be a grave mistake to conclude from this that the uncertainty of a theory, i.e. its hypothetical or conjectural character, diminishes in any way its implicit *claim* to describe something real. First of all, a conjecture *may* be true, and thus describe a real state of affairs. Secondly, if it is false, then it contradicts some real state of affairs (described by its true negation). Moreover, if we test our conjecture, and succeed in falsifying it, then we see very clearly that there was a reality—something with which it could clash.

Admittedly, if we do not know how to test a theory, we may be doubtful whether there is anything at all of the kind (or level) described by it; and if we positively know that it cannot be tested, then our doubts will grow; we shall suspect that it is a mere myth, or a fairy tale. *But if a theory is testable, then it implies that events of a certain kind cannot happen; and so it asserts something about reality.* (This is why we demand that the more conjectural a theory is, the higher should be its degree of testability.) Testable conjectures, at any rate, are thus

---

[1] See A. Tarski's work on the *Concept of Truth* (*Der Wahrheitsbegriff*, etc., *Studia Philosophica*, 1935, text to note 1: 'true = in agreement with reality').

conjectures about reality; from their uncertain or conjectural character it only follows that our knowledge concerning the reality they describe is uncertain or conjectural. And although only that is certainly real which can be known with certainty, it is a mistake to think that only that is real which is certainly real. We are not omniscient, and no doubt much is real that is unknown to us all. It is thus indeed the old Berkeleian mistake (in the form 'to be is to be known') which still underlies instrumentalism.

Theories are our own inventions, our own ideas; they are not forced upon us, but are our self-made instruments of thought: this has been clearly seen by the idealist. But some of these theories of ours can clash with reality; and when they do, we know that there is a reality; that there is something to remind us of the fact that our ideas may be mistaken. And this is why the realist is right.

Thus I agree with essentialism in its view that *science is capable of real discoveries*, and even in its view that, in discovering new worlds, our intellect triumphs over our sense experience. But I do not fall into the mistake of Parmenides—of denying reality to all that is colourful, varied, individual, indeterminate, and indescribable in our world.

With the belief that science can make real discoveries I take my stand with Galileo against instrumentalism. I admit that our discoveries are conjectural. But this is even true of geographical explorations. Columbus' conjectures as to what he had discovered were in fact mistaken; and Peary could only conjecture—on the basis of theories—that he had reached the Pole. But these elements of conjecture do not make their discoveries less real, or less significant.

There is an important distinction which we can make between two kinds of scientific prediction and which instrumentalism cannot make; a distinction which is connected with the problem of scientific discovery. I have in mind the distinction between the prediction of *events of a kind which is known*, such as eclipses, or thunderstorms, on the one hand, and, on the other hand, the prediction of *new kinds of events* (which the physicist calls 'new effects') such as the prediction which led to the discovery of wireless waves, or of zero-point energy, or to the artificial building up of new elements, not previously found in nature.

It seems to me clear that instrumentalism can only account for the first kind of prediction: if theories are instruments for prediction, then we must assume that their purpose must be determined in advance, as with other instruments. Predictions of the second kind can be fully understood only as discoveries.

It is my belief that our discoveries are guided, in these as in most other cases, by theory, rather than that theories are the result of discoveries 'due to observation'; for observation itself tends to be guided by theory. Even geographical discoveries (Columbus, Franklin, the two Nordenskjölds, Nansen, and Heyerdahl's Kon-Tiki expedition) are often undertaken with the aim of testing a theory. Not to be content with offering predictions, but to create new situations for new kinds of tests: this is a function of theories which instrumentalism can hardly explain without surrendering its main tenets.

But perhaps the most interesting contrast between the 'third view' and instrumentalism arises in connection with the latter's denial of the descriptive function of abstract words, and of disposition-words. This doctrine, by the way, exhibits an essentialist strain within instrumentalism—the belief that events or occurrences or 'incidents' (which are directly observable) must be, in a sense, more real than dispositions (which are not).

The 'third view' of this matter is different. I hold that most observations are more or less indirect, and that it is doubtful whether the distinction between directly observable incidents and whatever is only indirectly observable leads us anywhere. I cannot but think that it is a mistake to denounce Newtonian forces (the 'causes of acceleration') as occult, and to try to discard them (as has been suggested) in favour of accelerations. For accelerations cannot be observed any more directly than forces; and they are *just as dispositional:* the statement that a body's velocity is accelerated tells us that the body's velocity in the next second from now will exceed its present velocity.

In my opinion, *all universals are dispositional.* If 'breakable' is dispositional, so is 'broken', considering, for example, how a doctor decides whether a bone is broken or not. Nor should we call a glass 'broken' if the pieces would fuse the moment they were put together: the criterion of being broken is behaviour *under certain conditions.* Similarly, 'red' is dispositional: a thing is red if it is able to reflect a certain kind of light—if it 'looks red' in certain situations. But even 'looking red' is dispositional. It describes the disposition of a thing to make onlookers agree that it looks red.

No doubt, there are *degrees* of dispositional character: 'able to conduct electricity' is dispositional in a higher degree than 'conducting electricity now' which is still very highly dispositional. These degrees correspond fairly closely to those of the conjectural or hypothetical character of theories. But there is no point in denying reality to dispositions, unless we deny reality to all universals, and to all states of affairs, including incidents, and confine ourselves to using that sense of the word 'real' which, from the point of view of ordinary usage, is the narrowest and safest: to call only physical bodies 'real', and only those which are neither too small nor too big nor too distant to be easily seen and handled.

But even then we should realize (as I wrote twenty years ago[1]) that 'every description uses . . . universals; every statement has the character of a theory, a hypothesis. The statement, "Here is a glass of water " cannot be (completely) verified by any sense-experience, because the universals which appear in it cannot be correlated with any particular sense-experience. (An "immediate experience" is *only once* "immediately given"; it is unique.) By the word "glass", for example, we denote physical bodies which exhibit a certain *law-like behaviour* ; and the same holds of the word "water".'

[1]See my *Logic of Scientific Discovery*, end of § 25; also my 'Philosophy of Science: a Personal Report', especially §§ iv and v.

I do not think that a language without universals could ever work; and the use of universals commits us to asserting, and thus (at least) to conjecturing, the reality of dispositions—though not of inexplicable ones, i.e. of essences.

But if we are committed, or at least prepared, to conjecture the reality of forces, and of fields of forces, then there is no reason why we should not conjecture that a die has a definite *propensity* (or disposition) to fall on one or another of its sides; that this propensity can be changed by loading it; that propensities of this kind may change continuously; and that we may operate with fields of propensities, or of entities which determine propensities. An interpretation of probability on these lines might allow us to give a new physical interpretation to quantum theory—one which differs from the purely statistical interpretation, due to Born, while agreeing with him that probability statements can be tested only statistically. And this interpretation may, perhaps, be of some little help towards solving those grave and challenging difficulties in quantum theory which today imperil the Galilean tradition.

MAIN PUBLICATIONS

Logik der Forschung. Springer, Vienna. 1935.
The Logic of Scientific Discovery (translation of the foregoing with a *Postscript: After Twenty Years*). Hutchinson. 1956.
The Open Society and its Enemies. Routledge and Kegan Paul. 1945. Revised edition Princeton University Press, 1950, also Routledge, 1952.
Conjectures and Refutations. Routledge and Kegan Paul and Chicago University Press. 1956.
On the Theory of Deduction (I and II). *Proceedings of the Royal Dutch Academy*, 51. 1948.
Miseria dello storicismo. Editrice L'industria. Milano. 1954.
Misère de l'Historicisme. Librairie Plon. Paris. 1956.
    (These are translations in book form of 'The Poverty of Historicism', first published in *Economica* 11 and 12, 1944, 1945.)

THE ARGUMENT FROM ILLUSION

By H. H. PRICE

*Wykeham Professor of Logic in the University of Oxford and
Fellow of New College, Oxford*

THE ARGUMENT FROM ILLUSION

I DO not propose to state any views about philosophy in general, or even about the theory of knowledge in general. I shall confine myself to the particular department of the theory of knowledge which happens to interest me most, the epistemology of perception. A student of this subject cannot fail to be impressed by one feature of contemporary British philosophy. There is a widespread tendency to return to common sense. Nearly two hundred years ago, the common-sense philosopher Thomas Reid protested against the 'way of ideas'. In our own time, the terminology of sense-data has fallen into disrepute, and so have the more or less phenomenalistic theories, or analytical procedures, which were often associated with it. Some of this disrepute, I think, is due to misunderstandings of what the sense-datum philosophers were trying to say, as Reid perhaps also misunderstood what his predecessors were trying to say. The sense-datum philosophers might seem less paradoxical if more attention were paid to their remarks about visual depth, for example. Nevertheless, we should all like to hold a common-sense theory of perception if we could; and when distinguished thinkers assure us that we can hold such a theory, and even that we must, it is time to think again about the foundations of our subject.

There are three classical arguments which we ought to reconsider: the physiological argument, the argument from illusion, and the argument from inter-perceptual intervals. Whatever exactly these three arguments establish, it has been generally assumed, ever since the seventeenth century, that they do at least refute the 'Direct Realism' of common sense. In this essay

I shall only consider the argument from illusion, partly because I believe it is the most important of the three, and partly for a more personal reason. It is good to confess one's own errors, and I am persuaded that I myself have greatly over-estimated the force of this particular argument.

In the traditional expositions of the argument from illusion great stress has been laid on what are called the illusions of perspective, 'the seeming increase and diminution of objects according to their distance and the apparent variations in their figure', as Hume puts it. I now believe that this was a mistake. And if it was, it was an important mistake. For if perspectification is illusory, all vision is to that extent illusory. We cannot help seeing things in perspective if we see them at all.

Perhaps this last statement will be thought too sweeping. We are told, almost with menaces sometimes, that a man does *not* look smaller at twenty yards' distance than he does at three yards, and that a penny held in one's hand does not look oval when viewed obliquely, but circular. Certainly we must not neglect the phenomena of size-constancy and shape-constancy. But we must not exaggerate them either. They are less marked with unfamiliar objects than with familiar ones. They cease to occur when the object is cut off from its background, for instance by viewing it through a tube. They only occur at relatively short distances. From three hundred yards away the man really does look smaller than at three yards, and a circular pond or lawn seen from a distant mountain-top does look oval. The phenomena of size-constancy and shape-constancy could only show, at the most, that we *sometimes* do not see in perspective when it might have been expected that we should. There would still be plenty of perspectification left for the argument from illusion to exploit. But I think we must go farther. Even when there is size-constancy or shape-constancy, we are still seeing in perspective for all that. Certainly there is a sense in which a man ten yards away does not look larger as he walks towards us. Yet there is another sense in which he does; or, to speak more guardedly, there is still something about him which grows visibly larger as he approaches, whether or not we use the word 'looks' in describing it.

Thus if perspectival variations in the sizes and shapes of objects are illusory, we cannot avoid admitting that all our vision is to that extent illusory. And surely there *must* be something illusory about perspective? How can the same object really have many different sizes and shapes at the same time, when observer A is seeing it from one point of view, observer B from another, and C from a third? Surely the church spire on the horizon is not really smaller than it is when seen from across the street? If anyone wishes to answer this perspectival part of the argument from illusion, he cannot just wave the facts of perspective aside with a few words about size-constancy and shape-constancy. The facts are there, and are not to be abolished so easily. If a common-sense philosopher thinks that they have been misinterpreted in the traditional argument from illusion, he must offer a different analysis of them, one which is compatible with the Direct Realist assumptions of the ordinary man. Can this be done? I wish to suggest that it can.[1]

Let us begin with perspectival size, and consider perspectival shape later. Suppose we see a motor car which is approaching us along the road. As the motor car comes nearer, there is certainly something which grows larger, not merely appears to grow larger, but actually does; and that is, the proportion of one's field of view which that particular object takes up. ('The field of view' may be defined quite simply as the whole of what someone is visually aware of at a given time.) If the distance diminishes sufficiently, we may even find that the object takes up the entire field of view. It may do this, even if its physical size is quite small. A newspaper, for instance, can fill up the whole field of view. Again, a physically small object, such as a matchbox, if it is near enough, can 'cover' or 'eclipse' a very much larger object, for instance a large building two hundred feet long. It will be noticed that there is nothing

[1] Cf. J. Cook Wilson's essay on 'Primary and Secondary Qualities', *Statement and Inference*, vol. ii, especially pp. 790 ff.

'merely apparent' about the familiar facts I have just been describing. An object really does take up a larger portion of the field of view as it approaches, or as we approach it. A physically small object a short distance away really does cover or eclipse a physically larger object which is farther away; and if the small object is close enough, it really does take up the entire field of view. Conversely, of course, an object fills up a smaller and smaller portion of the field of view as it recedes from us, or as we recede from it, though its physical size remains the same. This again is not something which merely appears to happen. It really does happen. At the same time, the object's chance of being 'eclipsed' by nearer objects increases. Not only is its portion of the field of view diminished, but also its tenure of even that diminished portion is more precarious. A mere bush by the roadside may 'block out' a large mountain ten miles away.

It would be quite intelligible to speak of the 'field of view size' of an object. We could say that its field of view size is greater if the object fills up a larger part of some field of view, and smaller if it fills up a smaller part. That is what its perspectival size amounts to. Accordingly, we could sum up, so far, by saying that the field of view size of an object really does vary with the distance from which the object is seen. And so far as *this* sort of size is concerned, an object may have several different sizes at the same time. From here, where I am, this building fills up nearly the whole of the field of view. From the other side of the square, where you are, the same building fills up a much smaller part of the field of view. Of course it cannot have several different *physical* sizes at the same time. It cannot be at once fifty feet high and at the same time only five inches high. Perspectival size, or field of view size as I have called it, is something quite different from the physical size which is measured in feet and inches. The belief that there is something illusory about perspectival size, the belief that there is even a kind of contradiction in it (on the ground that the same object would have to possess many different sizes at the same time), a contradiction only to be avoided by saying that some perspectival sizes, or perhaps all, are 'merely apparent' and not real—these beliefs have arisen from confusing the two different sorts of size, field of view size on the one hand, and physical size on the other.

Nevertheless, it is a mistake to think that field of view size cannot be measured at all. And it is therefore misleading to say, as some have, that the physical size of an object is just its measurable size, as if field of view size differed from physical size by being *un*measurable. Field of view size cannot be measured in feet or inches, metres or centimetres. But it can be measured in angular magnitudes. The portion of the field of view which an object takes up can be measured in 'square degrees', e.g. 10° in the up-and-down dimension multiplied by 6° in the left-to-right dimension.

To make this clear, we have to introduce the notion of seeing in a direction. If I may say so, our seeing has a *multi-angular* character. Every object we see is seen in a direction; and any two parts of it which can be visually discerned are seen in different directions. From here I see the door of this room. The left-hand edge of the door is in one direction from here, and the right-hand edge is in a different direction from here. These two directions are at an angle to one another. I cannot say, without the use of surveying instruments, just what this angle is; about 10° perhaps. But if I consider not merely the door but the whole of the back wall of the room, I can easily see that this has a much larger angular magnitude from here than the door has. With every object which can be seen at all, its extremities are in different directions from 'here', the place where the observer is. And the *amount* of this difference (the angular magnitude of the object's height and of its breadth) is greater when the object is near and smaller when it is farther away. As the object recedes, the directions in which its extremities are seen differ less and less, until they differ only minimally. So far as its field of view size is concerned, the object is now a 'mere dot'; and after this, if it continues to recede, it is no longer seen at all. Suppose the object is a man. Let us fix our attention on his hands. As he goes farther and farther away, there is less and less difference between the direction in which his right hand is seen and the direction in which his left hand is seen. And we may notice that this is still so, even when he has phenomenal size-constancy during the earlier part of his journey.

If we bear in mind the multi-angular character of vision we can easily understand how a matchbox only three inches long can exactly 'cover' or 'eclipse' a building two hundred yards long. The two objects being placed as they are, the extremities of the matchbox are in the same directions from here as the extremities of the building. For similar reasons, a physically small object (if it is not transparent) can take up the entire field of view: that is, it can have the maximum field of view size. In every one of the directions in which I am seeing, I see only newspaper. The whole of the visually-available angular magnitude is appropriated by this one physically small object.

In the facts which I have been describing, about the proportion of the field of view which an object takes up, the angular magnitude it has in relation to the place from which the view is being seen, the way these quantities vary with the distance between the object and the observer—in all this, there is nothing illusory whatever. It is just an objective fact of Nature that the angle which an object subtends at a point P varies with the distance between the object and P. Even when there is no one in the lecture-room, the various objects in the room and outside the window are in different directions from a point P just in front of the middle of the blackboard. And it still remains true that the eastward edge of the table is in one direction from P, while its westward edge is in a different direction from P (likewise its southward and northward edges). Thus the table still has a perfectly definite angular magnitude in relation to P, and an equally definite but smaller angular magnitude in relation to another point P′ outside the window. There is nothing 'subjective' or 'merely apparent' about the difference between being north of a certain place and being north-north-west of it.

On the other hand, the facts I have been describing are not facts of physical optics either. In what I have been saying about the geometry of fields of view no mention has been made of light rays, nor of the complicated optical apparatus of the human eye. When I spoke of the multi-angular character of vision and pointed out that different parts of an object which we see are seen in different directions, I was not speaking of the way light rays from different parts of the object enter the eye from different directions. When I said that we always see in a direction, and in many different directions at once, it was seeing itself, the character of our actual visual awareness, which I was trying to describe, and not the physical causes of our seeing in that way. All the facts I have been describing could be detected by someone who was entirely ignorant of physical optics; and of course he could be equally ignorant of physiology too. Indeed, they were familiar to all mankind long before the science of physical optics was heard of.

If this account of perspectival size is acceptable, there should be nothing very puzzling about perspectival shape. Suppose there is a long wall, running east and west, and we view it obliquely from a place a few yards away from its eastern end. We are inclined to say that we see a 'perspectivally distorted' shape, tapering or converging towards its farther end. We then go to the farther end, stand a few yards away from it, and view the wall obliquely once more. Again we are inclined to say that we see a perspectivally distorted shape, but a different one, tapering in the opposite direction. But there is no distortion at all. When we see the wall obliquely, the nearer parts of it really do take up a larger portion of the field of view than the more distant parts. Let us suppose that the wall is divided into a series of thin vertical strips. Then, from the place at which we are, the nearer strips really do have a greater angular magnitude than the more distant ones. Whichever of the vertical strips we care to consider, we notice that its top end is seen in one direction and its bottom end in another direction. The *difference* between these two directions diminishes progressively as we progress along the series. There is nothing illusory about this, and there is no distortion either. To talk of a 'perspectivally distorted' shape is quite inappropriate. The perspectival taper which the wall has from here, its 'field of view shape' from here, as we might call it, is just a consequence of these differences in the respective field of view sizes of its parts. And as there is nothing unreal or illusory about these different field of view sizes, there is nothing unreal or illusory about the field of view shape which the wall as a whole has from this particular place. Suppose it is a place a few yards north of the eastern end of the wall. It is just a fact that in relation to this place the different vertical strips actually do have different angular magnitudes, decreasing steadily from east to west. And they would still have them even if there were no observer at the place; just as the objects in the lecture-room still have their different angular magnitudes in relation to a point in front of the middle of the blackboard, even when there is no one in the lecture-room to see them. In relation to another place, near the western end of the wall, it is the western end which has the greatest angular magnitude and the eastern end which has the smallest. And this too is still true even when there is no observer at *that* place. Thus there is nothing very puzzling about the fact that the wall can taper perspectively in two opposite directions at the same time. This sort of taper, unlike the physical taper of a wedge or of the letter V, exists only in relation to a place or point of view, and in relation to different places an object can taper in different directions and in different degrees at the same time.

If this account of perspectival size and shape is correct, there is nothing in the facts of perspective which need trouble a common-sense philosopher. He can maintain that in purely perspectival vision, uncomplicated by such phenomena as refraction or by physiological disorders, what we are visually aware of is the *directions* in which objects are from 'here', the place which is our present point of view; and if we consider just one single object which is visible from here, the wall for instance, what we are aware of is the directions in which the parts of the object are from here. It can be claimed that, in respect of the directions in which they are from here, all the different parts of the wall which are visible from here present themselves to the percipient as they really are, so long as his vision is purely perspectival. There is no illusion about it, and no distortion, however obliquely the object is viewed. Just because the wall actually has a rectangular shape—because of this, not in spite of it—the end of it which is farther away has a smaller angular magnitude than the near end has. In purely perspectival vision every visually-discernible bit of the wall's rectangular outline is seen in the direction in which it actually is.

So far as it relies upon the phenomena of perspective, then, the traditional argument from illusion seems to have no force at all, and no tendency to refute the Direct Realist epistemology which is the philosophical formulation of our common-sense assumptions.

But of course there *are* illusions, even though the phenomena of perspective are not among them. There are indeed many different kinds of illusion, and still more if we include hallucinations. There is no getting away from the fact that objects do quite often look other than they are; sometimes too they feel other than they are when touched, the noises they emit sound other than they are, etc. Sometimes, moreover, there appears to be an object which does not in fact exist at all, for example, the pool of water there appears to be on the tarmac when we experience a familiar kind of mirage. But if the phenomena of perspective are not illusory, the genuine illusions which remain in our hands are much less troublesome. It can be argued that they are just occasional abnormalities, and that they can be dealt with as it were piecemeal, by considering the various perceptual procedures which we use for detecting them and correcting them; whereas if the phenomena of perspective were illusions, as the traditional argument assumes, it would follow that *all* our visual perceptions have something illusory about them. We certainly could not say that perspective is just an occasional abnormality (as straight sticks occasionally look bent), because we always see in perspective whenever we see anything.

It would, however, be true that all vision is at least partially illusory, if Locke's theory of colour were correct. Indeed, his doctrine of Secondary Qualities entails that all perception whatever is at least partially illusory. Again, it would be true that all vision, and all touch too, is partially illusory, if the precisely localized surfaces and clear-cut boundaries which solids and liquids appear to us to have do not really belong to them, but merely appear to do so because of the limited acuity of our senses, as the study of physics has led some philosophers to suppose. These arguments, and not the traditional argument from illusion, are the most troublesome ones, if we wish to hold a common-sense theory of perception and the external world. I doubt whether one could answer them without departing in some degree from the assumptions of common sense; at the best, one could only hope to keep as close to these assumptions as the complexity of the facts permits.

MAIN PUBLICATIONS

Perception. Methuen. 1932.

Hume's Theory of the External World. Oxford University Press. 1940.

Truth and Corrigibility. Inaugural Lecture. Oxford University Press. 1936.

Thinking and Representation. Annual Philosophical Lecture to the British Academy, 1946. Oxford University Press.

Thinking and Experience. Hutchinson's University Library. 1953.

Some Aspects of the Conflict between Science and Religion. Eddington Memorial Lecture, 1953. Cambridge University Press.

BELIEF AND ACTION

By L. J. RUSSELL

Emeritus Professor of Philosophy
in the University of Birmingham

BELIEF AND ACTION

I

I HAVE been asked to deal with some particular problem, and I should wish to do so in such a way as to throw into relief my view of the nature and functions of philosophical activity at the present time. I use this last phrase in preference to either 'philosophy' or 'philosophical thinking' for various reasons. I want to avoid any suggestion, which the word 'philosophy' might convey, that there is a specific subject comparable in many ways with mathematics or physics or economics, with its own problems and methods, reaching conclusions which can be taken over and used by workers in other fields or by ordinary people as a help for the ordinary business of living; and still more to avoid the suggestion that something can be said about the nature and functions of philosophy without any time limitation. For this reason I have always preferred to speak of philosophizing rather than of philosophy, indicating an activity which has to be engaged in by each individual for himself rather than a set of doctrines which can be added to and improved on by successive workers. Not that the word 'philosophizing' negates the notion that philosophers can learn from their predecessors and contemporaries and profit from their mistakes, so that old problems come to be more precisely delineated, assumptions come to be more clearly stated and their implications analysed, blind alleys come to be charted, lines of fruitful exploration indicated. Indeed the word 'philosophizing' is useful just because it has no specific implications either way. You learn to do it by seeing what the people called philosophers have been doing and then gradually by doing it you form your own ideas of what it is that is to be done; and whether you decide in the end that all philosophers have been engaging in just the same kind of activity through the ages or that the activity has changed through time your decision is an integral part of your own philosophizing.

As an alternative to the word 'philosophizing' it is useful to have a more abstract term available; and I prefer to speak of 'philosophical activity' rather than of 'philosophical thinking' in order not to stress at the outset the suggestion that the activity is essentially one of thinking. Stress on thinking may lead to the assumption that philosophical reflection involves turning one-self as far as possible into a purely intellectual machine, getting rid as far as possible of one's emotions, leaving aside as far as possible all practical activities and all reference to practical considerations in one's treatment of one's problems. What I want to begin with is the suggestion that it is an activity engaged in by the whole person, and may bring into function all the sides of the person. What we like or dislike, what we could not bring ourselves emotionally to accept, affects our thinking, and the best way to ensure that our thinking will affect our likes and dislikes and our emotional attitudes is to bring them explicitly into the account as something that plays its part and must therefore undergo the discipline that all thinking imposes. As Otto Neurath said, there is no objection to wishful thinking so long as it is thinkful wishing. Further, it will be the main purpose of the present paper to discuss the part played by the practical decisions we make in social life, in determining our general system of beliefs, and to suggest that our study of the criteria of justifiable beliefs should include serious consideration of the ways in which our beliefs are related to our practical activities. 'Philosophical thinking' then would in my view overstress the intellectual factor; 'philosophical activity' commits us to less.

Finally, I speak of 'philosophical activity at the present time' in order to leave open the possibility that the activity functions differently in different epochs of social culture, with different aims and different methods. I do not know how the nature and functions of philosophical activity, taken timelessly, could be described or defined. It has been described by its practitioners in very different ways in different periods of its history.

II

I shall begin then with an attempt to show that our general system of beliefs is affected by our practical decisions about how to behave in practical life. Changes in the social structure often do lead members of the society, through practical considerations, to sanction types of action previously condemned or to condemn types of action previously sanctioned; and when this happens the system of ideas on which the previous approval or condemnation was based has to be changed, and replaced by a system of ideas more in harmony with existing attitudes. The evidence seems to suggest that at least sometimes the decision to accept one system of ideas and to reject others is not due to the fact that people have come to see that the one system is inherently sounder than the others, but rather to the fact that the type of social life in which they are engaged can be satisfactorily carried on only if certain forms of activity are approved and encouraged, and that in consequence a system of ideas is sought for which gives theoretical backing to this approval and encouragement.

If this can be made out, then the further question arises of the significance of these practical considerations when we are asking whether there are any criteria which enable us to distinguish between true and false beliefs.

III

Two illustrations, taken because there have been many studies of the facts by historians, will serve to bring out the point I want to make.

The first one concerns the attitude toward the taking of interest on loans (usury).[1] The taking of interest (however small)

[1]See e.g. *A Discourse on Usury*, by Dr. Thomas Wilson, with introduction by R. H. Tawney, London, 1925. H. M. Robertson, *The Rise of Economic Individualism*, Cambridge, 1933.

was condemned by the Church in the Middle Ages, and it is now an essential part of every day life. What was condemned was lending on condition of receiving back at a stated time not only what one lent but more, without the lender taking any risk. For this was an arrangement whereby money was enabled to beget money without its owner either doing or risking anything. If he contributed money as a share in a joint enterprise, taking the risks of the enterprise, he was allowed to share in any profits.

One can see the usefulness of encouraging neighbours in small relatively self-contained communities, depending on local crops, to lend to one another in cases of temporary difficulties; and so long as the economy was small-scale, trading being within a limited area, and capital playing a relatively small part in the organization of business, one can see that money lending as a way of making gains out of the troubles of one's neighbours would look unsavoury. But the history of the subject shows how difficult condemnation of interest on loans became, as the use of capital in business became more widespread and more important; and gradually both the Catholic and the Protestant churches had to change their attitude. The business man could put to gainful purposes more money than he himself possessed; he needed someone from whom he could borrow, and he was perfectly willing to pay interest. This kind of lending was not to tide over temporary difficulties, and so was not the kind of neighbourly act to be included under the heading of charity. However much one might object to an unscrupulous money-lender charging high rates of interest to people in distress, it was difficult to see why one should object to a person taking interest on a loan which a business man would use in activities profitable to himself.

In course of time the use of borrowed capital became a more and more important part of the economic structure. This change was not preceded by a change in ideas; it took place in opposition to them; and compromises which tarnish the theoretical purity of the ideas were introduced in response to pressure of the practical facts, until finally the old ideas were thrust almost entirely into the background.

The old arguments against usury owed their strength to factors of two different sorts. On the one side are those I have already referred to, viz. that the nature of the social structure was such that it seemed of primary importance to encourage neighbourly acts and discourage taking advantage of the distress of one's neighbour, while the disadvantages of the prohibition of usury as one of the ways of doing this were not so apparent. On the other side are the medieval Christian views about man's destiny and the nature of society, which R. H. Tawney has admirably described under the two heads of the functional view of class organization and the doctrine of economic ethics.[1] One result of this was to stress the view[2] that 'Labour —the common lot of mankind—is necessary and honourable; trade is necessary, but pernicious to the soul; finance, if not immoral, is at best sordid and at worst disreputable.' It is in this atmosphere that usury comes to be judged and condemned. But in addition to this system of ideas and closely integrated with it are more specific grounds for the condemnation of usury, viz. texts from the Old and New Testaments and from Aristotle's Politics. I need not go into these matters here; what is important for my purposes is the fact that texts from such sources had a special authoritativeness which enabled them to be separated from their particular context, and from the particular social circumstances to which they originally referred, and treated as pointers to timeless truth. This use of authority meets us in all fields of discussion right up to the seventeenth century, and in some fields even later. It was an important part of what I have called the general system of beliefs of the period, and affected many of the beliefs in that system.

The general point I want to put forward is this. In consequence of changes in the circumstances of society (in the present instance mainly through economic causes) more and more people want to behave in ways hitherto objected to, and find means of doing so. What was prohibited in the interest of

[1] *Religion and the Rise of Capitalism*, chap. i, § i, Pelican Edition, p. 37.   [2] P. 46.

certain social values comes to be looked on as itself having so much social value that people are unwilling to give it up. It gradually becomes incorporated into the set of accepted ways of behaving.

When such a thing happens, acceptance of the new type of behaviour calls for the acceptance of principles and points of view justifying the new type of behaviour, and weakens the prestige of the old arguments by which this type of behaviour was condemned. It also tends to weaken the whole system of ideas from which these arguments sprang.

If you start with such respect for the scriptures that any text may be taken out of its context and used as if it were a universal principle, the more often this leads to a condemnation of practices that are so essential a part of your lives that you refuse to condemn them, the more your respect for this kind of use of the scriptures becomes weakened. Again, the functional view of class organization (as described by Tawney) becomes weakened through the same processes of social change as weaken the objections against usury: people come to want to behave in so many ways which would be condemned by this functional view that it loses prestige.

IV

The second illustration concerns changes in the attitude of people in this country and elsewhere on the desirability of family limitation through birth control. Here again we have factors of two sorts, practical and theoretical. Under certain conditions of society, with a high death rate, a relatively self-contained family economy and a limited use of machines, large families are important partly for social survival and partly to lighten the burden of work. The favoured systems of ideas are those which strengthen the family. The view held by some Christians of chastity as better than marriage, which would by itself cut violently across these social needs, is cleverly used in the doctrine of marriage as a sacrament as a way of providing for them. The injunction to 'be fruitful and multiply'; the promise that 'God will provide' when it seems difficult to see how to make room for another child; doctrines against 'interfering with nature'; all combine to justify the kind of behaviour which, in certain circumstances of society, is generally held to be desirable.

The reasons leading first the professional classes and then the working classes in this country to limit the number of children are largely (though not entirely) practical. They follow in consequence of the new medical knowledge and the new sanitary arrangements which led in the nineteenth century to an enormous decrease in the death rate; of the changes in social institutions which opened up possibilities of social life outside the home, and in consequence not dependent on large families; of new business openings which required a longer and better education for children if they were to succeed; and so on. People wanted to do more for their children, and for this it was necessary to have fewer. They wanted a wider life for themselves now that a wider life had become possible.[1]

All this tends to weaken the old arguments against birth control, and in doing so helps to weaken the appeal of the whole system of ideas from which these arguments sprang. What people seek is a system of ideas through which they can justify the modes of behaviour which they regard as leading to a desirable life. Beliefs, we can say, are not wholly an affair of reason or intellect; certain types of argument owe their appeal partly to their plausibility in relation to the general system of ideas already accepted, partly to the way in which they fit in with, lead to the approval of, those social practices which are felt to be important for the maintenance of a satisfactory social life. Change the conditions of that social life, change in consequence some of the social practices and you alter the strength of appeal of the arguments. You may gradually change the whole system of ideas.

[1] I have mentioned only a few typical points. For fuller discussions see *Report of the Royal Commission on Population*, Cmd. 7695, pp. 39 ff., or *Population Policy in Great Britain*, P.E.P., London, 1948, pp. 65 ff.

V

An example of this kind of change which is taking place at the present time is to be found in the increase in the number of divorces and of remarriage of divorced persons. This is now coming to be regarded by many people as a desirable way of repairing an unfortunate mistake, and the condemnation of re-marriage of divorced persons, and especially of the injured and innocent person, is objected to. And any system of ideas which leads to such condemnation must in the end, I think, suffer a fate similar to the fate of the ideas leading to the condemnation of usury.

A closer analysis of this example would throw a good deal of light on the general point I am trying to make, and introduce an aspect which was left out in the consideration of the last example. I think there is no doubt that in both cases the change in social practice has been facilitated by widespread approval of a general system of ideas in which stress is laid on man's life in this world as important in its own right and not merely as a period of training, probation, expiation, in preparation for a life after death. There is no need to restrict this system to the view that pleasure is the only end to be sought in action; what is effective in it is the view that it is desirable to make life as satisfactory as possible for human beings on all sides of their nature, and that while renunciation and self sacrifice may sometimes be necessary, they are never good in themselves, but must always (as J. S. Mill insisted) be justified by reference to the way in which they contribute to a life of positive satisfactions for someone. But while this system of ideas helps to bring about the social change, it is not the sole factor, and it is reinforced by various practical considerations. What I want to suggest is that, however the social change has come about, its successful incorporation into social life gives strong support to the system of ideas which has helped to bring it about, or more generally to any system of ideas which justifies it. Of a system of ideas about the world or about man's place in the world you can ask, to what kind of life does it point as the most justifiable life; and if people find either that they cannot or that they do not want to live this kind of life (for whatever reasons) this will result in the condemnation of the system of ideas.

VI

Let me take a wider sweep and look at this interrelation between action and beliefs as it is shown in the working and in changes in the functions of social institutions.

The phrase 'a social institution' has been used in many different senses, so that it is important, if one is to use it, to indicate in what sense one is using it. I propose to use it here in a way which is very similar to the way in which it is used by Malinowski,[1] though there are aspects of his account which I do not quite understand. I use it to refer to an organization of persons within a community, existing for the performance of some social purpose or purposes. The purpose may concern members of the community as a whole, whether directly or indirectly (as in the case of the police force, hospitals, or universities) or it may be of interest only to a section of the community, as in the case of a football club or an operatic society. This gives the phrase a very wide use, but in what I have to say I am thinking mainly of social institutions which are of direct or indirect concern to all members of the community. Again, one could apply the phrase to a local organization of individuals (e.g. a particular football club) or to the system which results from the interrelations of such local organizations: this need cause no confusion.

Some persons may be members of the organization in a more special sense than others (e.g. the police force) though it may be a part of the duty of all members of the community to help the members of the organization in the performance of their tasks. The social purpose (or purposes) of the institution may involve different members having different duties; or it may involve behaviour of a particular sort from all members of

[1] *A Scientific Theory of Culture*, Chapel Hill, 1944.

the community. It may involve the possession by the organization of material resources, which are provided either by the community as a whole or by the members (e.g. universities, churches).

Behind each institution, growing up with it, changing as it changes, is a system of ideas which validates the institution in the eyes of the community, showing the importance for the community of the particular functions performed by the institution in the way in which they are performed; or, in the case of institutions affecting only particular groups (as e.g. chess clubs or drinking clubs) showing why the community should look kindly on, or at least tolerate, their activities.

The more the members of the community feel that their whole social life depends on the performance of these functions by the institution, the more important will it seem to them to maintain the institution, and the greater will be the prestige and the power over their minds of the system of ideas which validate the institution.

Malinowski has noted the way in which an institution may perform a variety of social functions, sometimes alone, and sometimes in association with another or with other social institutions; it can take on new functions; or again, a function performed by one social institution may come to be taken over by a different institution, whether one already existing or one developed for this specific purpose. In such ways the balance of importance of various social institutions can alter in the history of a community, and as this happens, the prestige of the sets of ideas validating the various institutions will be likely to change. All this seems to me of great importance for the student of ideas; and I think it is one of the main defects of Paul Hazard's admirable study of the changes of outlook in Europe at the end of the seventeenth century and the beginning of the eighteenth that he neglects changes in the working of social institutions, considering the intellectual changes as if they were entirely self-contained.[1]

[1]*La Crise de la Conscience Européenne* (1685-1715), Paris, 1935.

In order to give as much precision as possible to the thesis I am maintaining, I venture a suggestion about one way in which a social institution can diminish in importance in the life of the community, and in which in consequence the ideas validating the institution can lose prestige. The suggestion is not put forward as final, and I do not think that the general point I am trying to make depends on its soundness; but it will at any rate help to bring the issue into clearer relief.

What I want to suggest is that an institution which performs (or helps to perform) a great variety of tasks regarded as essential by the members of the community has very great prestige, and the ideas for which it stands will have a very great hold over their minds.

But if through social developments one after another of the tasks comes to be handed over to a different institution, if the old institution loses them without gaining new tasks, then its importance in the community will gradually diminish, and so will the power of the ideas for which it stands. New ideas arising in connection with the new institutions will dispute the field with its ideas. And if at the same time another institution comes to take on a greater and greater variety of tasks, this new institution will gain in importance, and the prestige of the ideas for which it stands will increase.

Something like this has occurred in Britain during the last three or four centuries in regard to religious organizations on the one hand and scientific organizations on the other. The sketch which follows lays no claim to be either exhaustive or original. It omits a great many qualifications and limitations. But I think it represents the line of development with sufficient accuracy for my purposes.

The Christian church embodies the ideas of the Christian religion. Its main function was to see to the spiritual interests of the members of the community. But in the Middle Ages, in doing this it did a great many other things as well, and continued doing many of them, in country districts, until the seventeenth and sometimes into the eighteenth century. The list is very lengthy and varies in different districts and at different times. It must suffice to give a brief selection by way of rough indication.[1]

The parson and the various clerics were often the only people able to read and write, with a knowledge of business. They wrote letters, made wills, and so on, for the people in their parishes. High ecclesiastics played important parts in public administration, and public servants were often rewarded for their services by ecclesiastical posts.

The church buildings were in many places the only buildings available for public meetings. Only the chancel was consecrated to exclusive religious use, and many activities went on in the nave of the church not themselves religious. There were village and town meetings, feastings and dancing and other entertainments. Herbert Maynard Smith[2] mentions the condemnation of buying and selling in York Minster in 1409, and a dispute between the town and the church authorities in Exeter as to who should collect the fees from those who set up booths in the Cathedral nave in fair time. He notes that Old St. Paul's was the one public place in the City of London which was under cover, and all sorts of business were done in it.

Travellers deposited their baggage in the churches for safety; pedlars sold their wares at the porch after the service and sometimes even during it. Curiosities of all sorts were displayed in the churches. Prominent people were buried there, or had their tombs or memorial tablets. The churches were the art galleries, the museums, the halls of memory of the community.

The monasteries provided alms for the poor, hospitality for travellers. Nunneries provided homes for unmarried women. Holy wells and shrines gave occasion for pilgrimages. G. M. Trevelyan notes that in the time of Elizabeth the medicinal spa began to take the place of the holy well, and touring and sight-seeing replaced the custom of visiting shrines.[3]

---

[1] An admirable popular account is to be found in William Addison, *The English Country Parson*, London, 1947. There are many specialized studies of the activity of the churches at particular periods.

[2] *Pre-Reformation England*, London, 1938, p. 108.

[3] *English Social History*, London, 1944, p. 160.

If we add the part played by the churches and the monasteries in education, in regard to marriage and burial, and in association with the agricultural round of life, we can see with how many sides of human activity they were closely connected. You couldn't live your life without the things that were provided through or in connection with the churches.

This I think accounts for a great deal of the influence of the Church in those times. It enabled the Church to control men's behaviour in a way impossible today except in some Catholic countries. The importance of doctrine was largely derived from its association with the many functions of the Church in social life.

In the last three hundred years there has been a steady taking over of these functions by institutions specially developed for the purpose. Education, care of the poor, marriage, burial, are all now possible independently of any church. The church building is not now the only place where even village activities are carried on. Motor transport has freed many villages from dependence on the churches for their social life, and in the towns there is for many people no need for any connection with church life at any time.

It is true that the churches have in modern times tried to develop new functions for various types of member, often very successfully. G. M. Young, for example, describes the influence of the Wesleyan Church as follows: 'By providing a far larger sphere of action for the laity than the Church or the older denominations furnished, it brought romance and ambition into a class which, under the pressure of a new civilization, was losing both purpose and aspirations; and the Wesleyan organization—the class meeting, the circuit, the conference, the Legal Hundred,—has powerfully affected the constitution of political parties and Trade Unions.'[1]

But on the whole it is true that the churches as a social institution are no longer as closely integrated with social life, no longer perform, in whole or in co-operation with other institutions, the many functions they performed in the past.

[1] *Portrait of an Age*, London, 1936, p. 65.

And I think that it is in this situation that a large part of the explanation is to be found of the lack of influence of the churches in modern times. Some part of the cause is due to changes in intellectual outlook arising in other ways; but the loss of social functions seems to me a very important factor.

If, on the other hand, we consider the development of scientific organizations and of the technological institutions based on and associated with science, we see a steady increase in the number and the importance of the social functions performed through or in co-operation with them. It is significant that the Royal Society was in its early days in the seventeenth century as much interested in inventions for practical purposes as it was in theoretical knowledge. It is now linked with the universities (many of which are predominantly scientific, where the earlier universities were predominantly religious), with research institutions, and with the research departments of many of the large industrial companies. Taken together all these can be described as a social institution whose functions are scientific and technological. Science and technology are linked in the closest possible way, and play an increasing part in making possible the performance of tasks on which the daily life of the community depends. Large cities must have a water supply and sewage disposal. One only needs to think of gas and electricity generators, of the motor industry, of the development of new drugs, new chemicals, new materials for building purposes, for textiles, etc., to see how dependent modern life is on the discoveries and techniques of science, and on the routine work of men trained in these techniques. What was true of the churches in the Middle Ages is now much more true of scientific and research institutions. Life could not be lived without them.

It is this I think which gives to the ideas for which these institutions stand the prestige which used to belong to religious ideas, which themselves have far less prestige than they had in earlier times. Thus when it is said that the modern trend away from religion is due to the spread of scientific ideas, as if the process were a wholly intellectual one, it would be more accurate to include as a conditioning factor the increasing importance of scientific institutions and the decreasing importance of religious institutions in social life.

The principle I would put forward for consideration is that the predominant ideas at any period are those which underlie and validate the predominating social institutions of the period.

VII

While providing a useful suggestion about the relation between practical activities and theoretical beliefs, this principle, or any principle of a similar kind which should turn out to be more accurate, does not take us the whole way in our survey of beliefs. For in a complex and changing society social institutions are not all of a piece or fully consistent with one another. Nor do predominant institutions cover the whole field. Not everybody approves of all the institutions of his society. Some people, e.g. think that our society is relying far too much on science and technology, some think it is not going far enough. There are still people who think that the old prohibition of usury, taken in the old sense, was sound. Many people still think of remarriage of a divorced person as against divine law. Thus there are conflicting ideas and beliefs current at any period concerning what ought to be done, and these ideas have many different sources and dates. Nor must the principle that acceptance or rejection of beliefs is conditioned by decisions about matters of practice be taken as if it asserted that practical decisions were the main determinants of belief. What is asserted is that people seek for a system of beliefs which will justify their behaviour, and that one strong reason for accepting the system of beliefs is that it does justify their behaviour. How far this takes us I shall consider in what follows.

VIII

The point I am trying to make, however limited, is important when the question, how our beliefs are to be justified, is being considered. It is not sufficient to distinguish this question sharply from the question how we come by our beliefs, and to assert that practical considerations are relevant only to the latter and not to the former question. Hume's theory of belief, says Professor Price[1] 'is not at all a satisfactory theory of *rational* belief, where we weigh the evidence for and against, and assent accordingly. But . . . it is quite a good theory of non-rational belief, or taking for granted.' Professor Price seems to suggest here that rational belief, where we have good reasons for what we believe, would be belief *par excellence;* but this still leaves open the question whether practical considerations can be good reasons for believing something. One line of approach to this question is to note that practical considerations vary from age to age, as we have seen in the case of usury. It would follow that, if practical considerations were good reasons, what was rational to believe would vary from time to time as the practical conditions varied. But, it might be argued, rationality is independent of time; and what we are seeking are considerations which would justify a belief under all conditions and at all times. The reply to this is that theoretical evidence equally varies from age to age, as new facts and new points of view are put forward; so that what has really to be shown is that practical considerations must be left out of account when valid beliefs are being sought, because they are in themselves irrelevant, independently of whether they vary or not. It may be answered that it is not difficult to show this. For practical considerations are largely dependent on what people want to do, on what kind of life they want to live, and in so far as this is not determined by objective facts (whether facts about what exists or facts about what is good or right) it is dependent on emotions, desires, caprices, which are non-rational or even irrational, and by their very nature have to be set aside by the seeker after truth.

If our thesis urging the relevance of practical considerations to theoretical beliefs is to be defended, we shall have to show that the above contrast is drawn on wrong lines, and that emotions, desires, and even caprices, as subjected to the pressures and disciplines involved in the practical tasks set by people

[1] *Hume's Theory of the External World,* Oxford, 1940, p. 44 note.

trying to live together in a community, play an essential part in the gradual discovery of the kind of life which will satisfy human beings in this world, and so make a contribution to the discovery of what man can be and what can be made of the world.

It must be remembered that the beliefs under consideration are not merely those concerned with simple facts such as where I put my gloves, who put the book on the table, how the boy got into the garden (though even the determination of such matters may be highly complex) but also those involving wider considerations of how truth is to be discovered at all on any matters. People have believed, e.g. that the way to discover the most important things about the world is to undergo some form of purificatory discipline, to retire from the bustle of everyday affairs, to suspend the bodily activities as far as possible, to make the mind receptive, to engage in the kind of contemplation which is akin to religious worship. This whether linked to or detached from a study of statements claimed to be received through revelation from God by chosen prophets or a divinely instituted church, represents a view of knowing (knowing by contemplation) which is in sharp contrast with that involved in modern scientific investigation, which, however much appeal may be made to imaginative penetration (a form of contemplation, rather different, however, from the form already mentioned) stresses the need for practical activities, guided and controlled by sense observation aided by instruments, as a fundamental condition of getting knowledge. In place of knowing by contemplation is put knowing associated with a special kind of doing. Neither of these contrasted views is capable of being verified, or proved, by deducing it from any more fundamental principles; but you have to have some view of this sort before you can engage in a search for truth.[1] It should be noted further

---

[1] For a discussion and defence of this view, I may refer to my paper on 'Propositions and Proposals'. An abstract of this paper is given in the *Proceedings of the International Congress of Philosophy*, Amsterdam, 1948, vol. i, Fasc. ii, p. 618. The full paper is printed in the *Australasian Journal of Philosophy*, December 1951.

28

that these contrasted views have actually led to quite different ideas about the kind of life desirable for man. The one view was designed to keep man humble in face of the facts, and it certainly left a whole range of information about processes of nature inaccessible to him, thus limiting his range of practical activities; the other view, by presenting men with statements of the form 'If you do so and so under such and such conditions, such and such results will occur', opened vast new possibilities of practical activity, and so tended to make a new life of activities desirable. It gave him a sense of power. Now if we are to find some way of assessing the value of these starting points, it will appear sensible (to say the least) to take into account the kind of life men are groping after in the trial and error process of social change, and tracing the effects of both views on this trial and error process. This is the kind of assessment men have been making for a long time, and are making at present, and it is the kind of thing, I think, that should be done by philosophers. Distressful pictures of the effect on modern life of science and technology may be taken as evidence that the way of exploration of the world through the senses is the way of illusion and sin;[1] or (more usually) as evidence that scientific knowledge is one-sided and needs the controls religious insight can provide. Equally distressful pictures of social life controlled by an authoritative religious organization have been taken as evidence of the inadequacy of an exclusively religious approach to knowledge. Whatever may be the merits of these views, I think it can be said that in taking into account the kind of life people live under the influence of a particular doctrine, and in using this as at least a partial test of the soundness of the doctrine, they are on right lines. We are here concerned with beliefs about the world which make some difference, whether directly or indirectly, to man's search for a satisfying life. A religious view does it directly; science does it indirectly by opening up new possibilities of action. In order to answer the question, is the

---

[1] From this point of view Marlowe's *Dr. Faustus* could be taken as a prophetic picture of consequences painted at the beginning of the modern era.

claim (e.g. of religion or of science) to provide genuine knowledge a sound one, we are entitled to take into account the effects on life that result from accepting or rejecting the claim. We must take these effects into account. We want beliefs which will lead to the encouragement of a life that, in the living, we judge satisfactory and would not wish to alter. I should go further and say that it is one of the tests of a true belief (in the range of beliefs under consideration here) that it should have this relation to life. It is only a partial test, and it shares with the ordinary accepted tests of factual or rational evidence the characteristic of being provisional and liable to revision as more satisfactory ways of life open up. No one would claim that a scientific theory is finally verified by being in harmony with all the evidence available to scientists at a particular period. New evidence against the theory may turn up. Similarly no one ought to claim that beliefs are finally verified by being in harmony with the practical decisions people are making or want to make at a particular period. These decisions may lead to ways of life people do not want to continue living. They are therefore provisional, and tests based on them are provisional. But though the tests are provisional, they are nevertheless tests continually applied, in my opinion justifiably, as tests of truth.[1]

IX

It is sometimes argued that a particular theoretical view (e.g. an emotive theory in ethics) should be rejected because the social consequences of its general acceptance would be disastrous. It does not seem to me to be satisfactory to put this argument aside as irrelevant. Nor is it satisfactory to accept it outright as final. Both practical and theoretical aspects of a doctrine

[1]They have no power of veto, and can be outvoted. Again, they come in only where they are relevant. If you have decided, partly on theoretical partly on practical grounds, to take the statements obtained by the use of scientific methods as your best guide to the facts, then you cannot turn round and reject particular statements because they are unpalatable. If you want to reject them you must rescind your original decision.

have to be fully considered, before we can determine whether to accept or reject the doctrine, and the theoretical examination has to be made with all the thoroughness of which we are capable, independently of what may be alleged about its practical consequences. But the statement about practical consequences has to be met. There are many cases in which it can be shown to be unsound, where, for example, it is based on the assumption that no changes in the existing social institutions or in the beliefs validating them can be made without social disaster. But it must be shown to be unsound. It is not necessary that those who defend a doctrine on purely theoretical grounds should have to show, as a condition of being listened to, that the doctrine can form part of a general system of beliefs which would be the basis of a satisfactory life. We do not know beforehand what kind of life would be satisfactory, we can only grope our way toward it, and views defended on theoretical grounds are often pointers along the way. But a purely theoretical defence is not a final defence. And if there is anything in the view I am putting forward, it is likely that among the fundamental principles on which the theoretical defence rests there will be some whose acceptance does not depend wholly on theoretical grounds, but rests partly also on practical considerations of the sort I have been discussing. Scientific method itself is not capable of being completely justified on purely theoretical grounds.

A further point must be mentioned, as it shows how much remains to be considered. It may be argued that certain types of doctrine should not even be discussed, because even this kind of publicity will have bad social consequences. This can be met in the way I have already suggested, but there is a wider issue connected with it, which turns on our view as to the kind of society we want and are prepared to fight for. If we reject the argument (as I should) we may do it on the ground that there is here a principle we are not willing to submit to any short term test of practical consequences. It is a guide to the future we will not dispense with. We are not willing to accept a society which cannot put up with free discussion. There are many principles of this sort, which express fundamental or obstinate decisions.

I do not want to suggest that these principles are beyond all tests in the long run. All I want to suggest is that they need further discussion than the discussion I have been able to give in this paper. And it may be that those who contend that we should rule out all references to practical consequences in our examination of beliefs, and base our acceptance or rejection of beliefs on wholly theoretical considerations, are resting their contention on a principle of this kind. But I think that the ultimate defence of such principles does turn on our decisions about the kind of life we regard as desirable for human beings; and this is, after all, a practical consideration.

SENSATION

By GILBERT RYLE

Waynflete Professor of Metaphysical Philosophy in the University of Oxford and Fellow of Magdalen College, Oxford

SENSATION

ONE of the things that worry me most is the notion of sensations or sense-impressions. It seems, on the one hand, very hard to avoid saying that hearing, seeing, and tasting could not happen unless appropriate sense-impressions were received; and yet also very hard to give a coherent account of what such sense-impressions are, or how the having of sense-impressions is connected with, say, our hearing a conversation or our seeing a tree.

There seem to be some very good reasons for saying that sense-impressions can occur in abnormal situations, when no perceiving occurs. For example, after looking at a bright light I have an after-image; or if I knock my head I seem to see stars or lightning flashes; or when I have a bad cold I have a singing noise in my head. One seems bound to say that in these situations I have optical or acoustic sensations or sense-impressions, and that it is just in the presence of these that the similarity consists between merely having an after-image and genuinely seeing a tree, or between merely having a singing in my head and genuinely hearing the choir singing in the concert-hall. In cases of genuine perception, we are inclined to say, we both have sense-impressions, produced or stimulated in the normal ways, and also contribute something of our own, namely, to put it too picturesquely, the interpretation or significance, without which we should not have perceived, say, an oak-tree. Yet the moment we start to press this tempting idea we are landed in familiar difficulties. Colours as we see them and sounds as we hear them seem at once to collapse into internal reactions or states of ourselves. The oak-tree is not really green and the tenor's voice is not literally shrill. The sense-impressions which were supposed to make perception of trees and choirs possible finish by becoming screens between ourselves and trees or choirs. The sensible qualities of things in the world cease to be qualities of those things and become, instead, momentary states of our own minds or nervous systems. They come to have the status of stomach-aches, caused, indeed, fairly indirectly by mechanical and chemical properties of external things, of the intervening medium, and of our own nervous systems, but no more to be equated with attributes of external things than my stomach-ache is an attribute of the uncooked beans which indirectly caused my stomach to ache.

There are further difficulties. First, the notion of sense-impression seems to be a technical or specialist notion. People without special theories or technical knowledge of physiology, optics, chemistry or psychology know well how to use the concepts of seeing, hearing and smelling, though not the concept of *sense-impression*. They have to be introduced to this notion by being introduced to the outlines of special theories about the physics and physiology of perception. Only after having heard a bit about the propagation of waves and the like, and then about the transmission of impulses up the nerves, and then perhaps also something about the psychology of stimuli and responses—only then can they begin to use the notion of *sense-impressions*. Consequently, in the ordinary contexts in which we talk about seeing, hearing and the rest, no mention is made of sense-impressions, any more than in ordinary contexts in which meat, vegetables, and fruit are discussed, any mention is made of calories or vitamins. As I might put it, the concept of *perception* is on a more elementary or less technical level than that of *sense-impression*. We can know all that is a part of common knowledge about seeing and hearing, without knowing anything about these impressions. But from this it follows directly that the concept of sense-impression is not any sort of component of the concept of perception, any more than the concept of *vitamin* is any sort of component of the concept of *dinner*.

Unfortunately, however, the logical situation is a confused one. For we are perfectly familiar with not one, but at least two quite different non-technical notions of *sensation*—and philosophers and psychologists have nearly always tried to equate their technical notion of *sense-impression* with one, or more often with both of these non-technical notions of *sensation*. They pass without apology from saying that without optical or auditory sense-impressions there is no seeing or hearing, to saying that seeing and hearing involve the having of sensations, as if the one assertion were a mere paraphrase of the other.

To get this point a bit clearer, let me examine in some detail the two non-technical notions of sensation.

First, there is the sense of the word 'sensation' or the word 'feeling', in which sensations or feelings are such things as pains, tickles, feelings of nausea, suffocation, thirst, and the like. A pain is what anodynes and anaesthetics exist to relieve or prevent. Sensations of this sort can be more or less acute or intense; they can be short-lived or protracted, and they are, in general, localisable in particular parts of the body. Most sensations, in this sense of the word, if not all of them, are in some degree distressing. Some philosophers, like Bishop Berkeley, have argued, quite fallaciously it seems to me, that the family which includes such things as pains, tickles and feelings of suffocation also includes such things as our sensations of temperature. When I bring my hand nearer and nearer to the fire, I begin by feeling increases in the heat, but at a certain point the heat is intense enough to hurt. Berkeley argues that therefore a feeling of warmth differs only in degree from the feeling of pain. So the feeling of warmth is a state of myself in the way in which a pain is.

But this will not do at all. For one thing, some weight must be attached to the fact that no one does suppose that painfulness characterises the fire, in the way in which they do suppose that warmth does. A child will say that the fire is so hot that it hurts his hand, and thus is already distinguishing between an effect which the fire has upon him from a property which the fire has, without which it would not hurt him. More-over, feeling, say with one's hand, that the fire is hotter than it was, is finding the answer to a question. The owner of the hand is discriminating something, finding out a difference. In some cases he would admit to having made a mistake. He had not been careful enough. But in having a pain there is no finding any-thing out, no discerning of similarities or differences, no place, even, for mistakes and so no room for carefulness or lack of carefulness. Feeling, in the sense of finding out or discerning, the warmth of things is a kind of perception, and a kind at which some people, like bakers and laundry-girls, become better than other people; it is the product of an acquired skill; but feeling, in the sense of suffering pains, is not a kind of per-ception, and there is no question of one victim being better or worse than another at feeling toothaches. In this sense of 'feeling' or 'sensation', pains are not things the feeling of which is the product of an acquired skill. So far from the feeling of warmth being merely a lower degree of the feeling of pain, the two things are 'felt' only in quite different senses of the word. They are not even species of one genus, as perhaps seeing and tasting are species of the one genus, perception. They belong to different categories from one another. The attempt to classify felt temperatures with felt pains, and so to show that felt warmth is a state or reaction in ourselves, as pain in some way is, was a logical mistake.

We need, therefore, to distinguish the sense of 'feeling' or 'sensation' in which we call pains and tickles 'feelings' or 'sensations' from the entirely different sense in which we say that we perceive some things not by seeing, hearing, smelling, or tasting, but by feeling—the sense in which we say that a person whose feet or fingers are numb with cold has lost sensation or the power of feeling things with his fingers and toes. Let me just remind you of some of the properties of external things which are perceived by feeling, as opposed to seeing, hearing, smelling or tasting. First, to detect how hot or cold something is, we have to feel it with the hands, or lips, or tongue, or, less efficiently, with other parts of our bodies. We cannot see, hear or smell how cold things are. Next, to detect the roughness, smoothness, slipperiness or stickiness of the surfaces of things, we normally have to handle them or finger them. Next, to detect whether something is vibrating, stiff, resilient, loose in its socket and so on, we usually have to touch it, and very likely also muscularly to manipulate it. Some people are much better than others at discrimination-tasks of these kinds. Doctors can feel the pulses of patients which are too faint for you or me to detect and the trained driver can feel the car going into a skid long before the novice could have done so.

We should notice that tactual and kinaesthetic detection is unlike seeing, hearing, tasting, and smelling in one important respect. What I detect by seeing, hearing, tasting, and smelling are with extremely few exceptions, properties or features of things and happenings outside me. What I detect tactually and kinaesthetically *may* be properties or features of external though contiguous things and events; but they may be and quite often are properties or features of anatomically internal things and events. I can detect, sometimes, the beating of my own heart, the distension of my own stomach, the straining or relaxing of my own muscles, the creaking of my own joints, and the fishbone in my own throat. A doctor, I imagine, learns to detect by feeling the congestion of his own lungs.

In this sense of 'feeling', feeling is a species of perception or perceptual discrimination. We have to learn to do it; we may be better or worse than other people at doing it. There is room for care and carelessness in doing it; and there is always the possibility of making mistakes. To be able to feel things, in this sense, is to have got a certain amount of a specific skill or family of skills, just as to be able to detect and discriminate things by seeing, hearing, tasting, and smelling is to have got a certain amount of a specific skill or family of skills. In all cases alike there can be trained or untrained observers. To detect or discriminate something, whether by sight or touch, is to achieve something, namely, to find something out by the exercise of an acquired and perhaps deliberately trained skill. This shows how enormously different is the sense of the verb 'feel' when used to denote detection by touch, from the sense of the verb 'feel' when used to denote the suffering of a pain or other discomfort.

But different though these two concepts of 'feeling' or 'sensation' are, still both are quite untechnical concepts. The child has learned to use both long before he has heard of any physiological, neurological or psychological theories.

So now we can ask whether it is true that all perceiving involves the having of sensations or the feeling of anything, in either of these senses. Well, to begin with, it is perfectly clear that usually when I see, hear, taste or smell anything, or detect something by touch, I do not suffer any discomfort or pain in my eyes, ears, tongue, nose or finger tips. Seeing a tree does not hurt my eyes; and hearing a bird singing does not set up the slightest sort of tickling-feeling in my ears. Sometimes, certainly, looking at things, like the headlights of motor cars, or listening to things, like the whistle of a railway-engine a few yards away, does hurt my eyes and ears. But not only is this exceptional, but still more important, these disagreeable sensations do not help, they hinder perception. I see much better when I am not being dazzled than when I am. Sensations, in this sense, are not usually present when perception occurs; and when they are present, they tend to impair perception. They are not *sine quâ nons* of perception.

But nor is it true that when I see, hear or smell things I feel anything with my eyes, ears and nose, in the sense of detecting something tactually or kinaesthetically. When I see a green tree, I do not concomitantly detect, with my eyes, the warmth or coldness, the smoothness or roughness, the vibrations or the resilience of anything. My eyes are very inferior organs with which to detect things tactually and kinaesthetically. My ears and nose are even worse. But whether they are good or bad, when I see things with my eyes, I do not therewith have to detect something else tactually or kinaesthetically with those eyes of mine and usually I do not; and similarly with my ears and nose. With my tongue the situation is slightly different. Usually when I taste things, I do also detect with my tongue the temperature and some of the tactually and kinaesthetically discoverable properties of the food or the drink in my mouth. But even this is a case of concomitance and not dependence. I can taste the taste of onions, when there is no longer anything in my mouth with a temperature of its own or with any shape or consistency of its own. In tasting, I often do in fact, but I do not in logic have also to feel anything with my tongue, in the sense of 'feel' in which I feel the roughness of the nutshell or the smoothness of the eggshell with my fingers or, sometimes, with my tongue. My tongue is, so to speak, a double sense-organ. I can both feel things with it and taste things with it. But I can feel the shape and surfaces of things like spoons without tasting anything; and I can taste, e.g. onions or pepper without feeling anything.

So when philosophers and psychologists assert that all perceiving involves the having of sensations or the feeling of something, either they are dead wrong, or else they are using a third, quite different notion of feeling or sensation. In particular, the notion of sensing or having sense-impressions which, they assert, is a component of the notion of perceiving, must be a notion quite different both from the notion of feelings like pains and tickles, and from the notion of tactual and kinaesthetic detection or discrimination.

But at this point there arises something of a crux. When a person has a pain we think that he must, in some sense of the word, be conscious or aware of the pain; and when a person detects or discriminates something by touch, his perceiving what he perceives must also be, in some sense of the word, conscious. A person cannot require to be told by someone else that he is in pain or that he has just perceived something. Well then, what of the sense impressions which, we are told, enter into perceiving? Are we conscious of them or do we have to be told of their existence by others, or, perhaps, infer to them ourselves in accordance with some more or less technical theory of optics or neurology or psychology? It is generally maintained that our sense-impressions are certainly and necessarily things that we are conscious of and cannot be unconscious of, as we cannot, with certain reservations, be unconscious of our pains and tickles and as we cannot see, hear or taste things unconsciously. Indeed it is apt to be maintained that if sense-impressions were things of which we were unconscious, then they could not do their proper business, namely, that of providing the basic *given* elements in seeing, hearing and the rest. Well then, are we conscious of having sense-impressions? Do people ever say, whether to themselves or to anyone else, 'I am having' or 'I have just had a sense-impression of such and such a description'? Or rather, since the actual term 'sense-impression' is obviously a somewhat technical, classificatory term, do people ever say, to themselves or others, 'I am having', or 'I have just had a so and so', where the concrete filling of the vacancy 'so and so' would be something which properly fell under the technical, classificatory term 'sense-impression'? Certainly people say that they see trees or have just heard some birds singing; but these verbs of perception carry too much luggage to be what is wanted. Certainly too, people sometimes say, more non-committally, 'I see something green', or 'I have just heard a twittering noise'. But these expressions also carry too much luggage. A person who said 'I see something green' might then learn that there was a tree in front of him, and say 'Then what I saw was a green tree, though I did not at the time know that the green thing I saw was a tree'. What is wanted, apparently, is some family of expressions, in constant and familiar use by everyone, in which they report, without inference or external information, the occurrence of a conscious experience unencumbered, as yet, with any beliefs or knowledge about the existence or properties of any external object.

Sometimes it is suggested that we do report such basic experiences in such utterances as 'I seem to smell onions' or 'I thought I heard birds singing' or 'It looks as if there is a green tree over there'. In reporting mere appearances, without committing ourselves to their veracity, we are, it is suggested, reporting the having of sense-impressions without the addition of any perceptual claims about the external world. But this will not do. We use such tentative, guarded or non-committal expressions in all sorts of fields or departments, in most of which there is no question of there being any appropriate sense-impressions to isolate. I can say, after a rapid piece of calculation in my head '15 × 16 appears to make 220'; I can say, after a cursory glance 'it looks as if the river here is about twice the width of the road in front of my house'; I can say 'She appeared to be half-angry and half-amused'; and I can say 'the period of general inflation seems to be coming to an end'.

Now all these are guarded statements of what I am tempted or inclined to judge to be the case, though I do not yet commit myself to their being the case. Yet no one supposes that in saying such things I am reporting the occurrence of any sense-impressions. Statements of the form 'it looks as if'—'there seems to be'—'Apparently, . . .' are not *ex officio* dedicated to the wanted reports of the experiences alleged to be basic ingredients in sense-perception. So we cannot, unless provided with some extra restrictions which are not in fact provided, adduce idioms of these patterns as being the untutored, uninferential deliverances of our consciousness of the postulated sense-impressions. We have, in fact, no special way of reporting the occurrence of these postulated impressions; we are, therefore, without the needed marks of our being conscious of such things at all. For there is surely something absurd in maintaining that we are constantly conscious of some things in the way in which we are conscious of pains, and yet have no way of telling ourselves or other people anything whatsoever about them.

We must acknowledge, therefore, that the view of some epistemologists and psychologists that there are sense-impressions is not arrived at at all in the way in which everyone comes to know that pains and tickles occur, or in the way in which everyone comes to know that we sometimes detect things by sight, hearing, taste, and touch. The view that sense-impressions occur is arrived at as a deduction from a theory, or perhaps from two or more seemingly interlocking theories.

I want to separate out two quite different theoretical allegiances which, in their different ways, drive people to postulate sense-impressions.

29

(1) If a child and a man are looking at the first word of the first line of a page, the man may say that he sees the word 'Edinburgh' misprinted, where the child may not detect the misprint but say only that he sees the word 'Edinburgh'. The child's eyesight is as good as the man's, but because he is worse at spelling, he fails to see the misprint that the man sees. If now an illiterate Esquimau looks at the same part of the page, though his eyesight is excellent, he will not see a word at all, but only some black marks.

Or if a countryman and a townsman, with equally good sight, are looking at the same field, the one may say that he sees a field of young wheat, while the other may say only that he sees a field of green stuff. In these and countless other such cases, the one observer claims to discern much more than the other, though admitting that their eyesight is equally good. It is natural and tempting to say that the observer whose eyes, somehow, tell him more is putting more into his report of what he sees or that he is giving to it a fuller 'interpretation' than the other can do. He has learned more spelling or more agriculture than the other, so he includes in his report of what he sees the extra information which his previous experience and education had equipped him with. His report of what he sees is inflated with knowledge or beliefs which the other man does not possess; in short it carries a mass of ideas or thoughts, which are absent from the other observer's report of what *he* sees. In detecting a misprint or a field of young wheat he seems, therefore, to be combining the piece of seeing, which, presumably, contains only what the townsman's seeing contains, with a piece of thinking, which the townsman is unable to supply. What is more, this extra thought-luggage may be right or wrong. The countryman may have misidentified the green crop.

Now there exists a view, which is accepted almost as an axiom, that all thinking, or anyhow all thinking which is intended to result in the discovery or establishment of truths, is inferring; and therewith that all errors and mistakes issue from fallacious reasoning. Accordingly, when philosophers and psychologists consider things like the detection of misprints or the identification of the green crop with young wheat, they automatically describe the thinking-element in this detection and identification with reasoning. The question at once arises Whence then do we get the initial premisses of our perceptual conclusions? On this view, the premisses must be ascertained at a level prior to any thinking, and prior therefore to any exploitation of knowledge or beliefs previously acquired. There must be a totally non-cogitative acceptance of some basic premisses for us to be able to move from these initial data to our correct or incorrect perceptual conclusions about misprints or young wheat. It is, I think, with this idea in mind that many thinkers use the expression 'sense-data' for the postulated sense-impressions which must be there to inaugurate our perceptual inferrings. For 'datum' ordinarily has the force of 'evidence' or 'reasons'. A datum is something that we reason from and does not itself have to be reasoned to.

This reason for postulating the existence of sense-impressions seems to me a bad reason, and bad on two scores. First, if it is not true that all thinking is inferring, then it need not be true that the thinking which enters into perceptual recognition, identification, comparison, etc., is inferring, and if it is not, then the search for its fund of premisses is a search for nothing. In multiplying we think out the answers to questions, but our results are not conclusions and our mistakes are not fallacies. This thinking does not start from any data or premisses; and the same might be true of the thinking that is supposed to go on in perceptual recognition, identification, etc. But second, it seems to me false or at least highly misleading to say that a man who detects a misprint or a farmer who identifies the green crop with growing wheat is necessarily *thinking* at all.

For one thing, the misprint and the nature of the crop might be discerned at sight or in a flash. As soon as his eye falls on the misprinted word, the man might start to pencil in the correction. There might be no moment, however short, in which he could be described as pondering, reflecting or putting two and two together. He might say, quite truly, that he saw the misprint

the moment his eye fell on the word, and that he did not have
time to think or even that he did not need to think.

To meet this sort of objection, epistemologists and psychologists sometimes say that though he does not remember doing
any thinking, and though the time available for thinking seemed
to be wanting, still he must have thought, and so his thinking
must have been done at lightning speed—and this might be the
reason why he cannot remember doing any thinking afterwards.
But we should mistrust these 'musts'. Why must he have done
any pondering, considering or putting two and two together?
All that the argument up to date has shown is that if he had not
previously learned to spell, he could not now recognise misprints at sight. But why must the exploitation of knowledge
previously acquired take the form of pondering? We ponder
when things are not obvious to us. But when previous training
results in things being obvious at sight, which would not
have been obvious without that training, why should we
have to postulate a present piece of pondering to explain the
immediate obviousness of the misprint? Ordinarily we account
for someone needing to stop to think by showing how something was, at the start, unobvious to him. But here, apparently,
the fact that the misprint is immediately obvious to him is
supposed to need to be explained not just by reference to his
prior education, but also by the postulation of the performance
by him of a piece of thinking, with the queer property of not
requiring any time for its performance.

So I maintain not only that perceptual recognition, identification, etc., need not embody any inferential thinking, but
that they need not embody any thinking at all. They involve the
possession and exploitation of knowledge previously acquired.
But this exploitation is not thinking. So the argument for the
occurrence of sense-impressions to be the data or premises for
the inferential thinking embodied is doubly broken-backed.

(2) There is another theoretical allegiance which helps to
drive philosophers, psychologists, physiologists, and physicists
into postulating the existence of sense-impressions. This is their
natural and up to a point proper allegiance to causal theories

of perception. We learn from optics and acoustics about the transmission of light and sound; we learn from physiology the structure of the eye and ear; we are learning from neuro-physiology about the transmission of impulses along the nerve-fibres. When we ask what makes seeing and hearing possible, and what makes them impossible or inefficient, we derive our answers, quite properly, from the relevant stretches of these scientific theories.

We trace the propagation of light from a light-giving source to the surface of a light-reflecting object and thence to the lens and the retina of the human eye; we then trace the nervous impulses set up at the retina to the right place in the brain. Some further transformation may then be supposed, such that the terminal neural impulse sets up, somehow, a psychic or mental reaction, and thus seeing takes place—or rather, since seeing a misprint requires a special education and maybe also, as is often supposed, a special act of lightning-speed thinking, we should perhaps say that the last neural impulse sets up a mental reaction which is the necessary spur or stimulus to seeing, though seeing consists not only in this stimulus but also in some part of our immediate response to it. This sort of account of perception operates naturally with the notions of propagation, transmission, impulse, stimulus and response, rather than with the notions of *data*, premisses, evidence, and conclusions. Sense-impressions are now thought of not as steps in a lightning-swift argument but as links in a causal chain. They are indeed often spoken of as 'given', but they are 'given', now, in the sense in which electric shocks are given, not in the sense in which Euclid's axioms are given, i.e. are the uninferred premisses for inferred consequences. 'Given' now means 'inflicted', not, as before, 'accepted without argument'. Sense-impressions are now thought of as things impressed on us, impulses transmitted through us, not as things found by us by some sort of pre-cogitative finding.

Now there can be no quarrelling with this sort of account, whether we are thinking of the stages covered by optics and acoustics, or whether we are thinking of the stages covered by physiology and neurophysiology. The final stage, covering a supposed jump from neural impulses in the body to mental experiences, or sense-impressions is, however, quite a different matter. It presupposes the Cartesian, body-mind view which I have found fault with at some length in my book. But, apart from this general objection, there remains the specific objection, that the existence of these sense-impressions is something postulated; they are not things which anyone reports who has not been convinced by the whole story of the chain of physical, neural and psychic impulses. Even if the Cartesian view were true, yet still we should be without the Cartesian grounds for asserting the existence of sense-impressions which we possess for pains and tickles.

What has gone wrong? It seems to me that this is what has gone wrong. The perfectly proper and necessary research into the physics of light and sound, and into the physiology of seeing and hearing came to be misrepresented as an enquiry which when completed would 'explain' seeing and hearing—explain it, that is to say, in the sense of 'explain' in which an earthquake is explained by seismological theory or diabetes is explained by a certain branch of pathology. The idea, then, is that what we need to know about seeing and hearing is the various physical and physiological conditions from modifications in which we could infer to the cessation or alteration of our seeing and hearing; in short, that our questions about perception are merely causal questions.

Now of course we have causal questions to ask about perception, and the sciences of optics and acoustics, ophthalmology and neurology have either already provided us with the answers to these causal questions, or can confidently be expected to provide them in the fairly near future. But not all our questions about perception are causal questions; and the proffering of causal answers to non-causal questions leads to inevitable dissatisfaction, which cannot be relieved by promises of yet more advanced causal answers still to be discovered.

Perceiving, as I have pointed out earlier, is exercising an acquired skill; or rather it embodies the exercise of an acquired skill. Seeing a misprint is an impossibility for someone who has not learned to spell. Now about the exercises of any acquired skills there are, of course, causal questions to be asked. If a tight-rope walker succeeds in walking along the stretched wire, we can, of course, ask and fairly easily find out the answers to all sorts of causal questions about his performance—mechanical questions about his equilibrium, physiological questions about his muscles and nerves, and pedagogic questions about the training he had received, and so on. But quite different from these causal questions are technical questions, questions, that is, about the nature of the task of tight-rope walking, about the various kinds of mistakes that are to be avoided, and the various kinds of attentiveness, courage and ingenuity which make for success—all the things which the tight-rope walker must either have been taught by his trainers or found out for himself. Lessons of this sort need not include much, if any, of the information which might be provided by the physicist, the physiologist or the psychologist. Nor does the chess player need to know anything about the physiology of his muscular system, despite the fact that he could not be good or even bad at chess if he could not move his fingers and hands where he wished.

In the same sort of way, I am arguing that some questions about perceiving, and particularly those which are of interest in epistemology, are not causal questions—though there are such questions, and many of them have been answered—but questions about, so to speak, the *crafts* or *arts* of finding things out by seeing and hearing—including questions about the nature of mistakes and failures in perception and their relations with mistakes and failures in thinking, spelling, counting, and the like.

It is not that hearing and smelling are queer happenings which are exempt from causal conditions, but that not all questions about hearing and smelling are questions about these causal conditions. Checkmating an opponent at chess is certainly a happening, and a happening conditioned by all sorts of known and unknown causes. But the chess-player's interest is not in these causes, but in the tactics or strategy or

sometimes just the luck of which the checkmating was the outcome. It is not the dull physical fact of the arrival of the Queen
at a particular square, it is the fact that this arrival constituted
the success or victory of the player, which is what is significant
for the players and spectators of the game. Similarly, finding out
something by seeing or hearing is, so to speak, a success or
victory in the game of exploring the world. This seeing or
hearing is of course susceptible of a complete and very complex
causal explanation, given in terms of optics or acoustics,
physiology, neurology and the rest; but the player's interest is
not primarily in the contents of this explanation, but in the
exploratory task itself and its accomplishment.

In other words, verbs like 'see' and 'hear' do not merely
denote special experiences or mental happenings, with special
causal antecedents; they denote achievements of tasks, or
successes in undertakings. There are questions of technique to
be asked about them as well as questions of causal conditioning,
and questions of technique are not answerable by any multi-
plication of answers to questions of causal conditioning; they
are questions of quite different types.

So I want to suggest that the postulation of sense-impressions
as causal antecedent of seeing and hearing, only an antecedent
not of a physical or physiological, but of a psychological kind
arose from two sources, (1) a proper realisation of the fact that
physical and physiological causal accounts of perception cannot
answer technical questions about perceptual successes and
failures; (2) an improper, non-realisation of the fact that what
was lacking to such causal accounts was not that they needed an
extra, psychological link in the causal chain; but that they were
answers to causal questions and not to questions of technique.
When we want to describe the differences between hearing,
mishearing, and non-hearing, no discovery or postulation of
causal links can give us what we want. Sense-impressions were
postulated as the missing causal links which would solve a
problem which was not a causal problem.

However, after all this has been said, I confess to a residual
embarrassment. There is something in common between

having an after-image and seeing a misprint. Both are visual affairs. How ought we to describe their affinity with one another, without falling back on to some account very much like a part of the orthodox theories of sense-impressions? To this I am stumped for an answer.

MAIN PUBLICATIONS

Philosophical Arguments. Inaugural Lecture. Oxford University Press. 1945.
The Concept of Mind. Hutchinson's University Library. 1949.
Dilemmas. (The Tarner Lectures.) Cambridge University Press. 1954.
Editor of *Mind*.

HOW I SEE PHILOSOPHY

By F. WAISMANN

Reader in the Philosophy of Mathematics
in the University of Oxford

HOW I SEE PHILOSOPHY

I

WHAT philosophy is? [1] I don't know, nor have I a set formula to offer. Immediately I sit down to contemplate the question I am flooded with so many ideas, tumbling over one another, that I cannot do justice to all of them. I can merely make an attempt, a very inadequate one, to sketch with a few strokes what the lie of the land seems to me to be, tracing some lines of thought without entering upon a close-knit argument.

It is, perhaps, easier to say what philosophy is not than what it is. The first thing, then, I should like to say is that philosophy, as it is practised today, is very unlike science; and this in three respects: in philosophy there are no proofs; there are no theorems; and there are no questions which can be decided, Yes or No. In saying that there are no proofs I do not mean to say that there are no arguments. Arguments certainly there are, and first-rate philosophers are recognized by the originality of their arguments; only these do not work in the sort of way they do in mathematics or in the sciences.

There are many things beyond proof: the existence of material objects, of other minds, indeed of the external world, the validity of induction, and so on. Gone are the days when philosophers were trying to prove all sorts of things: that the soul is immortal, that this is the best of all possible worlds and the rest, or to refute, by 'irrefutable' argument and with relish, materialism, positivism and what not. Proof, refutation—these are dying words in philosophy (though G. E. Moore still

[1] This article is in reply to a question put to me by the Editor.

'proved' to a puzzled world that it exists. What can one say to this—save, perhaps, that he is a great prover before the Lord?).

But can it be *proved* that there are no proofs in philosophy? No; for one thing, such a proof, if it were possible, would by its very existence establish what it was meant to confute. But why suppose the philosopher to have an I.Q. so low as to be unable to learn from the past? Just as the constant failure of attempts at constructing a perpetual motion has in the end led to something positive in physics, so the efforts to construct a philosophical 'system', going on for centuries and going out of fashion fairly recently, tell their tale. This, I think, is part of the reason why philosophers today are getting weaned from casting their ideas into deductive moulds, in the grand style of Spinoza.

What I want to show in this article is that it is quite wrong to look at philosophy as though it had for its aim to provide theorems but had lamentably failed to do so. The whole conception changes when one comes to realize that what philosophers are concerned with is something different—neither discovering new propositions nor refuting false ones nor checking and re-checking them as scientists do. For one thing, proofs require premisses. Whenever such premisses have been set up in the past, even tentatively, the discussion at once challenged them and shifted to a deeper level. Where there are no proofs there are no theorems either. (To write down lists of propositions 'proved' by Plato or Kant: a pastime strongly to be recommended.) Yet the failure to establish a sort of Euclidean system of philosophy based on some suitable 'axioms' is, I submit, neither a mere accident nor a scandal but deeply founded in the nature of philosophy.

Yet there are questions; (and arguments). Indeed, a philosopher is a man who senses as it were hidden crevices in the build of our concepts where others only see the smooth path of commonplaceness before them.

Questions but no answers? Decidedly odd. The oddness may lessen when we take a look at them at closer range. Consider two famous examples: Achilles and the tortoise, and the astonishment of St. Augustine when confronted with the fact of memory. He is amazed, not at some striking feat of memory, but at there being such a thing as memory at all. A sense-impression, say a smell or a taste, floats before us and disappears. One moment it is here and the next it is gone. But in the galleries of the memory pale copies of it are stored up after its death. From there I can drag them out when and as often as I wish, like, and yet strangely unlike, the original—unlike in that they are not perishable like the momentary impression: what was transitory has been arrested and has achieved duration. But who can say how this change comes about?

Here the very fact of memory feels mystifying in a way in which ordinary questions asking for information do not; and *of course* it is not a factual question. What is it?

From Plato to Schopenhauer philosophers are agreed that the source of their philosophizing is wonder. What gives rise to it is nothing recondite and rare but precisely those things which stare us in the face: memory, motion, general ideas. (Plato: What does 'horse' mean? A single particular horse? No, for it may refer to *any* horse; *all* the horses, the total class? No, for we may speak of this or that horse. But if it means neither a single horse nor all horses, what *does* it mean?) The idealist is shaken in just the same way when he comes to reflect that he has, in Schopenhauer's words, 'no knowledge of the sun but only of an eye that sees a sun, and no knowledge of the earth but only of a hand that feels an earth'. Can it be, then, that nothing whatever is known to us except our own consciousness?

In looking at such questions, it seems as if the mind's eye were growing dim and as if everything, even that which ought to be absolutely clear, was becoming oddly puzzling and unlike its usual self. To bring out what seems to be peculiar to these questions one might say that they are not so much questions as tokens of a profound uneasiness of mind. Try for a moment to put yourself into the frame of mind of which Augustine was possessed when he asked: How is it possible to measure time? Time consists of past, present and future. The past can't be measured, it is gone; the future can't be measured, it is not yet here; and the present can't be measured, it has no extension. Augustine knew of course how time is measured and this was not his concern. What puzzled him was how it is *possible* to measure time, seeing that the past hour cannot be lifted out and placed alongside the present hour for comparison. Or look at it this way: what is measured is in the past, the measuring in the present: how can that be?

The philosopher as he ponders over some such problem has the appearance of a man who is deeply disquieted. He seems to be straining to grasp something which is beyond his powers. The words in which such a question presents itself do not quite bring out into the open the real point—which may, perhaps more aptly, be described as the recoil from the incomprehensible. If, on a straight railway journey, you suddenly come in sight of the very station you have just left behind, there will be terror, accompanied perhaps by slight giddiness. That is exactly how the philosopher feels when he says to himself, 'Of course time can be measured; but how *can* it?' It is as though, up to now, he had been passing heedlessly over the difficulties, and now, all of a sudden, he notices them and asks himself in alarm, 'But how can that be?' That is a sort of question which we only ask when it is the very facts themselves which confound us, when something about them strikes us as preposterous.

Kant, I fancy, must have felt something of the sort when he suddenly found the existence of geometry a puzzle. Here we have propositions as clear and transparent as one would wish, prior, it seems, to all experience; at the same time they apply miraculously to the real world. How is that possible? Can the mind, unaided by experience, in some dark manner actually fathom the properties of real things? Looked upon in this way, geometry takes on a disturbing air.

We all have our moments when something quite ordinary suddenly strikes us as queer—for instance, when time appears to us as a curious thing. Not that we are often in this frame of mind; but on some occasions, when we look at things in a certain way, unexpectedly they seem to change as though by magic: they stare at us with a puzzling expression, and we begin to wonder whether they can possibly be the things we have known all our lives.

'Time flows' we say—a natural and innocent expression, and yet one pregnant with danger. It flows 'equably', in Newton's phrase, at an even rate. What can this mean? When something moves, it moves with a definite speed (and speed means: rate of change in time). To ask with what speed time moves, i.e. to ask how quickly time changes in time, is to ask the unaskable. It also flows, again in Newton's phrase, 'without relation to anything external'. How are we to figure that? Does time flow on irrespective of what happens in the world? Would it flow on even if everything in heaven and on earth came to a sudden standstill as Schopenhauer believed? For if this were not so, he said, time would have to stop with the stopping of the clock and move with the clock's movement. How odd: time flows at the same rate and yet without speed; and perhaps even without anything to occur in it? The expression is puzzling in another way. 'I can never catch myself being in the past or in the future', someone might say; 'whenever I think or perceive or breathe the word "now", I am in the present; therefore I am *always* in the present.' In saying this, he may think of the present moment as a bridge as it were from which he is looking down at the 'river of time'. Time is gliding along underneath the bridge, but the 'now' does not take part in the motion. What was future passes into the present (is just below the bridge) and then into the past, while the onlooker, the 'self' or the 'I', is always in the present. 'Time flows *through* the "now"', he may feel to be a quite expressive metaphor. Yes, it sounds all right— until he suddenly comes to his senses and, with a start, realizes, 'But surely the moment flies?' (Query: How to succeed in wasting time? Answer: In this way, for instance—by trying, with eyes closed or staring vacantly in front of oneself, to catch the present moment as it is flitting by.) He may come now to look at matters in a different way. He sees himself advancing through time towards the future, and with this goes a suggestion of being active, just as at other times he may see himself floating down the stream whether he likes it or not. 'What exactly is it that is moving—the events in time or the present moment?', he may wonder. In the first case, it looks to him as if time were moving while he stands still; in the second case as if he were moving through time. 'How exactly is it', he may say in a dubious voice, 'am I always in the present? Is the present always eluding me?' Both ring true in a way; but they contradict each other? Again, does it make sense to ask, 'At what time is the present moment?' Yes, no doubt; but how *can* it, if the 'now' is but the fixed point from which the dating of any event ultimately receives its sense?

So he is pulled to and fro: 'I am always in the present, yet it slips through my fingers; I am going forward in time—no, I am carried down the stream.' He is using different pictures, each in its way quite appropriate to the occasion; yet when he tries to apply them jointly they clash. 'What a queer thing time must be', he may say to himself with a puzzled look on his face, 'what after all *is* time?'—expecting, half-expecting perhaps, that the answer will reveal to him time's hidden essence. Ranged beyond the intellectual are deeper levels of uneasiness—terror of the inevitability of time's passage, with all the reflections upon life that this forces upon us. Now all these anxious doubts release themselves in the question, 'What is time?' (*En passant* this is a hint that *one* answer will never do—will never remove all these doubts that break out afresh on different levels and yet are expressed in the same form of words.)

As we all know what time is and yet cannot say what it is it feels mystifying; and precisely because of its elusiveness it catches our imagination. The more we look at it the more we are puzzled: it seems charged with paradoxes. 'What is time? What is this being made up of movement only without anything that is moving?' (Schopenhauer). How funny to have it bottled up! 'I've got here in my hand the most potent, the most enigmatic, the most fleeting of all essences—Time.' (Logan Pearsall Smith of an hour-glass.) For Shelley it is an 'unfathomable sea!

whose waves are years', a 'shoreless flood', for Proust—well, why not leave something to the reader?

But isn't the answer to this that what mystifies us lies in the *noun* form 'the time'? Having a notion embodied in the form of a noun almost irresistibly makes us turn round to look for what it is 'the name of'. We are trying to catch the shadows cast by the opacities of speech. A wrong analogy absorbed into the forms of our language produces mental discomfort; (and the feeling of discomfort, when it refers to language, is a profound one). 'All sounds, all colours . . . evoke indefinite and yet precise emotions, or, as I prefer to think, call down among us certain disembodied powers whose footsteps over our hearts we call emotions' (W. B. Yeats).

Yet the answer is a prosaic one: don't ask what time is but how the *word* 'time' is being used. Easier said than done; for if the philosopher rectifies the use of language, ordinary language has 'the advantage of being in possession of declensions', to speak with Lichtenberg, and thus renews its spell over him, luring him on into the shadow chase. It is perhaps only when we turn to languages of a widely different grammatical structure that the way towards such possibilities of interpretation is entirely barred. 'It is highly probable that philosophers within the domain of the Ural-Altaic languages (where the subject-concept is least developed) will look differently "into the world" and be found on paths of thought different from those of the Indo-Europeans or Mussulmans' (Nietzsche).

II

It may be well at this point to remind ourselves that the words 'question' and 'answer', 'problem' and 'solution' are not always used in their most trite sense. It is quite obvious that we often have to do something very different to find the way out of a difficulty. A problem of politics is solved by adopting a certain line of action, the problems of novelists perhaps by the invention of devices for presenting the inmost thoughts and feelings of their characters; there is the painter's problem of how to suggest depth or movement on the canvas, the stylistic problem of expressing things not yet current, not yet turned into cliché; there are a thousand questions of technology which are answered, not by the discovery of some truth, but by a practical achievement; and there is of course the 'social question'. In philosophy, the real problem is not to find the answer to a given question but to find a sense for it.

To see in what the 'solution' of such a 'problem' consists let us start with Achilles who, according to Zeno, is to this day chasing the tortoise. Suppose that Achilles runs twice as fast as the tortoise. If the tortoise's start is 1, Achilles will have to cover successively $1, \frac{1}{2}, \frac{1}{4}, \frac{1}{8}, \ldots$; this series is endless: so he can never catch the tortoise. 'Nonsense!' (a mathematician's voice), 'the sum of the infinite series is finite, namely 2, and that settles it.' Though perfectly true, his remark is not to the point. It does not remove the sting from the puzzle, the disconcerting idea, namely, that however far we go in the series there is always a next term, that the lead the tortoise has in the race, though naturally getting smaller and smaller, yet never ceases to be: there *can* be no moment when it is strictly zero. It is *this* feature of the case, I suggest, that we do not understand and which throws us into a state of confusion.

But look at it this way. Suppose that we apply the same sort of argument to a minute, then we shall have to argue in some such way as this. Before the minute can be over the first half of it must elapse, then one-quarter of it, then one-eighth of it, and so on *ad infinitum*. This being an endless process, the minute can never come to an end. Immediately we have the argument in this form, the blunder leaps to the eye: we have been confusing two senses of 'never', a temporal and a non-temporal one. While it is quite correct to say that the sequence $1, \frac{1}{2}, \frac{1}{4}, \frac{1}{8}, \ldots$ never ends, this sense of the word 'never' has nothing whatever to do with time. All it means is that there is no last term in the series, or (what comes to the same) that to any term, no matter how far out in the sequence, a successor can be constructed according to the simple rule 'halve it': that is meant here by 'never'; whereas in saying, for instance, that man will never find out anything to avert death, 'never' is meant in the sense 'at no time'. It is clear that the mathematical assertion concerning the possibility of going on in the sequence by forming new terms according to the rule does not state anything about actual occurrences in time. The mistake should really be obvious: in saying that, since the start is getting progressively smaller and yet can never cease to be, Achilles can never catch the tortoise, we jump from the mathematical, *non*-temporal to the temporal sense. Had there been two different words in our language to mark these senses the confusion could never have arisen, and the world would be poorer for one of its most attractive paradoxes. But the same word is as a matter of course used with different meanings. Result: something like a conjuring trick. While our attention is diverted, while, 'in our mind's eye', we stare fixedly at Achilles as he is speeding along, with each big bound diminishing his distance from the tortoise, the one sense is so innocuously palmed off for the other as to escape notice.

This way of bringing out the fallacy also holds when the other key term is used for presenting the puzzle. As there will 'always' be a next term in the sequence, i.e. a next step in the scheme of subdividing the race-course (the word 'always' looking just as spotless and innocent) we readily fall into the trap of concluding that the tortoise will 'always' be ahead of Achilles, eternally to be chased by his pursuer.

Many are the types of bewilderment: there is the obsessional doubt—can I ever know that other people have experiences, that they see, hear and feel as I do? Can I be sure that memory does not always deceive me? Are there really material objects and not only sense-impressions 'of' them? There is the doubt-like uneasiness—what sort of being is possessed by numbers? There is the anxiety-doubt—are we really free? This doubt has taken many different forms one of which I shall single out for discussion—the question, namely, whether the law of excluded middle, when it refers to statements in the future tense, forces us into a sort of logical Predestination. A typical argument is this. If it is true now that I shall do a certain thing tomorrow, say, jump into the Thames, then no matter how fiercely I resist, strike out with hands and feet like a madman, when the day comes I cannot help jumping into the water; whereas, if this prediction is false now, then whatever efforts I may make, however many times I may nerve and brace myself, look down at the water and say to myself, 'One, two, three——', it is impossible for me to spring. Yet that the prediction is either true or false is itself a necessary truth, asserted by the law of excluded middle. From this the startling consequence seems to follow that it is already now decided what I shall do tomorrow, that indeed the entire future is somehow fixed, logically pre-ordained. Whatever I do and whichever way I decide, I am merely moving along lines clearly marked in advance which lead me towards my appointed lot. We are all, in fact, marionettes. If we are not prepared to swallow *that*, then—and there is a glimmer of hope in the 'then'—there is an alternative open to us. We need only renounce the law of excluded middle for state-ments of this kind, and with it the validity of ordinary logic, and all will be well. Descriptions of what will happen are, at present, neither true nor false. (This sort of argument was actually propounded by Łukasiewicz in favour of a three-valued logic with 'possible' as a third truth-value alongside 'true' and 'false'.)

The way out is clear enough. The asker of the question has fallen into the error of so many philosophers: of giving an answer before stopping to consider the question. For is he clear what he is asking? He seems to suppose that a statement re-ferring to an event in the future is at present undecided, neither true nor false, but that when the event happens the proposition enters into a sort of new state, that of being true. But how are we to figure the change from 'undecided' to 'true'? Is it sudden or gradual? At what moment does the statement 'it will rain tomorrow' begin to be true? When the first drop falls to the ground? And supposing that it will not rain, when will the statement begin to be false? Just at the end of the day, at 12 p.m. sharp? Supposing that the event *has* happened, that the statement *is* true, will it remain so for ever? If so, in what way? Does it remain uninterruptedly true, at every moment of day and night? Even if there were no one about to give it any thought? Or is it true only at the moments when it is being thought of? In that case, how long does it remain true? For the duration of the thought? We wouldn't know how to answer these questions; this is due not to any particular ignorance or stupidity on our part but to the fact that something has gone wrong with the way the words 'true' and 'false' are applied here.

If I say, 'It is true that I was in America', I am saying that I was in America and no more. That in uttering the words 'It is true that—' I take responsibility upon myself is a different matter that does not concern the present argument. The point is that in making a statement prefaced by the words 'It is true that' I do not *add* anything to the factual information I give you. *Saying* that something is true is not *making* it true: cp. the criminal lying in court, yet every time he is telling a lie protesting, his hand on his heart, that he is telling the truth.

What is characteristic of the use of the words 'true' and 'false' and what the pleader of logical determinism has failed to notice is this. 'It is true' and 'it is false', while they certainly have the force of asserting and denying, are not descriptive. Suppose that someone says, 'It is true that the sun will rise tomorrow' all it means is that the sun will rise tomorrow: he is not regaling us with an extra-description of the trueness of what he says. But supposing that he were to say instead, 'It is true *now* that the sun will rise tomorrow', this would boil down to something like 'The sun will rise tomorrow now'; which is nonsense. To ask, as the puzzle-poser does, 'Is it true or false *now* that such-and-such will happen in the future?' is not the sort of question to which an answer can be given: which *is* the answer.

This sheds light on what has, rather solemnly, been termed the 'timelessness of truth'. It lies in this that the clause 'it is true that—' does not allow of inserting a date. To say of a proposition like 'Diamond is pure carbon' that it is true on Christmas Eve would be just as poor a joke as to say that it is true in Paris and not in Timbuctoo. (This does not mean that we cannot say in certain circumstances, 'Yes, it was true in those days' as this can clearly be paraphrased without using the word 'true'.)

Now it begins to look a bit less paradoxical to say that when a philosopher wants to dispose of a question the one thing he must not do is: to give an answer. A philosophic question is not solved: it *dis*solves. And in what does the 'dissolving' consist? In making the meaning of the words used in putting the question so clear to ourselves that we are released from the spell it casts on us. Confusion was removed by calling to mind the use of language or, so far as the use *can* be distilled into rules, the rules: it therefore *was* a confusion about the use of language, or a confusion about rules. It is here that philosophy and grammar meet.

There is one further point that needs elucidation. When we say of a given assertion, e.g. 'It is raining', that it is true we can hardly escape the impression that we say something 'about' the assertion, namely, that it has the property of trueness. To make such a statement seems, then, to say *more* than what was asserted originally, namely, that it is raining and that this assertion is true. That, however, leads to queer consequences. For in which sense does it say more? Consider first under which circumstances it would be appropriate to say of two given propositions that the one says 'more' than the other. 'This is red' says more than 'this is coloured' for the obvious reason that anyone can conclude from the first statement to the second but no one reversely; similarly 'today is Tuesday' says more than 'today is a weekday'. The criterion, then, suggests itself that, given two propositions p and q, p says more than q, if $\sim p . q$ is meaningful and $p . \sim q$ contradictory. The holder of the view that 'p is true' says more than p (p standing e.g. for 'It is raining'), may now be challenged to explain what he means by that. Is he using the word 'more' in the sense just explained? If so, the curious consequence ensues that it must *make sense* to assert the conjunction $\sim p . q$, that is in our case, 'It is not true that it is raining and it is raining'. Since this obviously is not what he had in mind, what *does* he mean? We are not contradicting him; we merely remind him of how these words have always been used by him, in non-philosophical contexts that is, and then point out that, if he still wants to use them in this sense, to say what he wanted to say lands him in an absurdity. All we do is to make him aware of his own practice. We abstain from any assertion. It is for him to explain what he means. Not that he cannot do it. In ascribing truth to a given statement, he might say, he wants to express perhaps either (i) that it is 'in accordance with fact' or something of the sort; or (ii) that he *knows* that it is true. In the first case he is faced with the same dilemma, namely, that it must make sense to say, 'It is not in accordance with the facts that it is raining and it is raining'; in the second fresh difficulties are breaking out. For one thing, the words 'it is true that—', when uttered by different people, would then mean different things; for another, and this is more fatal to the advocate of fatalism, in construing the words in this sense, he cuts the ground from under his own feet. No one would then be worried by the question whether, supposing that it is false now that he will write a certain letter tomorrow, it follows that it will really be impossible for him to write that letter, that this line of conduct is barred to him, logically barred. For since 'it is false now' means in the new sense 'he doesn't know yet' nothing follows and the whole question evaporates.

My reason for going into this tangle at some length is that the method applied in unravelling it presents some interesting features. First, we don't *force* our interlocutor. We leave him free to choose, accept or reject any way of using his words. He may depart from ordinary usage—language is not untouchable —if it is only in this way that he can explain himself. He may even use an expression one time in this, another time in that, way. The only thing we insist upon is that he should be aware of what he is doing. If we strictly adhere to this method— going over the argument, asking him at each step whether he is willing to use an expression in a certain way, if not, offering him alternatives, but leaving the decisions to him and only pointing out what their consequences are—no dispute can arise. Disputes arise only if certain steps in this procedure are omitted so that it looks as if we had made an assertion, adding to the world's woes a new apple of discord. This would be the true way of doing philosophy undogmatically. The difficulty of this method lies in presenting the subject in a manner which can easily be taken in—in arranging the cases and the ways in which they are connected through intermediate links so that we can gain a clear synoptic view of the whole.

Second, we do not use arguments in order to prove or disprove any 'philosophic view'. As we have no views we can afford to look at things as they are.

Next, we only describe; we do not 'explain'. An explanation, in the sense of a deductive proof, cannot satisfy us because it pushes the question 'Why just these rules and no other ones?' only one stage back. In following that method, we do not *want* to give reasons. All we do is to describe a use or tabulate rules. In doing this, we are not making any discoveries: there is nothing to be discovered in grammar. Grammar is autonomous and not dictated by reality. Giving reasons, bound as it is to come to an end and leading to something which cannot further be explained, *ought* not to satisfy us. In grammar we never ask the question 'why?'

But isn't the result of this that philosophy itself 'dissolves'? Philosophy eliminates those questions which *can* be eliminated by such a treatment. Not all of them, though: the metaphysician's craving that a ray of light may fall on the mystery of the existence of this world, or on the incomprehensible fact that it is comprehensible, or on the 'meaning of life'—even if such questions *could* be shown to lack a clear meaning or to be devoid of meaning altogether, they are *not silenced*. It does nothing to lessen the dismay they rouse in us. There is something cheap in 'debunking' them. The heart's unrest is not to be stilled by logic. Yet philosophy is not dissolved. It derives its weight, its grandeur, from the significance of the questions it destroys. It overthrows idols, and it is the importance of these idols which gives philosophy its importance.

Now it can perhaps be seen why the search for answers fitting the moulds of the questions fails, is *bound* to fail. They are not real questions asking for information but 'muddles felt as problems' (Wittgenstein) which wither away when the ground is cleared. If philosophy advances, it is not by adding new propositions to its list, but rather by transforming the whole intellectual scene and, as a consequence of this, by reducing the number of questions which befog and bedevil us. Philosophy so construed is one of the great liberating forces. Its task is, in the words of Frege, 'to free the spirit from the tyranny of words by exposing the delusions which arise, almost inevitably, through the use of a word language'.

III

What, only criticism and no meat? The philosopher a fog dispeller? If that were all he was capable of I would be sorry for him and leave him to his devices. Fortunately, this is not so. For one thing, a philosophic question, if pursued far enough, may lead to something positive—for instance, to a more profound understanding of language. Take the sceptical doubts as to material objects, other minds, etc. The first reaction is perhaps to say: these doubts are idle. Ordinarily, when I doubt whether I shall finish this article, after a time my doubt comes to an end. I cannot go on doubting for ever. It's the destiny of doubt to die. But the doubts raised by the sceptic never die. Are they doubts? Are they pseudo-questions? They appear so only when judged by the twin standards of common sense and common speech. The real trouble lies deeper: it arises from the sceptic casting doubt on the very facts which underlie the use of language, those permanent features of experience which make concept formation possible, which in fact are precipitated in the use of our most common words. Suppose that you see an object in front of you quite clearly, say, a pipe, and when you are going to pick it up it melts into thin air, then you may feel, 'Lord, I'm going mad' or something of the sort (unless the whole situation is such that you have reason to suspect that it was some clever trick). But what, the sceptic may press now, if such experiences were quite frequent? Would you be prepared to *dis*solve the connection between different sense experiences which form the hard core of our idea of a solid object, to *un*do what language has done—to part with the category of thing-hood? And would you then be living in a phenomenalist's paradise with colour patches and the other paraphernalia of the sense-datum theory, in a disobjected, desubstantialized world? To say in such circumstances, 'Look, it's just tabling now' would be a joke (for even in the weakened verb forms 'tabling', 'chairing' an element of the thing-category lingers on). That is why the sceptic struggles to express himself in a language which is not fit for this purpose. He expresses himself misleadingly when he says that he doubts such-and-such *facts:* his doubts cut so deep that they affect the fabric of language itself. For what he doubts is already embodied in the very forms of speech, e.g. in what is condensed in the use of thing-words. The moment he tries to penetrate those deep-sunken layers, he undermines the language in which he ventilates his qualms—with the result that he seems to be talking nonsense. He is not. But in order to make his doubts fully expressible, language would first have to go into the melting-pot. (We can get a glimmering of what is needed from modern science where all the long-established categories— thinghood, causality, position—had to be revolutionized. This required nothing less than the construction of some new language, not the expression of new facts with the old one.)

If we look at the matter in this way the attitude of the sceptic is seen in a new light. He considers possibilities which lie far outside the domain of our current experience. If his doubts are taken seriously, they turn into observations which cast a new and searching light on the subsoil of language, showing what possibilities are open to our thought (though not to ordinary language), and what paths might have been pursued if the texture of our experience were different from what it is. These problems are not spurious: they make us aware of the vast background in which any current experiences are embedded, and to which language has adapted itself; thus they bring out the unmeasured sum of experience stored up in the use of our words and syntactical forms.

For another thing, a question may decide to go in for another career than dissolving: it may pass into science. Frege, for instance, was prompted to his inquiries by philosophical motives, namely, to find a definite answer to the question about the nature of arithmetical truths—whether they are analytic or synthetic, *a priori* or *a posteriori*. Starting from this question and pursuing it with all possible rigour, he was led to unearth a whole mine of problems of a scientific nature; and proceeding along these lines, he came to fashion a new instrument, a logic, which in delicacy and range and power far surpassed anything that went by this name before, a subject revealing to this day new and unexpected depths. True, the question from which Frege set out was not too clearly defined owing to the imprecise nature of the Kantian terms in which it was expressed.

A whole chapter might be written on the fate of questions, their curious adventures and transformations—how they change into others and in the process remain, and yet do not remain, the same. The original question may split and multiply almost like a character in a dream play. To mention just a few examples: can logic be characterized completely in a formal way, i.e. without bringing in any extraneous ideas such as the use of language and all that goes with it? Can arithmetic be characterized in any such way, entirely 'from within'? Or will any interpretation include some *Erdenrest* of the empiric? These questions have given rise to extensive research on mathematical interpretation of formal systems. The query how far logical intuition is correct has got ramified into a bunch of questions pertaining to the theory of logical types, the axiom of choice, etc., indeed to a far more fundamental issue, namely, whether ordinary logic itself is 'right' as contrasted with the system of inferences evolved by the intuitionists. Or again, are there undecidable questions in mathematics, not in the restricted sense of Gödel, but undecidable in an absolute sense? Are there natural limits to generalization? It is interesting to watch how from a question of this sort, not too precise, somewhat blurred, new and better defined questions detach themselves, the parent question—in Frege's case philosophic *par excellence*—giving rise to a scientist's progeny.

Now something else must be noted—how these questions become, not only precise, but clear (which is not the same thing). To illustrate, can the infinity represented by all natural numbers be compared with the infinity represented by all points in space? That is, can the one be said to be less than, or equal to, the other? When it was first asked, the question had no clear sense— perhaps no sense at all. Yet it guided G. Cantor in his ingenious search. Before set theory was discovered—or should I rather say 'invented'?—the question acted as a sort of signpost pointing vaguely to some so far uncharted region of thought. It is perhaps best characterized by saying that it guides our imagination in a given direction, stimulates research along new lines. Such questions do not 'dissolve': they are solved, only not in the existing system of thought but rather by constructing a new conceptual system—such as set theory—where the intended and faintly anticipated sense finds its full realization. They are therefore of the nature of incitements to the building of such systems, they point from the not-yet-meaningful to the meaningful.

The question is the first groping step of the mind in its journeyings that lead towards new horizons. The genius of the philosopher shows itself nowhere more strikingly than in the new kind of question he brings into the world. What distinguishes him and gives him his place is the passion of questioning. That his questions are at times not so clear is perhaps of not so much moment as one makes of it. There is nothing like clear thinking to protect one from making discoveries. It is all very well to talk of clarity, but when it becomes an obsession it is liable to nip the living thought in the bud. This, I am afraid, is one of the deplorable results of Logical Positivism, not foreseen by its founders, but only too striking in some of its followers. Look at these people, gripped by a clarity neurosis, haunted by fear, tongue-tied, asking themselves continually, 'Oh dear, now does this make perfectly good sense?' Imagine the pioneers of science, Kepler, Newton, the discoverers of non-Euclidean geometry, of field physics, the unconscious, matter waves or heaven knows what, imagine them asking themselves this question at every step—this would have been the surest means of sapping any creative power. No great discoverer has acted in accordance with the motto, 'Everything that can be said can be said clearly'. And some of the greatest discoveries have even emerged from a sort of primordial fog. (Something to be said for the fog. For my part, I've always suspected that clarity is the last refuge of those who have nothing to say.)

The great mind is the great questioner. An example in point is Kant's problem 'How is geometry possible?' The way to its solution was only opened up through the rise of the 'axiomatic method'. Seeing that the axioms of geometry are capable of an indefinite number of different interpretations and that the particular way they may be interpreted is irrelevant to deductive purposes, Hilbert separated what belongs to the logical form of the axioms from what belongs to their intuitional (or other) content and turned the whole question by saying: a point, a straight line, etc., may be anything that satisfies the axioms. As the business of deduction hinges only on the relations in which the basic terms stand to each other and not on the 'content' we associate with them, and as these relations are fully set out in the axioms, the axioms in their totality determine what a 'point', a 'line', etc., is so far as it is sufficient for deductive needs. Through the rise of this technique it became apparent that the word 'geometry', as understood by Kant, covers, in fact, two totally different sciences, mathematical and physical geometry. It was the failure to distinguish between them that produced Kant's perplexity. 'So far as the laws of mathematics refer to reality, they are not certain; and so far as they are certain, they do not refer to reality' (Einstein). Kant's credit lies in having *seen* that there is a problem, not in having solved it.

But here a new problem presents itself: How do we know what will satisfy a given question? More generally: How does the answer fit the question? Questions of the current sort ('What is the right time?') show already by their form what sort of answer to expect. They are, so to speak, cheques with a blank to be filled; yet not always so: Augustine's question, 'How is it possible to measure time?' or Kant's question, 'How is geometry possible?' do not trace out the form of the answer. There is no *obvious* link between question and answer, any more than there is in the case of asking 'What is a point?' When Hilbert's idea—that the axioms of geometry jointly provide the 'implicit definition' of the basic terms—was first propounded it came totally unexpected; no one had ever thought of that before; on the contrary, many people had an uneasy feeling as if this were a way of evading the issue rather than an answer, amongst them no less a man than Frege. He thought the problem still unsolved.

Now is there anything one can do to make a man like Frege see that the axiomatic method provides the correct answer? Can it, for example, be *proved* to him? The point to which attention must now be drawn, though it should really be obvious, is that such a proof cannot be given, and it cannot because he, the asker, has first to be turned round to see the matter differently. What is required is a change of the entire way of thinking. Indeed, anyone who is puzzled by this problem and yet refuses to accept Hilbert's solution only betrays that he has got stuck in the groove hollowed out by the form in which the question is put. 'A point is —' he begins and then stops. What is to be done to help him to get out of the groove or, better still, to make him shift for himself when he feels 'cramped' in it, is a *discussion*, not a proof.

Frege behaves not so very unlike a man mystified by the question, 'What is time?' We may suggest converting the latter into the question how the word 'time' is being used (which would bring him down to earth). But aren't we cheating him? We seem to be holding out the answer to *one* question, but not to that one which he was asking. He may suspect that we are trying to fob him off with the second best we have in store, his original question still remaining an enigma. Similarly Frege: he considered it a scandal that the questions 'What is a point?', 'What is a number?' were still unanswered.

In either of these cases, the aim of a discussion, in the absence of a proof, can only be to change the asker's attitude. We may, for instance, scrutinize similar, or partially similar, cases, point out that the form of the answer is not always that of the question; by going patiently over such cases, the vast background of analogies against which the question is seen will slowly change. The turning up of a wide field of language loosens the position of certain standards which are so ingrained that we do not see them for what they are; and if we do this in an effective manner, a mind like Frege's will be released from the obsession of seeking strainingly for an answer to fit the mould. Arguments are used in such a discussion, not as proofs though but rather as means to make him see things he had not noticed before: e.g. to dispel wrong analogies, to stress similarities with other cases and in this way to bring about something like a shift of perspective. However, there is no way of proving him wrong or bullying him into mental acceptance of the proposal: when all is said and done the decision is his.

But here more is at stake than loosening a cramped position— it is a question of escaping the domination of linguistic forms. How often are we merely following the channels carved out by numberless repetition of the same modes of expression—as when we say, unsuspectingly, 'Time flows' and are, when confronted (say) with Augustine's paradox, suddenly shocked out of complacency. Existing language, by offering us only certain stereotyped moulds of expression, creates habits of thought which it is almost impossible to break. Such a mould is, e.g. the actor-action scheme of the Indo-European languages. How deep their influence is can perhaps be surmised from Descartes' conclusion from thinking to the presence of an agent, an ego, different from the thinking, that does the thinking—a conclusion so natural and convincing to us because it is supported by the whole weight of language. Frege's obsession with the question ' What is a number?' is another case. As we can speak of '*the* number five', five, Frege argued, must be the proper name of an entity, a sort of Platonic crystal, indicated by means of the definite article. (A Chinese pupil of mine once informed me that Frege's question is unaskable in Chinese, 'five' being used there only as a numeral in contexts like 'five friends', 'five boats', etc.). Again, when we say of a given statement that it is true, we seem to be saying something 'about' it—evidence of the power of the subject-predicate cliché. Indeed, so strong is the temptation to construe it in this way, namely, as a statement about a statement, that the idea of a different interpretation scarcely occurs to us. It is important to notice that in doing so we assimilate the expression to analogical forms; but it is no less important to notice that none of these analogies needs to be present to our minds: it is enough if they make themselves felt in a dim, inarticulated way. Such patterns have an effect on us like thousands of explicit analogies: they act upon us, one might say, like a field of force, a language field, that draws our mental gaze in a certain direction. And, I venture to add, it is precisely because of the fleeting, half-formed, shadow-like nature of these analogies that it is almost impossible to escape their influence. If we are taken in by them, it is our fault. A philosopher, instead of preaching the righteousness of ordinary speech, should learn to be on his guard against the pitfalls ever present in its forms. To use a picture: just as a good swimmer must be able to swim up-stream, so the philosopher should master the unspeakably difficult art of thinking up-speech, against the current of clichés.

Now for another point. When we dissuade a man like Frege from his search, we seem to be hindering him from reaching the aim he set out to reach. Does our discussion clash, then, with his search? And, if so, in which way? First of all, in no clearly definable way; for he is not yet clearly aware what he is aiming at, and the discussion brings him gradually to see things in a different light. How is this change brought about? Well, he first saw the question in analogy with other ones, and these analogies are, one by one, destroyed; or rather, in the course of the discussion they are seen to be misleading. In proportion as the whole conceptual background changes, he comes to see that something is wrong with the way he put his question, that the attainment of his object is no longer satisfying. It is not that he gives up because he has tried very hard, but in vain, and has now got tired: no, he gives up because he 'sees' the question differently. And in what does *this* consist? Well, in the fact that he is now well aware of the analogies which were misleading him, that he sees the question against a different linguistic background (a 'figure' sometimes changes when it is seen against a different 'ground'), that a certain strain disappears and that he says, with a sigh of relief, 'Yes, that's it'.

The philosopher contemplates things through the prism of language and, misled (say) by some analogy, suddenly sees things in a new strange light. We can cope with these problems only by digging down to the soil from which they spring. What we do is to light up the mental background from which the question has detached itself; in a clearer perception of some of the crucial concepts the question transforms itself into another one. Not that it has been answered in the current sense. Rather we have removed the factors that prompted the question by a more profound and penetrating analysis. The essence of this process is that it leads the questioner on to some new aspect—and leads him with his spontaneous consent. He agrees to be thus led and therefore ends by abandoning his search. We cannot constrain anyone who is unwilling to follow the new direction of a question; we can only extend the field of vision of the asker, loosen his prejudices, guide his gaze in a new direction: but all this can be achieved only with his consent.

By our critical analysis we try to counteract the influence of the language field, or (what comes to the same) we may help the questioner to gain a deeper insight into the nature of what he is seeking first of all,—make him see the build of the concepts and the moulds in which he expresses the question. What matters is more like changing his outlook than proving to him some theorem; or more like increasing his insight. Insight cannot be lodged in a theorem, and this is the deeper reason why the deductive method is doomed to fail: insight cannot be demonstrated by proof.

What it comes to in the end is that the asker of the question, in the course of the discussion, has to make a number of *decisions*. And this makes the philosophical procedure so unlike a logical one. He compares, for instance, the case before him with analogous ones and has to *judge* how far these analogies hold. That is, it is for him to decide how far he is willing to accept these analogies: he has not, like a slave, to follow blindly in their track.

Science is rich in questions of this type. They are not scientific questions properly and yet they exercise scientists, they are philosophic questions and yet they do not exercise philosophers.

What I have wanted to say in this section and have not said, or only half-said:

(1) Philosophy is not only criticism of language: so construed, its aim is too narrow. It is criticizing, dissolving and stepping over *all* prejudices, loosening all rigid and constricting moulds of thought, no matter whether they have their origin in language or somewhere else.

(2) What is essential in philosophy is the breaking through to a *deeper insight*—which is something positive—not merely the dissipation of fog and the exposure of spurious problems.

(3) Insight cannot be lodged in a theorem, and it can therefore not be demonstrated.

(4) Philosophic arguments are, none of them, logically *compelling*: they really screen what actually happens—the quiet and patient undermining of categories over the whole field of thought.

(5) Their purpose is to open our eyes, to bring us to see things in a new way—from a wider standpoint unobstructed by misunderstandings.

(6) The essential difference between philosophy and logic is that logic *constrains* us while philosophy leaves us free: in a philosophic discussion we are led, step by step, to change our angle of vision, e.g. to pass from one way of putting a question to another, and this with our spontaneous agreement—a thing profoundly different from deducing theorems from a given set of premises. Misquoting Cantor one might say: the essence of philosophy lies in its freedom.

IV

There is a notion that philosophy is an exercise of the intellect and that philosophic questions can be settled by argument, and conclusively if one only knew how to set about it. What seems to me queer, however, is that I cannot find any really good hard argument; and more than that, the example just discussed must make it doubtful whether any compelling argument *can* be found. Out of this plight I incline to come to a new and somewhat shocking conclusion: that the thing cannot be done. No philosopher has ever proved anything. The whole claim is spurious. What I have to say is simply this. Philosophic arguments are not deductive; therefore they are not rigorous; and therefore they don't prove anything. Yet they have force.

Before going into the matter, I want to show, quite summarily first, how unplausible the view is that rigorous arguments are applied in philosophy. A first alarming sign can perhaps already be seen in the notorious fact that the ablest minds disagree, that what is indisputable to the one seems to have no force in the eyes of the other. In a clear system of thought such differences are impossible. That they exist in philosophy is weighty evidence that the arguments have none of the logical rigour they have in mathematics and the exact sciences.

Next, arguments, in the way they are thought of, must contain inferences, and inferences must start somewhere. Now where is the philosopher to look for his premises? To science? Then he will 'do' science, not philosophy. To statements of everyday life? To particular ones? Then he will never be able to advance a single step beyond them. To general statements? If so, a number of questions raise their ugly heads. By what right does he pass from 'some' to 'all'? ('To Generalize is to be an Idiot', W. Blake.) Can he be sure that his premises are stated with such clarity and precision that not a ghost of a doubt can creep in? Can he be sure that they contain meat, are not analytic, vacuous, definitions in disguise and the like? Can he be sure that they are true? (How *can* he?) And even supposing, what is not the case,

that all these requirements could be met, there is still another
task looming before him when it comes to developing the consequences: can he be sure how to operate with the terms?
(How *can* he?) I am not letting out a secret when I say that the
ordinary rules of logic often break down in natural speech—
a fact usually hushed up by logic books. Indeed, the words of
common language are so elastic that anyone can stretch their
sense to fit his own whims; and with this their 'logic' is queered.
(Plenty of scope for a 'natural logic'; we know that we are
unhappy; so we *are* unhappy. We *know* that we are unhappy; so
we are *great*. Pascal. 'If she had perished, she had perished':
does this entail that she has not perished? If so, by what rule?
'If I believed that I should be very silly indeed': does this, or
does this not, entail that I don't believe it? Natural language
holds logical problems of its own, lots of them.)

This brings me to another point. Ordinary language simply
has not got the 'hardness', the logical hardness, to cut axioms
in it. It needs something like a metallic substance to carve a
deductive system out of it such as Euclid's. But common
speech? If you begin to draw inferences it soon begins to go
'soft' and fluffs up somewhere. You may just as well carve
cameos on a cheese *soufflé*. (My point is: language is plastic,
yielding to the will to express, even at the price of some
obscurity. Indeed, how could it ever express anything that does
not conform to the cliché? If logicians had their way, language
would become as clear and transparent as glass, but also as
brittle as glass: and what would be the good of making an axe of
glass that breaks the moment you use it?) But language is not
hard. And that is why it is dangerous in philosophy to hunt for
premisses instead of just going over the ground, standing back
and saying: look.

Most philosophic arguments, to ignore constructions *à la*
Spinoza, hinge on such points as what 'can' and what 'cannot'
be said or what sort of question it is 'proper' and what sort of
question it would be 'inappropriate' to ask. Much skill and
ingenuity has been spent in elucidating such questions as to
whether a certain metaphor is 'natural', a certain diction

'fitting'. It would not be right to burke the point that considerations such as these, while apparently pertaining to matters of style, contribute in fact largely to the forcefulness of an argument, indeed play a very real and decisive part in the way they make us look at the subject. In going over, examining and comparing the various modes of expression that centre around certain key notions, for instance, 'imagination', 'memory', 'pleasure', we catch the first glimpse of what is sometimes called the 'logic' of these notions. Now can any of these things be proved? Can it be proved, for example, that a certain diction is 'fitting'? (Remember, no such thing as a definition of a 'well-formed formula'.) No philosopher has ever made so much as an attempt. Everyone uses words in this way and he leaves it at that; and rightly so. For what sort of reasons *could* he give anyway? Here already, at the very threshold, the idea of a philosophic proof begins to ring hollow.

'Ah, but the ordinary use of language.' All right; but even so, it is not that one 'cannot' use language differently. To illustrate: 'frozen music'—does this 'tell' you anything? Perhaps not; yet a saying like 'Architecture is frozen music' (Goethe) drives the point home. To say 'The arms are full of blunted memories' sounds odd, until you come upon it in Proust's context. The 'will to understand' does not even flinch before those bogys of the logician, contradictions: it transforms them, wresting a new sense from the apparent nonsense. ('Dark with excess of light', 'the luminous gloom of Plato'—just to remind the reader of two examples of Coleridge.) There are about 303 reasons why we sometimes express ourselves in a contradiction, and understandably so.

Result: it cannot even be proved that a given expression is natural, a metaphor fitting, a question proper (or unaskable), a collocation of words expressive (or devoid of meaning). Nothing of the sort can be demonstrated.

Two other points reinforce what has been said. What we sometimes do in a philosophical discussion is not argue at all but simply raise lots of questions—a method brilliantly employed by Ryle. Indeed, a volley of perplexing questions can certainly not be described as an argument and *a fortiori* not as a logical one, yet it is no less effective in making one turn back in recoil to consider one's views. Lastly, though on the surface the philosopher seems to be engaged in much the same thing as a logician is, for instance, in testing an argument for any loose links in it or in building up an argument, this should not mislead us. For if he were to construct rigorous proofs, where are the theorems established by them? What has he to show as the fruit of his labours?

I have not raised any of these questions wantonly; they force themselves on everyone who tries to arrive at a clear and unbiased view of the matter. Should these difficulties not have their origin in the nature of philosophy itself?

V

I proceed now to consider philosophic arguments, especially those which are regarded as constituting a decisive advance. to see whether they give us any reason for modifying the view advocated here. There are only a few classical cases. One of them is Hume's celebrated argument to show that the relation of cause and effect is intrinsically different from that of ground and consequence. Now in what does this 'proof' consist? He *reminds* us of what we have always known: that, while it is self-contradictory to assert the ground and deny the consequence, no such contradiction arises in assuming that a certain event, the 'cause', may be followed not by its usual effect but by some other event. If it is asked 'Is this a proof?' what is one to say? It certainly is not the sort of proof to be found in a deductive system. Much the same applies to Berkeley's argument when he tells us that, try as he might, he cannot call up in his mind an abstract idea of a triangle, of just a triangle with no particular shape, any more than he can conceive the idea of a man without qualities. Is this a proof? He points out the obvious. (Only it wants a genius to see it.)

To take my own argument against logical fatalism, it is not strict. The decisive step consists in following a certain analogy with other cases. It is analogical, not logical. Similarly the argument used against Zeno is not conclusive. (I have no space to enlarge upon that.)

Now for two more examples, one of the current sort of argument applied today by philosophers, the other taken from Aristotle.

When we say of someone that he 'sees' or 'hears' an aeroplane, or 'descries', 'detects' a lark in the sky, or again that he 'tastes' or 'smells' roast pork, we do not ascribe to him an activity. That 'seeing' is not a sort of doing can be illustrated, e.g. by calling attention to the fact that we don't use the continuous present tense. We say 'I see the clock', not 'I am seeing the clock' (save G. E. Moore, who, oddly enough, regularly says that he 'is seeing his right hand'), whereas it is perfectly correct to say 'I am looking at the clock, listening to its ticking', and so in the other cases. Again, while it is proper to say 'I have forgotten to post the letter', no one would say 'I have forgotten to see the letter-box'. There is no sense in asking you, when you look at me, whether your seeing is easy or difficult, quick or slowish, careful or heedless, whether you see me deliberately and whether you have now finished seeing me. So, it is argued, perceiving is not a doing (an argument used by myself in lectures).

The point to be laboured is that this argument is not conclusive. Odd as it sounds, 'I have finished seeing you' *may* be said, though only in very special circumstances. A man with impaired eyesight who, unable to take in the shape as a whole, has perhaps to scan the face bit by bit in search of some characteristic marks might say, and understandably, 'Now I have finished seeing you'. We too are occasionally in a not much better position, as when, in magnesium light, we look at some scene, and afterwards complain, 'Too quick, I couldn't take it in'. It would seem then that there is no more than a difference in degree between this case and the normal ones. Odd cases, certainly; but what would you think of a mathematician whose theorems collapse when applied to slightly out-of-the-way curves?

For my next example I choose pleasure. Aristotle, in criticizing Plato, pointed out that if pleasure were a process going on in time I could enjoy something swiftly or slowly—an argument which is almost a bombshell in its destructive power. Certainly, to speak in such terms is very odd and sounds absurd. Yet, if I strain my imagination, I can perhaps bring myself to conceive of a set of circumstances under which it would not be entirely unnatural to say such a thing. In listening to music, for example, when I am following a slow and gentle movement, my enjoying it appears in some respects to be different from what I get when listening to an exciting piece of music. The very quality of my enjoyment seems to change as if something of the slow and gentle or of the wild, intoxicating flow of the music had entered into it. If I say, in the one case, that I was enjoying it leisurely like basking in the sun or sipping wine, in the other that I was suddenly carried away, breathlessly following its onrush and enjoying it like a storm at sea—does this sound like sheer nonsense? So there does seem to be a time factor in pleasure.

Amongst the most powerful weapons in the philosopher's armoury are *reductio ad absurdum* and infinite regress arguments. Before proceeding to an appraisal of these forms of reasoning, it will be well to consider how they work in their home land, mathematics.

Let me choose as a typical case the proof that $\sqrt{2}$ is irrational. If it were a rational number, we could find two integers m and n such that

$$m^2 = 2n^2 \qquad (1)$$

We may then argue as follows. As m^2 is even, m must be even; hence $m = 2m_1$. Substitution yields

$$2m_1^2 = n^2. \qquad (2)$$

As n^2 is even, n must be even; hence $n = 2n_1$. Substitution yields

$$m_1^2 = 2n_1^2. \qquad (3)$$

If, then, two integers m and n exist which stand in the relation (1), they must have halves which stand in exactly the same relation (3), and these must have halves which stand in the same relation, and so on *ad infinitum;* which is plainly impossible, *m* and *n* being finite. Therefore the tentative assumption (1) cannot hold, and $\sqrt{2}$ cannot be rational. Q.E.D. This is the prototype of a refutation by infinite regress.

Arguments of this type have been applied outside mathematics. However, when I come to look at them a bit more closely I begin to hesitate. An example will illustrate my doubts. An argument propounded against the use of mechanical models is this. If the elastic properties of matter can be explained as being due to electric forces with which the molecules act on each other, it surely is pointless to explain the action of the electric forces as being due to the elastic properties of a mechanical medium, the 'ether'. To do this is to go round in a circle: elasticity is explained in terms of electric force, and electric force in terms of elasticity; while the attempt to break out of the circle by supposing that the elasticity of the ether is due to 'electric forces' acting between the ether particles and these to the elastic properties of a second-order ether is to be pushed into an infinite series of reduction steps. Thus the mechanistic programme is faced with a dilemma both horns of which are equally fatal.

A formidable argument—or is it? I can well imagine an undaunted champion of the lost cause retort: 'Not a bit of a regress. Yes, the ether is elastic, not, however, in the sense in which a spring is: while elasticity of matter can be reduced to electric force, elasticity of the ether, being an ultimate postulate of the theory, cannot be reduced any further.' And with this the argument falls to the ground.

But this is unconvincing, it will be said. I agree; I am not such an imbecile as to plead for retaining mechanical models and the rest. My point is only to see whether this 'refutation' is compelling. *It isn't.* The advocate of models is not forcibly dislodged from his position. There is, it would seem, always a way of getting out of the dilemma—of wriggling out if you like —which foils the argument. What is shown in it is merely that to cling to models of this sort becomes, in the circumstances, very unnatural. But to say that something is unnatural is not to say that it is logically impossible: yet this is what the argument should establish. In the mathematical proof cited above no loophole was left for wriggling out. The whole deduction was a 'chain of adamant'—precisely the sort of thing the argument under review is not.

Consider now a similar argument. There cannot be any such thing as volitions, it has been said. Volitions were called in by theorists to provide causes not only for what we (intentionally) do but also for mental processes or operations such as controlling an impulse, paying heed to something, and the like. As a consequence of this, acts of will were supposed to be the sort of thing the presence of which makes an action 'voluntary', or which—somehow, in some unfathomable way—'gets itself translated' into a bodily or mental act. In fine, volitions were thought of as causes as well as effects of other, mental or physical, occurrences. Now the dilemma: if my pulling of the trigger were the result of a mental act of 'willing to pull the trigger', what of this mental act itself? Was it willed or unwilled? If unwilled, it cannot be called voluntary and therefore not a volition; if willed, then we must suppose, according to the theory, that it results from a prior act, namely, 'willing to will to pull the trigger', and that from another *ad infinitum*, leaving no possibility for me ever to start.

Brilliant as the argument is, the point to be brought up here is only whether it is logically fatal. Does it really prove that the assumption of acts of willing involves an infinite regress? A believer in such acts need not be cowed into submission. To ask of volitions whether they are themselves voluntary or involuntary acts, he may say, is plain nonsense. Only an *action* can be voluntary or involuntary, not an act of will. It is just the point that an act of will is an act of will and does not issue from any anterior act of will, any more than, in order to recall a thing I must first recall what I want to recall, and before I can even do that I must recall that I want to recall what I want to recall, and so on *ad infinitum*. Just as I can recall a thing without need to call in an act of recalling what I want to recall, so my pulling the trigger may be the direct result of an act of will without the latter issuing from a parent act of will. Thus the whole argument apparently crumbles away.

This is meant not to belittle the argument or detract from its force, but only to get clear as to *what sort* of force it has. If it were conclusive, it would, with its destructive power, do away with a good many more acts and states of mind, not only with volitions—with intending and desiring, for instance. Indeed, precisely similar arguments can be constructed 'to deal with them'. Intention: though clearly not the sort of thing to be classed as a simple 'act', it yet seems somehow to 'connect' with what goes on in us before we carry it into action—such as considering, planning, hesitating, choosing. I may, let us say, intend to find a flaw in a given argument, and when I subsequently turn it over in my mind, this will be the result of my intention. Some mental operations, then, *can* arise from an intention, they are 'intended'. So what of the intention itself? Is it intended or unintended? If the intention is not intended, it is not the intention, and if it is intended it must be due to another intention, and this to yet another *ad infinitum*. Similarly in the case of desire. Suppose that I feel a desire for a certain thing, is this desire itself desired or undesired? Either answer lands us in absurdities.

If the strength of the argument were to lie in its structure it would, with its devastating effect, apply after the exchange of some of its terms for other ones, e.g. 'volition' for 'intention'— provided, of course, that certain other circumstances essential to the reasoning are the same. Yet, while the first argument sounds, to say the least, very plausible, no one will be duped by its caricatures. So if it *has* any force it cannot owe it to its structure and consequently cannot be of a logical sort. It is meant to refute the existence of a kind of mental thrust; but then we should remember that to prove the non-existence of something is always a precarious business. 'No one has ever proved the non-existence of Apollo or Aphrodite' it has been observed; too much weight, then, need perhaps not be laid on this particular case. What is disturbing, however, is the ease with which arguments can be cast into pseudo-deductive moulds. And it is this fact to which I wish to call attention by examining the argument. As has been shown in the preceding discussion, it is not an isolated case. No philosophic argument ends with a Q.E.D. However forceful, it never forces. There is no bullying in philosophy, neither with the stick of logic nor with the stick of language.

VI

In throwing such strong doubts on the power of arguments as used by philosophers I may seem to deny them any value whatever. But such is not my intention. Even if they are lacking in logical rigour this certainly has not prevented an original thinker from using them successfully, or from bringing out something not seen before or not seen so clearly. So in the case I have discussed: something *is* seen in that argument, something *is* made clear, though perhaps not quite in the sense intended by the arguer. If so, something very important has been left out from the picture.

Perhaps our objections have been doing injustice to philosophic arguments. They were, quite mistakenly as I hope to have shown, supposed to be proofs and refutations in a strict sense. But what the philosopher does is something else. *He builds up a case.* First, he makes you see all the weaknesses, disadvantages, shortcomings of a position; he brings to light inconsistencies in it or points out how unnatural some of the ideas underlying the whole theory are by pushing them to their farthest consequences; and this he does with the strongest weapons in his arsenal, reduction to absurdity and infinite regress. On the other hand, he offers you a new way of looking at things not exposed to those objections. In other words, he submits to you, like a barrister, all the facts of his case, and you are in the position of the judge. You look at them carefully, go into the details, weigh the pros and cons and arrive at a verdict. But in arriving at a verdict you are not following a deductive highway, any more than a judge in the High Court does. Coming to a decision, though a rational process, is very unlike drawing conclusions from given premisses, just as it is very unlike doing sums. A judge has to judge, we say, implying that he has to use discernment in contrast to applying, machine-like, a set of mechanical rules. There are no computing machines for doing the judge's work nor could there be any—a trivial yet significant fact. When the judge reaches a decision this may be, and in fact often is, a rational result, yet not one obtained by deduction; it does not simply follow from such-and-such: what is required is insight, judgement. Now in arriving at a verdict, you are like a judge in this that you are not carrying out a number of formal logical steps: you have to use discernment, e.g. to descry the pivotal point. Considerations such as these make us see what is already apparent in the use of 'rational', that this term has a wider range of application than what can be established deductively. To say that an argument can be rational and yet not deductive is not a sort of contradiction as it would inevitably be in the opposite case, namely, of saying that a deductive argument need not be rational.

This alters the whole picture. The point to be emphasized is that a philosopher may see an important truth and yet be unable to demonstrate it by formal proof. But the fact that his arguments are not logical does nothing to detract from their rationality. To return to our previous example, the argument used against volition, though it is not what it professes to be, logically destructive, nevertheless has a force difficult to resist. Now to what is this due? It does not need much acumen to find the answer. It is the whole arrangement of so many felicitous examples, preceding the argument, and their masterly analysis, which breathes life into its bare bones; aided greatly by the fact that the connection between a mental thrust and a bodily movement is allowed to remain a mystery. The unsatisfactoriness of this position, together with the amassing of hosts of unanswerable questions and very striking examples—this makes the argument so convincing.

What do you find in reading Ryle or Wittgenstein? Lots of examples with little or no logical bone in between. Why so many examples? They speak for themselves; they usually are more transparent than the trouble maker; each one acts as an analogy; together they light up the whole linguistic background with the effect that the case before us is seen in the light they produce. Indeed, examples aptly arranged are often more convincing and, above all, of a more lasting effect than an argument which is anyhow spidery. Not that the 'proofs' proffered are valueless: a *reductio ad absurdum* always points to a knot in thought, and so does an infinite regress. But they *point* only. The real strength lies in the examples. All the proofs, in a good book on philosophy, could be dispensed with, without its losing a whit of its convincingness. To seek, in philosophy, for rigorous proofs is to seek for the shadow of one's voice.

In order to forestall misinterpretations which will otherwise certainly arise I have to concede one point: arguments on a small scale, containing a few logical steps only, may be rigorous. The substance of my remarks is that the conception of a whole philosophical view—from Heraclitus to Nietzsche or Bradley—is never a matter of logical steps. A *weltanschauung* like any of these or even a new approach like that of Wittgenstein is never 'arrived at', in particular it is not deduced, and once found it can neither be proved nor refuted by strictly logical reasoning; though arguments may play a part in making them acceptable. But some authors have disdained even that.

The one remaining question to be asked is this: if the philosopher's views cannot be derived from any premisses how has he ever arrived at them? How can he get to a place to which no road is leading? This leads to a new and deeper problem.

VII

To ask, 'What is your aim in philosophy?' and to reply, 'To show the fly the way out of the fly-bottle' is . . . well, honour where it is due, I suppress what I was going to say; except perhaps this. There is something deeply exciting about philosophy, a fact not intelligible on such a negative account. It is not a matter of 'clarifying thoughts' nor of 'the correct use of language' nor of any other of these damned things. What is it?

Philosophy is many things and there is no formula to cover them all. But if I were asked to express in one single word what is its most essential feature I would unhesitatingly say: vision. At the heart of any philosophy worth the name is vision and it is from there it springs and takes its visible shape. When I say 'vision' I mean it: I do not want to romanticize. What is characteristic of philosophy is the piercing of that dead crust of tradition and convention, the breaking of those fetters which bind us to inherited preconceptions, so as to attain a new and broader way of looking at things. It has always been felt that philosophy should reveal to us what is hidden. (I am not quite insensitive to the dangers of such a view.) Yet from Plato to Moore and Wittgenstein every great philosopher was led by a sense of vision: without it no one could have given a new direction to human thought or opened windows into the not-yet-seen. Though he may be a good technician, he will not leave his marks on the history of ideas. What is decisive is a new way of seeing and, what goes with it, the will to transform the whole intellectual scene. This is the real thing and everything else is subservient to it.

Suppose that a man revolts against accepted opinion, that he feels 'cramped' in its categories; a time may come when he believes, rightly or wrongly, that he has freed himself of these notions; when he has that sense of sudden growth in looking back at the prejudices which held him captive; or a time when he believes, rightly or wrongly, that he has reached a vantage point from which things can be seen to be arranged in clear and orderly patterns while difficulties of long standing dissolve as though by magic. If he is of a philosophic cast of mind he will argue this out with himself and then, perhaps, try to impart what has dawned on him to others. The arguments he will offer, the attacks he will make, the suggestions he will advance are all devised for one end: to win other people over to his own way of looking at things, to change the whole climate of opinion. Though to an outsider he appears to advance all sorts of arguments, this is not the decisive point. What is decisive is that he has seen things from a new angle of vision.

32

Compared to that everything else is secondary. Arguments come only afterwards to lend support to what he has seen. 'Big words, not every philosopher, etc.': but where should one get one's bearings if not from the masters? And besides, once tradition has given way there is always ample scope for specialists to reduce some 'pockets of resistance'. Unpalatable though it may be, behind the arguments so well-planned, so neat and logical, something else is at work, a will to transform the entire way of thinking. In arguing for his view, the philosopher will, almost against his will, have to undermine current categories and clichés of thinking by exposing the fallacies which underly the established views he is attacking; and not only this, he may go so far as to question the canons of satisfactoriness themselves. In this sense, philosophy is the re-testing of the standards. In every philosopher lives something of the reformer. That is the reason why any advance in science when it touches the standards is felt to be of philosophic significance, from Galileo to Einstein and Heisenberg.

If there is any truth in this, the relation of logic and philosophy appears in a new light. What is at issue is not a conflict between a formal and a less formal or informal logic, nor between the behaviour of technical and everyday concepts, but something radically different. It is the difference between drawing a conclusion and seeing, or making one see, a new aspect.

To put the matter in a nutshell, a philosophic argument does more and does less than a logical one: less in that it never establishes anything conclusively; more in that, if successful, it is not content to establish just one isolated point of truth, but effects a change in our whole mental outlook so that, as a result of that, myriads of such little points are brought into view or turned out of sight, as the case may be. Are illustrations necessary? Once Hume had exposed the fallacies of his predecessors when dealing with the notion of causality he had made it impossible for anyone to think along the lines of Spinoza whose world looks to us strange as the moon. Suppose that you look at a picture-puzzle: at first you can see in it only a maze of lines;

then, suddenly, you recognize a human face. Can you now, having discovered the face, see the lines as before? Clearly not. As with the maze of lines, so with the muddle cleared up by Hume: to recapture the mood of the past, to travel back into the fog has become impossible—one of the big difficulties of understanding history of philosophy. It is for the same reason that the rise of the linguistic technique in our day has put an end to the great speculative systems of the past.

A philosophy is an attempt to unfreeze habits of thinking, to replace them by less stiff and restricting ones. Of course, these may in time themselves harden, with the result that they clog progress: Kant, the *Alleszermalmer* to his contemporaries, yet proudly upholding his table of categories—which appear to us unduly narrow. The liberator of yesterday may turn into the tyrant of tomorrow.

It can now be seen that the philosopher is not doing what the logician does only less competently but doing something altogether different. A philosophic argument is not an *approximation* of a logical one nor is the latter the ideal the philosopher is striving for. Such an account totally misdescribes what really takes place. Philosophy is not an exercise in formal logic, philosophic arguments are not chains of logical inference, only bungled ones, nor can they by any effort be recast into deductive moulds. What is being confused here is the scientist's aim to find new truths and the philosopher's aim to gain insight. As the two things are so entirely out of scale it is small wonder that the philosopher cannot move in the logician's armour. Not even if the logician himself is fighting the battle. The clash over the law of excluded middle in mathematics is a clash between two parties, each in possession of clear and precisely defined concepts. Yet there seems to be no way of settling the dispute by cogent argument. If it were true that philosophical troubles arise from the loose nature of our everyday concepts, why should such conflicts break out in the exactest of the sciences?

There have never been any absolutely cogent reasons for parting with the law of excluded middle, accepting Darwinism, giving up the Ptolemaic system or renouncing the principle of causality. If any of these things could be demonstrated how does it come that there are always partisans of the 'lost causes'? Are they like the unlucky circle-squarers, wasting their time in trying to do what has been shown to be logically impossible? The truth is that conflicts of this type cannot be resolved, not entirely, either by adducing factual evidence or by logical demonstration. Both sides, of course, bring up arguments in the combat but they are not decisive. These are battles never lost and never won irrevocably. It is a typical situation, a recurrent theme in the history of human thought.

Whenever science arrives at a crucial stage where the fundamental notions become uncertain and are held as it were in solution, disputes of an odd kind are breaking out. The mere fact that leading scientists, in spite of differences in temperament, outlook, etc., take part in them, feel bound to do so, should make us reflect. Now what the protagonists avowedly or unavowedly are trying to do is to win their fellow scientists over to their own way of thinking; and to the degree to which their arguments are attempts at changing the whole intellectual attitude they take on a philosophical character. Is this co-incidence?

VIII

I have so far spoken of 'seeing a new aspect' without making an attempt to explain the term. I hope now to do so, though only perfunctorily, by giving one or two illustrations. There is a sort of paradox connected with the idea of certain discoveries. Descartes, for instance, was the discoverer of analytic geometry. But could he seek for it? To say that he spent years looking for it sounds downright absurd. What we are inclined to say in such a case is: to seek for analytic geometry is not possible—first because it was not seen and then because it was seen. But if he could not seek, how could he find? This leads us straight to the heart of the matter.

Consider first an entirely imaginary case. In the propositional calculus, as it was built up by Frege, two primitive ideas occur, 'not' and 'or'. It was later discovered by Sheffer that the whole calculus can be based on one single idea (his 'stroke' function). Of what kind was this discovery? Suppose that Frege, by a curious chance, had written all his logical axioms in the form

$$\sim(.\ .\ .\ .)\ \mathbf{v}\sim(.\ .\ .\ .)$$

i.e. as a sum of two negations, but had none the less mistakenly believed that *two* symbols were required for expressing these laws, namely '$\sim$' and '$\mathbf{v}$'. Imagine now that someone else looking at these formulae is struck by what, on our assumption, has escaped Frege, namely that they all have one and the same structure and require therefore only one symbol. In what exactly does his discovery consist? In his *seeing* the formulae in a new way, in his reading a new structure into them. What matters is his apprehension: so long as he does not see the structure of a new system in the old one he has not got it. Anyone may look at the formulae and yet not perceive what Sheffer has perceived, the occurrence of an identical structure. *This* is the discovery, not the introducing of a special symbol for a combination of the old ones. It would have been quite enough, for instance, had Sheffer merely pointed out the constant recurrence of this structure in all the laws without providing his 'stroke'; that is inessential.

This example may illustrate what is meant by the 'seeing of a new aspect'. Seeing such an aspect is often the core of a new discovery. If you look at the formulae, the moment you notice the new structure in them they suddenly seem to change —a phenomenon akin to seeing a figure, say, a drawn cube differently, now as solid and protruding, now as hollow and receding. The one pattern suddenly 'jumps' into the other. Similarly in our case, though there are also differences; thus the new aspect, once it has dawned, can steadily he held in mind and has not that perceptual instability. The apprehension of a new pattern in the formulae seems to hold in it actually more of a visual experience, anyhow to be more closely akin to it than it might at first appear. Seeing and interpreting, looking and thinking seem as it were to fuse here.

If it is now asked whether it is possible for anyone to *seek* for the new aspect, what is one to reply? Well, that something *can* be seen in a new way, is seen only when it *is* seen in this way. That an aspect is possible is seen only when the aspect has already flashed and not before: that's why the finding cannot be anticipated, not even by the greatest genius. It always comes unbidden and, as it would seem, in a sudden flash.

To take another case, is the calculation

$$(5 + 3)^2 = 5^2 + 2 \cdot 5 \cdot 3 + 3^2$$

at the same time a proof that

$$(2 + 3)^2 = 2^2 + 2 \cdot 2 \cdot 3 + 3^2 \quad ?$$

Yes and no—depending on how you look at it. (Does it strike you that the 2 in the middle term is a 'structural' 2, deriving not from the special numbers but from the general form of the operation?) A man, while reckoning with special numbers only, may yet conceivably do algebra if he sees the special sums in a new way, as the expressions of a general law. (Discovery of algebra as the discovery of an aspect of numerical calculation.)

What goes for these more or less trivial cases goes for Descartes and also for Einstein and Hilbert. They were unable to seek, Einstein for a conceptual gap in the idea of simul-taneity, Hilbert for the axiomatic method. Though these discoveries are of a different order altogether, the principle underlying them is the same. None of them has ever 'arrived' at his view because he was never travelling They did not seek, they found (like Picasso). And that is so wrong with the whole way in which such discoveries are so often presented—as if they were the result of a 'method' or 'procedure', as if the great men arrived at their solutions by drawing logical inferences. This leaves out the most essential thing—the flashing of a new aspect which is *non*-inferential. The moments of seeing cannot be foreseen, any more than they can be planned, forced controlled, or summoned by will-power.

Is there any truth in what I am saying? I shall not argue. Instead, let me remind you of some observations which will be familiar to you. It is notorious that a philosophy is not made, it grows. You don't choose a puzzle, you are shocked into it. Whoever has pondered some time over some dark problem in philosophy will have noticed that the solution, when it comes, comes with a suddenness. It is not through working very hard towards it that it is found. What happens is rather that he suddenly sees things in a new light—as if a veil had been lifted that screened his view, or as if the scales had fallen from his eyes, leaving him surprised at his own stupidity not to have seen what was there quite plain before him all the time. It is less like finding out something and more like maturing, outgrowing preconceived notions.

To give just one example of vision in philosophy: Wittgenstein saw through a big mistake of his time. It was then held by most philosophers that the nature of such things as hoping and fearing, or intending, meaning and understanding could be discovered through introspection, while others, in particular psychologists, sought to arrive at an answer by experiment, having only obscure notions as to what their results meant. Wittgenstein changed the whole approach by saying: what these words mean shows itself in the way they are used—the nature of understanding reveals itself in grammar, not in experiment. This was at the time quite a revelation and came to him, so far as I remember, suddenly.

The view advocated here is that at the living centre of every philosophy is a vision and that it should be judged accordingly. The really important questions to be discussed in the history of philosophy are not whether Leibniz or Kant were consistent in arguing as they did but rather what lies behind the systems they have built. And here I want to end with a few words on metaphysics.

To say that metaphysics is nonsense *is* nonsense. It fails to acknowledge the enormous part played at least in the past by those systems. Why this is so, why they should have such a hold over the human mind I shall not undertake here to discuss. Metaphysicians, like artists, are the antennae of their time: they have a flair for feeling which way the spirit is moving. (There is a Rilke poem about it.) There is something visionary about great metaphysicians as if they had the power to see beyond the horizons of their time. Take, for instance, Descartes' work. That it has given rise to endless metaphysical quibbles is certainly a thing to hold against it. Yet if we attend to the spirit rather than to the words I am greatly inclined to say that there is a certain grandeur in it, a prophetic aspect of the comprehensibility of nature, a bold anticipation of what has been achieved in science at a much later date. The true successors of Descartes were those who translated the spirit of this philosophy into deeds, not Spinoza or Malebranche but Newton and the mathematical description of nature. To go on with some hairsplitting as to what substance is and how it should be defined was to miss the message. It was a colossal mistake. A philosophy is there to be lived out. What goes into the word dies, what goes into the work lives.

MAIN PUBLICATIONS

Einführung in das mathematische Denken. Gerold & Co., Vienna. 1937.
Introduction to Mathematical Thought. (Translation of above.)

BIOGRAPHICAL NOTES

RICHARD I. AARON was born in 1901 and brought up at Ynystawe, South Wales. He received his university education at University College, Cardiff and Oriel College, Oxford, being elected a Research Fellow of the University of Wales in 1923. He became a Lecturer in the Department of Philosophy at University College, Swansea, in 1926 and was appointed to his present post in 1932. He has taken much interest in Welsh affairs, being the Editor of a Welsh philosophical journal, *Efrydiau Athronyddol*, and Chairman, for the maximum period of six years, of the Central Advisory Council for Education (Wales). Professor Aaron spent a year in America recently as a Visiting Professor at Yale. He was President of the Mind Association in 1955 and was elected a Fellow of the British Academy in the same year.

H. B. ACTON was born in London in 1908 and went to St. Olave's Grammar School, Tower Bridge. He became a Demy of Magdalen College, Oxford, in 1927, and a Senior Demy in 1930. From 1931 to 1935 he was an Assistant Lecturer in Philosophy at University College, Swansea, proceeding thence as a Lecturer to Bedford College, London, under the late Professor L. S. Stebbing. During the war he held posts as Temporary Principal in the Ministry of Supply. He was appointed to his present post in 1944, entering on his duties there in 1945. Professor Acton has added to his general work in philosophy a special interest in French Philosophy, and was a Visiting Professor in the University of Chicago in 1949. In 1952 he was President of the Aristotelian Society, his Presidential address being entitled: *Tradition and some other Forms of Order*.

A. J. AYER was born in 1910 and was educated at Eton College. He became a scholar at Christ Church, Oxford, in 1929 and a Lecturer in Philosophy at the same college in 1932. He also held the post of Research Student at Christ Church from 1935 to 1944, being then elected a Fellow (and subsequently Dean) of Wadham College in the same university. He was appointed to his present post in 1946. During the war Professor Ayer held a commission in the Welsh

491

Guards and in 1945 he was an Attaché at His Majesty's Embassy in Paris. In 1948-49 he was Visiting Professor at New York University, and he became President of the Aristotelian Society in 1951, and a Fellow of the British Academy in 1952. He is the editor of the Pelican series of philosophy books.

WINSTON H. F. BARNES was born in 1909 and spent his early life at Manchester, proceeding from the Grammar School there as a Scholar to Corpus Christi College, Oxford. He became the John Locke Scholar in the University of Oxford in 1932 and Senior Demy of Magdalen College in 1933. From 1936 to 1945 he was a member of the Department of Philosophy in the University of Liverpool (first as Assistant Lecturer and then as Lecturer), being appointed to his present post in 1945. During the war Professor Barnes served as an officer in the R.A.F.V.R. and as a Temporary Principal in the Ministry of Supply. He was President of the Mind Association in 1948.

C. A. CAMPBELL was born in 1897 and began his higher education in Glasgow Academy, in his home city, proceeding thence to Glasgow University. His career was interrupted by service, at home and in Egypt, in the 1914 war. Following two years of post-graduate residence in Balliol College, Oxford, he became a member of the Department of Moral Philosophy in Glasgow in 1924, first as an Assistant and then (in 1925) as Lecturer. He was appointed to the Chair of Philosophy in the University College of North Wales, Bangor, in 1932, and returned to Glasgow, to the Chair he now holds, in 1938. He has played a notable part in the organization of University Extra-mural Classes, the considerable expansion of these in the West of Scotland being largely due to his initiative. Professor Campbell was awarded an Honorary D.Litt. by the Queen's University, Belfast, in 1950, and was invited to deliver the Gifford Lectures in the University of St. Andrews in 1954 and 1955.

FREDERICK COPLESTON was born in 1907 and began his life near Taunton. He received his higher education at Marlborough College and St. John's College, Oxford. He entered the Catholic Church in 1925, becoming a member of the Society of Jesus in 1930 and being ordained in 1937. He was appointed to the Chair he now holds at Heythrop College in 1939 and became a Professor at Rome in 1952. Attracted in the first instance to what he "imagined to be Hegelianism" he has subsequently paid most attention to scholastic philosophy and to empiricism. He has travelled much on the Continent of Europe and lectured in Germany at the invitation of the Foreign Office and in Italy and Spain for the British Council.

A. C. Ewing was born in 1899 and educated at Wyggeston Grammar School, Leicester, and the University of Oxford, being a member there of University College and later, as Bishop Fraser Scholar, also of Oriel College. He became a Senior Demy of Magdalen College in 1921 and gained the John Locke Scholarship and the Green Prize in Moral Philosophy at Oxford; in 1926 he held temporary posts in Michigan University and Armstrong College, Newcastle, being appointed an Assistant Lecturer in Philosophy at University College, Swansea, in 1927. He became a Lecturer in Moral Science in the University of Cambridge in 1931, his post being converted to a Readership in 1954. Dr. Ewing was Visiting Professor at Princeton and Northwestern Universities, U.S.A., in 1949 and visited India as a delegate to the Indian Silver Jubilee Congress of Philosophy in 1950. He has attended many conferences of learned societies in Europe and was President of the Aristotelian Society for the session 1941-42. He was also made a Fellow of the British Academy in 1941.

J. N. Findlay was born in Pretoria, South Africa, in 1903, being, on his father's side, a great-nephew of Olive Schreiner and, on his mother's side, of Eugene Marais, the Afrikaans poet. He had his early education in South Africa and came to Balliol College, Oxford, as a Rhodes Scholar in 1924. His first university post which he held from 1927 to 1933 was that of Lecturer in Philosophy at Transvaal University College. This was the prelude to his tenure of several university chairs, first at Dunedin, New Zealand, from 1934 to 1944, then at Rhodes and Natal University College, South Africa, from 1945 to 1948, and, from 1948 to 1951, at King's College, Newcastle-upon-Tyne. He was appointed to his present post in 1951.

Stuart Hampshire was born in 1914 and educated at Repton, becoming a History Scholar of Balliol College, Oxford, in 1933. He was a Fellow of All Souls College, Oxford, from 1936 to 1945, being also a Tutor in Philosophy at The Queen's College for part of this time. He served in the Army during the war, and in the Foreign Office immediately after the war. From 1948 to 1951 he was Lecturer in Philosophy at University College, London, becoming a Fellow of New College, Oxford, in 1951. He became again a Fellow of All Souls in 1955.

H. A. Hodges was born in 1905 and brought up in Sheffield. He received his higher education at King Edward VII School, Sheffield, and the University of Oxford. He held a Classical Scholarship at Balliol College, Oxford, and became a Senior Demy of Magdalen College in 1926, being successful also at Oxford in gaining a Craven Scholarship, a War Memorial Studentship at Balliol College, and the

John Locke Scholarship. He was a Lecturer in Philosophy at New College, Oxford, in 1927, and held a similar post in the University of Reading from 1928 until his promotion to his present post in 1934. Professor Hodges has become known outside philosophical circles through his broadcast talks and the part he has taken in the Ecumenical Movement, the Student Christian Movement and other religious activities. From 1949 to 1951 he served on the Royal Commission on Betting, Lotteries and Gaming. He will deliver the Gifford Lectures in the University of Aberdeen in 1956 and 1957.

W. C. KNEALE was born in 1906 and went to school at the Liverpool Institute. From there he entered Brasenose College, Oxford, where he was elected to a Classical Scholarship and later to a Senior Scholarship in Philosophy. In 1928 and 1929 he studied at Freiburg and at Paris. After two years in Aberdeen and a year at Newcastle he returned to Oxford in 1932 as Lecturer in Philosophy at Exeter College. From 1940 to 1945 he served in the Ministry of War Transport, and for some years after the war he held the office of Senior Tutor in Exeter College. In the year 1949 he was President of the Aristotelian Society, and in 1950 he was elected a Fellow of the British Academy. His wife, who was formerly Miss Martha Hurst, is Fellow and Tutor in Philosophy of Lady Margaret Hall, Oxford.

H. D. LEWIS was born in 1910 and brought up in Waenfawr, North Wales. He received his university education at University College, Bangor, and Jesus College, Oxford, being Research Student of the University of Wales. He returned to Bangor as Assistant Lecturer in 1935 and was later promoted to the grade of Senior Lecturer. He held the Chair of Philosophy at Bangor from 1947 until his appointment to his present post in 1955. Professor Lewis has been for many years Secretary of the Philosophical Section of the Welsh Guild of Graduates and has taken part in other ways in the cultural and religious life of the Principality. He was President of the Mind Association in 1949 and became Editor of the Muirhead Library of Philosophy in 1950. He spent the session 1954-55 at Oxford as holder of a Leverhulme Fellowship.

J. D. MABBOTT was born in 1898 and brought up in Duns, Berwickshire. He received his higher education in Berwickshire High School, Edinburgh University and St. John's College, Oxford, gaining the John Locke Scholarship at Oxford in 1923. Two short spells of university lecturing, first in Classics at Reading and then in Philosophy at Bangor, preceded his appointment to his present post in 1924. During the war Mr. Mabbott served in the Foreign Office and was awarded the C.M.G. in 1946.

D. M. MACKINNON was born in 1913 and spent his early years at Oban, proceeding thence to Winchester College and from there to New College, Oxford, as a Scholar. A short period of lecturing in a junior capacity in the Department of Moral Philosophy at Edinburgh preceded his appointment as Fellow and Tutor at Keble College, Oxford, in 1937, a post which he combined for a period with a Lectureship at Balliol College. He was appointed to the Chair he now holds in 1947. Professor MacKinnon was Wilde Lecturer in Natural and Comparative Religion at Oxford from 1945 to 1947, and he was Scott Holland Lecturer in 1952. He has become known outside academic circles through his public lectures and broadcast talks.

H. J. PATON was born in 1887 and spent his early life at Abernethy, Perthshire. He received his higher education at the High School, of Glasgow, the University of Glasgow, and Balliol College, Oxford. From 1911 to 1927 he was Fellow and Praelector in Classics and Philosophy at The Queen's College, Oxford, being also Dean of his College for part of this time and Junior Proctor in the University. He spent the period 1925-26 as Laura Spelman Rockefeller Research Fellow in the University of California and became Professor of Logic and Rhetoric in the University of Glasgow in 1927. This post he relinquished to become White's Professor of Moral Philosophy in the University of Oxford from 1937 until his retirement in 1952. He has been a Fellow of the British Academy since 1946, was President of the Aristotelian Society in 1944, and has been given Honorary Doctorates by the Universities of Glasgow, St. Andrews, and Toronto. He gave the Forwood Lectures in the University of Liverpool in 1948 and was Gifford Lecturer in the University of St. Andrews from 1949 to 1951. In 1955 he was Visiting Professor in the University of Toronto. He is also Editor of the philosophical section in Hutchinson's University Library. Professor Paton served in the Intelligence Division of the Admiralty during the first war, and thereafter in the Foreign Office at the Peace Conference of Paris. He again served in the Foreign Office during the second war.

K. R. POPPER was born in 1902 in Vienna and studied at the University there from 1919 till 1928. Having published various papers and a book on scientific method, he gave lectures at several philosophic congresses and some English Universities. In 1937 he went to Canterbury College, University of New Zealand, as Lecturer and later as Senior Lecturer in Philosophy. In 1945, while still in New Zealand, he was appointed to a Readership in Logic and Scientific Method in the University of London (London School of Economics). He was made a D.Litt. of this University in 1948, and promoted to his present position in 1949. He gave the William James Lectures in Philosophy at Harvard University in 1950, and he has also lectured at various other universities in America and in Europe. He is a member of the editorial board of the *British Journal for the Philosophy of Science*, and was Chairman of the Philosophy of Science Group of the British Society for the History of Science from 1951 to 1953. He has been a member of the International Academy for the Philosophy of Science since 1948, and a member of the Council of the Association for Symbolic Logic since 1951.

H. H. PRICE was born in 1899 and began his life at Neath, South Wales. He received his higher education at Winchester College and New College, Oxford, of which he was a Scholar. He served in the R.A.F. in the 1914 war and resumed his studies at Oxford in 1919. He was a Fellow of Magdalen College from 1922 to 1923, and a Lecturer in Education in the University of Liverpool from 1923 to 1924. He then returned to Oxford as Fellow and Lecturer in Philosophy at Trinity College, a post which he held until his appointment to the chair he now occupies in 1935. He was Visiting Professor at Princeton, U.S.A., in 1948. Professor Price was President of the Society for Psychical Research in 1939, and President of the Aristotelian Society in 1943. He has also been on two occasions President of the Mind Association, first in 1946 and again in 1954. He was elected a Fellow of the British Academy in 1943 and given an Honorary D.Litt. by Trinity College, Dublin, in 1952, and an Honorary LL.D. by the University of St. Andrews in 1954.

L. J. RUSSELL was born in Birmingham in 1884 and spent his early years in Glasgow. He received his university education at the University of Glasgow and Emmanuel College, Cambridge. He returned to Glasgow as a Lecturer in Logic in the University in 1910 and became Professor of Philosophy in the University of Bristol in 1923, proceeding thence to the Chair of Philosophy in the University of Birmingham in 1925. He retired in 1950. In 1932 Professor Russell visited America as Acting Professor of Philosophy in Stanford University, California, and he went as Nuffield Visiting Lecturer to Australia in 1951. He was President of the Mind Association in 1933, and President of the Aristotelian Society in 1932. He was given an Honorary LL.D. by the University of Glasgow in 1948, and elected a Fellow of the British Academy in 1954.

GILBERT RYLE was born in 1900, his father, a general practitioner at Brighton, being an early member of the Aristotelian Society, to which he contributed some papers. He was educated at Brighton College and

The Queen's College, Oxford, of which he was a Classical Scholar. In 1924 he became a Lecturer in Philosophy and later a Student and Tutor in Philosophy at Christ Church, holding also for periods the offices of Junior and Senior Censor at Christ Church and Junior Proctor in the University. In 1940 he was commissioned in the Welsh Guards and after about a year with the regiment worked till the end of the war in Military Intelligence. In 1945 he was appointed to his present post and he became Editor of *Mind* in 1947. He was President of the Aristotelian Society in 1945 and gave the Tarner Lectures in Cambridge in 1953. Professor Ryle has had much to do with the organization of post-graduate studies at Oxford in recent years and he has paid visits to many universities abroad.

FRIEDRICH WAISMANN was born in Vienna in 1896 and received his education there, his original training being largely in mathematics. He was an Assistant to Professor Schlick from 1929 to 1936, and he then moved to Cambridge where he lectured at the invitation of the Moral Science Faculty from 1937 to 1939. He became a Lecturer at Oxford in 1939 and subsequently University Reader in the Philosophy of Mathematics. He was made a Fellow of the British Acdemy in 1955.

INDEX

33

GEORGE ALLEN & UNWIN LTD
London: 40 Museum Street, W.C.1

Auckland: 24 Wyndham Street
Sydney, N.S.W.: Bradbury House, 55 York Street
Cape Town: 58–60 Long Street
Bombay: 15 Graham Road, Ballard Estate, Bombay 1
Calcutta: 17 Chittaranjan Avenue, Calcutta 13
New Delhi: 13–14 Ajmere Gate Extension, New Delhi 1
Karachi: Haroon Chambers, South Napier Road, Karachi 2
Toronto: 91 Wellington Street West
Sao Paulo: Avenida 9 de Julho 1138–Ap. 51